Between the Lines

Recent Titles in
Studies in Military History and International Affairs
Jeremy Black, Series Editor

When Reason Fails: Portraits of Armies at War: America, Britain, Israel and the Future
Michael Goodspeed

A History of Modern Wars of Attrition
Carter Malkasian

When Men Lost Faith in Reason: Reflections on War and Society in the Twentieth Century
H. P. Willmott

Between the Lines

Banditti of the American Revolution

Harry M. Ward

Studies in Military History and International Affairs
Jeremy Black, Series Editor

Westport, Connecticut
London

Library of Congress Cataloging-in-Publication Data

Ward, Harry M.
    Between the lines : banditti of the American Revolution / Harry M. Ward.
      p. cm.—(Studies in military history and international affairs, ISSN 1537–4432)
    Includes bibliographical references and index.
    ISBN 0–275–97633–5 (alk. paper)
    1. United States—History—Revolution, 1775–1783—Social aspects. 2. Brigands and
robbers—United States—History—18th century. 3. Brigands and robbers—United
States—Biography. 4. War and crime—United States—History—18th century. I. Title.
II. Series.
E209.W36   2002
973.3—dc21   2001058038

British Library Cataloguing in Publication Data is available.

Library of Congress Catalog Card Number: 2001058038
ISBN: 0–275–97633–5
ISSN: 1537–4432

First published in 2002

Praeger Publishers, 88 Post Road West, Westport, CT 06881
An imprint of Greenwood Publishing Group, Inc.
www.praeger.com

Printed in the United States of America

The paper used in this book complies with the
Permanent Paper Standard issued by the National
Information Standards Organization (Z39.48–1984).

10 9 8 7 6 5 4 3 2 1

Contents

Illustrations

Preface

"The Revolution drives home the lesson that in war reality always seems to escape perception," noted one historian at the time of the Independence Bicentennial.[1] While there has been important scholarship on what may be called the underside of the war—including soldier discipline, camp followers, the home front, and the roles of women, African Americans, and Native Americans—there is little awareness that the conflict played out not simply as confrontations of armies but also in the context of a civil war, a very nasty one at that. Much of the destruction and plundering carried out by irregular forces and bandit gangs is attributable to "the Refugee War," wherein Loyalists and persons generally affiliated with the British cause incessantly conducted raids upon rebel civilians and militia, and met retaliation in kind. Wide sections of territory became virtual wastelands as a result of the military appropriation of livestock and provisions, the looting and destruction of homes, and the flight of civilians. Although the armies avoided a scorched-earth policy, British forces on several occasions during the southern campaigns did engage in such behavior. Most of the despoilation of private property came, however, at the hands of banditti.

During the war, citizens referred to those gangs engaged in wanton pillaging and highway robbery as banditti. These malefactors may be distinguished from most participants in the partisan warfare, which involved detached military units and militia.

Loyalist refugees as banditti form a major component of this book. There were, of course, many villains who were simply outlaws, who raided, plundered, and killed regardless of the Tory or Whig sympathies of their victims. When captured, these freebooters often claimed, albeit unsuccessfully, prisoner-of-war status.

The banditti phenomenon occurred chiefly in what may be referred to as war zones, within the range of military operations or at least in areas "between the lines." This was true in respect to both the freebooters and the bands connected with the military. In some of the contested areas, law and order were in disarray, to the extent of anarchy. Territory bearing the scars of relentless regular and internecine warfare became a no-man's-land.

Revenge and greed motivated the Revolutionary War banditti. In a sense many of the banditti were agents of retribution—oppressed Tories or outcasts of society who were attempting to even a score. The hostile atmosphere of a divided people invited despoilation and violence as means for waging war and put average citizens in harm's way from assaults by banditti.

Although outlaws roamed nearly everywhere in the new American states, the banditry that arose most directly from wartime conditions played out quite literally "between the lines." Hence areas excluded from the discussion of banditti are New England above Connecticut and Rhode Island and the interiors of New York, Pennsylvania, and the Chesapeake states, although the backcountry and frontiers of these areas (except New England) merit some review. Delaware, Maryland, and backcountry Pennsylvania and Virginia all experienced abortive Tory uprisings, but these events lay outside the banditti phenomenon. Also omitted is any examination of the mutual violence and depredations between rebels and Loyalists/Indians during the war.

The marauding and robber bands and their leaders discussed in this book are those who were the most prominent and representative of the banditti problem. The aim is to present the broad scope of banditti activity. The reader may find definitive treatment on the Pine Robbers in work by David J. Fowler, on James Moody by Susan B. Shenstone, and on the East Florida refugees by Wilbur H. Siebert.[2]

This work excludes the very large subject of privateering in the Atlantic coastal waters of North America. A connotative meaning of "banditti" is that of robbers by land. Marauding by "land pirates," via small sailing craft, is, however, considered for the regions of Long Island Sound, the New Jersey shores, and Chesapeake Bay. Omitted in this study is treatment of the picaroons in New England above Connecticut and Rhode Island and along the Carolina and Georgia coasts.

It is interesting that the term "banditti" caught on among the American revolutionaries. Banditti, as used then and now, is normally the plural for bandit, especially in reference to a band of robbers. As originally defined, a bandit is "one who is proscribed or outlawed; hence, a lawless desperate marauder, a brigand; usually applied to members of the organized gangs which infest the mountain districts of Italy, Sicily, Greece, and Turkey."[3] Generally, however, according to Eric Hobsbawm, "for the law, anyone belonging to a group of men who attack and rob with violence is a bandit."[4] Or one could say that banditti are armed gangs who move about committing robberies and depredations and then retreat to a secluded or protected sanctuary. During the Revolutionary War, Loyalist refugee bands found safety in places under military protection or across the southern international boundary. The more freebooting kind escaped to hideouts in out-of-the-way places in forests, hills, or swamps.

Historically some highwaymen and marauders in various countries have been viewed as social bandits, such as the legendary Robin Hood, who champion the poor and are aided by them. Social banditry, however, was not very evident during the Revolutionary War, although banditti often sought to redress wrongs, and a few refrained from taking advantage of destitute persons; there were no Robin Hoods. The bands of robbers/marauders of the Revolutionary era fit into two categories: those acting primarily from a cause and outlaws acting from greed. Generally in American history "outlaws are grimmer and more violent characters than the Robin Hood of the ballads"; the "American bandits do not ultimately make peace with the law as did Robin Hood; they are all unrepentent sinners to the moment of death."[5]

Hobsbawm comments on a typical profile of people who chose to become bandits (banditti): "Banditry is freedom." It appealed to young males before they were ready to settle down. Bandit recruits came largely from the margins of society—frequently, as was the case during the Revolution, soldiers, former soldiers, and deserters. "Ex-servicemen like deserters are natural material for banditry," explains Hobsbawm. Except for maroons, most of the Revolutionary War banditti at one time or another at least had ties, if not actual service, with the military. "Involuntary outcasts from the peasantry, such as ex-soldiers, deserters and marauders . . . abounded in periods of disorder, war or its aftermath."[6]

With the exception of James Moody, who acted under British military authority and avoided indiscriminate robbery, and a few others, the banditti of the Revolution were often brutal. They committed murder and arson and sometimes employed torture to terrify victims. Citizens lived in dread of nighttime assault. A favorite tactic of the banditti was to raid homes when the menfolk were gone to war. The invaders first sought money and then also any household valuables that could be sold to almost anyone. It is surprising to find that women's apparel was a much pilfered item. Horses and cattle were in demand by the banditti, especially when there was access to markets, such as in New York City.

Highwaymen, horse thieves, and rustlers existed throughout early American history. It was during the war, however, that instances of waylaying travelers and drivers became a common occurrence. Marauding bands were a product of the war.

For anyone undertaking this kind of study, there is the problem of separating fact from conjecture or legend. Much reporting was prejudicial or propagandist, depending upon a Tory or Whig viewpoint. From competing versions I have selected the report or composite that seems most authentic. Folklore is treated cautiously. For the most part I have considered as fairly reliable the reminiscences of persons directly involved with an event or persons who were bearers of a family oral tradition.

Acknowledgments

I am grateful to the following scholars for reading chapters relating to their areas of specialty: Edward J. Cashin, David J. Fowler, Woody Holton, Mark V. Kwasny, David B. Mattern, Holly A. Mayer, Philip Ranlet, Susan B. Shenstone, and Lynn L. Sims. Their suggestions improved this study. Collections of manuscripts and newspapers from the holdings of various libraries available on microfilm were valuable sources. Kim Ball and Jewell Anderson of the Georgia Historical Society, Andy Phrydas of the Georgia Department of Archives and History, and Melissa Bush of the University of Georgia Library provided copies of manuscript letters pertaining to Daniel McGirth. Steven Massengill of the North Carolina Department of Cultural Resources made a diligent search for illustrations. I thank collectively the members of the staffs of the Library of Virginia and the Virginia Historical Society, who gave ready assistance. At the Boatwright Library of the University of Richmond, Nancy Vick and Noreen Cullen carried on the almost uninterrupted task of securing interlibrary loans.

Chapter 1

Soldier-Straggler Plunderers

One May afternoon in 1779 four Virginia boys "on their way from Mr. Andrews's school near Suffolk, to their parents in Princess Anne county, were overtaken" by three light infantry soldiers belonging to the British force then scouring the lower Tidewater area. One boy was struck by a cutlass, and all four, amid "the most abusive language," were robbed of their shoes, knee buckles, handkerchiefs, money, "and all the clothes they had." The soldiers told the victims that "they might think themselves fortunate in not meeting with the Hessians instead of them, as they would not only have robbed them, but would have put them to death."[1] While other victims fared far worse, this occurrence is representative of the frequent oppressions visited upon the citizenry by military banditti.

War tempts soldiers and followers of the army to molest civilians living in zones between the contending forces. Much of the terror Americans, patriot and Loyalist, experienced during the Revolution came from assaults upon their persons and property by armies on the move and more substantially by individual or groups of soldiers acting outside the confines of military duty.

Both American and British commanders attempted to protect the citizenry from the ravages of war. It was recognized early in the war that victory depended upon winning the allegiance of citizens—an objective more incumbent upon the British as the invaders. Of course, the armies needed provisions and equipment from the countryside as they engaged in military operations or maintained encampments. Appropriating supplies from non-combatants was permissible when compensation was tendered, most likely in the form of promissary certificates to be submitted for future payment.[2]

Commanders and officers sometimes were allowed shares of certain captured goods, but plunder by soldiers without sanction of authority was a different matter. Violations entailed severe penalties, even punishment by death. Plundering by soldiers, nevertheless, often met with little or no censure or at least less than maximum punishment, although examples were made from time to time. It was difficult to prevent soldiers from plundering since so many enlistees in both armies hailed from the riffraff of society, destitute at the time of entering service or, in some instances, with a criminal past.[3]

Moving armies sometimes had to live off the land, as did General Charles Cornwallis's troops during the invasion of the Carolinas in 1780–81. It was important not to leave behind any supplies that could be used by the enemy. As the British army marched to the New Jersey coast after leaving Philadelphia in June 1778, according to one redcoat soldier, there was a "good deal of plundering going on," and General Augustine Prevost's army, while moving along the coast and Sea Islands of lower South Carolina and Georgia in 1779, engaged in systematic plundering.[4]

Large-scale military operations occasionally were aimed solely at gaining logistical advantage—to disrupt the flow of supplies going to the enemy. The hit-and-run raid conducted by British troops under General Benedict Arnold on Richmond, Virginia, and its vicinity in early January 1781 is a primary example of this kind of warfare. General Friedrich Wilhelm von Steuben, commanding American troops in Virginia at the time, commented that "a great part of the Inhabitants having removed, their Houses were plundered by the [British] soldiers." A Hessian officer observed, upon the conclusion of the raid, that "forty-two vessels were loaded with all kinds of merchandize for the corps' booty and sailed down the James River. . . . On the whole this expedition greatly resembled those of the freebooters who sometimes at sea, sometimes ashore, ravaged and laid waste to everything."[5]

While plundering by regular troops could be restrained in the major American armies, the militia presented a different situation. Even General George Washington recognized, as he told General John Lacey of the Pennsylvania militia, that "to excite the militia under your command and make them more active in their duty, I would have you to let every thing actually taken from persons going into and coming out of the city [Philadelphia], redound to the benefit of the parties who take them." But he cautioned against "plundering the innocent inhabitants."[6] Lacey was unable to exact any accountability, and he was soon complaining of "the most villainous robberies imaginable under the character of militia."[7]

In the Southern theater, in which a bitter partisan war waged from 1780 to 1782 with almost no regard for citizens' rights, the successful raising of militia volunteers depended largely on granting them permission to plunder at will. Even state governments were permissive. The patriot Executive Council of Georgia resolved in March 1778 that any person raising a company of fifteen or more volunteers "to go along with him . . . shall be entitled to a roving Commission into and against the provinces of East & West Florida and all plunder they shall take upon Condemnation agreeable to Law shall belong to themselves."[8]

Militiamen who voluntarily went on active duty seemed to have scarcely any motivation other than to plunder with impunity. General Nathanael Greene observed that Southern militia serving under Generals Francis Marion and Thomas Sumter "come and go just as they please, and are more allurd from the hopes of plunder than from a desire to serve the public."[9] Continental army officers dreaded having militia assigned to their command. Major John Armstrong complained to Greene that the militia with him could not be "a more disorderly Crew; plundering and Stealing in full Perfection."[10] A major problem occurred when militia from one locale "on Pretence" of being on their way to join Greene's army or some other military force plundered when they entered other neighborhoods.[11] Lieutenant Colonel Henry Lee, who commanded a Continental "legion," recognized the necessity of collecting militia into an embodied force as quickly as possible; otherwise, "they [would] indulge themselves in every species of rapine & plunder."[12]

Militiamen normally saw very short stints of active service, often for only a campaign or battle, and then they left for home, most likely to enter the field again at another time. Spoils of war were divided among the participants. One militiaman noted shortly after the battle of King's Mountain (October 7, 1780) that "in the evening, there was a distribution made of the plunder, and we were dismissed. My father and myself drew two fine horses, two guns, and some articles of clothing, with a share of powder and lead; every man repaired to his tent, or home."[13]

Seeking to raise several regiments of light horse in 1781, Thomas Sumter promised that enlistees would share in the spoils taken from Loyalists; each man could expect to receive at least one slave. This policy became known as "Sumter's Law." Sumter defended the slave award on the basis of appropriating resources from the enemy that could aid in "completing our ruin."[14] Sumter, however, found little backing for his scheme from other Southern American commanders. One widow, Mrs. Anne Lord, petitioned the South

Carolina legislature for redress for 74 slaves taken from her plantation in May 1781 "by Order of General Sumter and distributed among the State Troops," as well as twenty-two horses, one hundred head of cattle, and the like number of sheep, "besides other Considerable property."[15]

The Hessians, at least during the early part of the war, had a reputation for wholesale plundering. Although the British commander in chief, William Howe, asked Hessian officers to rein in their troops against "such outrages,"[16] little effort was made to mete out harsh penalties to Hessian marauders. Many of the German troops had been involuntary recruits, and they received no extra pay for foreign service. The German mercenaries were more likely to ravage the countryside than their British counterparts and, not knowing the language, did not distinguish between Whigs and Loyalists; "if they see any thing they want they seize it, and say 'rebel good for Hesse men.' "[17]

A British officer serving in the Southern campaign in 1780 complained that "the Hessians plunder methodically to a great distance in the Country."[18] General Howe's secretary lamented that "it is impossible to express the Devastations, which the Hessians have made upon the Houses & Country Seats of some of the Rebels. All their Furniture, Glasses, Windows, and the very Hangings of the Rooms are demolished or defaced"; along "with the Filth deposited in them," the houses become "so offensive, that it is a Penance to go into them." Citizens had such a "Dread" of the Hessians that "they almost run away at the name."[19]

Ironically, an independent corps in the Continental army, led by Baron von Ottendorff, composed mostly of Pennsylvania Germans, posed as Hessians for the purpose of plundering. John Carl Buettner, a member of Ottendorff's "foreign legion," explained,

The service of this corps was very hard. As we received no tents, we were obliged to patrol all night long. We also had to forage for cattle to be slaughtered for the use of the soldiers. As a rule we took the cattle from the planters who remained loyal to the king. . . . To discover their attitude in this matter, usually six men went into their houses, pretended to be Hessians and asked questions about Washington's army: how strong it was, where it was located at the present time, and such details. If these people seemed glad to see us, and gave us information about the North American army, soon the entire detachment entered and took possession of the plantation, drove away the cattle and often stripped the house. The duped people then sincerely regretted their frankness, gazed with tears in their eyes after their cattle that we were driving away, and seeing the "US" on our powder pouches, realized too late that we were soldiers of the United States. Such matters occupied almost every night.[20]

Other detached American military units could not resist the temptation to plunder. "All the horsemen were so infatuated with the itch for scouting," reported Lieutenant Colonel Aaron Burr from White Plains, New York, in January 1779, "notwithstanding Colonel [Noah] Littlefield's good intentions, I blush to tell you that the party returned loaded with plunder."[21]

Initially, Washington approved of plundering property belonging to Loyalists on a limited basis. In general orders of January 21, 1777, however, he stated his regret that permission "allowing the Plunder taken from the enemy to be divided for the benefit of the party that took it, has been so mistaken by some, and abused by others." Washington pointed out that the "indulgence was granted to scouting parties only, as a reward for the extraordinary fatigues, hardship, and danger they were exposed to upon those parties." He now made it clear that Continental and militia units were prohibited "in the most positive terms, the infamous practice of plundering the Inhabitants, upon the specious pretence of their being Tories." The commander in chief declared that it was the responsibility of civil authorities to seize property of "persons who are known to be enemies to their Country."[22] Not long after this order was issued, a New Jersey newspaper reported that "a Party of Rebel Light Horse" robbed Captain Thomas Crowell, a Tory who lived near Shrewsbury, New Jersey, of "all his Cattle, Sheep, Hogs and Horses."[23]

Some plundering occurred during foraging expeditions. One such episode so angered General Greene that he asked Washington permission to hang one of the culprits belonging to the foraging party that had "plundered a house" in full view of officers and had even threatened the officers when they interfered.[24]

Among the various detached units with an inclination for plundering were the 600 militia escorting the Convention (Saratoga) prisoners of war to Virginia for internment during 1778–79; this guard unit was regarded as "[e]xceedingly troublesome, robbing the inhabitants."[25] British grenadier companies (arranged as flanking parties) displayed, admitted a British officer, "a great inclination to plunder."[26] Even members of the Invalid Corps (disabled American soldiers), stationed to guard the hospitals and stores at Bethlehem and Easton, Pennsylvania, were accused of committing robberies. Colonel Lewis Nicola, the group's commander, denied the charges and informed Washington that those responsible for the crimes were former members who had been deemed "fit for service" and released, but who subsequently deserted.[27]

Two officers, Captain Eli Leavenworth and Captain Samuel Lockwood of the Connecticut Line, rank among the most notorious plunderers while commanding detached units in the field. It was brought to Washington's attention that the parties led by these men "employed to go on Long Island on pretence of procuring intelligence are mere plundering parties." Washington requested General Charles Scott, the army's intelligence chief, to press charges against Leavenworth and Lockwood. The two officers had stolen almost everything they could lay their hands on, including "several kinds of cloths, linnens, ribbands, some cases of knives and forks, wine glasses," and even "women's wearing apparel." Although the officers pretended to take property belonging only to Tories, Washington suspected "their rapacity makes very little distinction between friends or foes." Leavenworth and Lockwood sold their ill-gotten goods at public venue in Norwalk and Stamford, Connecticut, and in Bedford, New York. Scott soon relinquished his intelligence command, and neither he nor his successors pursued further investigation. The two offending officers were never brought to justice.[28]

Armies have always had stragglers: soldiers who accidentally or intentionally veer away from a main force after a battle or a line of march or slip out of camp. Civilians also follow the army in the wake of a battle or military action, hoping to find something to plunder. All these hangers-on pose a threat to civilians and their property.

Soldiers during the Civil War "were prone to roam about, 'see what they could find,' and in the process forage and pick up things—'capture' was their euphemism." Men sometimes view property rights differently when they are in uniform than when they are civilians.[29] It seems only fair that, when an opportunity presents itself, hungry and ill-equipped soldiers sponge off civilians, whom, after all, the military forces serve.

Civilians had a great fear of discharged militia returning home. The Moravian settlements of western North Carolina experienced frequent robberies, in 1780 and 1781, at the hands of various perpetrators, but the worst came from "mob violence of a released hungry militia." Officers of regular troops "kept good order among them, and the excesses were committed only by camp followers, single soldiers, and especially the militia."[30]

Reverend Henry Melchior Muhlenberg, from his parsonage at the Trappe (Collegeville), on the Schuylkill River, seven miles above Valley Forge, Pennsylvania, wrote, just after the battle of Brandywine, that "marauders who are following the American army are still stopping in to complain of hunger and thirst." The Lutheran minister worried most about the militia, who had "wicked men among them." The "militia is made up of all sorts of nationalities and cannot be kept in proper discipline." On December 8, 1777, Muhlenberg noted, "Our barn was also filled with marauders who, when begging will not get them far enough, know how to get what they want by pilfering."[31] To Muhlenberg, the riffraff in the area were much like the tramps of later American history, whom residents confronted with reluctant charity and fearfulness.

A North Carolina militiaman, William Dickson, described the terror among the farmers of southeastern North Carolina in 1781 after the battle of Guilford Courthouse. Cornwallis had withdrawn to Wilmington, North Carolina, and Greene had retreated to South Carolina. Marauders committed widespread depredations, carrying off farm animals and nearly everything else of value, including house furnishings and wearing apparel. "The outrages," declared Dickson, "were committed mostly by a train of loyal refugees," who "follow the camps and under the protection of the army enrich themselves." There were also "another swarm of beings (not better than harpies)" who caused great distress.

These were women who followed the army in the character of officers and soldiers' wives. They were generally considered by the inhabitants to be more insolent than the soldiers. They were generally mounted on the best horses and side saddles, dressed in the finest and best clothes that could be taken from the inhabitants as the army marched through the country.[32]

British commanders in the South recognized that women were among the marauders. Lieutenant Colonel Archibald Campbell, in charge of the British invasion of Georgia, in December 1778 issued orders for "advanced Centinels and Patroles" to "stop all Stragglers, whether Men or Women, Blacks or Whites," who "are found with Plunder, or committing any Act of Depredation" and to send them in irons to the provost. Cornwallis, in March 1781, called upon army personnel to be on the alert "to Detect & punish all Men & Women" involved in "the Shameful & Dangerous practice of plundering & Distressing the Country." When convicted of plundering, Army women, both American and British, faced whippings of up to 100 lashes "on the bare back" and being "drummed" out of the army.[33]

A Loyalist claimant, who filed for compensation for losses after the war, noted that, in December 1776, a "Party of the king's Troops & a number of women with them had plundered my house." Women with the British army often accompanied marauding parties. Tory militia bands in the South included women. While the American army allowed an indefinite number of women and children in the camps, the British had a fixed quota, six women or less per company. Women officially permitted to be with the British army were assigned barrack space, and, like the female followers of the American army, also partial rations. Many women hovered around the British camps and garrisons without being admitted into army stations or receiving provisions. Moreover, both British and American army women on a march had to position themselves on the "flanks" of the baggage trains. Thus those women detached from the regular body of troops could conveniently join soldier-plunderers. As Washington's army retreated toward the Hudson River, in early November 1776, after the battle of White Plains, American troops cruelly plundered local citizens and "many helpless women had even their shirts taken from their backs by the soldiers' wives."[34] The need for clothing of the women and children accompanying the armies accounts in large measure for the theft of women's and children's wearing apparel.

During Cornwallis's North Carolina invasion of 1781, blacks attached to the British army were used for foraging. To deter them from turning into marauders, they had to wear identifying insignia; those who did not comply were to be flogged. Furthermore, any black caught "in search of plunder" was to be executed on the spot. Nevertheless, reports came in "of Negroes Stragling from the Line of March, plundering & Using Violence to the Inhabitants."[35]

Straggling of all sorts continued to plague the British army. As General Howe's troops moved from the Head of Elk toward Philadelphia, beginning on August 28, 1777, 200 British and Hessian soldiers were captured while plundering.[36] A British officer observed that, just before the battle of Germantown, "Forty Seven Grenadiers and several other Parties straggling for Plunder were Surprised by the Rebels."[37]

As any good commanding officer knows, after a battle, especially during a retreat, it is imperative that soldiers be detailed immediately to round up army stragglers, if for no other reason than to prevent the depletion of military ranks. A court-martial dismissed Major General Adam Stephen from the Continental army in part as a result of the charge that during and after the battle of Germantown, when "it was necessary to cover straglers which were coming in," Stephen "went off under pretence to reconnoitre . . . and left his Division behind; for want of this necessary Disposition tis supposed many Stragglers fell into the Enemys Hands."[38]

Unauthorized leave from camp, which often led to marauding, was a persistent concern for both armies, more so for the American army because their forces were more likely to be stationed in rural areas. Unlike the soldiers of modern times, the ragtag enlisted men of the Continental army did not enjoy a regular privilege of authorized "liberty." It was an easy matter for a soldier to stroll out of camp and slip past the undermanned guard cordon. Soldiers were allowed to patronize farm vendors who were permitted to set up produce stalls just outside camp, but, without money, the temptation to roam the countryside to pick up vegetables, poultry, and the like proved irresistible. Unregulated sutlers, or civilian provisioners, sold spiritous liquors away from camp. General Cornwallis, from his headquarters at Hillsborough, North Carolina, in February 1781, expressed "great concern" that he "hears every day reports of Soldiers being taken by the Enemy, in consequence of their Straggling out of Camp in search of Whiskey."[39]

In a typical instance, four officers of the Pennsylvania Line, while serving with General Greene's army, one morning after breakfast "took a walk to the country," where they found a "number of Carolina soldiers straggling. ... We heard a musket fired, we pursued three of said soldiers and caught two of them, who had shot one of the poor negroes' hogs. We guarded them to camp and had them confined."[40]

Washington took a hard line toward soldiers who, using one artifice or another, left camp and plundered civilians. The dreadful winter at Morristown, December 1779 to February 1780, severely tested the commander in chief's resolve. The frequent and heavy snows, which made it difficult to bring in food supplies, accentuated the suffering. "Nothing to eat from morning to morning again," was the camp lament. Soldiers even resorted to eating tree bark.[41] During the worst part of the crisis, Washington relented on punishment for marauding by out-of-camp soldiers. "Some for their preservation have been compelled to maraud and rob from the Inhabitants," Washington declared, "and I have it not in my power to punish, or to repress the practice."[42] Washington wrote to local law officials asking for forbearance. The American soldiers, he pointed out, "have borne their suffering with a patience that merits the approbation of their Countrymen," but "their distress has in some instances prompted the Men to commit depredations . . . which at any other period would be punished with exemplary severity." The situation was "an unfortunate necessity."[43]

By the end of January 1780, Washington could return to stringent measures in curtailing marauding. "With a night scarcely passes without gangs of soldiers going out of camp and committing every species of robbery, depredation and the grossest personal Insults." Washington tightened camp security. More camp guards and patrols were provided, with authority to administer, at the discretion of an officer, 100 lashes on those persons caught outside camp without permission and from 100 to 500 stripes on those committing robberies.[44]

One way to diminish the number of men exiting camps was to limit passes. With Washington's army not engaging the enemy over long periods of time, officers became lenient in issuing passes. An enraged commander in chief, in orders issued from the army's brief encampment in Bergen County, New Jersey, expressed a renewed resolve to curtail the abuse:

It is with infinite regret the General is obliged once more to take notice of the disorderly conduct of the soldiers arising in a great measure from the abuse of passes: the whole country is overspread with straggling soldiers with the most frivolous pretences, under which they commit every species of robbery and plunder. In a ride he took the other day he found soldiers as low as Aquakanung bridge on both sides of the river and as far as he has ever yet gone round the environs of camp the roads and farm houses are full of them. To remedy these evils and to have the army ready for any sudden emergency the General does in most express and positive Terms forbid all but General Officers and Officers commanding Regiments to grant passes; and not more than eight from a regiment are to be given by the latter in a day, and those only to Soldiers of orderly conduct.[45]

Every enlisted man caught trying to "pass the chain of Sentinels" without proper authorization was to receive immediately 50 lashes.[46] Additional measures included frequent roll calls, nighttime searches of troops' quarters, and inspection of knapsacks. General Samuel Elbert, in command of the Georgia troops, required officers to accompany "any fishing or hunting parties in order to prevent their straggling."[47]

Military police played a role in maintaining camp security and apprehending absent delinquents. Congress established a provost corps in 1776.[48] With the increased problem of soldiers leaving camp for marauding, it was decided to create an elite unit with expanded provost duties. On May 27, 1778, Congress authorized a Maréchaussée Corps, so named after the mounted police in the French army. Besides performing regular provost duties, the Maréchassée was responsible for preventing marauding and spying and supervising camp breaking and marches to deter soldiers from drifting away. The new corps was mounted and accoutred as light dragoons. Most of the sixty-three members were German Americans from Pennsylvania. Washington preferred to staff military police with foreigners, who were expected not to be too sympathetic with the usual run of American soldiers. Four members had assignment as executioners. Captain Bartholomew Von Heer, formerly an artillery officer and a German immigrant, had the command of the Maréchaussée.[49]

The effectiveness of the Maréchaussée Corps as a wide-ranging police patrol was reduced by its occasional employment as a combat unit and by Washington's borrowing some of its soldiers for his "life guard." The unit often lacked sufficient upkeep. Continental army commanders continued to use a rear guard and flankers to apprehend those soldiers on a march who quit the ranks or went beyond the "hearing of a drum."[50] By 1782 the role of the Maréchauseé had been diminished "to the impotent level of the old provost marshalry."[51]

Deserters, singly and in groups, while on the lam, frequently resorted to robbery. Some of these delinquents absconded from the army after having already committed criminal acts inside or outside of camp.[52]

On Communion Day, June 22, 1776, four army deserters, with "godless and murderous intentions," rode into the Moravian town of Salem, North Carolina, and invaded the tavern and the house next door where they assaulted persons and smashed furniture; outside they beat up passersby. This was too much even for the pacifist Moravians, and a party of "Single Brethren" subdued the interlopers and carried them off to jail.[53]

A sampling of newspaper notices indicates a deserter-marauder problem.

A Philadelphia item published in December 1776 reported that "three villains," one of them an Irishman, John Watson, a member of the Pennsylvania rifle regiment, robbed a home near Princeton, New Jersey, and hauled off in knapsacks and bags nearly £200 worth of goods. A $100 reward was posted for the capture of the men, who were supposed to be "bound for Delaware [River], and so on to Shamokin" (an Indian village, now Sunbury, Pennsylvania).[54] A $500 reward was offered in a Charleston, South Carolina, newspaper in March 1779 for the capture of two brothers, John and William Martin, who had robbed a farmer. Both men had deserted from the Sixth South Carolina Regiment; one of the brothers had a missing ear, and the other, a missing forefinger of the left hand.[55]

In late September 1781, "the noted horse-thief Jerry King" was captured in Mendham, New Jersey, "on one of his nocturnal expeditions." King had deserted from Captain Thomas Clark's artillery company in 1777 and remained active in horse thievery for four years, escaping twice from jail. "As a reward for demerit," King was hanged at Morristown, New Jersey, on September 18, 1781.[56] A large reward for a deserter turned horse thief was offered by a Maryland newspaper in December of the same year.[57]

American deserters usually returned home, and, harbored by kin and neighbors, eluded arrest. Some deserters, however, wanted to avoid risk altogether and fled to isolated areas and the mountain fastness of the frontier. Southern New Jersey, the three Delaware counties, and especially Vermont provided refuge to military fugitives. Virginia deserters sought refuge in the western counties of Montgomery, Washington, and Hampshire and, during the early part of the war, northwestern North Carolina. The western sections of Pennsylvania and New York and Kentucky and Tennessee were "swarming with fugitives." Some deserters joined Indians and Tories in raiding army supply trains and plundering civilians.[58]

Numerous soldiers deserted the British. Some found employment; others, sparingly, were permitted to join American military forces. Still others for a while were footloose. A correspondent to the *Pennsylvania Gazette* in 1779 warned citizens "by no means suffer them to roam at large through the country, or go near our camps. . . . If they are idle, and won't accept of employment they are to be suspected, and treated as pernicious vagrants."[59]

Many escaped British prisoners of war, who had been held by the Americans, tried to make their way to New York City or other British army locations. These fugitives were able to take advantage of a sort of underground railroad, in which people fed them and acted as guides. Assisting the escape of prisoners was a capital offense.[60]

The brutal robbery of General William Maxwell's father and brother at their farmhouse in Sussex County, New Jersey, on April 19, 1780, led to the arrest of Robert Maxwell (no relation to the general) and John McCoy,

deserters from the Convention army (Saratoga prisoners of war). Both of
the accused had been working in the area for about a year. Despite the fact
that the assailants were not identified by the victims (the crime occurred
during pitch blackness) and strong evidence favoring their innocence, both
men were convicted in the county court and hanged.[61] (For James Moody's
involvement, see Chapter 6.)

As the war progressed, punishment for marauding increased in severity
in both armies, yet there was a disparity in enforcement. Some British officers preferred a hands-off approach to the plundering of property belonging
to rebels because such was a necessity in winning the war, and it provided
deserved compensation for soldiers and exacted revenge.[62] During the Pennsylvania campaign of 1777, Major John André observed,

> I have passed with the front of a brigade and seen dressing at the fires of a licentious
> regiment the greatest profusion of meat and poultry, whilst on their flanks other corps
> were living upon salt provision and inflicting a very severe punishment on such as had
> presumed to trangress orders.[63]

Army commanders regularly issued orders against robbing civilians. General Israel Putnam entreated all officers and men to do their utmost to detect
plundering "that Justice may be Done to the Ingered Inhabitants and the
Camp Cleansed from the Imputation of Robery and Theft."[64] Soldiers found
to have property belonging to "inhabitants" were subject for trial by a general court-martial.[65] Military personnel benefitting from stolen items were
deemed accessories and were equally liable to the punishment meted out to
the actual perpetrators. Thus a soldier warming himself by a campfire made
from stolen fence rails was as guilty as the actual thief.[66]

Stealing items even of little value was a capital offense. Penalties included
whippings (50 to 200 lashes), running the gauntlet "through the whole
army," and being placed in irons on a diet of bread and water. Sentences
were handed down by court-martial or summarily (whippings) by commanders of provost or field units.[67]

Army trials for theft from civilians numbered 197 of the 3,315 courts-
martial in the Continental armies (gleaned from 168 orderly books), according to James C. Neagles. The incidence represents 7.3 percent of all
courts-martial.[68]

Officers involved in any kind of robbery, of course, did not undergo whippings or, for that matter, suffer death. Consequences, nevertheless, were
severe. An officer involved in "Venduing of Plunder" had to make full
restitution in compensation for everything taken.[69] For plundering, he could
also be cashiered.[70]

At a brigade court-martial convened by General Lachlan McIntosh near

Savannah, Georgia, on October 9, 1779, a Captain Carter was tried on a charge of "Plundering Contrary to repeated Orders." Witnesses testified that Carter and a small party of soldiers came to a house where the owner refused them entry. When Carter shot at and missed the protester, he ordered a soldier to shoot, but the weapon misfired. The intruders, nevertheless, seized the victim and "tied him up to the Corn House & Whiped him" because he "would not tell where his money and other goods were." Carter and his men carried away all the household furniture and seven slaves. Carter's defense was that the victim was "supposed to be an Enemy to his Country, and that he did not mean to appropriate the things to his own use." A court-martial verdict dismissed Carter from the service and declared him to be ineligible to hold a military commission again. Carter was also remanded to civil authority for trial.[71]

George Washington, as he was wont to do regarding all capital convictions, permitted executions for men convicted of plundering on a selective basis, pardoning some condemned soldiers at the last moment. He advised General John Sullivan in one case that the execution "should be done in the most public manner . . . as it may serve to convince the rest of the Division that crimes of this dye will meet the most rigorous punishment."[72]

Several executions for plundering, occurring in Washington's army in New Jersey, may be noted. On April 20, 1779,

five soldiers were conducted to the gallows, according to their sentence, for the crimes of desertion and robbing the inhabitants. A detachment of troops and a concourse of people formed a circle round the gallows, and the criminals were brought in a cart, sitting on their coffins, and halters about their necks. While in this awful situation, trembling on the verge of eternity, three of them received a pardon from the commander-in-chief, who is always tenderly disposed to spare the lives of his soldiers. They acknowledged the justice of their sentence, and expressed the warmest thankfulness and gratitude for their merciful pardon. The two others were obliged to submit to their fate.[73]

On August 26, 1780, a soldier of the Pennsylvania Line, "having *ravished a farmers Daughter*, being found guilty of merauding inhabitants, was tried found guilty & executed immediately—others who had aid in otherwise abusing the people were flogged." After the execution, among the troops ordered to pass by the corpse, "one of comerades slaped him on the thigh & says 'well Jack you are the best off of any of us—it wont come to your turn to be hanged again this ten years.' "[74]

On September 12, 1780, David Hall of the Pennsylvania Line was executed "for robing an Inhabitant." He and three others, with blackened faces, had robbed a house at night, "but the Neighbors rallied, pursued & caught this man—& upon conviction was sentenced to suffer death." As the condemned man approached the gallows, "a number of women came thro' the

Provost to bid him farewell—one seizing him with both her hands, says—'great luck to you David.' "[75]

Like Washington, General Greene, commander of the Southern army, was hesitant to execute soldiers for marauding but felt he had to set examples. On March 1, 1782, two soldiers of the Maryland Line were hanged for robbing civilians.[76] As General Anthony Wayne's Pennsylvania troops moved through central Virginia in July 1781, a soldier, William Fitzpatrick, was convicted by court-martial and hanged for robbing a farmer.[77]

British commanders exacted harsh penalties for marauding, but sometimes enforcement lagged. From the beginning of the war, it was a capital offense for a British soldier to "plunder or pillage or to enter a house" unless ordered to do so. As General Howe's army opened the Pennsylvania campaign, on August 25, 1777, two British soldiers were hanged and five "severely whipped" for plundering, and on September 15 a "Light Infantry man" of the Fifth Regiment and a grenadier of the Twenty-eighth Regiment were executed for marauding, "the 1st Examples made, tho often threaten'd, & many deserved it."[78] There were other instances of stern justice, such as on November 24, 1779, when several soldiers were flogged "severely" for night marauding. As the British army completed its evacuation of Philadelphia on June 18, 1778, General Henry Clinton, in his orders, announced that any soldier found marauding or "straggling beyond the advanced Posts of the Army" without permission was to be executed on the spot.[79]

Clinton, however, showed reluctance in cracking down on plundering in the British-controlled area of Long Island, preferring to let civil justice take its course. In the summer of 1779, three privates belonging to the British Seventeenth Dragoons, commanded by Colonel Samuel Birch, burglarized a house near Hempstead, Long Island. During a scuffle one of the soldiers was killed. An Episcopalian clergyman wrote that he was not surprised by the robbery because Birch and his "worse than useless Regiment" had been roaming around taking whatever they wanted. The other soldiers escaped, but, having been identified, were arrested; however, they were soon freed. The dead soldier faced trial and was convicted and sentenced to be hanged in chains. General Henry Clinton approved the proceedings, and the sentence was executed upon the dead soldier. Birch informed the local citizens that justice had been done, and the case was closed.[80]

Clinton favored the use of civilian courts to try murder cases involving soldiers killing civilians. In the spring of 1781, three British soldiers robbed a house near Jerusalem, in Queens County, New York, and in so doing killed a man. The murderers were recognized and reported to British headquarters in New York City, where they were found guilty by a court-martial and sentenced to be hanged. The condemned men were never executed. Clinton thought the case should have been tried in a court of civil law, since the military code did not cover the murder of civilians. Thomas Jones, a former New York Supreme Court judge and a Tory, criticized the decision not to execute the culprits. He felt that since New York had a military-installed governor, General James Robertson, he could have ordered a trial in a civil court under a commission of oyer and terminer. The three criminals stayed in jail for three months and were then released.[81]

The plundering of civilians in the countryside by army detachments, militia, or stragglers remained a vexatious problem throughout the war. Civilians in the zones between the lines of the opposing armed forces had the worst of it. They were subject to indiscriminate looting, regardless of affiliation. General Greene tried unsuccessfully to mount patrols to stop the plundering.[82]

Possibly, by mutual accord of opposing commanders, an effective means to protect residents might have been accomplished. While Greene admitted, in reference to military hospitals, that for "armies operating in a neutral kingdom the commanding officers may with great propriety" enter into an agreement "from which both may derive equal advantage and at the same time promote the cause of humanity," he felt that such an arrangement would be "against the interest of a country invaded."[83]

For armies on the move, the British occasionally posted "safeguards" at homes near the line of march, with orders to kill any soldier caught plundering.[84] The safeguards were expected to protect private property against all comers. As could be anticipated, however, American soldiers and militia did not take kindly to lone redcoats guarding "helpless families."

Washington's army occasionally used safeguards in the vicinity of encampments to protect civilians from American soldiers. Safeguards, as in the southern theater, were impractical when contending regular and irregular troops were frequently in close proximity of each other.

Colonel Alexander Stewart, who shortly before had commanded the British troops at the battle of Eutaw Springs, complained to General Francis Marion that American militia had abused a safeguard. Stewart informed Marion that "upon every movement of the British troops" he would "send safe-guards to the neighboring plantations to protect the harmless neutral individuals," but he hesitated to do so because of "the fear of their being ill-treated by the mistaken zeal of the irregulars of your party." To prevent "the horrors of war being carried to extremes," it would be well to give "safe-guards the respect and sacredness which they receive in every civilized country."[85]

Indeed, the placement of "peace-keeping" details, by the mutual arrangement of both armies, for the protection of citizens and their property, might have averted much of the horrors of the war.

Chapter 2

Cowboys and Skinners

Bordered by opposing armies, Westchester County, New York, was a war zone, a no-man's-land constantly scoured by roving military bands and freebooters. It was dubbed the Neutral Ground, not because the inhabitants were noncommittal (there was almost an equal division between Tories and Whigs) but because it was "Debatable Ground." The county's resources were fair game to either army, and citizens were subject to being victimized regardless of affiliation or loyalty. One lived at greater hazard in the neighborhoods above and west of New York City (on Manhattan Island) than in the city itself, which was overrun with refugees, a riffraff soldiery, and a lawless and derelict element, many of whom were homeless or found shelter in the burned-out buildings left by the great fire of 1776. In Westchester County anarchy all but prevailed, more so in the lower part where a fleeting British military authority replaced civil jurisdiction. Still, with the capability of patriot military forces to penetrate into any part of the county, many leading Loyalists had to flee. Some were tainted with treason by the legislature and their property was confiscated; others became refugees because they feared bodily harm since they would not swear allegiance to the rebel cause. A high proportion of male Loyalists from Westchester County joined military units sponsored by the British. Often the refugees left behind unprotected family members.

Westchester County had been a prosperous farming community at the start of the war, populated by sturdy farmers of Dutch and English descent and tenants on the manorial lands of Frederick Philipse (roughly present-day Yonkers) and lesser estates. There were also marginal residents, those who lived in "Huts & Thatch Houses under the sides of Hills."[1] At the beginning of the war the county's population numbered about 22,000, 1,400 of whom were freeholders.[2] Although lacking an urban dimension, Westchester County had a scattering of little villages and hamlets, including Dobbs Ferry, Peekskill, New Rochelle, North Castle, Poundridge, Bedford, Rye, Scarsdale, Sing-Sing, Tarrytown, White Plains, Westchester, West Farms, Morrisania, Eastchester, Mount Vernon, and Mamaroneck.

The British outer lines extended from Philipse Manor on the Hudson River to Eastchester, backed up by posts at Kingsbridge (which connected the upper tip of Manhattan Island with the mainland), Fordham Heights, West Farms (central Bronx), and Morrisania (southwest Bronx). The American position in upper Westchester County stretched from Peekskill on the Hudson River eastward through the lower part of the Highlands, north of Croton River, and then veered southward near the Connecticut border, terminating at Mamaroneck on Long Island Sound.[3]

It did not take long for Westchester County farmers to be deprived of their livestock and a major portion of their sustenance. Army patrols and foraging parties of both sides combed the countryside and appropriated what they could find. Tory refugee bands and outright freebooters were soon on the scene and took their plunder to sell to the British army or at public vendue behind British lines. As one writer noted, the farmers were "tormented in the morning by marauders who shouted 'God and the King,' and at night by plunderers, who huzzaed for 'God and Congress.' "[4]

A French chaplain, Abbé Claude Robin, who traveled down the Hudson River, commented that

As we approached towards New-York, between the Lines of both Armies, we see more and more of the sorrowful vestiges of war and desolation,—the houses plundered, ruined, abandoned or burnt. These Americans so soft, pacific and benevolent by nature, are here transformed into monsters implacable, bloody and ravenous; party rage has kindled a spirit of hatred between them; they attack and rob each other by turns, destroy dwelling houses, or establish themselves therein by driving out those who had before dispossessed others.[5]

Reverend Timothy Dwight, chaplain to General Samuel H. Parsons's Connecticut brigade, stationed at White Plains in the fall of 1777, wrote about the dehumanizing effects upon the "unhappy people" of Westchester County caused by the ravages of war. The inhabitants feared everybody whom they saw, and loved nobody. . . . Their houses in the meantime were in a great measure scenes of desolation. Their furniture was extensively plundered or broken to pieces. The walls, floors, and windows were injured both by violence and decay. . . . Their cattle was gone. Their enclosures were burnt down where they were capable of becoming fuel, and in many cases thrown down where they were not. Their fields were covered with a rank growth of weeds and wild grass. Amid all this appearance of desolation, nothing struck my own eye more forcibly than the sight of this great road, the passage from New York to Boston. Where I had heretofore seen a continual succession of horses and carriages, and life and bustle lent a sprightliness to all the environing objects, not a single, solitary traveler was visible from week to week, or from month to month.[6]

An indication of what the residents of Westchester County were in store for became evident in late November 1775 when "border ruffians" from Connecticut, led by Isaac Sears, one of the patriot strongmen of New York City, cut a swath through the county, pillaging farmhouses.[7] In late August 1776, Colonel Edward Hand's Continental infantry regiment was accused of plundering "every Body in Westchester County indiscriminately"; the loot, including clothing and furniture, was "brought over to Morrisania and sold at publick auction."[8]

"Robbery, house burning, murder &c" in the Neutral Ground began, as one New England Continental officer noted, "as soon as the enemy fully possessed New York and the parts adjacent to it." Both the British and the Americans were offenders. To prevent use by the enemy as well as to supply American troops, the New York State Convention, on October 16, 1776, ordered the seizure of all horses, sheep, cattle, and threshed grain in Westchester County along the Hudson River and Long Island Sound.[9] As the American army retreated through Westchester County in early November 1776, the inhabitants were "cruelly plundered . . . in the general ravage, no discrimination was made by Whig or Tory."[10] The sack and burning of White Plains on November 5, 1776, by Massachusetts and Connecticut troops led by Major John W. Austin so infuriated General Washington that he had Austin cashiered.[11]

A food shortage in New York City, owing to substantial arrivals of British troops and refugees, increased pressure for securing provisions and livestock from Westchester County. It mattered little how supplies were obtained, thereby affording opportunity for persons to engage in the robbery of civilians. The needs of American troops left behind in the Highlands exacerbated the demand.

Two species of marauders in the Neutral Ground were the Cowboys and the Skinners. Cowboys generally were irregular British troops or Tories who were adept at rustling cattle for the purpose of driving the animals through British lines for sale to the army or at public vendue. Besides Westchester cattle, livestock driven from New England destined for the American army also fell prey to the Cowboys. "Cowboy," in eighteenth-century usage, had the connotation of "rogue," and indeed some of the Cowboys did engage in wholesale plundering. "Cowboys" was a term specifically applied to the Corps of Loyalist Westchester Refugees. Skinners were patriot troops, mostly militia, or freebooters ostensibly allied with the rebel cause, who plundered indiscriminately and stole just about anything, even the clothes off the backs of their victims.[12]

The Corps of Loyalist Westchester Refugees was created in 1777 by the British command to wage guerrilla warfare beyond British lines in Westchester County and to procure livestock and provisions. The unit consisted of mounted horsemen and light infantry; the former wore uniforms of green coats faced with white and brown cloth leggings, and the latter, civilian clothing. By the end of the war, the corps numbered nearly 500 members. Recruits were mostly refugees from Westchester and Dutchess counties and western Connecticut, who were seeking revenge for their rough handling by Whig neighbors. Members of the refugee corps served without pay, hence the motivation to profit from raids. There were frequent complaints that the Cowboys "in their excursions do not distinguish between friend and foe." Thomas Jones, a Tory judge, in his history of New York, observed that for the Cowboys "it was an established rule never to return empty handed." The Cowboys supplied one-third of the provisions for the New York market.[13]

Colonel Mansfield Baremore first commanded the Cowboys. Upon his capture on November 2, 1779, a Pennsylvania newspaper said of him that he was one of the "most active partizan officers, whose uniform endeavours have been to distress and injure the inhabitants" of Westchester County.[14] Baremore was exchanged after a few months; in November 1780, he was killed in a skirmish.[15]

DeLancey's Cowboys, as the Westchester refugee corps was known after James DeLancey assumed its leadership in 1780, kept Continentals and patriot militia on their toes. DeLancey directed countless raids by bands of his Cowboys, but he seldom went on missions himself. A "large fleshy man—florid—fine looking" but often "over-bearing and coarse,"[16] James DeLancey (1747–1804) hailed from one of New York's most powerful families. He was a nephew of Chief Justice James DeLancey and the grandson of the last de facto governor of New York, Lieutenant Governor Cadwallader Colden. At the age of twenty-three, DeLancey became sheriff of Westchester County, a position he held until 1777.

James DeLancey's trouble with the patriots began when he refused to sign the Association. Refusing to obey an order from the American army officers to stay at his house, he fled to British-held New York City. There he en-

James DeLancey. By unknown artist. From W. A.
Calnek, *History of the County of Annapolis*
(Toronto: William Briggs, 1897). Photo courtesy of
the Westchester County Historical Society.

gaged in a fistfight with a Hessian officer and was briefly confined to the provost jail. New York's military-installed royal governor, William Tryon, in March 1777, placed DeLancey in charge of raising Loyalist militia in Westchester County. As a member of the refugee corps he quickly rose in rank from captain to lieutenant colonel. In November 1777 DeLancey was captured by a rebel scouting party. He was found "under a bed, and for better defence, had himself surrounded with a bulwark of baskets. He was dragged from his humble redoubt, put under a proper guard" and then sent to the Hartford jail. He was exchanged for an American officer held by the British, and he was soon back in action with the Cowboys.[17]

James Holmes, DeLancey's second in command late in the war who most often substituted for his superior in leading raids, had been a large landowner from near Bedford and a justice of the peace. He first sided with the American cause and served as a colonel and commander of the 4th New York Regiment, from June to December 1775. Upon resigning his commission, he "lived retired" at his farm. In April 1778 Holmes was arrested "on suspicion of intending to join the British Army." After a two-day confinement he escaped to British lines. He resided in New York City and on Long Island until the fall of 1779 when he "was taken Prisoner being out of the Lines." After twenty months of imprisonment in Poughkeepsie, Holmes escaped in August 1781, making his way to New York City. He then accepted a commission as a lieutenant colonel in DeLancey's refugee corps, in which he served until the end of the war. Holmes's estate, like DeLancey's, was confiscated.[18]

The Cowboys also occasionally saw action in conjunction with other British military units. One such instance happened on November 17, 1777, when the Cowboys and a partisan corps of chausseurs under Captain Andreas Emmerich surprised a settlement in the Sawmill River Valley (Yonkers). They burned the houses of Cornelius and Peter Van Tassel, took the clothing even off the backs of their wives and children, and then tied the two Van Tassels to the tails of their horses and forced them to drive their cattle to British lines.[19] "Mounted refugees," in conjunction with British and Hessian troops, made a foray into American lines at Poundridge, twenty miles northeast of White Plains, on February 2, 1780. Of the 200 rebels engaged, 14 were killed, 37 were wounded, and 76 were made prisoners; the British loss was only 5 killed and 18 wounded.[20] Once in a while other British army units did the work of the Cowboys, such as Lieutenant Colonel Banastre Tarleton's light dragoons who raided near White Plains in July 1779; commented an American officer, "[T]hey, as usual plundered most of the houses they came to and set fire to several other houses."[21]

Typical of raids conducted by the Cowboys was one in January 1779 when they seized grain and flour in a magazine near White Plains and carried off "the entire store on 37 wagons."[22] In November 1780 a detachment of DeLancey's Cowboys, thirty mounted and twenty on foot, commanded by Captain Timothy Knapp and Lieutenant James Kipp, "went as far as Tarry-Town, where they took about 120 fat cattle, that were to be drove to Washington's camp."[23] The Cowboys extended their raids to include western Connecticut.[24] Washington kept army details in the field in constant pursuit of the Cowboys and even attacked their encampments, which were first located at Morrisania and then near Kingsbridge.[25]

One of Washington's infantrymen, Joseph Plumb Martin, a Massachusetts farmboy who enlisted at the age of sixteen, recalled after the war adventures in giving chase to Cowboys. In 1778, after a party of Cowboys had destroyed stores of flour and other provisions collected by a militia colonel for use of his troops, the colonel solicited volunteers from among Continental soldiers "to endeavour to capture the gang." Martin and eighty others answered the call. The detachment had difficulty in obtaining "any intelligence of the vermin we were in pursuit of." Traveling mostly at night through fields, swamps, "mire and woods," Martin and his comrades caught a dozen or so of the culprits, most of whom "belonged in the neighborhood."[26]

In 1781, as the American and French armies were "making preparations to lay siege of New York," Private Martin and thirteen other soldiers were sent out to locate "a party of Refugees, or Cowboys" thought to be near American lines. Martin and his group decided "to stretch our orders a trifle and go a little further." While in "a narrow wood," they "found themselves flanked" by about forty Cowboys. Both sides fired on each other. Then the Cowboys rushed forward, and Martin and his comrades, not having time "to reload our pieces," ran away as fast as they could. Martin, trailing the others, got his foot tangled in a tree stump. The commander of the Cowboy party came up and gave Martin "a stroke with his hanger [short sword] across my leg . . . which laid the bone bare." The assailant turned out to be one of Martin's boyhood "playmates"; the two had once gathered marsh hay together. The Cowboy leader had also served with Martin in the American army before deserting to the British. This commander of the "gang of Ref-ugee Cowboy plunderers" called Martin by name and promised him protec-tion if he surrendered. Martin in the meantime freed his leg, darted away, and eventually caught up with his companions. He marveled that the enemy did not fire at him as he sprinted across a field within easy range.[27]

The base reputation of DeLancey's Cowboys was largely undeserved. DeLancey himself pointed out, in a memorial of April 3, 1783, addressed to the British commander in chief in America, Sir Guy Carleton, that most of the crimes "which are indiscriminately charged against the Refugees" while under DeLancey's command were committed by persons who were not members of his corps. As noted by Catherine S. Crary, most of the plunder taken by DeLancey's unit was in accordance with the rules of war. According to Emmerich de Vattel's *The Law of Nations* (1758), "A nation has a right to deprive the enemy of his possessions and goods . . . which may augment his forces and enable him to make war."[28] Although regularly en-listed, the Cowboys, who did not receive any pay and were expected to conduct guerrilla-like raids, were held to less accountability than other Brit-ish military units. DeLancey merely dismissed from service one of his men who had robbed and murdered a French army sutler.[29]

Banditry behind American lines in the Highlands was often attributed to DeLancey's Cowboys, even though the refugee corps seldom went that dis-tance and then only to accomplish military objectives. Governor George Clinton, in July 1779, called upon a Dutchess County justice of the peace to issue arrest warrants because he had received "frequent Complaints" of "violent Outrages committed in this County and the adjacent Parts of West Chester by a Number of Persons stiling themselves Refugees, making free Quarters upon the Inhabitants and destroying and taking away Property and abusing their Persons."³⁰ A month later, Clinton heard from General William Heath, the American commander in the Highlands, that citizens in the vicinity of Sing-Sing and Tarrytown were being robbed and driven from their homes.³¹

On June 21, 1781, at about 9:00 P.M.,

a number of armed men burst open the door of Mr. Garret Storm in Hopewell [near Fishkill] and immediately demanded his hard cash, which, not instantly being complied with, they put a rope about the old gentleman's neck, though blind, and hung him up, but the rope breaking, he fell; when one of them took a knife, and cut a gash in his throat, but the rope being still about the old gentleman's neck, prevented it from being mortal . . . a Negro . . . got off . . . called a small guard, which happened to be near. . . . [T]he villains instantly run off taking about 14 1. [£] hard cash, a silver bowl, some silver spoons, and several other articles. . . . They had four or five horses to carry off their booty.—'Tis supposed they are some of DeLancey's thieving gang, all of which he is training for the halter.³²

The Peter Jay family endured a "cruel" robbery on April 12, 1781. Peter, old and infirm, and his wife, Mary Van Cortlandt Jay, had living with them at their farmhouse near Fishkill three sons—Frederick, Peter, Jr., who was blind, and James—and a blind daughter, Anna Maricka ("Nancy"). Another son, John Jay, at the time was on a diplomatic mission in Spain. Thirty armed men surrounded the house, twelve of whom, "with Fixed Bayonets," gained entry so silently that the occupants were not alerted until they were "in Custody." The intruders "seized all the Arms and then fell plundering every thing they could lay hands on." The robbers "continued with us" from 8:00 P.M. to 1:00 A.M. Fortunately, a few days later "a Party of ours fell in with them near Dobbs Ferry, killed one and retook the greater part of the Plate, a Sword and some small articles which we again got after paying nearly the Value."³³

Meanwhile, in the Neutral Ground, the refugee corps made raids with the least calculated risks. For example, as reported on September 6, 1781, "DeLancey's free booters, who were affraid to shew themselves while the confederate army lay near White Plains . . . are now more bold; some of them came out last week, picked up some prisoners, and, as is their custom, robbed them of their property."³⁴

The sudden appearance at a farm by a band of mounted Cowboys, with blackened faces and waving sabers, was enough to terrify the intended victims. Besides taking livestock and valuables, the intruders, out of revenge, burned crops and barns.³⁵ Freebooters, without any military affiliation, could be just as fearsome.

One of the most notorious of the freebooting "cowboys" was Shubal Merritt (1761–83). At the age of fifteen Shubal and his brother, Thomas (1758–

1842), left their home in Rye in the fall of 1776 and joined Lieutenant Colonel Andreas Emmerich's chaussers in New York City. Both brothers quarreled with their commander and were discharged. While Thomas went on to service with the Queen's Rangers for the duration of the war, Shubal became an independent freebooter. Shubal, usually in partnership with others, became well known throughout the Neutral Ground for many robberies. In July 1781 Shubal, Ned Merritt, and Tom Saxton waylaid and murdered a French sutler attached to the Comte de Rochambeau's army. Not long afterward, while Shubal and Benomi Newman were robbing the house of a Mrs. Sherwood near Horseneck (Greenwich), Connecticut, they were surrounded by an American detachment led by Colonel Elisha Sheldon. Newman was shot dead, and Shubal Merritt was taken prisoner. For some reason, Merritt was soon released. He had other encounters with rebel troops but escaped.

Shubal Merritt's downfall resulted from his robbery of a Loyalist, one Holcroft, near New Rochelle; Holcroft engaged in a profitable illicit trade with the British. The victim complained to Colonel James DeLancey, who summoned Merritt to his camp near Kingsbridge and ordered Merritt to return the stolen money. Merritt complied, but Holcroft was still bent on revenge. Holcroft secured the services of Samuel Reynolds, who himself had been shot and wounded while being held prisoner by Merritt, to track the outlaw. Reynolds and a party of whaleboaters discovered their quarry in Mamaroneck, gave chase, caught up with Merritt at a tavern in New Rochelle, and shot and killed him. Long after the war, from oral interviews, it was discovered that many of the old-time residents of Westchester County had regarded Shubal Merritt as a hero.[36]

On the patriot side, the Skinners, mostly freebooters and local roughneck militiamen, competed with the Cowboys in stealing livestock and other property. Ostensibly plundering only Loyalists, the Skinners frequently did not concern themselves with the allegiance of their victims. "The Skinners generally 'skinned' their victims first and inquired about their politics afterward."[37]

Because of the disintegration of law and order in the Neutral Ground, patriot Westchester County militia were not called up for duty elsewhere. There was plenty of temptation to rob the property of Tories since New York law awarded the value of the property taken from Tories to the captors.[38]

Even some Continental soldiers behaved in Skinner fashion, as did their counterparts among the local militia. Colonel Aaron Burr, in command of a post at White Plains, in 1778 and 1779, was horrified to find widescale plundering by his troops. On one occasion a detail had scarcely returned a half an hour when six or seven civilians came before Burr "with piteous applications" for restoring their stolen horses and goods. Burr arrested the more obvious culprits and ordered restitution. Several of the offenders were publicly flogged. These measures had their effect, for afterwards "there was not a single instance of robbery" by Burr's men.[39]

The apprehension of Skinners from time to time was reported in the loyalist newspaper in New York City. Lieutenant Colonel Tarleton, in July 1779, captured American militiamen near Bedford. "Amongst the prisoners is one of the Vantassel's from near Tarry-town, of a pedigree partly Indian, partly Batavian; this despicable caitiff has of late" engaged in "*flagellating* numbers of inoffensive women, whom he had suspected of frequenting the New-York markets; four of this handy varlet's brothers also are in safe custody."[40] A notice of February 6, 1782, mentioned that DeLancey's men had captured "seven of the Horseneck gentry, commonly called Skinners," near Mamaroneck "in the very act of plundering the sleigh of a poor defenseless inhabitant."[41]

Skinners resorted to atrocities in efforts to persuade persons to forfeit money and other valuables. Techniques included sprinkling hot ashes on the body, hanging until unconscious, hanging by the thumbs, and ducking in closed water sacks. One young woman was shot while traveling the Boston Post Road; the body was stripped naked and a finger was almost cut off from trying to remove a ring.[42]

It was not unusual for Skinners and Cowboys to be allied in securing plunder. Skinners sold stolen property to the Cowboys and received in exchange goods brought up from New York City, or Cowboys turned over to Skinners illicit goods to be disposed above American lines. Both shared in the profits.[43]

Skinners also stole cattle within American lines. After crossing over into Neutral Ground, they staged a sham battle and, pretending to have captured cattle from Cowboys, returned to sell their prize. General William Heath, commandant at West Point, in November 1780, informed Governor George Clinton of "wanton abuses" being

practiced on the Lines, by persons who stile themselves refugees &c. which are loudly complained of both by the officers and well affected inhabitants. These people are represented as devoting themselves to an almost continual plundering of the Inhabitants below the Lines in a manner disgraceful to the laws of humanity, honor or arms. . . . [S]ome of these people have driven off the Cattle of the Inhabitants above the Lines, and having got them on the other side of the Croton, have kindled fires, discharged muskets &c. and then drove the cattle up, pretending that they had defeated a party of cow boys, and retook the cattle, which they claim as lawfull prize, and sell at vendue.[44]

Trying to prevent cattle rustling by both the Cowboys and the Skinners at the same time frustrated Lieutenant Colonel John Jameson, who commanded the American post at North Castle.

The Militia and Cow-boys are very busy in driving, and it is out of my power to prevent them. If I send the troops down below to prevent the Cow-boys the Militia are driving off in the rear, and if I have the troops above, the lower party are driving downwards; and the inhabitants are left destitute without any prospect of redress.[45]

Washington advised several of his commanding officers "to employ some trusty Man or Men to Dog and follow" persons driving cattle "in droves or small parcels" in order to determine if the cattle were destined for the enemy.[46]

With so many Skinners and Cowboys prowling the Neutral Ground, identities became blurred, especially since the plunderers often were not uniformed. Here and there an espionage agent needed cover. James Fenimore Cooper wove an episodic narrative of duplicity in *The Spy: A Tale of the Neutral Ground* (1821). The author, who lived in Westchester County when he wrote the novel, incorporated anecdotes gleaned from interviews with old-timers. In one instance in the story, the hero, a spy for the patriots who was undercover as a peddler, is accosted by a British patrol. To protect himself, the newcomer declares to the military commander,

I have been a poor deluded man who has been serving the rebel army, but, thank God, I've lived to see the error of my ways, and am now come to make reparation by enlisting under the Lord's anointed.

To which the commander of the party responded,

Umph! a deserter—a Skinner, I'll swear, wanting to turn Cow-Boy. In the last brush I had with the scoundrels I could hardly tell my own men from the enemy. We are not over well supplied with coats, and as for the faces, the rascals change sides so often that you may as well count their faces for nothing.[47]

In one of America's most famous spy encounters, Major John André, an adjutant general of the British army, out of uniform and acting as a courier between Generals Benedict Arnold and Henry Clinton, faced the dilemma of whether to pass himself off as an American or as a British operative. The Arnold-André affair is quite familiar. It will suffice here to mention André's capture by Skinners.

In a typical foray, John Yerks of the patriot First Westchester militia organized a "scout" with his comrades—John Dean (the oldest at age 25), John Paulding, James Romer, Isaac See, Isaac Van Wart, and Abraham Williams. Van Wart and Paulding were cousins, as were Paulding and Romer. The group obtained permission from their militia commander to go into the countryside to intercept any Cowboys driving cattle toward New York City. There was ample incentive: success meant dividing money received from sale of the cattle. The party set out in early afternoon, on

John André about to be captured by American militiamen. From *Harper's Weekly*,
October 2, 1880, p. 629.

September 22, 1780, and was joined by David Williams, who had extra
motivation in wanting to avenge a neighbor who had been killed and his
property taken a few days earlier.

After reaching Tarrytown at 7:30 A.M., on Saturday, September 23, the
group had breakfast at the home of John Romer and then proceeded on
their mission southward. Not far from Tarrytown, the Westchester Eight
divided: Paulding, Van Wart, and Williams staked out a position along the
Old Post Road, and the other five took a position at Davis Hill on nearby
Bedford Road. While waiting for their prey, Paulding, Van Wart, and Williams played cards. By arrangement, either of the two groups would fire a
shot as a signal if they needed assistance. Several friendly acquaintances
passed by unmolested. Eventually a man who had a gentlemanly appearance
came galloping up while looking at a map.

Paulding, Van Wart, and Williams greeted the stranger. Paulding, who
had escaped from the North Dutch Church prison in New York City where
he had been held as a prisoner of war, was wearing a Hessian jager's jacket
(green faced with red). Noticing Paulding, André thought he was in safe
company. When asked where he was going, André replied, "I hope you
belong to our party."

"What party?"

"The lower. I am a British officer and have been up the country on
particular business, and would wish not to be detained a minute."

The three Skinners told André to dismount and identified themselves as "Americans." André, surprised, declared, "God bless my soul, a body must do anything to get along now-a-days."

André presented Benedict Arnold's pass. Paulding, the only one of the three captors who was literate, read it, which revealed André's alias, John Anderson. Not entirely satisfied, the three militiamen brought André into a thicket at the side of the road and removed his outer clothing and boots. The incriminating papers relative to the defenses of West Point were discovered in André's stockings. The search also yielded 100 guineas and a gold and a silver watch, which, along with André's horse and its saddle and bridle, was worthwhile loot. The three Skinners were not above stealing; Isaac Van Wart and David Williams only a short while before had been involved in a robbery in which they hung up the victim to get him to reveal the whereabouts of his money.

André, in desperation, offered to have 1,000 guineas and dry goods delivered from New York City if his captors would set him free. The proposal did not have much appeal. It was feared that a British detachment sent out to seal the bargain might not be trustworthy, and Paulding, a prisoner of war escapee, might again be taken into custody. The three militiamen quickly realized they had a spy. By turning André over to the American military authority, they would be able to keep what André possessed when captured and also share in the glory as heroes and perhaps receive other rewards. André was delivered to Colonel Sheldon's light dragoons posted twelve miles distant at North Castle. Lieutenant Colonel John Jameson, acting in Sheldon's stead, received the prisoner. Jameson, unaware of Arnold's connection with the prisoner, sent André on to West Point. Major Benjamin Tallmadge, Washington's intelligence chief, was suspicious, and he reversed the order. André later confessed to full complicity in the treason plot.[48]

All of the Westchester Eight shared in the bounty from André's capture. Paulding, Van Wart, and Williams, however, were singled out as heroes. They received the plaudits of Congress and the commander in chief. Congress provided each of the three men a $200 a year lifetime pension and ordered that each man be given a silver medal: "Fidelity" inscribed on one side and "*Vincit amor patriae*" on the other. Washington presented the medals to the three heroes at his headquarters on Verplanck's Point. The state of New York also voted for each man a farm valued at £500.[49]

The reputation for the uncommon patriotism of Paulding, Van Wart, and Williams remained untarnished until 1817, when Colonel Benjamin Tallmadge, then a congressman from Connecticut, made a speech in the House of Representatives in reference to a proposal to raise the pensions for the three men. Tallmadge accused Paulding, Van Wart, and Williams of having searched André in quest of plunder and not to detect a spy and that they brought André in only because of the expectation of reaping a greater reward. Tallmadge declared that had he been out on patrol the day of André's capture, he would just as likely have apprehended Paulding, Van Wart, and Williams as he would have André.[50]

Some of the worst marauding and atrocities committed in Westchester County occurred as the war was winding down and British and American troops were pulling out of the area. In May 1782 the British command forbade "offensive measures" against the rebels.[51] In October 1782 the British abandoned and demolished all their posts on the British side of the Harlem River, including the Kingsbridge fort.[52] The American army withdrew from the upper reaches of Westchester County on October 27–28, 1782, and reestablished camp across the Hudson River at New Windsor. On March 23, 1783, news arrived that the British government had formally proclaimed cessation of hostilities, and Congress did the same on April 11, four days before its ratification of the preliminary peace treaty. Congress also granted Continental soldiers indefinite furloughs, and by mid June 1783 most of the army had departed for home. The last of the British troops in Westchester County left in mid May 1783.[53]

While the New York state government was slow to reestablish full civil jurisdiction over the Neutral Ground, it was not remiss in persecuting Westchester County Tories. Efforts continued to complete the confiscation process in ridding Loyalists of their real and personal property and to force them into exile. Loyalists who had fled to British protection were not allowed to return to their places of abode. Given the anarchy in the county, there was an ongoing temptation to raid abandoned estates and the property of Loyalist families who had remained. The search went on for persons suspected of disloyalty to the American cause, even at war's end.

Following in the footsteps of the Commission for Detecting and Defeating Conspiracies in the State of New York, which had been authorized to arrest Loyalists and seize the estates of those who had gone over to the enemy, the inquisitorial process was extended on March 6, 1777, by the creation of commissioners of sequestration. Three of these officials, who served seven-year terms, were appointed for each of seven counties. Westchester was the only county in the Southern District to have the commissioners (the British controlled the rest of the district during the war). Loyalist families remaining behind could keep necessary furniture and wearing apparel for only three months. The commissioners of sequestration had the power "to enter any house or place" in search for goods, call upon the militia for assistance, and imprison anyone who refused to be examined on oath as a witness. At war's end especially, the commissioners acquired a reputation for "barbarous measures."[54]

David Colden, a New York Loyalist, observed that "the spirit of persecution and violence does not appear to abate in any degree, since the cessation of hostilities." Loyalists "are not suffered to go into the country even to take a last farewell of their relations." Colden also noted that James DeLancey of Cowboy fame, who was among those named in an act of attainder, "has no expectation of recovering his estate: he has gone to England." Oliver DeLancey, Jr., a cousin of James, although he professed to being a patriot throughout the war, was "turned off the old family estate at West Chester since the cessation of hostilities by commissioners acting under authority of the state, who gave him and several others a severe whiping, lest they should forget the Orders they had got to remove."[55]

One of the most vicious perpetrators of violence during the transition period was Israel Honeywell, Jr., a sequestration commissioner. At the head of a party of fifty, Honeywell searched for and punished Tories. On May 16, 1783, Honeywell and his followers went to the home of Joseph Orser. Honeywell, without saying a word, struck Orser with "a large Club," which ripped the "Scull bare." Others of the group beat Orser and "then left him weltering in his blood." Orser had declared himself a neutral during the war and did not bear arms for either side. John Orser was savagely attacked on the same day and left unconscious; the assailants stole three horses from him. According to historian Philip Ranlet, there were many other "savage incidents committed by Honeywell and his men." Honeywell's gang beat and robbed Oliver DeLancey, Jr. Other violence, as Governor Clinton commented, stemmed from "mere Acts of Individuals unauthorized and uncountenanced by Government."[56]

To restore order in Westchester County, both Governor Clinton and General Washington established military protection. Clinton sent in state troops, and Washington obliged by dispatching Colonel William Hull and eight companies of light infantry. The stated purpose of the federal troops was to assist the civil authority. Washington cautioned Hull to "pay the strictest Attention to prevent the Troops from committing any outrages or excesses on the persons or property of the Inhabitants under pretext of their having been disaffected."[57]

Meanwhile, Governor Clinton ordered Chief Justice Richard Morris of New York into Westchester County "to establish the Civil Authority" in that part of the county "lately relinquished" by the British and "concert with the Civil Officers of the County the most effectual Measures for preventing any Act of Violence which may be construed in the least Degree against the Spirit of the Treaty."[58]

The military-imposed security quickly had the desired effect. Washington informed a member of Congress on June 14, 1783, that "the Chief Justice of the State, supported by a Regiment of Continental Troops, is now administering Justice" in Westchester County, and he anticipated that very soon "good Order and Regularity of Government may prevail in that distressed County."[59]

Colonel Hull happily reported on July 7 that his troops "are now extended from Fort Independence [the site of the former British post on the Harlem River] to New Rochelle" and "a perfect Harmony subsists between the civil and military Officers, and likewise between the Soldiers and Inhabitants of the County." Furthermore, Hull had established "a friendly Intercourse" with Brigadier General Thomas Musgrave, who commanded a British outpost, and expected Musgrave's cooperation if necessary "to suppress those Enormities" which "some of the People even yet practice."[60]

For over seven years, Westchester County, as the Neutral Ground, endured a civil war, neighbor against neighbor, and terror visited upon the once placid farmers. DeLancey's Cowboys, among the losers in the war, gained greater opprobrium than their counterparts, the Skinners, who were equally or more culpable for outrages against persons and property. James DeLancey tried to abide by the rules of war, but greed and a desire for revenge among his followers while on their hit-and-run missions resulted in extensive depredations. The embroilment in the Neutral Ground was but one phase of the Revolution's brutal refugee war.

Chapter 3

Long Island Marauders

"Everywhere one sees real quality and abundance," wrote a Hessian officer in September 1776, impressed by the prosperity of the Dutch farm communities on Long Island, New York.[1] Seven years later a Maryland Loyalist, recently discharged as an officer in the Queen's Rangers, saw a different picture. The farmers of Dutch extraction were "constantly inveloped in dirt and nastiness." There was no "society amongst these people," and they had the same "share of sensibility and sentiment" as their hogs and cattle.[2] Even discounting some ethnic bias of the two writers, the contrast in the descriptions reveals the dreadful effects of the war on the residents of Long Island. Most Dutch farmers and villagers stayed put during the war and gave nominal allegiance to the British. Citizens of patriot persuasion who fled found, upon their return, their "dwellings empty, furniture smashed and their cattle gone forever."[3]

The devastation in western Long Island was caused primarily by bivouacking British and German troops who appropriated fences, timber, livestock, and crops. Robbery and plundering throughout most of Long Island worsened the situation. Tories and Whigs from each side of the Sound made raids inland, from Connecticut into Long Island, and from Long Island along the Connecticut shores. The British suffered economic setbacks from the heavy toll taken on shipping by New England privateers operating off

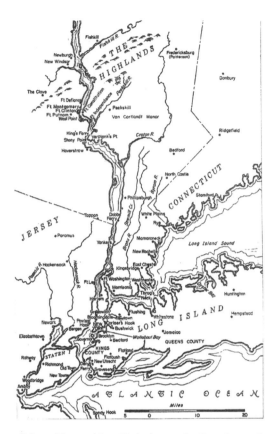

"Map of Lower New York during the Revolution."
Redrawn from a section of C. J. Sauthier's *Choro-*
graphic Map of the Province of New York . . . ,
London, William Faden, 1779. From *Revolution in*
America: Confidential Letters and Journal of Adjutant
General Major Baurmeister of the Hessian Forces, ed-
ited by Bernhard A. Uhlendorf. Copyright © 1957
by Rutgers, The State University. Reprinted by
permission of Rutgers University Press.

Long Island and from imported goods illicitly making their way from New
York City into Long Island and on for sale on the mainland.

British control extended to the two western counties of Long Island,
Kings (Brooklyn) and Queens. Suffolk County, covering the middle and the
eastern half of the island, was sparsely populated, and British influence was
practically nil there. Yet Suffolk was not immune to plundering raids.

After the victory at the battle of Long Island, on August 27, 1776, the
British army moved to secure the western section of Long Island. Martial

law was declared, and for the remainder of the war no elections were held. While New York City had a military Board of Police, no such authority was established on Long Island (except in Jamaica, beginning in 1780).

The number of British troops stationed on Long Island varied, according to the needs of military campaigns, with a high of 8,117 soldiers in August 1778 and a low of 1,158 in October 1782. Loyalist militia-refugees were relied upon primarily to garrison defensive posts on the coasts. At the beginning of the war, Oliver DeLancey's Loyalist "New York Volunteers" had a major role in the "defense of Long Island," but in 1778 two of the brigade's three regiments were sent to Georgia. Only three British posts on Long Island remained in British hands at the end of the war: Oyster Bay, headquarters of the Queen's Rangers; Fort Franklin, on Lloyd's Neck, located on a hill between Oyster Bay and Huntington; and Fort Golgotha at Huntington.[4]

The British fort at Sag Harbor, near the eastern end of Long Island, was captured on May 24, 1777, by Colonel Jonathan Return Meigs, leading an assault party conveyed from Connecticut in whaleboats. Two American attacks (August 21–22 and December 10, 1777) failed against a British post at Setauket (opposite Fairfield, Connecticut), but in January 1778, it was abandoned.[5]

Fort Franklin was quite a nuisance. Five hundred Tories, embodied as Loyalist militia, were stationed there, and "in the rear of the garrison a large band of marauders encamped, who, having boats at command, continually infested the Sound and our shores," noted Major Benjamin Tallmadge of the Second Continental Dragoons and George Washington's intelligence manager. During the night of September 5, 1779, Tallmadge and a detachment of 130 men debarked from Shipam Point near Stamford and landed on Lloyd's Neck. The attack was so "sudden" that most of the garrison was captured.[6]

Fort George, on the south shore of Long Island in Suffolk County, held more than 200 refugees from Rhode Island—"worthless Vagabonds, thieving banditti." Leaving from Fairfield, Connecticut, and crossing Long Island by land, on November 23, 1780, Tallmadge and eighty dismounted dragoons surprised the garrison: 7 of the Loyalist militia were killed and 54 were made prisoners, along with 154 noncombatants.[7]

On October 3, 1781, Major Lemmuel Trescott and 150 dismounted dragoons from Norwalk, Connecticut, captured Fort Slongo (present-day Northport), which like the other forts was a rendezvous for Tory raiders. One of the rebel attackers commented,

[we] surrounded the fort, and on being hailed by the sentinel, the words, "Groton, god-damn you," rang all around our lines, alluding to the taking of Fort Griswold [by General

Benedict Arnold on September 6, 1781]. I never saw fellows more frightened. They cried "Quarters! gentlemen, quarters!" and immediately surrendered.[8]

Small-scale whaleboat marauding from Long Island Sound followed two patterns: American refugees from Long Island who lived in Connecticut crossing the Sound to Long Island, and Loyalists in reverse, from Long Island to the Connecticut shores. Much of the activity degenerated into gang plundering.

Whaleboats were ideal for hit-and-run tactics—committing a robbery and making a quick getaway. There were plenty of whaleboats around despite the near disappearance of whaling off the Sound. Whaling companies still existed; a dozen or so men collectively owned a boat. Whaling craft varied in size, from twenty-six to thirty-five feet in length and six feet wide, with a single sprit sail. Equipped with eight or more oars, muffled with leather to deafen the sound, the boats did not depend on wind or tide, and, with shallow draft, could glide swiftly through water. Usually a whaleboat used for raiding had a squirrel gun (similar to a large musket), and the crew of from fourteen to twenty-four hands carried pikes, muskets, pistols, and cutlasses. The boats were light enough that upon reaching some obscure inlet they could be brought ashore and concealed in the underbrush.[9]

Like privateersmen holding marque and reprisal commissions, some whaleboaters out of Connecticut, who made raids on Long Island, had government sanction. Governor Jonathan Trumbull of Connecticut issued about a hundred commissions, conferring authority "to take and capture the enemies of the united States" and "illicitly exported" British goods; sufficient bonds were required "not to plunder any of the inhabitants of the said island or exceed the instructions."[10]

Approval for official raids paved the way for those with commissions, not to mention freebooters without any permission, to rob persons of a variety of personal property and to kidnap persons for ransom.

Governor Clinton of New York protested to the Connecticut government that goods were being stolen indiscriminately on Long Island. The New York legislature passed resolutions requiring Clinton to prohibit the plundering of Long Island inhabitants, but the Connecticut government at first dragged its feet on the grounds that retaliation was necessary against Loyalists marauding in Connecticut.[11]

"There are some men on this side the Sound," noted Benjamin Tallmadge, who behaved "most villionously towards the inhabitants of Long Island by lying on the road and robbing the inhabitants as they pass"; persons "under sanction of Commissions for cruising the Sound land on Long Island and plunder the inhabitants promiscuously."[12]

Instead of repudiating the commissioning system, Connecticut's Council

Spider Catcher (whaleboat). Reprinted from *Pirates and Patriots* © 1984 by C. Keith Wilbur with permission from the Globe Pequot Press, Guilford, CT 1–800–962–0973, *www.globe-pequot.com.*

of Safety and governor favored holding individual whaleboaters selectively accountable for their actions. In August 1778 Jonathan Vail and Jeremiah Rogers, "commanders of boats," were required to answer charges that they "have unjustly and cruelly plundered many of the friendly inhabitants" on Long Island; in the meantime, the two men were forbidden "to make any hostile descent" upon Long Island.[13] At least the American army command did its part in trying to end the wholesale plundering. Washington enjoined his officers, in accordance with a congressional resolution of June 22, 1779, to "use their exertions" to prevent any military parties from going to Long Island "under the idea of seizing or destroying Tory property."[14]

Plundering by commissioned whaleboaters continued. The predators sought out persons who were known to be in substantial possession of money and other valuables. Those who were patriot refugees from Long Island often acted out of retaliation against their previous oppressors, some of whom had acquired estates confiscated by the British. Surprise was essential in order to meet minimal resistance. Sometimes, however, if unknown in a community, the would-be robbers, posing as nonchalant visitors, lingered in a community for days at a time, sizing up opportunities and risks.

The vicinity of Islip, Long Island, took a number of hits in 1779. In a notice, "Cautions to Travellers on Long Island," printed in a Loyalist New York newspaper in March 1779, readers were alerted to a "party of rebels," who, over a ten-day period, had robbed many houses and persons riding on horseback or in wagons. Two of the thieves were known—Nicholas Tilloston and Stephen Woodhull; "the former is son of Daniel Tilloston of the Branch, owner of the barn . . . which the rebels made use of as a look-out to waylay passengers." The "loyalists in this part of the country . . . are few in number and unable to defend themselves from the frequent incursions of the parties who land from Connecticut."[15] A report in another Loyalist newspaper several months later mentions that "a party of rebels and plunderers" had stolen furniture, clothing, and money from two residents of Islip; "these villains are commissioned by Gov. Trumbull to take everything below highwater mark."[16] It seemed that "scarcely a night passes" but Loyalist citizens "are plundered by the sons and other relations of those rebels who fled to Connecticut when the King's troops landed on the Island."[17]

Even one of Washington's espionage agents on Long Island, Abraham Woodhull (code name, Samuel Culper, Sr.), was afraid to order invisible ink. "It is too great a risque to write with ink in this country of robbers," Woodhull said. He recounted an incident that "saved my life." Woodhull, traveling on a road that went through a woods, "was attacked by four armed men, one of them I had frequently seen in N. York." The robbers "searched every pocket and lining of my clothes, shoes, and also my saddle. . . . I had but one dollar in money about me. It was so little they did not take it, and so came off clean."[18]

Woodhull, who lived in Setauket, became increasingly disturbed over whaleboaters from Connecticut persisting in their robberies. He asked Major Tallmadge to bring some of the culprits to justice. "I cannot put up with such a wanton waste of property," Woodhull informed Tallmadge. Although most victims "are enemy's to our cause," their property "should not go amongst such villians." Woodhull also noted that "night before last a most horrid robbery was committed on the houses of Coll. Benj. Floyd and Mr. Seton, by three whale boats from your shore, commanded by Joseph Hulce and Fade Danolson, and one other master of boat." The thieves took "household goods, Bonds and Notes, of Three Thousand Pounds. They left nothing in the houses that was portable. They even took their clock and all their looking glasses, and all Seal Gold Cloths."[19] On another occasion, Connecticut whaleboaters even stole the "communion plate" from the Setauket church.[20]

Whaleboat banditti from Connecticut did not hesitate to use torture or to commit murder to force victims to reveal the whereabouts of their valuables. With no adequate redress coming from the Connecticut government, Long Island residents brought to the attention of Governor Clinton of New York reports of the constant robberies and acts of violence inflicted on Long Islanders in hopes that he could do something to put a stop to the marauding.

Lieutenant Caleb Brewster of Setauket alerted Clinton to atrocities in August 1781. Brewster, serving in Tallmadge's intelligence network, carried spy dispatches in a whaleboat across the Sound to Connecticut. In reporting on "the Conduct of the plundering boats lately," Brewster said that on August 14 two boats landed at Miller's Place, and at midnight the crew of one boat went to the house of Captain Ebenezer Miller, who admitted the visitors and gave up his arms;

his son hearing a noise below stairs got up out of bed shoved up the chamber windo. One of the party without ever speaking to him, shot him dead in the windo; the other boate's crew at the same time went to Mr. Andrew Miller's demanded Entrance in the like manner; as soon as Mr. Miller got the door open, one of the party struck him with the breech of his gun, broke the bone over his eye, tore his eye all to pieses, broke his cheek bone and left him for dead. . . . They have been over at several other times at the Westward, at Oyster Bay. Went to the houses of Mr. Simon Flint's and Gilbert Flint's, plundered their houses of their furniture, hung Mr. Gilbert Flint till he was so near dead, that they had to apply the dockter to fetch him to and abused their families to a shameful rate. Another time they went to great Neck plundered Major Richard Thorn and hung him up to make him tell where his money was till they thought him dead, then cut him down and after awhile finding life yet in him, one of the party took his knife and cut him under his jaw from one ear to the other, as he ment to cut his throate, then went to Esqr. Coulne and hung him up in the same manner to get his hard cash and plundered his home. Theres not a night but they are over; if boates can cross peopple cant ride the roades but what they are robbed.[21]

A "Memorial" of September 1781, addressed to Governor Clinton, from residents of Southold and Shelter Island in Suffolk County, also gave a lengthy report of various instances of thievery and rough treatment inflicted by Connecticut commissioned whaleboaters.[22]

Kidnapping was prevalent. Usually the abductees were Loyalists of some prominence. The prisoners were turned over to military authorities for the purpose of making exchanges for like captives held by the British. Non-military captors could expect rewards.[23]

Not infrequently a neighborhood on Long Island would be sufficiently alarmed so that a pursuit party could be sent out, resulting in the killing or capturing of some attackers. Captive Connecticut whaleboat robbers were sent to British prisons in New York City, particularly the notorious Sugar House.[24]

The abuses committed by the commissioned whaleboaters could not be ignored. The infuriated New York governor asked Trumbull point-blank to revoke the commissions.[25] Clinton also forwarded to Congress all the information that he had on the depredations caused by the Connecticut whaleboaters. Congress, on August 7, 1781, announced its findings that the commissions issued by the Connecticut government "are attended with many abuses dangerous to the public as well as distressing to citizens and friends of these United States . . . some of whom, under pretext of the powers contained in such commissions, have been plundered of their property, and otherwise evilly treated." Congress, therefore, voted a resolution, desiring that the Connecticut governor "immediately to revoke the said commissions . . . so far as they authorise the seizure of goods on Long Island, or elsewhere, on land not within the State of Connecticut."[26]

In response to the pressure, the Connecticut government, on November 23, 1781, ordered that the "commissions granted to commanders of armed vessels in this state . . . are hereby revoked and recalled." Furthermore, Brigadier General David Waterbury, Jr., was authorized to secure "all boats and small craft" on shore between New Haven and the western boundary of Connecticut, and Colonel Samuel McClellan, "commandant of the fort at New London and Groton etc.," was to take charge of "all boats and small craft" from the eastern border of the state to Branford.[27]

The measures taken to control raids on Long Island by Connecticut whaleboaters had the desired results, but unauthorized assaults continued. As late as fall 1782, two such instances were reported. In mid September, "two armed boats from Connecticut crossed the sound and landed at the Canoe place (so called) on Long Island." The crews went about two miles inland and "plundered sundry of the inhabitants of cash and clothing." The next morning a posse of residents was raised and, "finding the boat crews on a beach dividing their goods, they fired upon them," killed three of the raiders, "badly wounded" two others, and took five prisoner.[28] A month later about twenty whaleboaters "landed near Cow Neck" and "attacked the houses" of James Burr and one Burtis, a blacksmith. "They killed Burr, and robbed his store of everything valuable, but in the attack of Burtis, their leader, a Captain Martin . . . was killed, which occasioned the rest to retreat, carrying off three of their party, supposed to be badly wounded."[29]

Besides having to brace themselves against rebel-bandit forays from the northern shore of the Sound, residents, most of whom were Loyalists, on the western end of Long Island endured almost nightly attacks by whaleboaters from New Jersey. The New Jersey vessels came out mainly from the vicinity of New Brunswick on the Raritan River.[30] A typical incursion occurred one night in June 1781 when the "crews of two rebel whale boats" entered the home of Nicholas Schenck, three miles south of Flatbush, while "the family was at supper." A lodger, Peter Bogart, was bayoneted in the side, and the intruders "took away his money and the plate of the family."[31]

The short career of Adam Hyler (died 1782) stands out as the most prolific and daring of the New Jersey raiders of Long Islanders. An accomplished seaman, Hyler also had great success in privateering in coastal waters. The robbery of Colonel Jeromus Lott at his home in Flatlands, on August 4, 1781, had a surprise for Hyler. In searching Lott's house, Hyler and his men found two bags which they thought contained guineas. The intruders took Lott, two of his slaves, and the two bags with them. While sailing up the Raritan the robbers opened the bags and discovered only half-pennies belonging to the church at Flatbush. At least Hyler had some satisfaction in forcing Lott to "ransom" his two slaves at New Brunswick.[32]

The New Jersey government also gave out privateering-type commissions to whaleboaters. The recipients were soon abusing the privileges by engaging in wholesale marauding inland. John Taylor, a resident of New Brunswick and a former militia colonel, sounded his indignation over New Jersey patriots being involved in banditry. Writing to Governor William Livingston of New Jersey in June 1781, Taylor pointed out that

the whale-boatmen from this place are daily guilty of robbing the Inhabitants of Long-Island, and of Staten-Island, and, in their last [cruize?] they have murdered an old man because he defended his property in his own house. From principles of humanity, from principles of friendship for my Country and from a principle of self interest as an Inhabitant of this Town I sincerely wish a stop might be put to their depredations. They certainly do not render their Country any essential Service; but do it much injury and increase the calamities of war.[33]

Governor Livingston eventually took some minimal action to curtail abuses by whaleboaters. Three weeks after Congress had entreated governors to suspend the commissions to seize enemy property given to boat captains if there were "malconduct," Livingston rescinded the commission of Baker Hendricks for "illegal intercourse" with the enemy and "mal-conduct in quality" as captain of whaleboats and other vessels.[34]

While patriot whaleboaters were descending on Long Island from Connecticut, Loyalists were conducting incursions in reverse—into Connecticut. As early as October 1777, the citizens of Norwalk, Connecticut, complained that "the Enemy frequently Just at Night cross the Sound" and "take away our Stock and plunder us." The petitioners wanted the state government to provide an armed sloop to patrol the coast in the vicinity of the town.[35]

Some "refugees went over to Greenwich in Connecticut," in June 1779, and "returned with thirteen prisoners, among whom is a PRESBYTERIAN PARSON, named Burritt, an egregious REBEL . . . 48 Head of cattle and 4 horses."[36] About the same time, a party of Loyalists from Long Island first went to Green's Farms at Fairfield and "plundered the household of Dr. Jesup of all they could carry off." The next day the raiders landed at Stamford where they made prisoners of nine persons and stole between thirty and forty head of cattle, which they conveyed in their boats back to Long Island; "they likewise plundered all they could lay their hands on, broke windows, &c. and committed many outrages."[37]

Sometimes Loyalist raiders from Long Island went beyond the Connect-icut boundary and into New York. It was reported in July 1779 that a "party of refugees crossed to Westchester" and brought off, "with assistance of the guard ship below City Island," fifty milk cows, twelve to fourteen horses, and 250 sheep, "which they drove to Jamaica Plains."[38]

Middlesex County, Connecticut, was greatly "infested" with marauders from Long Island. In summer 1780 a militia company was stationed "as a guard on each side of Five Mile River" to intercept incoming predators.[39]

Some of the Loyalist marauders had great success, only to be put down by rebel militia crews. For example, in March 1780, a band of seven ma-rauders from Long Island, led by Alexander Graham, a deserter from the American army, landed at Branford, and moving inland damaged or carried off £5,000 worth of property. The group hid out for a number of days in cellars or barns belonging to local Tory sympathizers. Finally returning to the coast, they set out for Long Island in their whaleboat, only to be vig-orously pursued in the Sound by two rebel whaleboats. Graham and his men were captured; subsequently, he was hanged and his crew was imprisoned.[40]

The British establishment of a refugee corps accentuated the raiding along the Connecticut shores. On November 21, 1780, the Honorable Board of Associated Loyalists was organized, headquartered in New York City. The board, consisting of prominent Loyalists, with Governor William Franklin of New Jersey as its first director, had charge of embodied Loyalist volunteers who assisted the British war effort by "annoying the seacoasts of the revolted colonies and destroying their trade." Since they did not receive pay, the Associators were prone to engage in actions solely for the purpose of plun-der. All goods captured by the Associators, when not acting in conjunction with regular troops, were divided among themselves.[41] A Tory judge, Tho-mas Jones, had a derogatory opinion of the Board of Associated Loyalists; he said it "certainly encouraged" the member refugees "to infest the rebel coasts, and plunder the inhabitants indiscriminately, without any distinction of Whigs or Tories, Loyalists or rebels."[42] Although the Associated Loyalists directed their attention mostly to the New Jersey coasts, they also made raids into Connecticut.

During 1780 and 1781, Loyalist refugees returned in force to Lloyd's Neck, which became a staging area for Connecticut raids. To cite an ex-ample, on Sunday, July 22, 1781, "a Party of Refugees from Lloyd's Neck" went to Darien, Connecticut, and crashing an afternoon Methodist church service, they brought off the minister, Reverend Moses Mather, and fifty men of the congregation, "tying their captives two by two." The raiders also came away with forty horses. The prisoners from the congregation were delivered from Lloyd's Neck into New York City.[43] Travelers were also robbed. Connecticut citizens learned to "keep a good look-out" for any "sulking tories" who might be "concealed in the bushes" near a road, ready to waylay a passerby.[44]

Partisan whaleboat crews frequently made kidnapping a primary objective in their raids. Prominent military or civilian personnel could be held for ransom or turned over to the respective armies as prisoners of war to be exchanged for persons held by the other side. A sort of equilibrium developed, with a quid pro quo being maintained. Of course, robbery almost always accompanied the taking of prisoners.

The best-known example of reciprocal kidnappings of prominent persons were those of General Gold Selleck Silliman from Connecticut and Judge Thomas Jones from Long Island. The British commander in chief, Henry Clinton, made known his desire to capture Silliman, the commander of Connecticut's coastal militia. During the night of May 1, 1779, a party of nine refugees, out of Lloyd's Neck, crossed the Sound and headed for the Silliman mansion, two miles from Fairfield. Mary Silliman, the general's wife, recalled the harrowing moments of the raid.

At a midnight hour, when we were all asleep, the house was attacked. I was first awakened by the General calling out, "Who's there?" At that instant there was a banging at both doors, they intending to break them down . . . with great stones. . . . My dear companion then sprang up, caught his gun and ran to the front of the house, and as the moon shone brightly saw them through the window, and attempted to fire, but his gun only flashed and missed fire. At that instant the enemy burst in a window, sash and all, jumped in, seized him and said he was a prisoner. . . . [T]heir appearance was dreadful. . . . I heard them breaking the windows, which they wantonly did with the breeches of their guns. They then asked him for his money, he told them he had none but continental, and that would do them no good. Then they wished his papers. He said his public papers were all sent abroad, and his private papers would be of no use to them. Then some wanted one thing and some another. He told them mildly he hoped he was in the hands of gentlemen, and that it was not their purpose to plunder. With these arguments he quieted them so that they plundered but little.

Actually the intruders took "a fusee, a pair of elegant pistols inlaid with silver, and an elegant sword." Silliman and his eldest son, William, were brought to New York City and eventually confined at Flatbush.[45]

To secure the release of Silliman, the Americans had to capture someone of equal prominence. At the time neither Washington nor the British command could agree upon a suitable prisoner in British custody for an exchange. Some Connecticut militiamen decided to take the matter into their own hands. On November 6, 1779, Captain David Hawley of Newfield (now Bridgeport) and Captain Samuel Lockwood of Norwalk, with a crew of twenty-five volunteers, crossed the Sound in a whaleboat and landed near Smithtown, Long Island. Upon disembarking, the group marched fifty-two miles to the residence of Judge Thomas Jones. Not suspecting any trouble, Jones was easily captured. Because of the presence of British soldiers in the area, the kidnapping party had to find cover in the woods for a day. Though six of the party lagging behind were captured by British troops, the kidnappers and their prize made it back to Connecticut. Mrs. Silliman even had Jones as a house guest for a few days. Jones was then sent for detainment at Middletown. In May 1780 Jones and Silliman were exchanged for each other.[46]

The kidnapping of Connecticut citizens by Loyalist refugees became more the goal of raids along the north shore of Long Island Sound. Connecticut's treason act of 1776 was a harsh one, making aid to the enemy a capital offense. Only one person, Moses Dunbar, who held a commission to gather recruits for the British army at two dollars a day, was hanged (March 19, 1777) under sentence of a civil court. Two others, David Griswold and Robert Thompson, also in 1777, met the same fate handed down by military courts-martial. The revised treason act of February 1781 struck fear among Connecticut's Loyalist refugees and their abettors by assigning the death penalty to a new category of offenses. The 1781 law declared that a person formerly a "subject" of Connecticut or the United States "who shall come into the State and rob or plunder" anyone "of their goods or effects" was liable to the death penalty. Thus, with the risks in raiding escalated, Loyalist marauders made it a point to secure hostages as a means of insurance against execution for themselves or their friends if captured by the rebels.[47]

The threat of severe penalties did not deter the whaleboat marauding, and no one was executed under the 1781 treason act. Depredations and kidnappings continued at full pace, and it seems that collusion frequently existed between Loyalist and rebel whaleboaters. Judge Jones averred that "these depredators grew so civil to each other, that they mutually gave notice of the persons most proper to be made prisoners of, the situation of their houses, and where the most plunder was likely to be obtained." Jones recounted an instance in May 1781 when

four rebel whale-boats from New Rochelle, upon the main . . . actually went to the British guard ship which lay at the Two Brothers, small islands in the Sound, about a mile below Whitestone, and nearly midway between the main and Long Island, and made presents of poultry, lamb, veal, and vegetables, to the Captain and other officers, and in return their crews were regaled with wine, punch, and grog. In the evening they took leave, went directly to Long Island, broke open the house of Thomas Hicks, Esq., robbed him of several hundred pounds in cash, his plate, his linen, his library, and returned with their spoil directly to New Rochelle. As they passed the guard ship upon their return, they gave three cheers, which the ship cordially returned.[48]

The success of the Loyalist refugees on Long Island in their raids into Connecticut often depended upon the collaboration of Tory sympathizers.

Because "many distressing robberies and plunders are frequently committed on the good people of this State living on the sea coasts by our open and secret enemies," which "in many instances" were "countenanced at least if not aided and supported by our internal and domestic foes," the Connecticut legislature in November 1780 enacted a law ordering "the civil authority and selectmen of any town who may . . . think themselves in danger of being robbed or plundered by any attempt of such open or secret enemies" to make a list of any persons suspected of being involved in illicit trade with the enemy "or who are reputed to countenance, and or assist, any plundering parties, or who shall be generally reputed to be dangerous and inimical persons." Upon application from a town, the legislature would send a special committee to the town, "empowered to compel the appearance of any listed person before the committee." Anyone from the original list who would be declared dangerous would be placed on a new list, and whenever "any depredation, robbery or plunder" should be committed within a town, persons on the list of dangerous persons would be assessed sums toward reimbursement for the losses of victims.[49]

The legislation was a response to a situation such as the one that existed in Greenwich, Connecticut. "A number of evil minded and designing men who live from 8 to 14 miles eastward of the said town," forming themselves into "parties and clubs" and "without any authority," were plundering the town's inhabitants of their cattle and "other valuable effects." The stolen property was delivered back to the rightful owners only if the robbers received payment of nearly full value of the property. When local militia guards impounded the ill-gained items from the robbers, in order for the original owners to recover their possessions they had to compensate the guards "one quarter of the value of such property for salvage, which they are obliged to pay without any legal process."[50]

It is sometimes difficult to discern from contemporary reports whether perpetrators of robberies and assaults had any affiliation, however loosely, with the British or American cause. For example, what is one to make of the report that, during the night of October 15, 1779, at Bushwick, Long Island, five men, "disguised, meanly habited with faces blackened," forced their way into the home of George and Peter Duryea, who with their wives lived as one family? The attackers, "armed with a gun, bayonet fixed, a pistol, a number of clubs and a cutlass," badly wounded the two male victims, though Peter Duryea managed to escape to warn neighbors. One of the wives, Catherine (Mrs. Peter Duryea), "was seized by the throat, thrown on the floor and almost choked to death." The thieves got away with £200 in hard cash and various silver pieces.[51]

An unknown assailant was involved in a murder in April 1779: "One of the conductors in the [British army] waggon department, proceeding to the

East End of Long-Island, perceived a dead body, apparently a gentleman lying in the road stripped with his throat cut."[52] Even in confronting criminals, victims often did not try to surmise identity. In October 1779 "a party of men attempted to break into the house of the widow Platt, of Huntington, on Long-Island, where Mr. James Houston and John Stewart kept store." The attackers met a hail of gunfire, but "one of the villains got into the kitchen where John Stewart killed him." With the arrival of armed neighbors, the bandits fled; "the man that was killed was buried the next day by Mr. Stewart."[53]

While the names of the many raiders and desperados remain unknown, certain individuals stand out for their infamy. John Degraw, a British refugee soldier at Lloyd's Neck, in January 1779 left the garrison and, with six comrades, broke into the house of Parmenas Jackson. Degraw's sister, a servant with the family, had informed Degraw that Jackson kept a large amount of money in the house. After mutilating and killing Jackson the outlaws started to work on his father-in-law, Thomas Birdsall. To save her father, Jackson's wife revealed the location of the money. The tormentors left with $3,000 in hard cash and household valuables. Colonel Gabriel G. Ludlow, the commandant of the garrison at Lloyd's Neck, was immediately notified. The robbers were soon caught, and the stolen property was returned. The criminals were conveyed to New York City, where they were tried. Degraw went to prison where he soon died; the others were sent to labor in mines in South America.[54]

William Crosson (or Crosden, Crossing), a refugee from Newport, Rhode Island, and a member of a Loyalist corps, committed many depredations and robberies on the eastern New England shore of Long Island Sound. Captured in 1778, he was imprisoned in Providence. After escaping, he linked up with British forces in Newport and left with them when they evacuated Rhode Island.[55]

Richard Barrick is a good example of a freebooter. An illiterate Irishman (b. 1763), he had once been a member of a gang of thieves in England. Arrested and convicted in England, he had arranged to go to America as a convict servant in lieu of execution. Transportation to America under pledge not to return to England for fourteen years (if before, subject to the death penalty) had been a common practice since 1717. Barrick served his indenture on Long Island, where he learned the trades of papermaking and basket weaving. Barrick eventually reverted to his old ways and participated in a series of gang robberies on Long Island. In between escapades, he found refuge in Greenwich and Stamford, Connecticut. Barrick was jailed for a while in New York City. After his release, his criminal activities ranged from Philadelphia to various places in New England. Finally convicted of highway robbery, he was hanged at Cambridge, Massachusetts, on November 18, 1784.[56]

Lydia Minturn Post, a Long Island housewife, left a remarkable journal of the anxieties and tribulations of a patriot family, written for the benefit of her husband, Edward Post, who was away for most of the war serving with the American army. With her husband absent, Mrs. Post and her three children moved into the home of her father, an Anglican clergyman. She had to put up with British (especially Hessian) troops in the neighborhood, "but worse than all, robbers come over from the main shore in boats, and keep us in constant alarm! They belong to no party, and spare none; freebooters, cowardly, midnight assassins, incendiaries, indiscriminate, bold, and daring."[57]

Mrs. Post related many atrocities, including murder and mutilation as the robbers, whom she usually called "Runners," tried to wring booty from their victims. On one occasion the predators tied up a whole family in a house, which they then set afire; fortunately the victims managed to escape.[58] At one point in her journal, Mrs. Post states that "house-breaking, horse-stealing, and depredation are so common, that I am weary of noting them down."

The Runners, some of whom were Loyalist refugees, did not hesitate to back off when they came across a house amply defended. Mrs. Post was amused at one ploy used against the Runners.

Last night the Runners appeared round a house near West-Town, and were about forcing a door in front when they were discovered. John Rawlins, the owner, sent a negro up stairs to fire when the word was given. It was a bright moonlight night, and he saw the creatures step up to the door from a window near it with a pane of glass out. In alarm, he looked out for something wherewith to defend himself; seeing the broom, he . . . ran it through the broken window. It touched the shoulder, and grazed the cheek of one of the villains, who supposing it to be a loaded gun, cried out piteously, "Oh Heavens, don't kill me" as though he had never an evil intention towards any one.

The signal was now given, and the man above fired; they soon scattered, leaving John Rawlins aiming his broomstick through the broken window-pane![59]

One protection against marauders was to scare them away before they had a chance to strike.

The farmers have devised a scheme to make known through the neighborhood the presence of the "Runners." They are generally seen lurking about at twilight, spying the points most favorable for attack; if observed, they walk on in an unconcerned manner, whistling or singing. Sometimes they will stop, and inquire the way to some place; suddenly disappearing, they are unexpectedly seen again in the edge of the wood, or from behind a hay-stack in the field, peering about, terrifying every body, above all women and children. These signs are not to be mistaken. We are on our guard; the "great gun" with which all are provided, is loaded and fired off. Pop! Pop! go the answering guns for five miles round; each house takes up the alarming tale, and thus it spreads, warning of impending danger, and frightens away the enemy, for *that* time at any rate.[60]

As the war drew to a close, whaleboat marauding diminished. In May 1782 raids made by Loyalist refugees stationed on Long Island came almost to a halt, as General Henry Clinton, soon to be replaced as commander in chief by Sir Guy Carleton, ordered that no excursions be made except by his permission. In October 1782 the Loyalist refugees abandoned their fort at Lloyd's Neck and moved to New York City; at the end of the war, they became exiles in Canada.[61]

Even so, during 1783, a few plundering raids occurred, most likely by banditti without any affiliation. For example, on March 4, 1783, "a number of villains entered the house" of Maurice Lott of Kings County at nighttime and "violently assaulted and robbed him of between 4 and 500 guineas, chiefly in gold, a silver watch, 6 silver teaspoons, tea-tongs, a pair of round gold buttons." Two Long Island residents, Richard Thompson and Isaac Bunting, were charged in this robbery and lodged in the provost jail in New York City.[62] During the evening of October 24, a "gang of thieves" robbed the house of Michael B. Grant, "near Brooklyn Church," of £90 in hard cash and "plate in great quantity, clothing, &c."[63]

Gradually some of the 5,000 American refugees from Long Island who had left, chiefly for Connecticut, to escape British sanctions began to return to their homes. Most of the refugees had been poor and, finding their property wasted, had to start over again. Those who had some wealth were in much the same predicament, and many had to mortgage their lands. The returning refugees were not the only ones in dire straits; those who had stuck it out under the British occupation discovered that their claims for compensation for livestock and other goods impressed by the British army were being ignored. General Guy Carleton, in April 1783, established a Board of Commissioners to settle outstanding demands on the army for taking private property. Unfortunately, members of the board left for England before allowing compensation, and the claimants went unpaid. Adding to the hardship, the New York legislature in 1784 levied a $100,000 tax collectively on the residents of the Southern District of the state for the purpose of paying down the state's war debt.[64]

Despite the distress of so many Long Islanders at the end of the war, the prospect of peace bid expectations of future happiness. On December 2, 1783, a week after the British evacuation of New York City, the inhabitants of the Dutch farming village of Bushwick, in northeast Kings County, celebrated. Patriot exiles were welcomed back into the town. An ox was roasted. Military salutes boomed, and citizens imbibed in thirteen toasts. An observer commented on the "cheerfulness" that prevailed "once more beholding the metropolis of the State, emerging from that scene of ruin and distress."[65]

Chapter 4

New Jersey Refugees

Loyalist refugees fought their own war along the coasts of New Jersey. Most of the raiders were native New Jerseyans who, by choice or from severe repression inflicted by their Whig neighbors, had fled their homes. Like the refugees in southeastern New York, the New Jersey raiders were bent on retaliation and revenge. As early as 1778 the state began confiscating estates belonging to Loyalists,[1] and Loyalists almost everywhere in the state were subjected to intimidation and harsh penalties. Simply adhering to the British cause could bring about the death penalty, although very few suffered this punishment. Refugees poured into New York City, where, one observer noted, they "are in distressed circumstances, several large families being obliged to crowd in one small room, and other families . . . live on board ships in the harbour, and provisions amazingly scarce and dear."[2] Not surprisingly, large numbers of New Jersey refugees welcomed the opportunity to even the score with their former neighbors.

George Washington, under authorization from Congress, on January 25, 1777, issued a proclamation from Morristown compelling any New Jersey citizen who had taken a loyalty oath to Great Britain preferred by General William Howe to repudiate that oath and swear allegiance to the United States. Those not complying were "to withdraw themselves and families within the enemy lines." Anyone deemed to be an adherent to the King of

Great Britain was to be treated as "common enemies of the American States."[3]

Although mostly steadfast in the pursuit of military objectives, those Loyalist refugees from New Jersey who took up arms engaged in plundering, destruction of property, and kidnapping. Despite having only minimal and reluctant support from the British command in America, the armed Loyalists performed the valuable service of demonstrating that the British army had the continued ability to strike at will. The success of the raids by Loyalist refugees along New Jersey's shores derived from a relatively unprotected coastline. By stealth and cover of darkness, raiders conducted hit-and-run missions before local militia could be collected and brought into pursuit. Washington refused to commit any large number of troops to secure areas where Loyalist raiders had made inroads, particularly in Bergen County, as recommended by Generals Charles Lee and Adam Stephen. The commander in chief kept his eye on the grand strategy, holding his army together to engage the full strength of the enemy. Still, during much of the war, regiments of the New Jersey brigade were stationed in the Elizabethtown-Newark sector. The task of these troops was not so much to guard the coasts from small enemy incursions but to serve as a covering van for the American army should the British army cross into the state in force from New York City or Staten Island (for example, in June 1780).

Many of New Jersey's 5,000 "active male Loyalists"[4] bore arms for the British cause. A few joined John Graves Simcoe's Queen Rangers and other provincial units. Probably as many as 1,500 served at one time or another in the New Jersey Volunteers, raised almost exclusively from among New Jersey Loyalists. The unit was the largest American Loyalist military organization. Formally called the Royal New Jersey Volunteers, it was also known as Skinner's "Greens." Brigadier General Cortlandt Skinner, a former attorney general and speaker of the assembly in New Jersey, raised the brigade-size unit and commanded it. Not achieving the goal of five completed battalions (totaling 2,500 troops), the New Jersey volunteers normally had 800 enlistees; the largest number in service at one time was 1,001 in May 1778. The Volunteers made successive raids into northeastern New Jersey where they attacked local militia and destroyed war matériel. They also took part in British army operations, including service of the second battalion in the southern campaigns of 1780–81.[5]

Refugee militants who preferred not to be regularly enlisted in British army units were brought under the general supervision of the Board of Associated Loyalists in New York City (see Chapter 3). The board had authority to approve or deny intended operations of the Associated Loyalists, and by accepting this condition the Loyalist refugees received, in turn, some military supplies and permission to divide spoils. As a Philadelphia

Brigadier General Cortlandt Skinner. From *History of Staten Island* by I. K. Morris, vol. 1, p. 261. Negative number 21018, © Collections of The New-York Historical Society.

newspaper noted in 1781, the British provided the refugees "with armed boats, provisions and warlike stores, all at free cost to go and plunder on the rebel shores (as they call them) and to cruize in the rivers, to distress the persons who live near the water."[6] The Associated Loyalists were organized into three "societies": DeLancey's corps in Westchester County, New York; the refugee whaleboaters at Lloyd's Neck, Long Island; and the group that harassed the New Jersey coasts, based on Staten Island and at posts on the New Jersey shore.[7] During the final years of the war, the Associated Loyalists largely replaced the New Jersey volunteers in bringing irregular warfare to New Jersey.

The establishment of the Associated Loyalists seemed a sensible way to deal with the nonattached armed refugees. The British army did not want the burden of taking them into regular service, nor did this class of refugees desire to join the provincial corps. The Associated Loyalists would prove useful in keeping a foothold along New Jersey's coasts, discouraging rebel privateering, and most important aid in gathering supplies for the British army—forage, livestock, provisions, horses, and wood. The problem was that the refugees still engaged in a predatory war, often wantonly plundering and destroying private property. Historians have generally dismissed the Associated Loyalists as "a band of thieves and murderers" and "licensed outlaws." In actuality, the control exercised by the Board of Associated Loyalists mitigated the propensity for extreme violence.[8]

Loyalist refugees conducted their raids in New Jersey primarily from four stations. Lieutenant Colonel Abraham Buskirk's fourth battalion of New Jersey Volunteers held post on Staten Island. Separated from Manhattan by the five-mile-wide Narrows, which connects the upper and lower New York Bays, Staten Island's western shore was only 500 feet from the New Jersey coast.[9] Fort DeLancey, a small stockade at Bergen Point (Neck) at Newark Bay, just below present Bayonne, New Jersey, was also used as a seat of operations by refugees. Captain Thomas Ward, who deserted from the Continental army in 1777, commanded at the post, which was burned and abandoned on September 1, 1782.[10] Armed Loyalists also maintained a fort at Bull's Ferry, three miles below Fort Lee and opposite present-day New York City (100th–110th streets).[11]

Refugeetown provided a maroon-like safe haven for militant Loyalists, under the protection of nearby British warships. It was located on Sandy Hook, a cedar-covered sand sprit, five and a half miles long, at the entrance to lower New York Bay. Once connected to the New Jersey mainland, the area became an island as a result of erosion from the winter storms of 1776–77. Before 1781 some of the New Jersey Volunteers were stationed at Sandy Hook. Eventually Sandy Hook became the main haven for Associated Loyalists. Livestock and other property seized from the rebels were taken to Sandy Hook and transported by ships to New York City. Refugeetown and Fort DeLancey were way stations for runaway slaves, many of whom joined the armed refugee bands.[12]

Armed Loyalist refugees, principally bands of New Jersey Volunteers before 1781, frequently raided the coasts of Essex and Monmouth counties.[13] Captain Thomas Ward, on November 21, 1780, with 100 men, went to the Newark vicinity "on a picarooning expedition," gathering up "a number of hogs, cattle, and sheep." An alerted rebel militia, however, soon recovered most of this property.[14]

The continual Tory raiding and counterthrusts of rebel militia in Bergen County, especially in the Hackensack Valley, left the area a virtual Neutral Ground. In summer 1780 Schraalenburgh was "reduced to a heap of rubbish by a party of Refugees and Runaway Negroes, the inhabitants being mostly friendly" to the rebel cause.[15] In May 1779 armed refugees burned most of the houses and barns in the village of Closter, "a settlement abounding with many violent rebels and persecutors of loyal subjects, and who are almost daily affording some fresh instance of barbarity." After the raid, patriot militia stripped the body of a Loyalist raider who had been killed and hanged up the corpse, with a placard pinned to it, declaring "No quarter to refugees."[16] As late as September 1781, a Bergen County resident noted that Closter was "very much exposed" and "entirely open to the Depredations of the Refugees, who are indefatigable in making nocturnal Expeditions for Horses, Cattle, & Prisoners."[17]

Armed Loyalists, sometimes in conjunction with British regulars, kept up the pressure on the rebels by crossing from Staten Island to New Jersey. Raiding parties, upon withdrawing from their missions, fought skirmishes with detachments of militia or Continental troops. The New Jersey sector closest to Staten Island, which included such towns as Rahway, Woodbridge, and Elizabethtown, was hit the hardest.[18]

Rebel raiders returned the favor by plundering farms on Staten Island, but with difficulty because of the large number of British forces stationed on the island. A sizeable Continental army detachment on two occasions made incursions into Staten Island, first led by General John Sullivan on August 22, 1777, and then by General Lord Stirling on January 14–15, 1780, for the purpose of breaking up the bases used by the enemy raiders. The missions failed miserably. In the latter expedition, 500 civilians accompanied Stirling's force and indulged in widespread plundering of Staten Island farms. Stirling was so infuriated that he ordered that "all persons possessed of any articles of plunder, taken on the island" to "immediately deliver the same" to Reverend James Caldwell at Springfield "to the end that they may be returned to their proper owners." Caldwell, a Presbyterian minister, was at the time an assistant quartermaster general. Not much of the booty was returned, but some property was sent back to the original owners.[19]

During the night of January 30, 1780, thirteen "mounted Refugees" crossed over from Staten Island on the ice and "in the vicinity of Elizabethtown surprised Mr. Wyants, a lieutenant of the rebel militia" and eight privates, who "were all found at a *fandango*, or merry-meeting, with a party of ladies, who became planet-struck at this sudden separation from their *Damons*." The intruders returned with three sleighs and ten horses.[20]

This little venture was followed up the next day by Lieutenant Colonel John Graves Simcoe and his Loyalist Queen's Rangers, who tried to accomplish a "march by very secret ways . . . to arrive near Gen. Washington's Quarters by day-break . . . to storm the quarters" and take Washington prisoner. Washington reportedly was staying at the time "at a considerable distance from the army." Simcoe had to cancel the high-risk mission because "the snow prevented all possibility of marching, but on the beaten road." So as not to come up empty-handed, the Queen's Rangers fought with local militia and did some looting before returning to Staten Island.[21]

The blockhouse at Bull's Ferry became increasingly a nuisance for the rebels. Bergen County woodcutters, who sent their rails across the Hudson to supply the British army in New York City, found protection from the small garrison of seventy men and could flee to within the bounds of the blockhouse, surrounded by an abatis and a palisade on three sides and a perpendicular cliff overlooking the Hudson on the other. Cattle destined for the British army were also herded nearby. The armed refugees from the garrison occasionally went out on plundering raids. In July 1780 the commandant at the post, Lieutenant Colonel Abraham Cuyler, was absent, and Captain Thomas Ward, later to command at Fort DeLancey, acted in his stead.

Brigadier General Anthony Wayne persuaded Washington to erase this trouble spot, which General Henry Clinton described as "a trifling work," defended by a "small body of loyal refugees . . . poor people." Wayne had a different perspective of the blockhouse defenders; they were "refugees & a wretched banditti of Robbers horse thieves &c." On the morning of July 21, 1780, Wayne and two Pennsylvania brigades, "the flower of Washington's army," headed for the blockhouse. Anticipating that General Clinton might send reinforcements from across the river, Wayne placed more than half his force at different passes to intercept the enemy. With the remainder of his troops, Wayne began the attack on the blockhouse with an intense cannonading; however, the volly of six-pound cannonballs from the "grasshoppers" (artllery light enough to be carried on horseback) did not penetrate through the log walls. Foolishly, without orders, some of Wayne's troops tried to storm the fort, but entangled in the abatis and meeting a withering fire, had to back off, suffering heavy casualties (64 killed or wounded). Wayne withdrew from the scene, heading back to the army's camp at Totowa, New Jersey.[22]

The heroism of Thomas Ward and the armed refugees received much praise. Even King George III commended "the very extraordinary courage shewn by the Loyal Refugees—the brave SEVENTY."[23]

Major John André, Clinton's aide-de-camp, ridiculed Wayne's misfortune in failing to capture the greatly outnumbered garrison and coming off only with some cattle. André penned the *Cow-Chace*, a seventy-two-stanza poem, in the form of the old Scottish ballad, *Chevy-Chace*. The three cantos of André's opus were published in New York's *Royal Gazette*, the last on

Block-House Point, Hudson River. From *Magazine of American History*, vol. 5 (1880), p. 165.

the day he was captured as a result of the Benedict Arnold treason plot. The first three stanzas of *Cow-Chace* set the tone of derision for Wayne and the caliber of his troops.

> To drive the kine one summer's morn
>   The Tanner [Wayne] took his way;
> The calf shall rue, that is unborn,
>   The jumbling of that day.
>
> And Wayne descending steers shall know,
>   And tauntingly deride;
> And call to mind, in every low,
>   The tanning of *his* hide.
>
> Let Bergen cows still ruminate,
>   Unconscious in the stall
> What mighty means were used to get—
>   And lose them after all.

André also poked fun at the American claim that none of the cannonballs did any damage:

> Five refugees, 'tis true, were found
>> Stiff on the block house floor,
> But then, 'tis thought, the shot went round
>> And in at the back door.

The final stanza was sadly prophetic:

> And now I've closed my epic strain,
>> I tremble as I shew It,
> Lest the same warrior-drover Wayne
>> Should ever catch the poet.[24]

On August 9, 1780, the refugees burned their blockhouse at Bull's Ferry and went to Fort DeLancey on Bergen Neck. For two years the armed Loyalists from Fort DeLancey conducted raids into the countryside. Militia and Continental army detachments tried to take the post but failed, owing to firepower from the British ships nearby in the Hudson River.[25]

It seemed to one American observer that during the winter and spring of 1780 the British army was "reduced to mere marauding parties."[26] During January and February the water passage between Staten Island and mainland New Jersey froze to a depth of six inches; every few days, armed refugees crossed over the ice to plunder and cause havoc in the vicinity of Elizabethtown, New Jersey. The successful raiding encouraged General Wilhelm Knyphausen, with a 6,000-man expeditionary force, to invade New Jersey in mid June 1780. After burning Connecticut Farms and Springfield, Knyphausen, quickly checkmated by a large number of troops sent by Washington from Morristown, withdrew back to Staten Island.[27]

Two of the most despised armed Loyalists involved in raids at the Elizabethtown sector were Cornelius Hatfield and his distant kin, John Smith Hatfield. Cornelius Hatfield, a farmer of Essex County, went over to the British in December 1776 and was appointed a captain of refugees in February 1779; John Smith (usually referred to simply as Smith) Hatfield, an Elizabethtown carpenter, joined the British in 1778. Both men, having expert knowledge of the coastal topography, served as guides and pilots for British military incursions and frequently, on their own, led marauding bands into New Jersey, in which they excelled in abducting prominent civilians and military officials. On one raid, Cornelius Hatfield burned the Presbyterian church (where his patriot father was a deacon) and the courthouse in Elizabethtown. Both Hatfields had a cruel streak. In an act of revenge for the Americans having hanged a Tory spy, the two Hatfields summarily hanged a civilian trader, an action repudiated by British military authority. Smith Hatfield was captured by the Americans in 1782, but he soon escaped. Both Hatfields were tried for the murder by the British but were acquitted. In 1788 Smith Hatfield, captured while returning to New Jersey from Nova Scotia, was put on trial for murder in the Essex County court, but, with no witnesses apearing against him, he was released on bail. A short time afterward he fled, with a lynching party at his heels.[28]

Continental army troops, who maintained guard stations at Elizabeth-town, Newark, and Woodbridge, were never able to respond quickly enough to prevent depredations by bands led by the Hatfields or their co-horts. In the early summer of 1780, Connecticut troops were spelling the regiments of the New Jersey brigade who normally had the coastal guard duty. Private Joseph Plumb Martin of the Eighth Connecticut Regiment described a typical hit-and-run raid made by the armed Loyalists from Staten Island, such as led by the Hatfields. At the time Martin had duty at the "Elizabethtown station." Soldiers on watch at the house of Caleb Hal-sted, on Halsted's Point, reported hearing "boats pass and repass, during the night." A number of refugees had already landed, but it was "next to im-possible to detect them" because they had "so many friends" in the area. Hoping to confront some of the refugees before they committed depreda-tions, several soldiers consulted Caleb Halsted, who advised that the en-emy would come at the place most unexpected "about the time of the setting of the moon." A sentinel was stationed at the location where Hal-sted predicted a landing. The raiders indeed appeared as expected; the lone guard, not heeding a warning, fired his musket to sound an alarm for the other guards at the house. In fleeing, the sentinel "got entangled" in bushes and was bayoneted thirteen times by the raiders. The other guards "had taken the alarm and left the house." The armed refugees then entered the Halsted home.

When they could find none to wreak their vengeance upon, they cut open the knapsacks of the guard and strewed the Indian meal about the floor, laughing at the poverty of the Yankee soldiery who had nothing but hog's fodder, as they termed it, to eat. After they had done all the mischief they could in the house, they proceeded to the barn and drove off five or six head of Mr. Holstead's young cattle, took them down upon the point and killed them, and went off in their boats, that had come across from the island for that purpose, to their den among the British.

Martin rued the brutal death of his friend, the guard.

Such maneuvers the British continued to exhibit the whole time we were stationed here, but could never do any other damage to us than killing poor Twist [the name of the young man]. Unfortunate young man! I could not restrain my tears, when I saw him the next day, with his breast like a sieve, caused by the wounds. He lost his own life by endeavoring to save the lives of others; massacred by his own countrymen, who ought to have been fighting in the common cause of the country instead of murdering him.[29]

While marauding had become a common occurrence in Bergen and Essex counties, New Jersey, the large-sized Monmouth County, stretching from Raritan Bay southward to Little Egg Harbor, was "more afflicted" by the enemy's "marauding parties, than all the rest of the state combined" and "suffered severely from its intestine enemies, particularly the refugees, who took up arms against their former neighbors and friends."[30] Not only were there raiders from Refugeetown (Sandy Hook) and elsewhere, but local banditti abounded, claiming refugee status (see Chapter 7). In June 1779, 436 patriot inhabitants of Monmouth County signed articles of agreement, formed themselves into an "association," and pledged to combat the outlawry. The Articles stated that

Whereas from the frequent incursions and depredations of the enemy (and more particularly of the refugees) in this county, whereby not only the lives but the liberty and property of every determined whig are endangered, they, upon every such incursion, either burning or destroying houses, making prisoners of, and most inhumanly treating aged and peaceable inhabitants, and plundering them of all portable property, it has become essentially necessary to take some different and more effectual measures to check said practices, than have ever yet been taken.

The signees, therefore, "solemnly associate for the purpose of retaliation." A nine-man committee, elected by the associates, would determine action. For any property belonging to an associator destroyed or stolen, restitution would be made from local "disaffected" citizens.[31] The association was most effective as vigilantes in ridding the county of its worst outlaws.

Although the Monmouth "Associators" turned out as militia for the "defence" against enemy incursions, they were only minimally successful in thwarting raids by refugee Loyalists.[32] As late as November 1781, a Monmouth militia captain informed the governor that in the "Lower parts" of Monmouth County and also in Burlington County "the Refugees go & Come there unmolested & Repeatedly Joined by the Inhabitants in their mischiefs under the Cover of the Night."[33] At the same time villagers of Little Egg Harbor complained of the "ravages & Devastations of the Refugees which they are Committing Every Day."[34]

Raids in northern Monmouth County continued late into the war. An example of a good haul is one of February 8, 1782. About fifty "refugees, pillagers and kidnappers," under the command of Lieutenant James Steelman, "left their lair on Sandy-Hook and crossed over to the mainland." Treading deep snow, they raided farms, taking prisoners as they went. "The freebooters seized from the various farms five large woodsleds . . . the carrying capacity of which they greatly increased by means of hay-shelvings and planking." These they loaded with applejack, pork, flour, bacon, hams,

butter, and potatoes. "The marauders covered the loads with blankets, clothing, and portable plunder of the more valuable sort, and hung to every
projecting point, a string of slaughtered poultry." The "bandit band" then
marched "slowly and ponderously through the hampering snow" toward
Sandy Hook. Captain John Schenck, however, managed to gather a party
for pursuit, recovered some of the loot, and took several prisoners before
the refugees made it to safety.[35]

Blacks played a major role in the raiding along the New Jersey coasts. At
the time of the Revolution, New Jersey had about 11,000 slaves, 8 percent
of the state's total population.[36] Runaways could easily join up with British
forces on the march or stationed at posts, such as those at Perth Amboy,
New Brunswick, or Paulus Hook. Refugeetown on Sandy Hook and the
several other Loyalist military installations on the Hudson River beckoned.
British-held New York City and its environs and Staten Island also offered
freedom. Free blacks and slaves joined the New Jersey Continental regiments, and free blacks in New Jersey did militia duty.[37]

While many blacks in the American armies did not bear arms and served
chiefly as pioneers (manual laborers), orderlies, or in other special capacities
such as guides and boat pilots, most units of regular soldiers were racially
mixed, and one black regiment was sustained from 1778 to the end of the
war. While blacks were all but absent among regular British troops, they
were employed for special services similar to the American army practice,
and in the South there were several all-black military units.

Many blacks served with the Associated Loyalists. Thomas Ward's refugee
band in Bergen County, New Jersey, was largely African. Asher Holmes, a
Monmouth County militia colonel, observed that many "Depredations have
. . . been committed by the Refugees (Either Black or White)."[38]

The British offered enticement for slaves to desert their rebel masters.
Following Governor Lord Dunmore's emancipation directive in Virginia in
November 1775, General Sir Henry Clinton, from his headquarters at Phi-
lipsburg (in present-day Yonkers, New York) issued a proclamation on June
30, 1779, forbidding "any Person to sell or claim Right over any NEGROE,
the Property of a Rebel, who may take Refuge with any Part of this Army"
and promising any black "who shall desert the Rebel standard, full Security
to follow within these Lines, any Occupation which he shall think proper."[39]
By joining up with the Associated Loyalists, runaway blacks found not only
refuge but also an instant livelihood, being allowed to share in the booty
from marauding.

One mulatto runaway slave, who emerged as the leader of a band of
mostly black refugees, struck terror among patriots in Monmouth County.
His slave name was Titus, but he became known as Colonel Tye. The
British customarily conferred honorary rank on blacks of outstanding ability

serving with the military forces. Tye (Titus) was a slave of his Quaker master, John Corlis, of Colts Neck near Shrewsbury in Monmouth County. The Corlis farm bordered the Navesink River, which ran into the Atlantic Ocean. While a slave, Tye gained experience as a river pilot and knowledge of the topography of Monmouth County. The Shrewsbury Friends (Quaker) Meeting tried to convince Corlis to free Tye, but Corlis refused.[40]

Tye instantly recognized the opportunity brought about by the outbreak of the Revolutionary War. Corlis gave notice of Tye's running away in a Philadelphia newspaper of November 22, 1775.

THREE POUNDS REWARD

RUN away from the subscriber, in the county of Monmouth, New-Jersey, a NEGROE man, named TITUS, but may probably change his name; he is about 21 years of age, not very black, near 6 feet high; had on a grey homespun coat, brown breeches, blue and white stockings, and took with him a wallet, drawn up at one end with a string, in which was a quantity of clothes. Whoever takes up said Negroe, and secures him in any gaol, or brings him to me, shall be entitled to the above reward of *Three Pounds* proc. and all reasonable charges, paid by John Corlis, Nov. 8, 1775.[41]

Tradition has it that Tye fled to Virginia where he joined Governor Lord Dunmore's Ethiopian Regiment. If he wanted to take cover under British military protection, this was a good probability. The only alternative at the time was to make contact with General Howe's army in Boston, not a likely possibility. Rosters for Dunmore's Ethiopian Regiment for May 1776, however, do not mention Tye.[42] Tye could have been on his way back to New Jersey by then. The little army of the "piratical peer" was already forced by the rebels to remain shipboard and in July would leave Virginia waters. Disease was rampant among Dunmore's sailors and soldiers; "jail fever" (ty-phus) and other maladies claimed the lives of over half of the Ethiopian Regiment, certainly a good reason for Tye not to hang around very long with the Virginia governor's ill-fated venture.

The next known appearance of Tye was at the battle of Monmouth in 1778. An American militia captain, Elisha Shepard, declared he was made a prisoner by "Captain Tye" and delivered to the Sugar House prison in New York City.[43]

On July 15, 1779, Tye began to make a series of raids in Monmouth County—for plunder and retaliation. In the first raid, Tye, at the head of fifty blacks and white refugees, landed at Shrewsbury and plundered the inhabitants of nearly eighty head of horned cattle, twenty horses, wearing apparel, and household furniture, and he took two prisoners.[44] The July 1779 raid set a pattern: "a combination of banditry, maroonage and commissioned assistance to the British army."[45]

On March 30, 1780, Tye and his band captured several rebel militia officers, looted and burned the home of John Russell, whom they killed, and wounded his son. In April Tye's marauders abducted Matthias Halsted from his home, and came away with furniture, wearing apparel, and eight cattle. In June 1780 Tye and his men, at least this one time aided by armed white refugees and some of the Queen's Rangers, netted a great deal of plunder at various locations, including the Hornet's Nest, the residence of Captain Barnes Smock, which served as a rendezvous for rebel militia. Tye and his band murdered Joseph Murray at his home near Colts Neck in retaliation for Murray's having participated in the execution of Tories. In each of the raids, Tye's raiders made prisoners of militia officers and men, whom they turned over to British army authorities.[46] According to historian Graham R. Hodges, "Tye's incursions in early June caused great fear among New Jerseyans. In one week Tye carried off much of the officer corps of the Monmouth militia"; furthermore, he "destroyed their cannon and demonstrated his ability to strike at will against a weakened patriot population. If before he was a banditti in service of the British, he now became an important military force."[47]

In reporting two skirmishes between Monmouth militia and presumably the Tye band, Samuel Forman informed Governor Livingston that "our men retook" horses that the enemy had stolen and "wounded one Negro"; in the second engagement, "the enemy got off their plunder." The New Jersey Assembly made an effort to empower the governor to declare martial law in Monmouth County, but the measure failed to pass.[48]

Tye's marauders returned after their raids to their base at Refugeetown: sometimes, they hid out in swamps if they were on successive missions. For the captured rebel militia prisoners and the stolen loot, Tye and his men earned hard cash from the British military authorities in New York City or Staten Island.[49]

Tye's last exploit had one goal: to capture the notorious Joshua Huddy. A Monmouth militia captain, lawyer, and tavern owner from Colts Neck near Shrewsbury, Huddy was a most wanted man by the Loyalist refugees. He had assisted in the execution of Loyalist prisoners. Huddy boasted that in his role in the hanging of a refugee, Stephen Edmunds, from an oak tree near Monmouth Courthouse, he had "Greased the Rope well."[50] With a mixed party of blacks, white refugees, and some of the Queen's Rangers, Tye, on September 1, 1780, attacked Huddy's house at Colts Neck. Huddy and two women—his friend, Lucretia Emmons, and a servant—were the only occupants of the house. Since there was usually a guard detail stationed at the house, Huddy had access to a number of muskets, which the women loaded and he discharged through different windows, creating the impression of many defenders. Finally, with the house set afire, Huddy surrendered. Tye's troops beat a quick retreat, with Huddy in tow, as American militia began to appear. Tye's refugee followers wanted to kill Huddy, but Tye protected his prisoner. As Tye was conducting Huddy by boat to Refugee-town, a rebel militia party sailed up, and Huddy jumped overboard and swam to his rescuers, only to have a fatal rendezvous with refugee Loyalists at a later date. During the assault on Huddy's house, Tye was wounded in the wrist; lockjaw set in, and he died shortly afterward.[51]

Colonel Stephen Bleuke, a freeborn black from Barbados and formerly of the British-sponsored Black Pioneers, replaced Tye as the leader of the black refugee raiders.[52] Toward the end of the war, several black refugee bands were still active. On February 1, 1782, "a party of refugees, consisting of blacks and whites, having formed a plan to intercept the people of this side [Elizabethtown vicinity] as they passed into the meadows for salt hay, came over and concealed themselves in a swamp." Ambushing the passersby, they captured a dozen people along with horses and sleighs. An "alarm" was sounded, and the raiders were "pursued so close" that two of them were taken prisoners, and all of the raiders' captives were recovered.[53] On June 1, 1782, forty whites and forty blacks, commanded by Captain Richard Davenport, landed at Fork River in southern Monmouth County and proceeded along the shores of Barnegat Bay, burning saltworks and plundering local residents.[54] A "number of refugees" went on a robbery spree in Burlington County, near Mount Holly in December 1782. Local militia managed to capture "one Kimble Stackhouse, a white man, and the notorious negro Lot, with three of his black party." A cache of stolen goods was found in "the houses where these villains were secreted." The prisoners were first lodged in the Burlington jail and then moved to Philadelphia for trial.[55]

The long refugee war of retaliation came to a bitter climax over an event of March–April 1782. Having almost snatched their quarry in 1780, two years later the armed Loyalist refugees were still determined to get militia Captain Joshua Huddy, the feared nemesis of all Monmouth County Loyalists.

The Board of Associated Loyalists, from its New York City headquarters and under the direction of William Franklin, authorized a raid on a block-house at the village of Dover (now Toms River) in southern Monmouth County (in present Ocean County); at the installation, "none but a piratical set of [rebel] banditti resided." Near midnight, on March 23, 120 Loyalists (eighty oarsmen and forty Bucks County, Pennsylvania, refugees), commanded by Lieutenant Blanchard, who had set out from Sandy Hook, arrived in whaleboats at Toms River. Reinforced at daybreak, on March 24, the Loyalist attackers surrounded the six- or seven-foot palisade enclosing the blockhouse, which was defended by Huddy and twenty-six men. A fierce fight ensued. When the patriot defenders ran out of ammunition, the Loyalist refugees stormed over the palisade and into the blockhouse, bayoneting some of the defenders. Nine rebels were killed, and Huddy and eleven others (two of whom were wounded) were captured; several other defenders escaped into nearby swamps. Two of the Loyalists were killed, and six were wounded.[56] Huddy and the other prisoners were taken to New York City, where they were lodged first in the Sugar House prison and then in the Provost jail.

Six days after Huddy's capture, Philip White, a Loyalist refugee and former neighbor of Huddy, was apprehended by patriot militia. While being brought by a three-man guard toward Monmouth County Courthouse jail, White, allegedly trying to escape, was killed by one of the guards. John Russell, who fired the fatal shot, had a score to settle; White and a band of refugees had previously raided Russell's house in Shrewsbury, killing Russell's father and wounding Russell and his young son. The refugees claimed that White's death was wanton murder and that the victim had also been mutilated, a charge denied by the patriot militiamen who viewed the corpse. From the refugee viewpoint, White's death demanded retaliation.

Captain Richard Lippincott received permission from the Board of Associated Loyalists to gain custody of Huddy for the purpose of an exchange, although there was to be strong testimony that Lippincott was orally informed that he should execute Huddy in retaliation for the murder of White. As Huddy was being transported aboard a British warship to Sandy Hook for exchange, Lippincott, with a guard of sixteen Loyalists and six sailors, on April 12, went aboard the man-o'-war and put Huddy into their custody. The prisoner was immediately conducted to Gravelly Point, directly across from the southern point of Sandy Hook. Huddy was placed atop a flour barrel, under a gibbet made of three fence rails and hanged. Lippincott and his crew left the site, without cutting down the body. On Huddy's chest was pinned a placard bearing the inscription:

> We the Refugees having with Grief Long beheld the Cruel Murders
> of our Brethren and Finding Nothing but Such Measures Daily
> Carrying into Execution
> We therefore Determine not to Suffer without taking Vengeance
> For numerous Cruelties and thus begin and have made use of Captn
> Huddy as the First Object to present to your Views, and Further
> *Determine* to Hang Man for Man as Long as a Reffugee is left Existing.
>
> UP GOES HUDDY
>
> FOR
>
> PHILIP WHITE[57]

Four hours later, local patriots discovered Huddy's body and carried it to the home of Captain James Green, near Monmouth Courthouse. On April 14, the day before the funeral, nearly 400 persons gathered at the courthouse and drew up a petition to General Washington. The document depicted the whole series of events concerning Huddy's death. It accused the refugees at the Toms River attack of having "inhumanly murdered" five of Huddy's men after they surrendered, and also noted that Huddy had been deprived of any kind of judicial proceedings. Huddy, just before his execution, had demanded the charge against him. One of the refugees, John Tilton, replied that Huddy had captured Philip White, and, after journeying with him about six miles, had cut off White's arms, "broke both his legs, pulled out one of his eyes, and most cruelly murdered him." The petition pointed out that all this was patently a lie, if for no other reason than that Huddy had been in custody when White was killed. Application was made to Washington, in whom "the sole power of avenging our wrongs is lodged," to "hang a British officer of the same rank." For justification, the Monmouth citizens cited a resolution by Congress of October 30, 1778, authorizing an ultimate resort to retaliation; "the law of nature and of nations points to retaliation as the only measure," which can provide "any degree of security that the practice shall not become general."[58]

After receiving the Monmouth County petition and affidavits pertaining to the murders of White and Huddy, Washington forwarded the documents to Congress. The commander in chief stated his intention to exact retaliation. Washington also convened a council of war on April 19 at General William Heath's headquarters at West Point, whereupon all the member officers voted unanimously for retaliation unless Lippincott were surrendered. Washington wrote to General Henry Clinton about his decision on April 21. The British commander in chief responded by condemning the Huddy murder, but he refused to turn over Lippincott, who, he promised, would face trial by a British army court-martial. Not expressed, but certainly in Clinton's mind, and for that matter, also a concern for Washington (though not voiced), was the fear that unremitting retribution would be unleashed if Lippincott were given over to the patriots.[59] General James Robertson, the British interim commander in chief for a few days in May, reminded Washington that fourteen Loyalists had been put to death by patriots in Monmouth County, and further retaliation at "the hands of incensed Men" could only lead to "universal Horror and Barbarity."[60]

The British court-martial of Richard Lippincott was delayed because of a jurisdictional dispute between the Associated Loyalists and the regular army command. Lippincott had joined the New Jersey Volunteers in 1777, and a year later switched to the Associated Loyalists, being commissioned captain in 1781.[61] Since the Associated Loyalists was an autonomous group, only remotely connected to the British high command and not with the army itself, it was argued that a member of the Associated Loyalists could not be tried by a British court-martial; furthermore, Lippincott's execution of Huddy was a military act of war—retaliation for an offense committed by the other side. General Sir Guy Carleton, who replaced Clinton on May 8, ordered the court-martial to convene on June 13. One intriguing argument for the decision was that the crime had been committed in New Jersey, and, although a semblance of civil courts functioned in New York under British military rule, such courts could not try a New Jersey case. The court-martial went its course, and Lippincott was acquitted, chiefly upon testimony by witnesses that Lippincott had acted under oral orders by William Franklin and the Board of Associated Loyalists.[62]

Even before the Lippincott court-martial, Washington set in motion the process for retaliation for Huddy's death, which gained Congress's approval.[63] On May 3 Washington ordered Brigadier General Moses Hazen, commandant of the American prisoner guard at Lancaster, to designate by lot a British captain "who is an unconditional prisoner" or a lieutenant "under the same circumstances" from among the prisoners in Pennsylvania (at Lancaster, York, or Reading) or Maryland (at Frederick Town) and send the designee to the secretary at war in Philadelphia, who would then determine the place for the retaliatory execution.[64]

Eight captains and five lieutenants on parole gathered at Lancaster on May 25, 1782. In a room at the Black Bear Tavern, with twenty mounted American guards in the inn's yard, they drew pieces of paper, all of which were blank except for one marked "unfortunate." Captain Charles Asgill, nineteen years old and the son of a former mayor of London, got the unlucky draw. The technicality that Asgill was a "conditional" prisoner, that is, protected by the Yorktown surrender agreement and not subject to any kind of retaliation, was overlooked.

Asgill was sent to the encampment of the New Jersey Line near Morristown to await execution. Asgill's hanging was postponed as long as possible. Congress agreed to consider the situation again. As members wrapped up a three-day debate over the Huddy-Lippincott-Asgill affair, during which "much ill blood appeared in the House," Congress received a letter from the king and queen of France along with a letter from Asgill's mother, Lady Asgill (Thérèse Prativiel), both pleading clemency. The letters "operated like an electrical shock" among the Congressional members, who finally concluded their review with the freeing of Asgill as a "compliment to the King of France."[65] Asgill returned to England in December 1782.

Although Congress and Washington were not satisfied that the British command had made no retribution for the murder of Huddy, they were contented that General Clinton, before his departure, had severely curtailed the activities of the Associated Loyalists, and Clinton's successor, Sir Guy Carleton, in December 1782, disbanded the Associated Loyalists altogether. Carleton's decision elicited from Washington the hope "that the savage kind of desultory War which we have long experienced is at an end."[66]

Cessation of all hostilities became official in April 1783.[67] By that time, some 6,000 Loyalists had set sail from New York City for the maritime provinces in Canada; many of them were New Jersey refugees who had borne arms.[68] A few refugees who had stayed behind conducted plundering raids in the Hackensack Valley through the spring of 1783.[69]

The constant raiding by the armed Loyalist refugees, in the long run, did more harm than good, from the British viewpoint. While the activities demonstrated the capabilities of attacking almost anywhere along the New Jersey coastline, the reckless marauding only further embittered citizens against the British cause. As one writer observed, the armed refugee Loyalists "wanted not only victory but vengeance," and "by openly advocating a war of depredation and revenge," they "willingly burned their bridges behind them. They could never again accommodate themselves with their countrymen."[70] Having forfeited their own property, the land the British government provided to the north and the remuneration eventually received by a few amounted to scant compensation for the refugees' long, high-risk guerrilla service.

Chapter 5

Highlands Gangs

From their nests in the rugged terrain of the New York Highlands, banditti swooped down into the surrounding countryside to prey upon farmers and villagers. The Highlands, lying next to the southeastern part of the Adirondack Mountains, diagonally connect the hills of northern New Jersey to the Taconic Mountains of western Connecticut and Massachusetts. The Highlands mainly encompass the New York counties of Orange, bordering the west bank of the Hudson River, and Dutchess, on the east side. The highest elevation is Butter Hill (1,529 feet). The "rugged mountains" of the Highlands begins, according to one traveler in 1774, about forty miles north of New York City and stretches for about twelve miles before leading into "a tolerable level country." Dr. James Thacher, a military physician, commented that in June 1779, as Washington's army marched "over the prodigious highland mountains," his "curiosity was excited by a vast number of huge rocks marked by fissures and cavities, occasioned by some stupendous power beyond our comprehension." Brooks "winding in every direction, among rude clefts and precipices, afford a singular and romantic landscape. Our path was narrow and rugged, and probably will not again be traversed but by savages and wild beasts."[1]

The Highlands banditti specialized in the theft of livestock, but they also stole anything that could bring a price in New York City. Ostensibly the members of the gangs were Tories, but they acted independently of any military affiliation. Like their counterparts elsewhere, the most notorious of the banditti had short careers. The Highlands outlaws were relentlessly hunted down, and many of them were executed, usually after conviction for crimes less than murder. The gangs had ready recruits from escaped Convention (Saratoga) army prisoners of war[2] and from disaffected persons, who had been persecuted by local patriots.

The Highlands gangs particularly infested the Ramapo River Valley, which, bordered by steep mountains and marshy ravines, extends from just inside the tip of northeastern New Jersey to about fifteen miles below West Point, in New York, on the Hudson River. Smith's Clove (near Monroe, New York) formed the northeastern entrance into the valley. One army officer said of Smith's Clove that it was "a most villainous country, rough, rocky" and filled with "rattlesnakes and robbers. . . . It was an infringement on the right of wild beasts for man ever to enter this Clove."[3]

During the war a roadway was cut from King's Ferry on the west side of the Hudson River diagonally southward through Smith's Clove and the Ramapo Valley on through Haverstraw and Kakiate to provide a main artery between Washington's army when it was stationed at New Windsor, in the Highlands on the west bank of the Hudson, and Morristown and Philadelphia.[4] Robbers soon found easy marks on this "Continental Road."

Claudius Smith became the best-known, and most wanted, of the Highlands desperados. Regional authors have celebrated Smith as a Robin Hood. In the ample literature Smith is the "Cowboy of the Ramapos" and "the Scourge of the Ramapos."[5]

The Claudius Smith gang committed depredations throughout the southern part of Orange County, in and around the towns of Monroe, Cornwall, Bloominggrove, and Goshen. The outlaws had a remarkable hideout in the woods in Smith's Clove near the Continental Road. The refuge was a double cave. As one writer described it, "The upper cave was used as a temporary storage place for booty and as a camp-site for the bandits. The lower cave stabled their horses and stolen cattle." A spring ran between the caves. "To secure themselves further, the gang, at great labor piled large boulders around the front and sides of the upper cave with a secret-covered exit leading out from one end."[6]

Smith's gang consisted of Claudius Smith and three of his sons—Richard, James, and William—and various refugee outlaws who drifted in and out of the loose bandit network, such as Edward Roblins, William Cole, John Mason, Matthew Dodson, John Ryan, Thomas Delamer, and James Gordon. Claudius Smith's other son served in the patriot army.

The Smith family, originally from England, had been in America for a long time. Claudius's father, David Smith (1701–87) and mother, Jerusha Ramsey, had lived in Brookhaven, Long Island, where Claudius was born

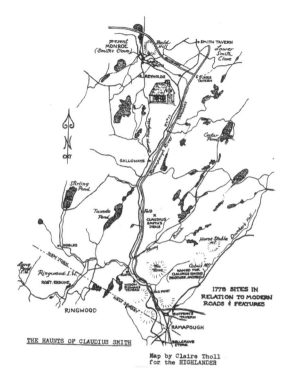

"The Haunts of Claudius Smith." From Claire K.
Tholl, "The Career of Claudius Smith," *North Jersey
Highlander*, vol. 4, no. 3 (1968).

in 1730, and Southold, Long Island, before moving to near Monroe village
in Smith's Clove sometime before the war. David Smith, who refused to
sign the Articles of Association prescribed by the New York Committee of
Safety and Observation, had his own run-in with the patriot authorities,
but he was left unmolested for his Toryism. The father was known to carry
provisions to Claudius's hideout. David Smith was fined £25 in 1780 "for
his son [other than Claudius] agoing to and joining the enemy." Before he
died David Smith became blind and hit his wife with his cane whenever
she came near him.[7]

Claudius Smith does not appear as an outlaw until well into middle age,
yet reportedly he had a vicious streak even as a youth, and his mother told
him, "Claudius, you will die like a trooper's horse, with your shoes on." One
of Claudius's first thefts was that of some iron wedges, which bore the
owner's initials. Claudius's father, who himself seems to have had thieving
ways, helped him grind out the letters. Next, in July 1777, for stealing oxen

"belonging to the continent" Claudius Smith and John Brown were jailed in Orange County.[8] It is probable that Claudius escaped confinement.

Claudius Smith now committed himself fully to banditry. Although he had a compassionate side, he was willing to use violence to achieve his objectives. At the start of his outlaw career one episode reveals Claudius's better self. On October 7, Judge William Bodle met Claudius Smith on a road. The men were acquainted, but Bodle had heard local talk that Smith had become a highwayman. Calling Bodle by name, Claudius gave him a friendly greeting and extended his hand. After inquiring about the news, Claudius said, "Mr. Bodle, you are weary with walking, go to my dwelling yonder." Pointing to a place near the road, Claudius continued, "Ask my wife to give you a breakfast, and tell her I sent you." Judge Bodle, who himself is the source for this story, related that he thanked Claudius, "seeming to accept his offer, and bade him good morning, but when he was out of sight, he changed his course toward home, nor felt himself safe until he was a far way on his journey."[9]

A year later, Claudius Smith learned that a wealthy miser, Abimal Youngs, had declined to lend money to a needy wife of a patriot lieutenant colonel, James McClaughry of the militia, who had been captured at the surrender of Fort Montgomery on October 6, 1777, and was a prisoner of war in New York City. McClaughry's former wife, who had died in 1762, was the sister of New York's Governor George Clinton. Youngs did not want to assume the risk of a loan to someone whose husband was a prisoner. Going to Youngs' home late at night, in October 1778, Smith and his gang demanded money, but Youngs said he had none. Thereupon the robbers threw a rope over a well pole and strung up Youngs. Letting him down, money was again demanded, and again Youngs refused. In all, Youngs was suspended three times before being let go. The band searched the house and came away with valuable papers, including deeds, bonds, and mortgages; presumably Mrs. McClaughry reaped some benefit.[10]

The same night (October 6) of the Youngs raid, the Claudius Smith gang visited the home of Major Nathaniel Strong at midnight. Strong, aroused from sleep, was shot dead while going for his pistols. All the robbers came away with were two bridles and a saddle. Ebenezer Woodhull was robbed at his home about the same time. During fall 1778 the Smith banditti raided various villages and farms to the south and west of Schunemunk Mountain, about twelve miles west of the Hudson River. Claudius's son William was shot by pursuers on the mountain, but he escaped. After getting down the mountain, William hid in a barn for a while and then entered a swamp, where he hid in a hollow log. His pursuers caught him there, and on his way to the Goshen jail he died of his wounds.[11]

The murder of Strong made Claudius Smith a much wanted fugitive.

Governor George Clinton, acting upon a legislative resolution, posted rewards of $1,200 for Claudius Smith and $600 for each of his two sons, James and Richard.[12]

Claudius Smith fled first to New York City, where he deemed he was unsafe, and then to Long Island, where he lodged with a widow near Smithtown, located in an area under British control. But Claudius Smith's luck had run out. Major John Brush, who owned a farm nearby, had gone to Connecticut as a patriot refugee, leaving his property in the hands of tenants, but occasionally returned secretly. On one of his trips to his homestead, he learned that Claudius Smith was living in the neighborhood. Brush had heard of the reward for Smith. Brush returned to Connecticut and told a Mr. Titus, a strongly built man who also had resided on Long Island, and the two agreed to apprehend Claudius Smith. With three others enlisted for the mission, the kidnapping party crossed the Sound late one night; upon landing one man was left with the boat, and the others went to the house where Smith was staying, about a mile distant. They opened the door and saw the landlady sitting by a fire. After some prodding she admitted that Claudius Smith was upstairs in bed and agreed to call him. Brush refused the offer and, taking a candle, he and the three other men went upstairs and seized Smith while he slept. Smith "awoke and made violent resistance, and endeavored to get his pistols which were under his pillow. They bound his arms with a cord and led him to the boat, immediately crossed the Sound and landed early next morning. Then they had him ironed and put under guard."[13]

Major Brush delivered his prisoner to Governor Clinton at Poughkeepsie, the makeshift capital of New York. Clinton then sent Claudius Smith to Fishkill, where he was picked up by the sheriff of Orange County, Colonel Isaac Nicoll, and in the company of militia cavalry brought to the jail in Goshen. Smith was bound in irons, hands and feet, and chained to the floor; a "strong guard" kept watch. Orders were given to shoot Smith if his followers attacked the jail. Smith languished in confinement for two and a half months before coming to trial.[14]

On January 13, 1779, a special court of oyer and terminer, consisting of two justices of the New York Supreme Court, Robert Yates and John Sloss Hobart, and a local justice of the peace, Elihu Marvin, sat in judgment of Smith. Customarily, in this kind of court there was no jury. Claudius Smith was tried and convicted, not on any counts of murder, but for capital felony in robbing the houses of John Earle, Ebenezer Woodhull, and William Bell; stealing horses belonging to James Savage and William Armstrong, Jr.; and robbery "on the Highway" of Simon Fink. Tried and convicted on the same day along with Smith on robbery charges were Matthew Dodson, John Ryan, Thomas Delamer, and James Gordon. The court sentenced to death all the defendants and also Amy Augur, "late Mary Jones," a "young woman" who two days earlier had been convicted for the murder of her bastard child. It appears that Dodson, Ryan, and Augur were reprieved or pardoned.[15]

Claudius Smith, along with Gordon and Delamer, were hanged on January 22, 1779, from a balm of Gilead tree in the jail yard of the Goshen courthouse. On the gallows Claudius Smith "was dressed in a suit of rich broadcloth, with silver buttons, and with his large form and manly air, presented really a noble appearance." He bowed to several acquaintances. Abimal Youngs approached the gallows and asked the condemned to tell him where he had hidden the papers that had been stolen from him. Claudius replied that this was hardly the time for such matters and that the issue could be settled in the next world. Claudius, who apparently had harbored a resentment toward his mother, kicked off his shoes, thereby making the prophecy of his mother that he would die with his shoes on a lie. When the cart was pulled away, Claudius "swung to and fro perfectly straight, determined . . . to evince no feeling; when senseless he twitched a little, and exhibited signs of life after he had hung a long time."[16] Although buried in the Presbyterian Church cemetery, as tradition has it, his skull, filled with mortar, was placed in the masonry above the entrance of the courthouse, and a wristbone was made into a handle for a carving knife. Well into the twentieth century fortune hunters were still searching the Ramapo Mountains for Claudius Smith's ill-gained loot.[17]

The execution of Claudius Smith spurred his followers to seek revenge. Richard, Claudius's youngest son, appears to have taken charge of the gang, the core of which included James Flewelling, James Ramsey, James McCormick, and Daniel Keith (a deserter from General John Burgoyne's captive army). Various Highlands banditti drifted in and out of the Smith group. James Smith, Claudius's other bandit son, had the misfortune of being captured at the home of Nathan Miller only three weeks after his father's execution.[18]

Richard Smith, as did his brothers and other Highlands banditti, claimed to be a Loyalist and declared his deeds benefited the British cause. The Smith gang regarded Claudius's hanging to be a result of the maliciousness of patriot leaders. One month after Claudius Smith's death, Richard performed his first act of revenge. Smith, with six others, including David Badcock, John Mason, and Thomas Ward, went to the house of John W. Clark near Warwick, Orange County. The visitors knocked on the door and were admitted. One of the men pulled out a watch and told Clark it was midnight and by 1:00 A.M. Clark would be a dead man.

Clark inquired why they would take his life; they answered "you have killed two Tories & wounded a third. . . . Clark replied, "I never killed a man in my life, but I believe I did wound the man you mention & I was then under the command of my proper officer & therefore did my Duty. They said . . . they were determined to hang him. . . . They drank very freely of sundry sorts of Liquor, of which there were three Barrels in the house, filled their Bottles & stove the Casks; took 3 Bushels of salt & strewed upon the Ground so as it could not be collected: filled Bags with Meat, Bread, Meal & many other things, took about £200 in Cash & gave Mrs. Clark a Paper written as follows Viz:

A Warning to Rebels:

You are hereby forbid at your peril to hang no more Friends to government as you did Claudius Smith.

You are warned likewise to use James Smith, James Flewelling & Wm. Cole well and ease them of their Irons, for we are determined to hang six for one, for the Blood of the innocent cries aloud for vengeance; your noted Friend, Capt. Williams & his Crew of Robbers & Murderers we have got in our Power, & the Blood of Claudius shall be repaid; there is particular Companies of us that belong to Col. Butler's army, Indians as well as white men, & particularly Numbers from N. York that are resolved to be revenged on you for your cruelty & Murders. We are to remind you that you are the beginners & agressors, for by your cruel oppressions & bloody actions drive us to it. This is the first & we are determined to pursue it on your Heads & Leaders to the last til the whole of you is Massacred. Dated New York Feb'y 1779.

The intruders then led Clark out of the house and began to argue about whether to hang him or shoot him. Richard Smith settled the dispute by shooting Clark through the breast. After the assailants had taken his shoes, Clark rose and ran away but was shot again in the shoulder. He reached his wife and informed her that Smith had shot him; shortly afterward, Clark died. The assailants left and stopped at the house of Gideon Maces down the road. Next they robbed a traveler. "After this they went in to the Mountains."[19]

Richard Smith's ultimatum had a contrary effect. The Orange County, New York, and Bergen County, New Jersey, authorities relentlessly pursued the outlaws. In Hackensack, New Jersey, William Cole and Thomas Welcher were tried and executed on April 9, 1779.[20] James Smith (Claudius's son), James Flewelling, Daniel Keith, and James McCormick were hanged at Goshen, New York, on June 8, 1779.[21]

Nothing more was ever heard from Richard Smith, who most likely found refuge in New York City or elsewhere. In April 1779 there were reportedly forty or fifty banditti "now in the mountains" in the vicinity of Smith's Clove.[22] The crackdown on the outlaws forced many of them to leave or lie low, although every once in a while a Highlands gang-type robbery occurred.

Success against the Highlands bandits came largely after the authorities learned the identities of about three dozen outlaws and their abettors, even those who were responsible for specific crimes, thanks to the cooperation of William Cole. The most tragic figure among those who were apprehended, Cole, himself not an outright Loyalist and one who was minimally involved in robberies, hoped to avoid execution by providing all the information he could about the Highlands gangs. Two depositions given by Cole at New Barbadoes Township in Bergen County, one upon examination by Judge John Cleves Symmes of the New Jersey Supreme Court on March 23, 1779, and the other, a confession of March 29, 1779, gave the names of just about everyone who had ever been involved in robberies over the past two years and also the names of those who had given them any kind of aid. Cole told of several underground caves dug by Isaac Maybee and his sons, spaced at distances apart to shelter the outlaws, and also of a series of way stations, culminating with a privately owned landing site on the Hudson River through which "large quantities of all sorts of provisions" passed, destined for New York City.[23]

William Cole's misfortune began after the British capture of Fort Montgomery in October 1778, during which he served in a Tory regiment commanded by Colonel John Bayard. When he became sick, he was allowed to stay at the home of Moses Clement, and then he went to New York City for a while. He returned to Orange County in the company of a gang, headed by John Mason, but also consisting of Thomas Ward, John Everet, Jacob Acker, James Cowen, George (alias Thomas) Harding, David Badcock, James Twaddle, Martinus Lawson, and Peter Lawson. Cole soon split off from the group. He admitted to participating in only two robberies: taking a gun from Hendrick Odell and, in the company of George Bull, Jacob Low, James Flewelling, Archibald McCurdy, and Thomas Welcher, robbing a Mr. Ackerman. Cole was arrested in early March 1779 at the home of Jacobus Peek in Schraalenburgh (in Bergen County).

Among the robbers Cole identified for the authorities were members of the Mason gang, with whom he had briefly associated but did not participate in their crimes. According to Cole, this group had conducted the robbery of the Robert Erskine manor house in Ringwood, New Jersey, on November 11, 1778. Erskine was the manager of the ironworks at Ringwood, as well as the geographer and surveyor-general of the Continental army. The Ringwood ironworks had fallen on somewhat difficult times; only 40 of the 400 employees remained. Because the mansion and the counting house (thirty yards distant) had escaped robberies during the war, there was not much concern for security. With information regarding valuables, probably supplied by one of Erskine's employees, the opportunity for a bandit strike was ripe.

Erskine was on one of his regular jaunts to Washington's army, seventy miles to the east. The only persons at home were Mrs. Erskine, Ebenezer Erskine, Jr., a nephew who was visiting from Scotland, and two boys staying in the garret ("a Negro [Cato] and a Blacksmith boy"). Two clerks, Robert Monteith and one Gordon, occupied the counting house. Ebenezer, quite shaken, recorded a complete description of the ordeal in his diary.

About 9:30 P.M. the robbers silently approached the counting house, gained entry, and tied up the two clerks. The intruders approached the main house, knocked on the door, and declared that they were a detachment of Continental soldiers. They were admitted by Mrs. Erskine. Ebenezer, who shared a room with his traveling companion, James Arthur, came downstairs and soon discovered five pistols pointed at his face.

"Don't move or you're a dead man!" several of the robbers shouted.

After securing all the residents and locking Gordon, Monteith, and Arthur in the cellar, the bandits began their quest for loot. Mrs. Erskine had hoped to conceal most of the valuables, especially her gold watch, but the robbers knew of their existence, and so she surrendered them. Taking six horses from the stable, the thieves loaded on all the plunder they could; among the stolen goods were four silver watches, the gold watch, rings, firearms, papers of Robert Erskine, and cash. The victims were told not to open the cellar door or leave until 6:00 A.M. Two hours after the robbers left, however, Mrs. Erskine sent several of the men down the road to alarm the neighborhood. After they left the Erskine home, the thieves robbed the homestead of a Mrs. Sidman, coming away with "a quantity of negroes, horses and plate."

A militia company pursued the robbers "to the Ramapo mountains," recovering in the process the "negroes" and horses. The remaining loot went to New York City, where one member of the gang, George Harding, presented Mrs. Erskine's gold watch to David Matthew, mayor of the city, and John Mason, the gang's leader, gave Robert Erskine's rifle to Major Lord Cathcart, commander of the Scottish Legion.[24]

Wiert C. Banta, who often could be found in a Highlands bandit gang, became "notoriously known for his complicated villainous thefts and robberies." Born in 1743 and raised near Hackensack, New Jersey, Banta worked as a carpenter before the war. At the beginning of the conflict he spent ten months in an Albany jail for being "a dangerous Tory." He then served as a guide and intelligence gatherer for Loyalist and British military forces. He provided information that assisted in the British capture of Fort Montgomery and General Charles "No Flint" Grey's massacre of Colonel George Baylor's American dragoons at Tappan, New York, on September 28, 1778. On February 2, 1779, he was appointed a lieutenant in the King's Militia Volunteers.

According to Cole, and supported by a memorandum written by Thomas Ward, Banta was a nearly illiterate son of an ironworker who later achieved military success as a captain of Loyalist refugees (see Chapter 4). Banta, along with John Mason, Thomas Ward, James Smith, Nathaniel Biggs, and

Richard Smith, after being frustrated in trying to rob the mails, pulled off one of the most daring coups of the war. The group crept into the American camp at Kakiate, and, disarming a guard consisting of a sergeant and thirteen men, abducted General Joseph Ward, the muster master general of Washington's army, and his deputy, Colonel William Bradford. Banta and his comrades also came away with the muster rolls of the Continental army. Although soon hotly pursued by American soldiers, the kidnappers made it safely across the Hudson River with their prisoners, who were delivered to British headquarters in New York City. Lord Cathcart paid the band 100 guineas, to be shared by each abductor.

On March 28, 1779, as Banta and thirty other men ("embodied Refugees") were trying to steal horses and plunder inhabitants near Closter, they were attacked by American militia. Although he escaped, Banta was shot through the knee. The amputation of the lower leg ended Banta's bandit-military career. After the war he settled in Nova Scotia, where he resumed his trade as a carpenter.[25]

John Mason, a principal leader of the Highlands outlaws during late 1778 and 1779, is a tragic figure. A Loyalist, Mason sought British protection in New York City and then returned to his native Orange County as one of the Highlands banditti. He participated in many robberies. Mason was with the Richard Smith gang when they murdered John Clark. He was probably the author of "The Warning to Rebels," which the assailants left behind at Clark's murder. In any event, Mason made a lengthy revision of the "Warning," which he presented British General Henry Clinton. Mason's document called for vengeance: the patriots must release all Loyalist prisoners, and there was the threat to kill six persons for every one executed by the patriots. Mason declared that "we Embody not with the British Army; but keeps by our Selves." Mason threatened that "two titular Governors" (George Clinton of New York and William Livingston of New Jersey) would "meet with their Just Deserts." Mason pledged that "the Blood of . . . men; and the crys of the Widows; and Fatherless; will be heard; and be Recompensed with the Almighty's Wrath." The "Warning" concluded with poetry:

On your Governors

> You Infernal Bloodhounds; now Desist
> And in your Murders; no more persist
> Unless you Repent, you'll tormented be
> With Incarnate Devils; to all Eternity
> Signed in Behalf of the Loyalists
> John Mason
> Dated at Rabels Defiance March 27th, AD 1779
> N.B. the above lines is wrote in a low Stile Sutable to your Capacities.

Most likely this "Warning" did not reach Washington's headquarters as the first one had.

Mason's return to New York City was not welcomed as he expected it to be. He irked British authorities by indiscriminate plundering on Long Island, trading with the enemy, and encouraging a British soldier to desert. A court-martial sent him to the Provost jail, where for two months his wife was also a prisoner. Seeking freedom for himself and his wife, Mason volunteered to enlist as a sergeant in a planned British military expedition against the Spaniards in Nicaragua; the project, however, did not materialize. Also, in seeking release from jail, Mason volunteered to go as a spy behind American lines.

Unfortunately for him, John Mason received a spy assignment of the most dangerous kind. He carried a message from General Henry Clinton, wrapped "in a piece of tea-lead," enticing the mutineers of the Pennsylvania Line in the Continental army to go over to the British army. The mutineers arrested Mason and James Ogden, a young New Jersey farmer who had served as Mason's guide, and turned them over to an army court-martial. Both men were hanged, on January 12, 1781, at the Cross Roads near Trenton.[26]

Little is known about one of the most notorious of the Highlands ban-ditti—John Berry, alias John the Regular. A militia officer noted that Berry had boasted of killing forty-eight persons. Berry frequently served as an operative for the British army. Berry met his end when, on May 27, 1780, he and five comrades came across an American militia patrol, under the command of Captain John Huyler and Captain Thomas Blanch, near Bull's Ferry on the Hudson. Berry was mortally wounded when he refused to sur-render. All members of the militia party shared equally in the $1,000 reward provided by the New Jersey government for the capture of Berry, dead or alive.[27]

As Washington moved his army for a short stay in Smith's Clove in June 1779 and then up to New Windsor, in the northern foothills of the High-lands,[28] banditti, in conjunction with Loyalist military parties, had newer, riskier targets, in attacking detached soldiers and army supply wagons. In early June 1779,

six daring villains, in Smith's Clove, had the audacity to fire on two of our light-horse as they were passing in the rear of the army, one of which they wounded in the body, and broke the thigh bone of the other: They were immediately pursued by a party from the army, taken, and one hung; the other five were conducted to headquarters, and a court-martial being held on them, they were found guilty, and received sentence of death; pursuant to which four were hanged, and it being insinuated to the fifth, that if he would discover his accomplices, he would be pardoned, which offer of clemency he eagerly embraced, and conducted a party of our people to a cave in the mountains, the depository of all their plunder, where lay concealed five more, whom they secured. Various articles of plunder were found in their den.[29]

On April 30, 1780, two wagons on their way from Fishkill to Morristown were stopped in Smith's Clove "by a party of the enemy and robbed of most part of whatever was valuable in them." The robbers took away three trunks, containing hats, clothing, and books belonging to private citizens; many books and "some trifling articles" were discarded in the woods. Two of the persons whose property was robbed "with a party of continental troops scoured the Mountains . . . and searched all the disaffected houses in the neighborhood of the clove," but with "little success."[30]

The presence of the Continental army nearby contributed to security against outlaw raids. Furthermore, the New York Commissioners for Detecting Conspiracies in 1779 rounded up persons suspected of assisting Highlands banditti and detained them.[31] Anyone found "selling continental cattle" was jailed.[32] The immediate vicinity of West Point, in Orange County on the Hudson, was declared to be under martial law in reference to "certain offenses," such as stealing public property.[33]

Every now and then an event served as a jolting reminder that some Highlands banditti were still on the loose. In July 1782 robbers viciously assaulted the Henry Reynolds family at their farmhouse in Smith's Clove. The episode was vividly recalled many years later by an old neighbor, who had obtained his information first hand from the victims themselves.

Late that fateful night, Benjamin Kelly, who had lived a half mile down the road, and Edward Roblins knocked on the door of the Reynolds' home. The visitors announced that they were a party searching for American deserters. The request did not seem surprising since Washington's army was stationed a few miles north at New Windsor. Henry Reynolds, though a Quaker, himself had seen active military service as a militiaman. When he opened the door of his house, Reynolds suddenly realized the true identity of his would-be guests, and he darted outside. The intruders quickly caught him and dragged him back into the house.

Roblins grabbed a servant boy, put him up against a wall, and told him that if he moved, his head would be cut off. The lad stayed in a fixed position during the whole of the awful proceedings that followed. Mrs. Reynolds and her oldest child, Phebe (age twelve), entered the room. Mrs. Reynolds was pregnant, ready to give birth. Reynolds, who had received wounds from the intruders' knives and swords, lay on the floor bleeding. Mrs. Reynolds fainted. Her young son, Caleb, came in and was kicked unconscious. His body lay on top of his mother's.

Henry Reynolds was hanged from a beam, whereupon the bandits began searching the house. Phebe cut down her father and placed him in a bed.

The robbers came up to Phebe, who stood in front of the bed, wielding a knife, declaring she would kill the first one who tried to harm her father further.

Benjamin Kelly yelled, "Get away you little rebel or I'll run my sword through you."

"You may kill me, for if you will kill my father I do not wish to live," responded Phebe.

Kelly lunged at Phebe with a sword, which Phebe managed to knock from his hand. Kelly tried to catch it but received a deep wound in his wrist. Another robber stabbed Phebe in the breast, and she threw herself on her father's body. Someone grabbed Phebe and tore off her clothes. Phebe then received a lashing on her bare body from the rope that had been used to hang her father. Mrs. Reynolds and Caleb, having regained consciousness, hovered nearby. The robbers again hanged Reynolds from the beam. As the assailants again searched the house, Phebe again cut her father down and threw herself over his body. She was stabbed twice more. The bandits put Henry Reynolds into a chest and closed the lid. They left with their loot, after placing a large stone against the door of the house. Phebe removed her father from the chest, and Mrs. Reynolds pried open her husband's mouth with a spoon and forced water into his mouth. Reynolds, who seemed dead, revived. Before leaving the property, the robbers had set fire to some flax and two beds, which Phebe extinguished. All the while the servant boy refused to budge, and Phebe went out to alarm the neighborhood. A doctor was brought in from Goshen. A posse, who went in pursuit of the bandits, discovered their hiding place in the mountains. All the bandits, however, escaped, although Kelly was wounded and was later found dead.

During the traumatic event, Henry Reynolds sustained thirty wounds and was nearly killed by hanging; Phebe also had wounds. Mrs. Reynolds gave birth to a girl (Polly) the next day. Remarkably Henry Reynolds lived to the age of ninety (d. 1830), and Phebe, who married Jeremiah Drake, lived to be eighty-three (d. 1853). It is not known whether any other perpetrators of the horrible proceedings were taken alive. Edward Roblins fled to Canada. Many years later, his sons visited Orange County to search for hidden plunder of their father and other gang members.[34]

Highlands gangs east of the Hudson River also caused terror. Dutchess County, from the Fishkill Mountains to the steep river banks, with an intervening valley containing the Great Swamp between two large ridges, offered a protective terrain for robbers seeking quick refuge.[35]

Before his execution in 1779, William Cole fingered "a gang of the same kind [as the Claudius Smith outlaws in Orange County] on the East Side of the Hudson River whose names are Mandeville Leonerbeck, Peter Wood,

William Heiliker, William Danford, Aaron Williams, James Houston and others, who plundered and brought some cattle and Horses from Tarrytown to New York."[36]

During 1778 and 1779 robbers plagued the eastern Highlands. "Complaints of the frequent Robberies committed on the East Side of the River are become intolerable," noted the Commissioners for Detecting Conspiracies at their Albany meeting on July 27, 1778.[37] Robber gangs regularly attacked the homes of tenants on Livingston Manor[38] and residents of the Claverack district. Inhabitants of the towns of northern Dutchess County and of Livingston Manor petitioned Governor Clinton to provide protection against robbers. The petitioners complained that they "have been despoiled and Plundered of all their arms and great part of their Ready money, cloathing and Valuable Effects by a Gang of Robbers pretending to be Subjects of the King of Great Britain."[39]

A company of about thirty militia rangers, commanded by Captain Jacob DeForest, went "in quest of the Perpetrators," with orders to search "every suspected House for Papers & stolen Goods" and to "apprehend all Strangers" who had not "sufficient Authority to be at large."[40] The Commissioners for Detecting Conspiracies proscribed for arrest certain persons, naming the locale where the suspected criminals committed robberies or where they might be found: John Smith and Jonathan Wickwire (Livingston Manor); Hugh Frere and Thomas Wood (New Britain); Martinus Kimmel and Frederick Querin (Poestenkill); and Thomas Garnet, Roeliff Van der Kar, John Stoner, John Cafert, and Stephen Miller (Peesink). Jacob Coatman was wanted for the murder of Abraham Van Ness (Nine Partners precinct).[41]

The rangers apparently did their job because the robbery problem abated for a while. Eventually the banditti returned. Like their counterparts across the river, the eastern Highlands malefactors were usually Loyalists who had been ill-treated by their neighbors and who had lost their estates, as well as British agents sent out to commit depredations against substantial Whigs. General Alexander McDougall observed that "from long Experience it is well known that many of those miscreants come out in winter and return to the Enemy in the Spring."[42]

On April 26, 1781, the *New-York Packet* carried a notice that, on Sunday night, April 1, the house of Comfort Sands, in Charlotte precinct, Dutchess County

was robbed by a gang of villains who went off some time ago to New-York, and are the very persons who robbed Zaccheus Newcomb . . . the preceding week one of the villains name is Hoog, of a brown complexion, black hair tied, a cocked hat, with silver button and loop, about five feet four inches high. One named Joseph Earle, about five foot high, thin visage. One named Storm, about five foot eight inches high, thin visage. One they called Nickerson—another name unknown, about five feet three inches high, full face, brown complexion, black hair; and others that were about the house that cannot be described. Two of them had regimental coats faced with red—one had a short red coat, the others brown over clothes.

As these persons are so far out of the enemy's lines, it must necessarily take them some time to return, and as they said they had no other way to live, having lost their habitations, and their effects been sold by the state, but to plunder.

The robbery victim who posted the notice was quite determined. He called upon every Whig to try to apprehend "such atrocious villains, and to search disaffected persons houses, who harbour and comfort them." A reward of $25 "new emission" money was offered for each of the robbers captured and brought to justice; a double amount and also a "generous reward of such of the goods as may be taken" would go to a person killing any one of the culprits. It seemed like a heady revenge for the victim, whose loss consisted mainly of silverware and tableware, clothes, silver buckles, a small silver watch, tablecloths, and pillowcases.[43]

Captain Pearse of Pawling's Precinct in Dutchess County took upon himself to lead a law enforcement campaign against eastern Highlands banditti. In May 1781 he and a posse captured seven robbers who had been hiding in a cave; some of the captives "received the reward due to their deserts." On September 6, Captain Pearse,

having heard of a party of robbers being seen in the mountains, collected a few men to go in quest of them; Having divided them in three parties, one of them discovered four villains playing cards near a small house in the woods; our men fired on them, and killed the noted thief, Vaughan, on the spot; Hoog, Proffet and the other got off. One of them (supposed to be Hoog, by his hat which was left) was wounded, by the blood which was discovered in considerable quantities on the road. Several papers were found on Vaughan, giving an account of the division of their plunder. . . . In the house, near where the fellows were discovered, were cooking for them, two quarters of mutton, and two more hanging up: They pulled down the house which harboured the robbers, and took bail of the disaffected man who possessed it.[44]

In the summer of 1782 banditti killed three persons near Fishkill. One of the victims, Robert Oakley, "an active friend of freedom," who lived near Philips's Precinct in Dutchess County, was "most barbarously murdered" on June 19 while traveling on a road that went through Wiccopee Pass in the Fishkill Mountains. The attackers led Oakley into the woods, made him kneel down, and killed him with a musket shot. The murderers took Oakley's money and his horse. A newspaper editorial commented that the "perpetrators" were "some of the thieves and robbers sent out by the enemy."

Of the two other victims, one "was found hanging in the woods." The other was missing for a long time and presumed dead; his horse was discovered killed and the saddle "cut to pieces."[45]

Disgusted that so many robbers committed crimes with virtual impunity because they had ample assistance and protection from friends and Tory sympathizers, the New York legislature finally confronted the problem head on and, on November 21, 1781, provided the death penalty for accessories as well as principals involved in robberies.[46]

One person by the last name of Wynne was hanged at Poughkeepsie in early July 1782, "on conviction of having harboured, victualled, and given intelligence to the robbers . . . so as to enable them to elude the pursuits made after them." A newspaper commented that "it is indeed high time something efficacious should be done" because the robbers "murder all those that are either active in bringing them down, or could be evidences against them."[47]

The Highlands gangs flourished as long as they did because of a community divided between patriots and those Loyalist sympathizers who sheltered and assisted the robbers in making their get-away and moving stolen property. It had been difficult to convict persons of being accessories, and the practice of requiring the posting of bond for future good behavior by suspected accomplices had not been effective. Setting an example by executing accessories certainly made brigandage more hazardous. The connection between the British army and some of the banditti had been tenuous at best, but nevertheless it was important. The cessation of hostilities and the declaration of peace ended all British encouragement and collusion, putting the banditti into further isolation and vulnerability.

Chapter 6

James Moody

"Moody is out!" "Moody is in the country!" The cries of alarm excited patriot militia of northern New Jersey to go "hunting" for the ever ubiquitous and evasive Loyalist raider and spy, James Moody. One legend has it that mothers warned their children, "If you don't come in Moody will get you."[1]

James Moody had no fight to pick with the British. When war came, he was residing quietly on his farm in northwestern New Jersey, and he expected to avoid taking any side during the conflict. He was mistaken. Local patriots hounded him and forced his hand. Moody decided on revenge, and the transformation from simple farmer to one of the Revolution's most daring warriors began. Moody may be more properly regarded as an abductor and spy rather than as a plunderer, although occasionally in his outings he and his men seized property. In serving the king, Moody preferred to steal human beings (setting free imprisoned Loyalists and capturing patriot leaders), rob mails, and perform espionage behind American lines.

Moody has been styled the "Scarlet Pimpernel of New Jersey." Like the hero of Baroness Emmuska Orczy's popular novel (1905 et seq.), the Englishman Sir Percy Blakeney, who made incursions into France to rescue aristocrats from the guillotine,[2] Moody performed a similar task on behalf of his fellow Loyalists, but he went a step further by usually returning from his missions with his own prisoners of war.

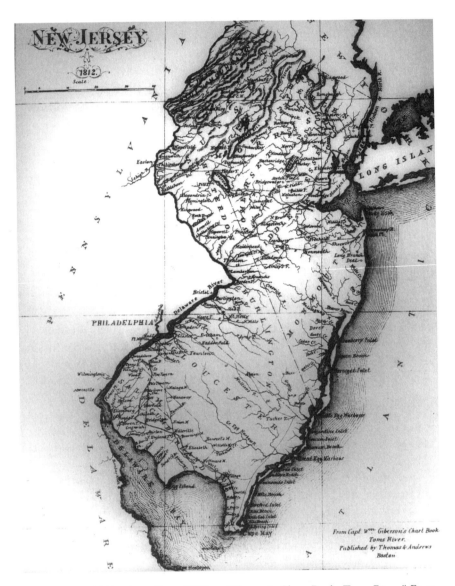

"New Jersey, 1812—from Capt. William Giberson's Chart Book, Toms River." From
T. F. Rose, H. C. Woolman, and T. T. Price, *Historical and Biographical Atlas of the
New Jersey Coast* (Toms River: Ocean County Historical Society, 1985, originally pub-
lished in 1878). Courtesy of the Ocean County Historical Society.

James Moody (1744–1809) was born in the New Jersey township of Little Egg Harbor. His father, John, was a merchant; his mother is known only as Mrs. Holden, formerly a widow. Though his parents were Anglican, according to a brief, authoritative sketch, he probably attended a local Quaker school. As a young man, Moody settled on a 500-acre farm his father had given him in Sussex County (that part which is now Warren County), near the Delaware River Water Gap; he raised mainly sheep and cattle. Moody said of himself that at the beginning of the war he was a "happy farmer," with "a beloved wife, and three promising children."[3]

Despite eschewing politics, Moody believed strongly that "rebellion is the foulest of all crimes; and that what was begun in wickedness must end in ruin." Moody refused to take the oath of abjuration (renouncing loyalty to the British crown) and of allegiance "to the government established" in New Jersey "under the authority of the people." The local committee of safety deployed militia through the community to persuade citizens to adhere openly to the patriot standard. Tory hunters assaulted Moody, "having first flourished their *tomahawks* over his head," and at another time, on March 28, 1777, while walking in his fields with a neighbor, William Hutchinson, a roving band of armed men shot at him three times, fortunately missing their target. Moody and his friend fled into Moody's house and barred the door and windows. The patriot attackers fired into the house several times before leaving. For his own safety, Moody did not need further convincing "to take shelter behind the British lines."[4] He assumed the risk that his family would be unmolested during his absence and trusted he could send for them at a later time.

Just a week or so after the incidence of harassment, in April 1777, Moody and seventy-three like-minded neighbors headed toward New York City, fighting off militia attacks along the way. In Bergen County, Moody and his followers met Lieutenant Colonel Joseph Barton's troops, who were part of Brigadier General Cortlandt Skinner's New Jersey Volunteers. Barton, before his defection, had been a wealthy farmer in Sussex County, a land agent for the East Jersey Proprietors, a surveyor, and an assemblyman. Moody's offer to serve with the New Jersey Volunteers without receiving an immediate commission and without pay was accepted. Moody had the assignment of going into the interior of New Jersey and gathering recruits for British service. By June 1777, Moody, with the help of his friend, William Hutchinson, Lieutenant John Troup, and Sergeant Peter Saunders, had lined up 500 men willing to bear arms against the rebels. Moody expected that the new recruits would assist the British army in securing the state of New Jersey. It came as a shock to him when, in the summer of 1777, General William Howe put his army shipboard, with the apparent intention of shifting the theater of war, and went up the Chesapeake to capture

Philadelphia, abandoning New Jersey. Most of Moody's enlistees left altogether because of the danger of operating in New Jersey without full military support. Furthermore, they did not want to be forever separated from their homes and families.[5]

Just before crossing from the Jersey coast to British-held Staten Island, Moody and his remnant group of about seventy men were attacked by New Jersey militia under Colonel John Munson. Some sixty of Moody's band were captured; Moody and eight others escaped and safely reached British lines. If Moody had been captured, he probably would have been hanged. Under the treason ordinances of New Jersey's Provincial Congress, simply "adhering" to the enemy was a capital offense. As it was, two of Moody's enlistees, Lieutenant John Iliff of the New Jersey Volunteers and John Mee, a British soldier, taken while recruiting for the New Jersey Volunteers, were convicted of high treason in a New Jersey Court; both men were hanged at Morristown on December 2, 1777. The other captured Moody recruits were reprieved on condition of joining the Continental army, which they did. Governor William Livingston commented that Iliff and Mee could just as well have been executed for being spies.[6]

Undaunted by the turn of events, Moody twice again in 1777 returned "into the country." He came away with nineteen recruits during the first venture, and during the second, he obtained "forty-two young men as fine soldiers as are in the world; some of whom had but escaped from jails, where they had been confined for their loyalty." Moody conducted them safely to "the King's army."[7]

Moody's exploits gained the attention of Brigadier General Cortlandt Skinner, commander of the New Jersey Volunteers, on whose orders he set out, now as a commissioned ensign, on May 18, 1778, for "the interior parts of the Rebel Country," to stay out as long as he could and "render such service" to the British as opportunity presented. Moody especially was to learn of any operations and plans of Lieutenant Colonel John Butler and his Rangers, who consisted of Loyalist refugees based at Niagara. Rather than make the long trek to meet Butler, Moody sent a "trusty Loyalist" in his stead. Moody's agent accompanied Butler on the raid of American settlements in the Wyoming Valley of the Susquehanna River on July 3, 1778, which resulted in the Tory and Indian massacre of nearly 300 persons, some of whom were horribly tortured. In a few weeks, the British command in New York received a lengthy report of the event, written by the agent and presumably forwarded by Moody.[8]

During his long stay in northwestern New Jersey during 1778, Moody seems to have remained mostly in Sussex County. He knew all the roads there and was acquainted with Tory sympathizers, from whom he could draw assistance. According to legend, Moody and his men had a secure hideout at "Moody's Rock," in an area known as Muckshaw, which contains numerous ponds, quagmire, and limestone ridges and whose overhangings provide cavelike recesses. The many islands (including "Moody's Island") in Lake Hopatcong, in Morris County at the Sussex border, also offered refuge.[9]

When Moody finally decided to return to New York City, he captured Isaac Martin, a Sussex County justice of the peace and chief commissioner of forfeited estates, "a man remarkable for his spite and cruelty" toward suspected Loyalists. Unfortunately, a rebel militia band quickly rescued Martin from Moody's custody. Moody commented that the ordeal for Martin made him "much more mild and humane" toward his "loyal neighbours." Moody returned to British lines on September 13, 1778.[10]

As an ensign in Lieutenant Colonel Joseph Barton's first battalion of the New Jersey Volunteers,[11] Moody could now wear the dress uniform of the Volunteers: a green coat with yellow trim and tan breeches (later red jackets faced with blue). If captured in uniform, Moody could claim prisoner-of-war status. The nature of Moody's missions behind American lines, however, meant he had to travel as incognito as possible—in civilian clothes—although at times he donned his uniform and carried his commission in his pocket for protection.[12]

During most of 1779, Moody, in Barton's regiment of the New Jersey Volunteers, may have gone out with his unit for quick raids along the New Jersey coast. On June 9, 1779, Moody and his friend, William Hutchinson, a lieutenant in the Volunteers since 1776, accompanied by twenty-two men and several guides, crossed over to Sandy Hook, and the next day went ten miles to Tinton Falls, in Shrewsbury Township in Monmouth County. At this location the Americans had a large depot of military stores and provisions, including flour. The Volunteer detachment captured the militia guard, among whom were a colonel, a lieutenant colonel, a major, and two captains. The arms from the depot were broken, and the seized powder was thrown into a pond. Moody's comrades slaughtered some of the livestock, and with the meat loaded on wagons and 300 animals in tow—sheep, cattle, and horses—the raiders headed back toward Sandy Hook. Thirty pursuing militia attacked the Volunteers. Fortunately for Moody, he obtained a position on Jumping-point Inlet, where his flanks were protected and the captured livestock were corralled on ahead. After a "warm engagement" lasting forty-five minutes, Moody and his men ran out of ammunition. A bayonet charge, however, forced the rebel militia to retreat. A flag for a cease-fire from the rebel side brought about an arrangement in which the rebels would be allowed to remove their dead (eleven persons) and wounded, and Moody's Volunteers would move on with the captured military supplies and prisoners. In New York City the booty netted £500, which was divided equally among all members of the raiding party, except Moody who kept nothing for himself. The casualties for the Volunteers amounted to two officers and two privates wounded.[13]

In the field again as a spy, from October to December 1779, Moody sent intelligence to the British command on the size and disposition of Continental army troops. General Clinton sent him to report on General John Sullivan's army, which had just returned from an expedition against the Iroquois in western New York. This was an easy assignment since Sullivan's troops arrived at their original base at Easton, Pennsylvania, across the Delaware from Moody's stamping ground, Sussex County, on October 15, 1779, and then proceeded across Sussex County a few days later to make contact with Washington's army along the Hudson. Moody also checked on troops under the command of General Horatio Gates at Pompton, New Jersey, and the arrival of Continental soldiers at Morristown in late November for the ensuing winter cantonment.[14]

A rebel gallows almost punctuated the end of Moody's remarkable adventures of 1780. Moody's long foray into enemy territory began when he received orders, dated May 10, 1780, from General Wilhelm Knyphausen, through his aide-de-camp, George Beckwith:

You are hereby directed and authorized to proceed without loss of time, with a small detachment, into the Jerseys, by the most convenient route, in order to carry off the person of Governor Livingston, or any other acting in publick station, whom you may fall in with in the course of your march, or any person whom you may meet with, and whom it may be necessary to secure for your own security, and that of the party under your command.

Should you succeed in taking Governor Livingston, you are to treat him according to his station, as far as lies in your power; nor are you, upon any account, to offer any violence to his person. You will use your endeavour to get possession of his papers, which you will take care of, and, upon your return, deliver to headquarters.[15]

Moody kept this letter with him so that, if he were captured, he could show he was on a military rather than a spy mission. On the other hand, since he wore civilian clothing over his uniform, the letter could implicate him as a spy.

Moody started out with "four trusty men," eventually adding two more to his party—Sergeant William Brittain, Sergeant William Carrel, and Private Phillip Boughner (all from Moody's Knowlton Township in Sussex County), Corporal Joseph Lowery of Oxford Township (Sussex), Corporal Martin Boyles of Hardwick Township (Sussex), and a private from Pennsylvania. Moody expected to surprise the New Jersey governor at his home in Elizabethtown and whisk him away before an alarm could spread. Unfortunately for Moody, Governor Livingston was away at Trenton, and Moody and his men decided to bide their time hiding in Sussex County.

During this interim, Lowery decided to visit a woman friend. Both were walking near Moravian Mills when approached by Major Robert Hoops, a militia commissary officer. Hoops had learned that Moody was in the vicinity, and he was determined to find him, first by checking up on local suspected Loyalists. Although he had forgotten to bring his pistol with him, Hoops ordered Lowery and his friend to halt and then to follow him to his house. After going a short distance, the two suspects darted off in different directions. Hoops caught up with Lowery and stabbed him with his sword. Hoops discovered that the fugitive was wearing a Volunteers uniform and, grabbing his opponent's pistol held it to Lowery's head, declared he would shoot if his prisoner did not explain his circumstance. The captive gave his true identity and said that he was of a party led by Moody intending to kidnap the governor. Hoops conducted Lowery to a military guardhouse in Newton. Acting on information provided by Lowery that Lowery was to join Moody at nighttime four days later at the top of Jenny Jump Mountain, Hoops and the militia laid a trap for Moody. Apparently warned by local Tories, however, Moody did not show up for the rendezvous.[16]

Lowery's confession, of course, had "blasted the whole project" of kidnapping Governor Livingston, who, after learning of the plot, "took every precaution to prevent a surprise." Not wanting to return empty-handed, Moody decided to blow up the American army magazine at Succasunna, in Morris County, sixteen miles above Morristown. The guard at the magazine, however, had been recently increased to more than 100 soldiers, and the project had to be abandoned.[17] A British expeditionary force of 5,000 troops under General Knyphausen invaded New Jersey June 7–23, 1780, resulting in the battles of Connecticut Farms and Springfield. Continental troops met the challenge in thwarting the invasion, but militia forces also poured out for active service. Afraid to move about the countryside during this situation, Moody and his little band returned to their safe haunts in Sussex County.

Moody learned that several prisoners were confined in the Sussex County jail at Newton "on various suspicions and charges of loyalty." One of the prisoners, Robert Maxwell, had been sentenced to death. John McCoy had already been executed on May 12, 1780. Maxwell won a reprieve, extending his sentence to September 29.[18] Both men were reported to be deserters from the captured Saratoga army. They had been in the Sussex County area briefly, one as a coal pit worker in the county and the other as a common laborer from just across the Delaware River in Pennsylvania. Moody's recollections, however, differ somewhat from other contemporary sources. He referred to Maxwell as "a Scotsman, who had a good education." McCoy and Maxwell had been condemned for the brutal assault and robbery committed on the aged father of an American general, William Maxwell, at the family's farmhouse in lower Sussex County. It was generally thought at the time that both of the condemned men were innocent; yet they were to be hanged. Reverend Uzall Ogden, the popular Anglican clergyman in Newton, provided a powerful brief, ably arguing the innocence of the two men, to the New Jersey government, but to no avail. There were no witnesses to identify the true culprits since the crime had been committed in pitch darkness; no incriminating evidence was found relating to the accused; both men had credible alibis; and, regrettably, the trial judge denied defense counsel.[19]

Moody was infuriated that the government's answer to Reverend Ogden's plea for clemency for Robert Maxwell was that, even if Maxwell were innocent of the crime charged against him, he was "deserving to die, as an enemy to America." Concluding that "there was something so piteous, as well as shameful, in the case of this ill-fated victim to republican resentment," Moody "determined, if possible, to release both him and his fellow-prisoners."

Late one July night, Moody and six companions entered Newton, the little county seat of about thirty houses. At the jail, an aroused keeper called out from an upper window, demanding to know what business the visitors were upon.

"I have a prisoner to deliver into your custody," replied Moody.

"What! One of Moody's fellows?" queried the jailor.

"Yes," said Moody.

The jailor requested the name of the prisoner, and one of Moody's men, whose name was well known in the area, identified himself. Although highly pleased to have one of Moody's men in his custody, the jailor refused to take charge of the prisoner, saying that he had strict orders not to open the door to anyone after sunset, and therefore he would not assume custody until morning. Since his stratagem had not worked, Moody decided upon a direct confrontation.

Moody addressed the jailor: "Sirrah, the man who now speaks to you is Moody. I have a strong party with me; and, if you do not this moment deliver up your keys, I will instantly pull down your house about your ears."

At this moment, as Moody recalled, his men, "who were well skilled in the Indian war-whoop, made the air resound with such a variety of hideous yells, as soon left them nothing to fear from the inhabitants of New Town." The "panic-struck" villagers shouted, "The Indians, the Indians are come!" and fled to the woods. There was good reason to fear an Indian atack; at this very time, Iroquois warriors were raiding in Northumberland County, just across the river in Pennsylvania and in New York near the Sussex County, New Jersey, boundary.

James Moody's rescue of a condemned prisoner. Drawn and engraved by Robert Pollard, London, published February 19, 1785. Reproduced from the collections of the LIBRARY OF CONGRESS.

The jailor finally appeared and conducted Moody to the "dungeon" where "the poor, forlorn, condemned British soldier" was fast asleep. Upon awakening, the prisoner thought his rescuers were his executioners. Suddenly there was a scene of joy, and Moody and his party were soon leading the condemned man and several other prisoners to safety.[20] Unfortunately, Robert Maxwell, the prisoner Moody had saved from execution, was later recaptured and hanged.[21]

Still wanting to be "more useful," Moody and his party of now seven men rounded up eighteen rebels—militiamen, including several officers and "sundry Committee Men." These men Moody released when they agreed to take parole or swear an oath of neutrality.[22]

Moody was now a wanted man more than ever, and, as he said, he was like "a partridge in the mountains." The governor and council called upon militia colonel Jacob West of Sussex County and his regiment of forty men to have as their sole mission the apprehension of Moody and his associates. Colonel Aaron Hankinson and a detachment of Sussex militiamen also joined in the search. Lieutenant Colonel Lewis Morris, Jr., who, as aide-de-camp to General Nathanael Greene had been sent from Washington's camp at Preakness to secure quartermaster supplies at Hackettstown and at the Sussex County courthouse in Newton, accompanied one of the pursuit parties. Back at camp, on July 15 he wrote his father that "I have had a very fatigueing tour in Sussex—tramping the woods after Mr. Moody and his gang, but without discovering or hearing anything of them."[23]

Constantly on the run, hiding in "dens and caves," Moody barely eluded the militia hunters hot on his trail. There was no alternative but to make a beeline over some seventy miles to New York City. On his journey, Moody picked up "a few more of Burgoyne's men," so that his party now numbered thirteen. Moody managed to reach the Hudson River, but there his "former good fortune" ended, and he "was soon doomed to feel all those bitter calamities from which it had been the object of his exertions to extricate others."

On July 21, Moody had the "ill hap" to be in the neighborhood of Anthony Wayne's unsuccessful attack on the blockhouse at Bull's Ferry, defended by Captain Thomas Ward and Loyalist refugees. Moody was seized by a detachment of Continental soldiers, and he and two of his men were sent to a place called the Slote for confinement. Over the next several weeks, Moody was detained at the Beverly Robinson house, across from West Point, and in jails at Fishkill and Esopus. In mid August he found himself in irons and handcuffs inside an unfinished powder magazine at Fort Putnam (part of the West Point complex). Colonel John Lamb, in charge of Fort Putnam, wanted to send Moody to the custody of Governor Livingston, but apparently was overruled by higher military authority. Moody suffered greatly during this confinement: the ragged inside of his handcuffs tore the flesh off his wrists; the roof over his cell consisted only of loose planks; and he slept on a wooden door, resting on four stones, just above the level of the water, mud, and "filth" in the cell. The only food Moody had to eat was "stinking beef, and rotten flour, made up into balls or dumplins, which were thrown into a kettle and boiled with the meat," served in "a wooden bowl which was never washed" and "contracted a thick crust of dough, grease, and dirt." Moody's pleas to General Benedict Arnold, commandant at West Point, went unheeded, but eventually an officer sent by Washington visited him and ordered his irons removed.[24]

The incarceration of Moody at West Point occurred while Benedict Arnold was finalizing his arrangement to surrender West Point to the British. It has been a mystery how Arnold came by Sir Henry Clinton's secret cipher, used in Arnold's letter to John Anderson (John André) agreeing to the betrayal of West Point. One historian insists that it was Moody who supplied Arnold with the code.[25] While this is a probability, it seems that Moody would have taken credit for this in his *Narrative*, in which he is silent on the subject.

On September 1, Moody was removed to Washington's temporary camp at Tappan (Orangetown), New York, and in a few days went with the army when it set up a new camp at Steenrapie (now River Ridge), along the Hackensack River in New Jersey. He was confined in a barn at the center of camp. Moody, who was wearing his uniform and carrying his commission when he was captured, expected the move was to accommodate his being exchanged as a prisoner of war. At this time Moody was handcuffed only; Colonel Alexander Scammell, the army's adjutant general, observed Moody's lacerated legs and gave orders that no irons be placed on Moody until his legs healed. After about two weeks' detention with Washington's army, Moody was shocked when he learned that in several days he would face a court-martial on charges of the murder of two American officers (Captain Chadwick and Lieutenant Hendrickson) during the Tinton Falls raid of June 10, 1779, and recruiting men for British military service, which was considered treason under New Jersey law and spying under military jurisdiction. Governor William Livingston was asked by Washington to send material witnesses.[26]

Fully realizing that the gallows awaited him, Moody desperately looked for a means of escape. A guard was placed in his cell, another just outside, and four more nearby. During the night of September 17, Moody made his bid for freedom. The inside guard threw a "watch-coat" across Moody's shoulders when he complained that he was cold. Thus Moody could conceal any manipulation of his handcuffs. By twisting the bolt of his handcuffs in a hole in a wooden post, while his guard looked another way, he freed his hands. Rushing past the "interior sentinel," Moody quickly grabbed a musket from the next guard, knocking him to the ground. As he darted out of the compound, all the guards sounded the alarm, and, "in a moment, the cry was general—'Moody is escaped from the Provost!'"

Everyone in the camp was in a "bustle" looking for Moody, "and multitudes passed him on all sides." Moody shouldered the musket he had taken from the guard. It being a dark and "drizzly" night no one discovered his identity. Luckily for him he managed to crawl through the chain of sentinels placed around the camp by Washington. Realizing that his pursuers would assume that he would head toward the British army on the most direct route possible, Moody "made a detour into the woods on the opposite side." For four days he wandered through the "most dismal woods and swamps," employing the Indian tactic of "occasionally groping and feeling the *white-oak*" to get his directions (the south side of the bark is rough and the north side is smooth). Moody subsisted by chewing and eating leaves of beech trees. Traveling only at night and with assistance from some Tories he knew, Moody reached the small British post at Paulus Hook.[27]

After his miraculous escape, Moody, the most wanted man in New Jersey, played it safe for a while and remained behind British lines until spring. He received a promotion to lieutenant in the Volunteers.[28]

Mail robbery became another of Moody's specialties for gathering secret information from the rebels from March through June 1781. Acting on a request from Lieutenant Colonel Oliver DeLancey, the adjutant general of the British army, on March 6, 1781, Moody "readily consented" to enter New Jersey in order to intercept Washington's dispatches. Heading toward Morristown, Moody, two others, and a guide traveled twenty-five miles and then hid in a swamp for a day. The guide refused to go any farther, and Moody and his comrades redirected their route toward the Ramapo Mountains, along the Hudson. After learning that the post had already gone by, Moody made haste to catch up with the mail, seized it, and took it to New York.

DeLancey wanted Moody to go after "another rebel mail." Moody complied, and on March 16, scarcely across the river, he and four companions were confronted by seventy militia, who surrounded the Moody party on three sides. Moody realized that he had been betrayed "by intelligence from New York." The only alternative to "surrender or perish" was to leap from a high cliff, not knowing what lay below. The besieged Volunteers made the jump, landed on soft ground, and escaped. After avoiding another militia party by lying prone, upon reaching the Hudson River Moody and his men were attacked by a detachment of militiamen. A heated exchange of fire ensued, and several shots went through Moody's clothes; one went through his hat, and another grazed his arm. By "doubling" upon the enemy, Moody gave them the "slip" and returned to New York City.

The next night, May 18, Moody and four others set out again, going into Bergen County. Moody dispersed several small rebel parties by yelling for his "rear to advance," and he also employed a stratagem of having a Loyalist, who had the general appearance and voice of Moody, to enter a neighborhood at nighttime, arouse the inhabitants, and then flee, thus diverting militia "hunters" from the area where Moody actually had gone.[29]

On June 1, 1781, James Moody seized some dispatches which included General Washington's letters to Congress, General Rochambeau's letter to the minister of France, and "Southern mail," some of which included letters to General Lafayette in Virginia. Major Frederick Mackenzie of the Royal Welsh Fusiliers expressed the pleasure of the British high command in Moody's accomplishment. In his diary for June 5, 1781, mistakenly crediting Moody's younger brother, John, he commented,

Ensign John Moody [actually James Moody], came in early this morning with a Rebel Mail which he intercepted a few days ago, near Sussex Court House, going from Washington's quarters to Congress. The information obtained by the Commander in Chief

[Clinton] from the despatches and letters found in this Mail, is of the utmost consequence, as they contain the particulars of the conference held the 17th of May at
Weathersfield in Connecticut, between Washington and Rochambeau, and the whole
plan of their operations for the ensuing Campaign.

The Capture of this Mail is extremely consequential, and gives the Commander in
Chief the most perfect knowledge of the designs of the Enemy.

James Moody received a reward of 200 guineas for this service, of which he
kept 100 guineas for himself and gave the rest to his comrades.[30]

In the long run, the British military command had little to celebrate over
the capture of Washington's mail. The information that Washington and
Rochambeau planned a concerted attack by the American and French armies, assisted by a French fleet, on New York City caused General Clinton
to deny reinforcements to Cornwallis's army in Virginia and also to recall
to New York some of the British troops there, thus preventing the British
from securing Virginia and ultimately contributing to the British capitula-
tion at Yorktown. Washington did not use cipher in his dispatches and
relied on public mail service. It is conjectured that he anticipated that his
dispatches would be stolen and may have made arrangements to that effect.[31]

Three weeks after the June 1 mail robbery, Congress tightened postal
security by directing the postmaster general to apply to the Board of War
to provide an escort for any carrier passing through an area where there was
danger of robbery. The problem of robbing postal riders, however, continued.[32]

John Moody, James's younger brother, was involved in a robbery of Washington's mail near Philadelphia in early August 1781. Upon taking the mail
he and his party were attacked by an escort: two of his men were captured
and part of the mail was recovered. John Moody made his escape and went
on to seize "several persons and horses."[33]

Governor William Livingston issued a proclamation on August 8, 1781,
offering a $200 reward for anyone apprehending John Moody or any of three
named other persons, all of whom had been known to have "committed
diverse robberies, thefts and other felonies." James Moody, who considered
that the governor had actually meant to signal him out rather than his
brother, John, responded by declaring his own "HUE and CRY," promising a
reward of two hundred guineas for the capture of Livingston, "a lawless
Usurper, and incorrigible Rebel," who was responsible for "attrocious
crimes," including treason. "If the WHOLE person cannot be brought in, half
the sum" would be paid for his "EARS and NOSE, which are too well known,
and too remarkable to be mistaken."[34]

John Moody had joined the Fourth Regiment of the New Jersey Volunteers in 1777; and in 1778, he was in the First Regiment with James. John Moody was probably less even tempered than James Moody since he was listed once as being confined to the regimental guardhouse. At the age of twenty-three in 1781, John Moody had the reputation of being one of the young Loyalists in New Jersey who stole horses, something James Moody refrained from doing. William Clarke of New Jersey reportedly stole more than 100 horses between 1776 and June 1782, when he was lured into a trap near Woodbridge and shot dead. Several New Jersey counties regularly had patrols for the purpose of looking for horse thieves. The crime of horse stealing in New Jersey carried the death penalty.[35]

Persons stealing horses for the benefit of the enemy could be considered spies. On June 15, 1780, four young Loyalist refugees on military assignment, who had come over from Staten Island, stole horses behind American lines and were apprehended hiding in a barn near Scotch Plains, New Jersey. One was killed while resisting, and the other three—Ludovic Lassick and William Hutchinson of Morris County and nineteen-year-old Jonathan Clawson, Jr., of Woodbridge, "a smart and active lad"—were tried by court-martial at Morristown on June 18 and hanged the next day as spies.[36]

James Moody selected his brother John to perform the extremely dangerous part of his last cloak-and-dagger mission. James Moody had confidence in John, and he knew that failure would mean the gallows for both men.

At the end of October 1781, Captain George Beckwith, aide-de-camp to General Knyphausen, suggested a scheme to James Moody: "nothing less than to bring off the most important books and papers of Congress." This required breaking into the State House in Philadelphia and pilfering the "secret" archives of the Continental Congress.

The key to the plot was Thomas Edison, an immigrant from England in 1775, who had worked as a clerk in the office of Charles Thomson, the secretary of Congress. Unhappy about his low salary and Congress' keeping it in arrears, Edison resigned his congressional position in 1781. Subsequently captured on an American ship by the British, he was brought to New York City as a prisoner of war. In a meeting with Beckwith, Edison said that "he was resolved to be revenged on Congress" and that "he would engage, if he was set at liberty, to go to Philadelphia, and take out of the Secretary's Office, all the most interesting private papers of Congress," including "instructions to their Ministers at Foreign Courts." The plan was approved, and Edison was "sent out on parole." Edison was to deliver the Congressional papers to James and John Moody and Laurence Marr, who agreed to join the undertaking. James Moody was suspicious of Edison, but Edison swore an oath not to inform on his cohorts. A fitting "reward" was promised to all the participants.[37]

Edison went ahead to Philadelphia. In the morning of November 1781 the two Moodys and Marr left Staten Island in two armed whaleboats, landed near Egg Harbor, then made their way to the Delaware River adjacent to Philadelphia. John Moody and Marr went into Philadelphia, and James Moody remained on the east bank of the river, where he obtained lodging in a ferryhouse by posing as a soldier in the New Jersey brigade.

Edison betrayed his comrades. On November 8, John Moody and Marr were arrested. About 11 A.M. on November 9, James Moody, from his second-story room on the New Jersey side of the river, heard a man tell someone at the door that "there was the devil to pay." The plot to break into the State House had been discovered, and one of the would-be burglars had informed on his accomplices. Moody also heard that a detachment of Philadelphia's light horse troops had just crossed the river and were searching for the remaining conspirator.

Moody grabbed his pistols and ran out of the house. After he had gone just a short distance, he saw soldiers entering the house. With the whole area swarming with pursuers, Moody had no recourse but to lie face down in a ditch; fortunately for Moody, the soldiers who came to the ditch examined only the "thickety part" of it. One soldier did spot him, but from a sense of "humanity," he did not "discover" him. Later, looking out from the ditch, Moody saw soldiers running their bayonets into "stacks of Indian corn-fodder." Since this inspection was already accomplished, at nightfall Moody put himself into one of the stacks, where he stayed for two days, unable to sit or lie down, and without water or food. Eventually he went to the river where he found a canoe and rowed a long way upstream. When he met persons passing on the river, Moody was clever enough to address them with the "less polished phrases" of rivermen, thus avoiding suspicion. After leaving his boat, Moody followed a "circuitous" route, receiving some assistance from local Tories, and he finally arrived in New York City.[38]

Moody learned here of the sad fate of his brother. John Moody and Laurence Marr had been interrogated for two days. The Congressional Board of War ordered a court-martial to try the two men as spies. With General Lafayette presiding, a court-martial, on November 11, convicted the prisoners and sentenced both to die. John Moody was hanged on the Philadelphia Commons on November 13. The day before his death, John penned a touching letter to his brother, advising him "not hereafter so often venture yourself out of British lines." Laurence Marr was reprieved, on condition of giving information incriminating other "disaffected Persons." Apparently he did not supply worthwhile information concerning the Philadelphia caper, but in 1782 he informed a Sussex County court of persons who had harbored James Moody and his men in 1780. After the war, Marr settled first in New Brunswick (province) and then in Upper Canada.[39]

Thomas Edison did not become quite the hero he had expected. On December 5, 1781, Congress praised him for his loyalty to the United States and granted him $266, to which amount $335 was later added. Many persons thought Edison had turned state's evidence only to save himself. Edison pestered Congress for reappointment to his old position as clerk, but to no avail. The best Congress could do was to recommend Edison for a clerkship in the Comptroller's Office, which did not materialize.[40]

There was a fear that James Moody would revenge his brother's execution. Governor Livingston incorrectly informed Washington on January 1, 1782, that Moody had gone again into New Jersey and intended to kidnap a member of Congress in Philadelphia.[41] Moody, however, did not exhibit any inclination of taking a member of Congress hostage. Several reports claimed that "Moody's banditti" during November 1781 and April 1782 attempted to rob the mails in Orange County, New York.[42]

Moody's Philadelphia expedition to seize the papers of the Congress in early November 1781 proved to be his last mission. His wife, Elizabeth Brittain Moody, died in February 1782, apparently from falling off a horse, leaving Moody with three motherless children. Moody, however, quickly married again. On March 21, 1782, he wed Jane Robinson Lynson, a Loyalist widow in her early twenties from Newark. On May 13, 1782, Moody sailed with General Henry Clinton for England, armed with affidavits and certificates to substantiate his claims for war compensation. His family joined him in fall 1783.[43]

Moody and his family stayed in England until 1786. He was given a yearly allowance of £100 while in England. He also received half pay for life as a retired lieutenant in the New Jersey Volunteers. Moody published his *Narrative* in November 1782, which was intended to bolster his claim for compensation from the British government. The Royal Commission on the Losses and Services of American Loyalists granted Moody £1,608 for the loss of his property and £1,330 toward his expenses during the war in recruiting men for British military service. In 1788 Moody learned that he was the recipient of £5,000 from the will of Henry Niols, an Englishman who had been impressed by Moody's *Narrative*.[44]

Moody and his family settled at Sissiboo (Weymouth), Nova Scotia, in 1786. He became a successful shipbuilder but fell into financial straits when he had to pay the debts of his son, John, who drowned in a ferry accident. A much respected citizen in Nova Scotia, Moody served as a magistrate, a militia colonel, and a member of the House of Assembly from 1793 to 1806.[45]

Method and lifestyle set Moody apart from the usual Loyalist refugee raiders and freebooters. Moody always conducted himself humanely and avoided wanton depredations. Under military orders, he ventured behind enemy lines with only a few companions, keyed primarily to espionage. As Malcolm G. Sausser has noted, if Moody had been given "a regiment at his back" to "strike where he thought best, not a patriot" in New Jersey "would have felt safe."[46]

Moody led a double life. He endured extreme hardship over long periods of time, and his life was constantly in peril. After 1780, during intervals between his forays, when he was attached to British headquarters, he and his family lived in New York City; before that, Moody stayed with his New Jersey Volunteer regiment based on Staten Island. He lost his livelihood and property, and he served without pay during the first year of his British service. Moody also spent £1,300, inherited from an uncle, on expedition expenses. He nevertheless appeared as a gentleman. Moody formed close associations with New Jersey's last royal governor, William Franklin, and many high British officers. He regularly attended church services, and he became a close friend of Reverend Charles Inglis, the rector of Trinity Church in New York City and later the first Anglican bishop of North America. Moody, like George Washington, did not take communion. As his biographer notes, Moody "liked good company and good food." Moody was a Master Mason, and presumably he attended the many balls and the British army's theatrical productions in New York City.[47]

At the time Moody departed for England, Reverend Inglis wrote, Moody "is one of the most active partizans we have, and perhaps has run more risque than any other man during the war."[48] Clever, resourceful, and having an uncanny ability to anticipate the movements of his adversaries, Moody survived.

Chapter 7

Pine Robbers

Outlaw gangs flourished briefly in certain parts of the Pine Barrens region of New Jersey. Locale and wartime conditions blended perfectly for the encouragement of brigandage. The thinly distributed population and civil authority, the wilderness refuge, the isolated farm households on the fringes of the Pine Barrens, and the carting inland of goods brought off privateer vessels all invited depredations. Individual travelers on the few roads could be waylaid. Some stolen goods could be assigned to Loyalist refugees for transportation and sale in New York City.

The Pine Robbers were mostly local young thugs from the poor and propertyless segment of society. David J. Fowler notes that they "regarded themselves as avengers and agents of retribution." In the forming of gangs, usually consisting of six to ten persons, army deserters and runaway servants were included as members. The robbers stayed close to their hideouts by day, in the thickets or caves burrowed out of sand hills and covered with brush, and nocturnally went in search of victims.[1]

The Pine Barrens area stretches southwestward from the vicinity of Asbury Park, in a belt about ninety miles long and thirty to forty miles wide, comprising most of the tidewater portions of the counties of Monmouth (including present-day Ocean County), Burlington (including present-day Atlantic County), Salem, and Gloucester (including present-day Camden County). The Pine Barrens were distinguished by white, sandy soil, cedar and spruce trees, fallen timber covered with green moss, and in some places an undergrowth rising to between fifteen and twenty feet in height.[2] Here and there one could find huts of woodcutters and squatters. While traveling along the coastline of Great Egg Harbor, Philip Vickers Fithian noticed "many straggling, impertinent, vociferous Swamp-Men."[3]

The first to use the Pine Barrens as a hideout was the Woodward gang of Upper Freehold Township, Monmouth County. These banditti were different from other Pine Barrens outlaws: they were staunch Loyalists, forced to go on the defensive; most were older, in their forties and fifties; they had been substantial landowners; and the Woodward family had been residents in Monmouth County for several generations. The Woodwards were Quakers, and in their depredations never seriously injured or killed anyone.

The Woodwards were harassed for being "disaffected" to the patriot cause. By December 1776 Anthony (Little Anthony) Woodward, Jr., age fifty-one, had gathered followers who set about disarming rebels and taking their wagonloads of supplies. Eventually the gang robbed patriots generally. The core of the Woodward gang consisted of Little Anthony, Jr., and his brother, Thomas Woodward; their cousins, Jesse, Anthony (Black Nat), and Thomas Lewis Woodward; Little Anthony, Jr.'s, nephews, Samuel, Robert, and John Woodward; and various non-kinsmen, including Thomas Fowler, Nicholas Williams, John McGinniss, Richard Robins, and John Leonard. The gang found refuge in the forested area of Upper Freehold Township.

One of the victims of the Woodward gang, Lewis Bestedo, raised a posse on March 1777, and, in a confrontation with part of the gang, shot and killed Nicholas Williams and captured Thomas Fowler, who turned informant but was imprisoned anyway. Most other members of the band were caught, imprisoned, and served their time or escaped, as did Little Anthony, Jr., several times. Jesse Woodward remained in jail for three years. Little Anthony, Jr., was named in an indictment for burglary, involving the notorious Doane gang, committed in Burlington County in 1783. Most of the Woodward gang went into exile in Canada and New Brunswick. Little Anthony, Jr., and several other family members eventually returned to New Jersey.[4]

Monmouth County authorities succeeded in the summer of 1778 in breaking up a band of desperados. A court of oyer and terminer, held at Freehold in June, meted out death sentences for eight persons. Convicted and condemned to die for burglary were John Wood, Michael Millery, William Dillon, Robert McMullen, and Thomas Emmons. Emmons and Wood were executed, and the other three were pardoned. Sentenced to be executed for high treason were Ezekiel Forman, John Polhemus, and William Grover; there is no record of their sentences being carried out, and they were probably reprieved and possibly executed at a later time. McMullen reverted back to his old ways; he apparently ended his criminal career when, being pursued, he swam his horse into the mouth of the Toms River and boarded a British vessel.[5]

Jacob Fagan (or Phagin), age twenty-two in 1778, led a band of cut-throats, among whom was his brother, Perrine. The Fagans were a poor family who lived on or near Manasquan Creek in northeast Monmouth County. Jacob and Perrine, as youths, entered a life of crime by stealing clothes and horses. An advertisement in the *Pennsylvania Gazette*, on May 22, 1776, offered a reward from a person in Burlington County, New Jersey, for the return of horses

supposed to be stolen by JACOB PHAGIN, alias Jamison, 19 or 20 years of age, a lusty well set fellow, about 5 feet 5 or 6 inches high, straight black hair, with some freckles in the face; and Perrin Phagin, 16 or 17 years of age, about 5 feet high, dark complexion, with short black hair.

Both brothers were convicted in a Burlington County Court of horse steal-ing, and each received a sentence of twenty lashes. While Jacob had no ongoing military service, in December 1777 he was listed as a private in Lieutenant Colonel John Morris's second regiment of the New Jersey Vol-unteers.[6]

During summer and early fall 1778, the Fagan gang undertook a fast and furious crime spree. For a while the Fagan brothers used the family home as a base for their operations; their parents, fearful of retaliation, moved to Trenton. With the trail heating up, the Fagan gang hid out in caves and thickets between Ardena and Farmingdale.[7] Jacob Fagan and his cohorts made the same mistake as did other Pine Robbers: they did not seek the safety of a distant area.

The Fagan gang could be quite ruthless if their victims did not reveal the whereabouts of possessions. If the victims cooperated, they were robbed but left unharmed in places that would impede sounding an alarm; at the bot-tom of a well, on a rooftop with its trapdoor secured from the inside, or tied up in a stable.[8]

In late September 1778, Jacob Fagan, Stephen Emmons (alias Burke), and John Van Kirk, who was actually an undercover agent known to the outlaws by the last name of Smith, set out to rob the home of Captain Benjamin Dennis of the Monmouth militia. It was known that captured British goods were stored on the premises. Dennis was absent at the time. Dennis's home was on the south bank of the Manasquan River, in the same neighborhood where the Fagans had lived. Smith (Van Kirk) went ahead of the other two men, ostensibly to be sure the way was clear, but he used the opportunity to warn Mrs. Dennis and her two children. Mrs. Dennis hid $80 worth of money in a bed tick, and the fourteen-year-old daughter, Amelia, fled for safety in a nearby swamp. When Fagan and Emmons arrived, Mrs. Dennis denied having any money. The robbers suspended her by the neck from a cedar tree. At the same time, the outlaws saw John Holmes approaching in a wagon. When the robbers ran toward Holmes, Mrs. Dennis freed herself and escaped. Amelia had been able to warn Holmes, who found safety in the woods. The robbers then left.[9]

Upon his return home, Captain Dennis sent his family under guard to Shrewsbury. Van Kirk (Smith) was able to absent himself from the two robbers, and he informed Dennis that Fagan and Emmons would return to Dennis's house the next day. True to this report, Van Kirk (Smith), riding in a wagon, and Fagan and Emmons, on horseback, approached the Dennis house, only to face an ambush. Both Fagan and Emmons escaped; Fagan, however, was mortally wounded, and his body was discovered in the woods a few days later. The posse buried Fagan's body, but the next day a large group of people went out to the burial site and disinterred the corpse. Fagan's body was taken to a place on the side of the road leading to Colts Neck, a mile from the Monmouth Courthouse, and, wrapped in a tarpaulin and irons, was suspended from a chestnut tree. The body remained hanging until the skeleton, rotted away and picked clean by birds, fell in pieces to the ground. Legend has it that the skull was fixed against a tree with a pipe in its mouth.[10]

Meanwhile, Governor William Livingston, unaware of Fagan's death, issued a proclamation, on October 15, promising a $500 reward each for the capture (no mention of killing) of Jacob Fagan and Stephen Emmons (alias Burke) and $100 each for the apprehension of other Pine Robbers: Samuel Wright, William Vannote, Jacob Vannote, Jonathan Burdge, and Elijah Groom.[11]

Captain Dennis was determined to root out other members of the Fagan gang. On January 26, 1779, Dennis and a party of militia, having advance knowledge that some of the bandits would be on the seashore to load booty aboard British ships, which would take the cargo to New York City for sale, surrounded Stephen Emmons, Stephen West, and Ezekiel Williams, who begged for quarter, but Williams was shot to death and the other two were killed by bayoneting.

Although he split a $500 reward with Dennis for putting an end to the Fagan gang, John Van Kirk, who had risked his life by infiltrating the outlaw band, was unsuccessful in petitioning the legislature for further compensation. Van Kirk's usefulness, however, as an undercover agent, was at an end. "We were at first in hopes of keeping Van Kirk under the rose," so read a newspaper account, "but the secret is out, and of course he must fly the country." Van Kirk moved forty miles distant to Hopewell Township.[12]

Lewis Fenton rivaled Jacob Fagan in notoriety. Fenton, who had learned the blacksmith trade in Freehold and was in his mid-twenties, began his 1779 crime spree by robbing a tailor shop in Freehold Township. A vigilante committee formed and warned Fenton that if he did not return the stolen goods he would be hunted down and shot. Fenton gave back the property with a note declaring his own warning: "I have returned your d——d rags. In a short time I am coming to burn your barns and houses and roast you all like a pack of kittens."[13]

On July 5, as he traveled from Coryell's Ferry on the Delaware River toward Shrewsbury, Captain Benjamin Dennis was shot and killed "by some freebooters that harbours" in Monmouth County. The assailants were believed to have been Fenton and some of his gang. On July 21, the home of the Andrews family was robbed by the Fenton outlaws. A local tax collector, found murdered on the south side of the Manasquan River, was also thought to be the victim of the Fenton gang.

At midnight on July 31, 1779, Fenton and his accomplices attacked the home of Thomas Farr in the vicinity of Imlaystown in Upper Freehold Township. Farr and his wife, who were both elderly, and their daughter bolted the front door with rails. Failing in the use of a log as a battering ram, the robbers fired into the house. One shot broke Thomas Farr's leg. After forcing their way through the back door, the gang murdered Mrs. Farr and mortally wounded Mr. Farr as he lay helpless on the floor. Although the daughter was severely wounded, she escaped. Thomas Farr lived long enough to swear to an affidavit naming Fenton as one of the assailants. Governor Livingston declared a reward of $500 to anyone who would bring in Fenton and $250–$300 for any of his accomplices.[14]

On September 23, 1779, eighteen-year-old William Van Meter was riding through dense pinewoods toward Longstreet's Mill on an errand for his father. Suddenly, from out of nowhere, Lewis Fenton grabbed the bridle of Van Meter's horse and pulled the rider to the ground. Fenton was accompanied by his brother, John Fenton, and John DeBow. The robbers took the saddle. When Van Meter denied that he had any money, DeBow lunged toward him with his musket and bayonet. Van Meter deflected the blow with his arm but sustained a deep flesh wound. At this moment, a wagon carrying five or six persons approached, and the outlaws fled into the woods. Van Meter tore off part of his shirt to bind his wound, jumped on his horse, and rode bareback to Monmouth Courthouse in Freehold.

Major Henry Lee and his Continental dragoons were stationed at the courthouse. It was decided to pursue the bandits immediately. Van Meter, Sergeant Matthew Cusick, Corporal John Wright, and another soldier, posing as farmers going to a local saltworks, set out in a wagon carrying two barrels, in between which two of the riders with cocked pistols were concealed under the hay. They had two bottles of applejack with them. Hardly had Van Meter and his companions gone two miles when someone in a loud voice cried, "Halt!" Fenton, obviously inebriated, approached with a cocked rifle in one hand and a pistol in the other and another pistol in his belt. Fenton taunted Van Meter for being foolish enough to venture out on the road again. The outlaw then asked for rum and was given one of the brandy bottles. In taking a drink Fenton dropped his rifle butt to the ground and tucked the pistol into his belt. The sergeant, from four feet away, shot Fenton in the breast. As Fenton wheeled around, the other soldiers rose and shot off the top of Fenton's head; the outlaw's brains splattered on the side of the wagon. Fenton's accomplice, who had hitherto remained hidden, fired his rifle at the avenging party and, though pursued, escaped. Fenton's body was carried to Monmouth Courthouse. Subsequently, four of Fenton's gang were captured and lodged in the Monmouth County jail. Their fate is unknown.[15]

Captain John Bacon has been described as the "foremost Tory guerrilla of the seacoast and pinelands regions"[16] and "one of the most noted and desperate of the Tory bandits who infested Monmouth County during the later years of the Revolution."[17] While there is no certainty about Bacon's background, he probably hailed from the southern Pines region, in Monmouth or Burlington county, and worked as a farm laborer before the war.[18]

For a while Bacon had military standing among the New Jersey refugees but then went his own way as the leader of a band of marauders. Most of his activities occurred in that part of Monmouth County that is now Ocean and Burlington Counties although he was known to range as far northward as the Shrewsbury area. Unlike many of the Pine Robbers, Bacon preyed almost exclusively on property belonging to patriots. He fought pitched battles with militia. Although considered more honorable than the other banditti generally, Bacon's occasional killings earned him the nickname of "Bloody John."[19]

Bacon appears as an outlaw leader in early 1780. At the end of April he and a band of sixteen men committed robberies of the John Holmes house in Forked River (village) and the homes of Reverend John Price and William Price in Goodluck. The band engaged in other robberies off the coast of Barnegat Bay, using a tavern owned by David Bennet in Waretown and later a secret hiding place in Manahawken Swamp to stash their loot.[20]

Having visited New York City, Bacon, in December 1780, prevailed upon three farmers from lower Monmouth County, who had brought produce to sell in the city, to give him return passage on their whaleboat. After arriving at a beach near Cranberry Inlet, Bacon and his newfound companions, who were afraid of being associated with a wanted criminal, lay low for the night. Word got out of their presence, however, and a group of local militia under

Lieutenant Joshua Studson concealed themselves near the inlet, waiting for the Bacon boat to pass by. When this occurred, Studson demanded that Bacon surrender, whereupon Bacon refused, and, standing up in the boat, shot and killed Studson. The militiamen fled, and so did the whaleboat crew a little later. Having been with Bacon, the crew members were afraid to return home. They went to the British army for protection and were forced into military service. Later the inducted crewmen took advantage of a proclamation issued by George Washington offering protection to British deserters, and finally they returned home.[21]

Bacon led raiding parties off the coast of Little Egg Harbor. On December 30, 1781, residents of the area, fearful that their property would be plundered, assembled local militia under Captain Reuben F. Randolph to intercept the marauders. Confronting Bacon's band as it came toward the village of West Creek, the militia found that they were surrounded and retreated. Bacon's men fired on their withdrawing opponents, killing one patriot, Linus Panghorn, and wounding another, Sylvester Tilton, and then proceeded to West Creek, plundering patriot estates along the way.[22]

Indicted for high treason in Monmouth County, Bacon was captured in early 1782. While in the county jail awaiting trial, he escaped. In the summer of 1782, several robberies were attributed to Bacon, including the theft of a large sum of money from the house of Thomas Fenimore, the tax collector of Burlington County, and also the robbery of James Woodmancy of Dover Township. The Bacon banditti, maintaining British ties, also were engaged in conveying Loyalist and prisoner-of-war escapees to New York City.[23]

The fear of the Bacon banditti was widespread in the southern pinelands. The residents of New Mills (Pemberton), Burlington County, suspected that the Bacon gang might be in their vicinity in late September 1782. Bacon's wife lived in the village. A strange incident confirmed the fear. About 8:00 P.M., September 24,

a man armed with pistols passed through the town. He being wrapped in a great coat, excited the curiosity of some boys who were playing in the road to interrogate him whither he was going, on which he knocked one of them down, this dispersed the rest, and he made his escape to the pines.

Neighbors considered it fruitless to pursue the stranger in the woods in the dark, but sentinels were posted. About midnight, two of them

spied a man coming from the woods, who proved to be the same that had been in the town in the evening—he was properly hailed seven or eight times, but refused to answer, and still kept advancing towards them; one of the sentinels attempted to fire, but his piece did not go off; the man on seeing this rushed on them as fast as he could run, evidently appearing with an intent to seize on the sentinel, but the other who was not discovered by him fired and wounded him in the thigh, so that he died this morning. He was very obstinate, and refused to give any account of himself other than he was one of Cornwallis's men [Yorktown prisoners of war], and had made his escape from Lancaster in Pennsylvania; but as this is the full of the moon, at which period the infamous Bacon and his plunderers infest the country; and as we have had information that they were in the neighbourhood, it is believed here that this man was one of that banditti sent here as a spy; and it is hoped he has met his just deserts.[24]

Since the mysterious figure who was slain admitted to being an escaped prisoner of war, it is likely that a sort of underground railroad ran through the Pine Barrens, which the escapee availed himself of, in hopes of gaining the assistance of the Bacon gang for conveyance to New York City.[25]

John Bacon's vilest moment is known as the Long Beach Massacre of October 27, 1782. Captain Andrew Steelman and a crew of twenty-five aboard an American privateer, the *Alligator*, had captured a British cutter, which, blown off course from its route from Ostend, Belgium, to Saint Thomas in the West Indies, had grounded on Barnegat Shoals on the north end of Long Beach. Steelman and his men spent a whole day unloading cargo from their prize. At night, Bacon and his gang crossed over from the mainland in a whaleboat. Finding Steelman and his crew sleeping at their camp on the beach just south of Barnegat Lighthouse, the intruders engaged in slaughter, killing Steelman and all but four or five of his crew.[26]

On December 27, 1782, Captain Richard Shreve of the Burlington County light horse and Captain Edward Thomas of the Mansfield militia, "having received information that John Bacon, with his banditti of robbers were in the neighborhood of Cedar Creek," which empties into Barnegat Bay, immediately assembled a party and went in pursuit. The two groups met at Cedar Creek Bridge. Although Bacon and his men "being on the south side had greatly the advantage," Shreve and Thomas decided to charge the enemy. "The onset on the part of the militia was furious, and opposed by the refugees with great firmness for a considerable time, several of them having been guilty of such enormous crimes as to have no expectation of mercy should they surrender." The militia were on the verge of winning, when "unexpectedly" they were fired upon "from a party of inhabitants near that place, who had suddenly come to Bacon's assistance." Bacon and his men were able to escape. Of the militia, William Cook, Jr., was killed, and Robert Reckless was mortally wounded. One of Bacon's followers, Icabod Johnson, "for whom the government offered a reward of 25£" was killed; Bacon and three others were wounded. The militia went in pursuit and also made prisoners of seven local citizens who had fought with Bacon at the bridge and who were then lodged in the Burlington

County jail. In "searching some suspected houses and cabins on the shore," the militia appropriated a large quantity of stolen goods.[27]

The hunt for Bacon intensified but with no success. The authorities raided houses for contraband items gained in the "London trade," whereby local citizens exchanged livestock, provisions, and lumber for illegal imported British goods. Bacon, mending his wound, lay low, moving among his many hideouts.[28]

John Stewart, a militia captain of Arneytown, Burlington County, was determined to capture Bacon. Stewart formed a little posse including himself, Joel Cook (brother of the slain William Cook), John Brown, Thomas Smith, John Jones, and one other person. They combed the Barnegat shore where they apparently learned of Bacon's whereabouts from an informer. It was discovered that Bacon was separated from his band and at a tavern belonging to William Rose, between West Creek and Clamtown (present Tuckerton) in Burlington County. Smith was sent ahead and spotted Bacon through a window. Captain Stewart went through the tavern doorway, and demanded that Bacon surrender. Bacon sprang to his feet and was about to fire at Stewart but Stewart wrestled Bacon to the floor. Bacon asked for quarter, which was granted, and Stewart, holding Bacon, called to Cook, who, enraged, remembering that Bacon had killed his brother, bayoneted the captive. Bacon fell but made an effort to escape by the back door. Stewart pushed a table against the door. Bacon shoved it away and knocked Stewart to the floor, whereupon, rising to his feet, Stewart shot and killed Bacon. Bacon's body was taken to Jacobstown and, through the entreaty of his brother, was allowed a family burial.[29]

John Bacon was an independent marauder, but he worked closely with Loyalist refugees and raiders frequently present in the Barnegat Bay–Little Egg Harbor area. Because there were so many collaborators with the enemy and an inadequate number of militia in the thinly populated region to patrol the pinelands and extended seashores, Bacon operated virtually with impunity. While atrocities were charged to Bloody John, it should be noted that he killed only in self-defense; even the Long Island Massacre was a situation of killing or being killed by a superior force.

One of the more notorious Pine Robbers, Joseph Mulliner, in his late twenties or early thirties, had a sociable bent and loved dancing. Like Bacon, he was married; his wife lived near Pleasant Mills. Well educated, handsome, and over six feet tall, Mulliner often appeared in a uniform carrying a sword and a brace of pistols. Mulliner came from a family that had emigrated from England and had settled in Little Egg Harbor Township of Burlington County. Two brothers served in the rebel military forces.[30]

Before turning to marauding, Mulliner had been a seaman. He even received a commission from the British to engage in privateering. Governor

Livingston observed that Mulliner "before he plundered on shore, committed many depredations at Sea." Mainly with deserters and escaped prisoners of war, Mulliner formed a gang of about a dozen persons, though at times he had forty or more followers. Most of Mulliner's activities were confined to the Mullica River region. His hideouts, at the head of the river, were known to be in Mordecai, Hemlock, and Cold Spring swamps. Legend asserts that Mulliner's wife supplied him with valuable information from time to time. Her cabin in a swamp on the south side of the river was across from her husband's main rendezvous. Mulliner trained a dog to act as a courier between himself and his wife, who sent messages to him by fastening them to the animal's collar. Mulliner's year-long career as a marauder was consistent with one who might be in Loyalist military service, chiefly robbing and kidnapping patriots, whom he held as prisoners of war. There is no evidence, however, that Mulliner had any association with British military authority other than that of his privateering commission.[31]

Mulliner was not known for wanton destructiveness, but the pack he led had its villains. When Mulliner was not with them, his gang appeared on a Sunday afternoon at the small farm of a widow, one Mrs. Bates, in Washington Township in Burlington County, just as she and her four young sons were returning from religious services. Mrs. Bates had four grown sons in Washington's army. She excoriated the bandits for taking her silverware, a family heirloom, and when told to keep quiet she refused. The robbers set fire to the farmhouse and for a while strapped Mrs. Bates to a tree. Afterward, neighbors pitched in to rebuild the destroyed homestead. Mrs. Bates received a $300 donation from an unidentified person, believed to have been Joseph Mulliner, who had disapproved of the actions of his gang. Hence a touch of the Robin Hood persona is attached to Mulliner.[32]

Stories have been told of Mulliner's fondness for dancing. On one occasion he popped in at a dance in an inn near Clamtown (Tuckerton). Mulliner demanded that the fiddling and dancing continue and that he dance with the prettiest girl. He ordered all the men to leave, but one man was defiant and slapped Mulliner. Instead of being vengeful, Mulliner shook hands with the man and, assuming his partner was the best-looking woman present, danced with her and then left. Another time, Mulliner crashed a wedding ceremony, in which the groom, an outlaw himself, was an enemy of Mulliner. The prospective bride had met Mulliner previously and confided in him that she was unhappy with the marriage. Mulliner pulled out a pistol and ordered the groom to leave, which he did, abandoning the wedding altogether. Allegedly Mulliner danced with the would-be bride, drank heavily, and then rejoined his gang.[33]

One night in July 1781, Mulliner again could not resist the temptation of socializing away from his ruffian cohorts, and he appeared as an uninvited guest at a dance held in New Columbia, Monmouth County. During the entertainment, one man at the party left to inform the local militiamen. A militia detachment interrupted the frolic and seized Mulliner, who was carted off to the Burlington jail. Tried for robbery and high treason in a special court of oyer and terminer, consisting of Chief Justice David Brearley and three associate justices of New Jersey's Supreme Court, Mulliner was convicted and sentenced to hang. The attorney general of the state, William Paterson, served as prosecutor. It is alleged that Mulliner presented his commission as a privateersman for the British, but to no avail. Normally the commission would have given Mulliner protection as a prisoner of war rather than being liable for trial in a state court.

Loyalist refugees had caused such havoc in Burlington and lower Monmouth counties that it was considered that an example had to be made. Mulliner had committed no murders, and the incendiarism he was blamed for actually were deeds perpetrated by his gang members; of course, robbery and treason were capital offenses in New Jersey and other states as well. Mulliner was the only leader of the Pine Barrens banditti to be capitally convicted in a court and executed. Newspaper notices of Mulliner's trial and execution, to give assurances to good Whigs, exaggerated Mulliner's notoriety. An account of August 15 said that Mulliner "had become the terror of that part of the country" and "had made the practice of burning houses, robbing and plundering all who fell in his way, so that when he came to trial it appeared that the whole country, both whigs and tories, were his enemies."[34]

The hanging of Joseph Mulliner on August 16, 1781, took place in a carnival atmosphere. A huge throng of spectators, who arrived from different parts of the state in a variety of conveyances, assembled on Gallows Hill. A military detachment was drawn up, and doleful music sounded as the prisoner came upon a wagon, accompanied by a procession of people. For the some six weeks that Mulliner had been in jail before his execution, he was frequently visited by three evangelical Methodist preachers—Caleb Pedicord, Joseph Cromwell, and William Budd. From the entreaties of these divines, Mulliner "repented most sincerely, confessing all his baseness" and showed "positive proof" that "God for Christ's sake, had pardoned all his sins."

At the execution site, Mulliner talked at length, acknowledged his guilt, and then, sitting down, closed his eyes, appearing to be "in an agony of prayer." To complete the ritual, the Reverend Pedicord "preached a suitable sermon," and one of the other preachers offered a prayer, while the "people wept and sobbed." Mulliner then rose and requested a hymn. At the end of the singing, Mulliner clapped his hands, exclaiming, "I've found Him! I've found Him! Now I am ready." Mulliner adjusted the rope, said farewell to the preachers and to several other persons, and then declared, "I am ready; drive off." In the words of a later Methodist minister, who had learned of the details of the hanging from the reminiscences of a man, who at the age of seventeen had ridden from Mount Holly to witness the event, after the wagon pulled away Mulliner "swung a few turns, struggled once, for a moment, then all was still. The spirit of the daring refugee, now an humble Christian, was in the presence of God." Mulliner's body was sent to his wife, who was still living near Pleasant Mills, and was buried along the side of Weekstown Road (today County Road no. 542, where there is a marker for the burial site).[35]

The names of many of those who joined the robber gangs are unknown, and, for those whose identities are established there is frequently a lack of information concerning their specific activities. Several Pine Robbers, however, of lesser fame than Fagan, Fenton, or Mulliner may be noted.

Jonathan West was captured at Toms River in a fight, in which one of his arms was so badly mangled that it had to be amputated. Lodged in the Monmouth County jail, West managed to escape into the pinelands and became "more desperate than before." Using his arm stump to hold his musket, West demonstrated "great dexterity" in shooting. Tracked down again, he refused to surrender, and was killed.[36]

Henry Sellers was sentenced to death for robbery by a court of oyer and terminer at Freehold in December 1780. In response to a recommendation by Chief Justice David Brearley, the governor and council pardoned Sellers on condition of his serving aboard a Continental war vessel for the duration of the war.[37]

William Giberson, Jr., from a well-established family in Monmouth County, of whom all were royalists, did not begin his banditti career until 1781. Governor Livingston, on August 3, 1781, offered a $200 reward for the capture of Giberson, wanted for "divers robberies, thefts and other felonies." Giberson was indicted in Monmouth County for stealing horses, which he had taken to Sandy Hook and New York City for sale to the British army. He was apprehended while hiding at a girlfriend's house in Little Egg Harbor but soon escaped by diverting the attention of his captors. Lieutenant Benjamin Bates, determined to snare his quarry, returned to the same location the next night. Finding Giberson outside the house, Bates exchanged fire with the bandit, leaving Giberson wounded in the leg. While fleeing to a nearby swamp, Giberson was captured and brought to the Burlington jail. He escaped by a clever ruse; when his sister, who bore a strong resemblance to Giberson, visited him in jail, he traded clothes with her. Giberson made it to New York, and, as did many members of his family, settled in Nova Scotia.[38]

Richard "Dick" Bird, a gang leader from Potter's Creek (Bayville), involved himself in the contraband trade and robberies. He hid out primarily in a cave on a hillside along Cedar Creek. Bird eventually met his end when a militia patrol traced him to a cabin belonging to a young woman, whom Bird was known occasionally to visit. A militiaman, looking through a window, spotted Bird sitting on the woman's lap. Alerted, Bird sprang up and, while reaching for his weapon, was shot dead. When the militiamen entered the cabin, they found the woman searching through Bird's pockets.[39]

During the war, according to Samuel Forman, who helped erect the gallows, as reported in a nineteenth-century history of Monmouth County, "no less than thirteen pine robbers, refugees and murderers were executed at different times on one gallows" near the Monmouth County Courthouse.[40] This figure probably includes the hanging of the bodies of two robbers in chains after they had been shot to death, and the number may also be overstated because of clemency granted in certain cases. Joseph Mulliner may have been the only Pine Robber, per se, to have been executed in Burlington County during the war.

Vigilantism at the hands of members of the Monmouth County Association for Retaliation may have accounted for one or more lynchings. The organization of 436 members, founded on July 1, 1780, if not very successful in resisting Loyalist military incursions along the New Jersey shore, seems to have had some effect in intimidating Pine Robbers. The group was pledged to retaliate in kind upon "disaffected persons" for any depredation committed upon any Whigs or their property, including kidnapping and arson. Members of the association were sworn to secrecy, and all who learned of their actions were likewise compelled to be silent upon threat of penalty. For this reason, the lack of names of persons hunted down and resultant actions, for the most part, have not come down to posterity.[41]

David Forman served as chairman of the Committee of Nine, which directed the activities of the Monmouth Association for Retaliation; his successor, in late 1781, was Kenneth Hankison, one of the state's commissioners for forfeited estates. Forman had attended the College of New Jersey but did not graduate, and he served as a Continental army officer and brigadier general of the New Jersey militia. During the war he became a wealthy landowner by acquiring confiscated Tory estates. Forman lost no time in plundering Loyalist property. He had a reputation of great brutality and earned the nicknames of "Devil David" and "Black David." In 1777 he personally performed the hanging of a Tory.[42] As chairman of the Retaliators, Forman, according to a historian of Monmouth County, "either openly led, directed, determined, or, in the background counselled, aided, encouraged, supported, and controlled the little patriot bands" that "in scavenger packs, hunted with dogs, as men hunt tigers down, the malefactors."[43]

While little is known about the vigilantism of the Retaliators, presumably most culprits taken alive were detained for legal punishment. One account, however, heard from the son of one of the Retaliators, tells of a vigilante action presided over by General Forman (although secrecy was such that Forman's name was not mentioned). Two "foot-pads, tied with ropes," who had been captured were brought before Forman, seated on a stump. After looking over the prisoners, Forman pointed a finger at the one considered the worst offender, then to the rope binding him, and then to a limb of a nearby tree. Forman did not say a word as the accused man was hanged. After a while Forman "looked the other fellow over, motioned that he was to be freed from his ropes, pointed down the road and said, 'Scat.' " Forman said no more,

but everybody knew that he looked for the man, a sort of feckless fellow, more weak than bad, to be a kind of walking warning to others of his ilk of what they might expect, just like they sometimes tie a little bell around the neck of some old rat and turn him loose, to scare others away.[44]

The Pine banditti operated in a subregional context—in Monmouth County and contiguous areas of Burlington County. The activities of the robbers, as David J. Fowler notes, were a "manifestation of a larger phenomenon of guerrilla warfare," comparable to situations elsewhere between the lines of the armies. Although the banditti were "criminally-inclined" opportunists, their coming from the poorer segment of society gave them an "ethic of self-redress" and a sense of "primal honor."[45]

Depredations against patriots and their property were condoned by the British authorities. Proximity to British military forces was requisite to success for the bandits, especially in having a market for stolen goods.

The Pine Robbers staked out their bases for operations in their own neighborhoods or those close by. They took advantage of their detailed knowledge of the terrain, their networks of friends and kin, and the inadequacies of government in policing the sprawling, sparsely populated townships. Yet the narrow confines of their movement proved to be a major factor in their undoing. Refuge in the woods and swamps could offer only so much security. To survive and to conduct raids, the outlaws had to leave their hideouts. There were makshift roads through the sandy wilderness, and many residents on the fringe of the Pine Barrens had about as much familiarity with the topography as did the outlaws, who, therefore, found it necessary to change their locations frequently.

As elsewhere, the distinction between refugee-partisan warfare and sheer banditry was blurred. Some simply discarded the connection and became true villains. Emboldened by instant success, the Pine banditti, as has happened so often in the annals of crime, assumed risks that brought about their own destruction.

Chapter 8

Doane Outlaws

In March 1777 Congressman John Adams complained that one-half of the population of Philadelphia had "removed into the Country." Those who remained "are chiefly Quakers as dull as Beatles. From these neither good is to be expected nor Evil to be apprehended. They are a kind of neutral tribe, or the Race of the insipids."[1] Adams obviously had not made the acquaintance of the members of a Quaker family living near Plumsteadville in nearby Bucks County—the villainous Doanes.

The Quakers of Pennsylvania endured many hardships as pacifists during the war. Refusing to take up arms, attend militia musters, materially support the war in any way, affirm allegiance to the rebel cause, or pay taxes and fines, they faced imprisonment and loss of property. Yet the gentle Friends contributed substantially to poor relief and turned over their meetinghouses for use as military hospitals. A few Quakers, however, could abide only so far by their tenets of nonresistance, and these protested through riots and by breaking into jails to free their brethren.[2] It was anger over the repression of Quakers that primarily motivated the Doanes to enter on the path of crime.

Unlike other gangs, the Doanes had extraordinary success over a long time span, one that persisted beyond the war. The large, disaffected population, many of whom were Quakers, showed little inclination to turn in members of the Doane gang because they exacted retribution from oppressors and were capable of retaliating against informers. The Doanes adhered to the principle of *lex talionis*, of getting even with anyone who dared to cross them. A Robin Hood legend accompanying the exploits of the Doanes has little basis in fact.

Of the six family members of the Doane banditti, five were the sons of Joseph Doane, Sr.—Moses, Joseph, Jr., Aaron, Mahlon, and Levi—and the other was Abraham, the son of Joseph, Sr.'s brother, Israel, Jr., who lived a half mile distant from Joseph, Sr.'s 100-acre farm. In 1775 Moses, Joseph, Jr., Aaron, and Mahlon were in their twenties, and Levi and Abraham were both seventeen years old. Almost nothing is known of the background of the young Doanes, although reportedly Moses had tried the trade of weaver, and Joseph, Jr., the only one of the group who married (to his cousin, Abraham's sister), taught at a log cabin school in Plumstead Township. Moses quarreled with his father and, allegedly, went off and lived with Indians in northeastern Pennsylvania for several years before the war. Claims that Moses served as a spy and guide for the British army, with feats including delivery of a note to Colonel Johann Rall on the eve of the battle of Trenton which Washington was planning to attack, are wholly unsubstantiated.[3]

Moses Doane was the dominating figure in the gang. According to John F. Reed, "Of all the gang, he was the greatest rider, jumper (except perhaps Abraham, though it is said Moses could clear the body of a Conestoga wagon), runner, wrestler, brawler, planner, thief and evil spirit, though his youthful cousin, Abraham, eventually excelled the rest of the desperadoes in sadistic acts."[4] Another writer has commented that Mahlon was "a thin-visaged, slender man, not more than five feet eight inches in height. He was the smallest of the brothers, but though lacking in size and brute strength, he was wiry and active."[5]

Characteristic of the modus operandi of the Doane renegades were going out on their ventures at nighttime, appearing in disguise and often intoxicated, dividing the band and even committing depredations individually, and selling their loot in Philadelphia and Baltimore.[6] Because the Doane banditti went out in disguise, it was impossible for victims to identify them positively, and several years passed before they were publicly proclaimed as outlaws.

Several house robberies on the night of August 7, 1777, "near the borders of Bucks and Philadelphia counties, by a gang of five armed villains" may have marked the beginning of operations by the Doane banditti. The intruders, who obtained a large haul in money and silverware, behaved "in a very insolent manner, uttering many horrid oaths and imprecations, with frequent threats against the lives of those they robbed, and of others in their families." The ringleader, who was armed with a "pitching axe," appeared to be about five feet ten inches tall, "of a slender active make, a thin long visage, long nose, bold impudent look, his hair black and clubbed, and about 30 years of age." The "next most active person, who was armed with a pistol and bayonet, was a well set square shouldered man, about 5 feet 8 or perhaps 9 inches high, and full visage."[7]

At nighttime in December 1777, the Doane gang attacked Thomas Smith's house at his mill near present-day Conshohocken. Smith had forewarning and rallied his neighbors. Under heavy fire, the gang withdrew, leaving one of their members, Jacob Harwood, dead.[8]

By the end of 1777, the Doane banditti were set on a course of frequent robberies, without making much distinction as to the victims' allegiance or religious faith. They did not hesitate to use torture to force persons to reveal the whereabouts of their valuables: the favorite method was to place hot coals in the victim's cupped hands. The gang constantly switched hideouts in the hilly and forested environs of Bucks and present-day Montgomery counties.[9]

The Doanes caroused in the less than respectable taverns of Philadelphia's Hell-Town. In early 1778, when both men were inebriated, Moses Doane and James "Captain Fitz" Fitzpatrick got into a brawl at a Philadelphia tavern. Fitzpatrick already had a price of $200 on his head for robberies in Chester County. Although Fitzpatrick was powerfully built, Moses emerged the victor. Thereafter the two became friends, and the Doane gang occasionally joined with Fitzpatrick for depredations in Chester County; Fitzpatrick reciprocated by accompanying the Doanes on raids in Bucks and Philadelphia counties. Captain Fitz was captured and hanged at Chester on September 26, 1778.[10]

"Foxy Joe" Condit became a member of the Doane band in early 1778. "A physically, mentally and spiritually misshapen creature," according to Reed, Condit was "even more depraved than the Doanes were rapidly becoming." Condit was eventually hanged for murder in New York City in 1785.[11]

In February 1778 Mahlon and Abraham were in British-occupied Philadelphia. Mahlon, who, posing as an American army deserter, appeared at the residence of a Quaker, Isaiah Hallowell, and said that he was starving. He gained admittance, and was given lodging for the night. When the members of the household were asleep, Mahlon admitted Abraham into the house, and the two men pilfered silverware and a watch before leaving.[12]

In the spring of 1778, the gang, joined by Fitzpatrick and Condit, broke into the house of Israel Lucas, who lived in southern Chester County. Lucas grabbed a pistol and fired at Levi Doane, wounding him in the arm. The robbers then seized Lucas and savagely beat him; Moses's interference saved Lucas's life. Not long afterward the Doane gang again attacked Thomas

Smith's residence and were repelled as before. This time Moses was wounded in the right shoulder. He recovered and took refuge in New Jersey. Moses hesitated to go behind British lines because he was wanted by British military authorities for having killed a redcoat soldier for assaulting a woman.[13]

The Doanes continued their robberies through 1779 and the first half of 1780. They eluded posses hot on their trail. For a while they were in New Jersey, and allegedly (but not likely) they were in the forefront of burning and pillaging houses at the battles of Connecticut Farms and Springfield during the attack of General Wilhelm Knyphausen's troops on American forces in June 1780.

In July 1780 the gang robbed a tavern between Elizabethtown and Newark belonging to "Foxy Joe" Condit's father-in-law, one Van Tienck. Dressed as Quakers, Abraham and Levi took lodging at the tavern and, during the night, admitted other gang members. The intruders debauched themselves from the liquor supply and destroyed furnishings. Abraham raped Foxy Joe's wife, with the consent of the husband. Finally, after gathering up the money, the gang set the tavern afire and left. The Doanes lay low in New Jersey for the remainder of 1780.[14]

In the fall of 1781 the Doanes discovered that the easiest and most lucrative kind of larceny was robbing county tax collections, which were usually unguarded and in the custody of a lone individual. The Doanes were not the only people who engaged in this endeavor, but they were the most persistent and successful. Some of the other robbers, but not the Doanes, were British operatives. One author estimates that as many as sixty-two persons were charged in Pennsylvania for committing robberies of tax collections as principals or accessories. Of twenty-seven principals, five were executed (two for murder), and one was killed by a posse. Fourteen of thirty-five persons accused of being accessories were tried: five were convicted (one of whom was hanged) and nine were acquitted.[15]

Finding a safe haven at the farm of John Tomlinson near Wrightstown in Burlington County, fifteen miles across the Delaware in New Jersey, the Doanes planned to rob tax collectors in Bucks County, Pennsylvania. On the night of October 21, 1781, the gang robbed Ralph Williamson, collector of militia fines, who himself was in cahoots with the robbers, having informed Tomlinson when he would have a sufficient amount of money collected to make a robbery worthwhile. Williamson shared in the take.

The next night, October 22, the Doanes pulled off their biggest robbery, at Newtown, the county seat of Bucks County. This raid had been delayed because, with Washington's army having gone to Virginia for the Yorktown siege, local militia had been called out and were encamped on the town's green. The militia dispersed when news arrived of Washington's impending success at Yorktown. The Doanes enlisted another dishonest tax collector, Moses Winder, who informed the outlaws when he had a large amount of tax money on hand. The gang at this time numbered about a dozen members, including Solomon and Jesse Vickers (cousins) and several desperados from New Jersey. Abraham and Levi were absent. The band went to the house of John Hart, the county treasurer. Some of the robbers wore linsey-woolsey coats or hunting shirts bound at the waist with large handerker-chiefs, knee breeches, and soft felt hats with round crowns. All had pistols; some had heavy clubs, swords, or muskets. With the door unlatched, the robbers entered the residence, where they found Hart sitting near the kitchen fire with Mary Hellings, the housekeeper, and a neighbor, Robert Thomas. The outlaws ransacked the house and found some money, but were told by Hart that most of the tax funds were deposited in the Prothonotary's Office (county treasury) nearby. Threatened by the robbers, Hart gave up the key to that building. No violence was done to Hart, Thomas, or Hellings on condition that they not sound an alarm for one hour. The haul amounted to £735 17s. 9½d., mostly in silver, and £1,307 in state currency (at face value).

The gang divided the loot at the Wrightstown School House. Twelve full shares were doled out, at $280 each; three accessories—John Tomlinson, John Atkinson, and Moses Winder—each received $40. The outlaws, as did Winder, hid out for the time being in Burlington County, New Jersey. In later confessions Jesse and Solomon Vickers identified all the participants in the Newtown robbery: Ned Connard, formerly a blacksmith from Maryland; Caleb and John Paul, brothers from Warminster; Solomon Vickers; Robert Steele; George Burns; John and Samuel Woodward, from New Jersey; Aaron, Mahlon, and Moses Doane; and Jeremiah Cooper. John Atkinson, Moses Winder, John Tomlinson, and one Meyers, a German doctor, were identified as accessories.[16]

For the time being, however, the actual identities of the robbers of the Newtown treasury were unknown. The Supreme Executive Council of Pennsylvania, three days after the robbery, issued a proclamation, offering a reward of £100 for the capture and conviction of each of the "perpetrators," reduced to £50 a month later, which sum was extended in July 1782 to pertain to all robbers.[17]

During the rest of 1781 and in 1782, the Doane banditti struck other tax collectors. In November and December 1781, the Doanes robbed, in separate instances, tax collectors David Petit and Job Barton of Bucks County and Frederick Taylor and John Brown of Chester County.[18] In mid-January 1782, some of the Doane outlaws showed up at the residence of James Snodgrass, the collector for New Britain Township, near Doylestown. Snodgrass and his wife were absent; only several children were at home, and the robbers came away with only nine Spanish dollars and $80 in paper money.[19]

On February 16, 1782, four members of the Doane gang appeared at the residence of John Keith, the collector for Upper Makefield Township. Keith was absent; only his sister (Sarah), stepmother, and a boy were at home. Keith, fearful of robbery, had kept his funds on his person, and the robbers came away with nothing. Sarah Keith gave a description of two of the robbers.

The One who came into the Home appeared about 5 Foot 10 Inches high—about 22 or 23 years old with black Hair, dark Complexion, Smooth face, a little Out-mouthed—had on a large Scolloped Hat. A light gray Coloured Bears Skin great Coat with a large falling Collar of the same, buttoned up so that his Other Cloaths could not be seen—except his pale blue yarn Stockings & Calf Skin Shoes with Silver Buckles of the French Pattern. The Man who stood at the Kitchen Door, this Deponent judged to be near the same Height—had a Great Coat on with the Cape buttoned close to his Face—had a Gun in his Hand, and when this Deponent went to the Door with a candle, he turned his Face from her, and walked towards the Garden Pales. This Deponent saw two other men at the other Doors.[20]

In March 1782 the Doane banditti struck at the homes of Ralph Williamson of Wrightstown Township (for the second time), Nicholas Hole of Tinicum Township (also for the second time), one Smith of Quakertown, and one Weaver of Tinicum; in the robbery of these tax collectors, the Doanes came off with only a few coins and small amounts of paper money. Except for taking a watch, the robbers seem not to have stolen any household articles. Other robberies of tax collectors attributed to the Doane gang in 1782 were those of Daniel Hough of Solebury, Joseph Dyer of Plumsteadville, and Jonathan Stout of Tinicum.[21]

The tax collection robberies hit hard the state of Pennsylvania. With an empty treasury, there was difficulty in meeting the demands of state creditors and filling the quota of supplies for the American army.[22]

During winter of 1781–82 the Doane banditti stole about 200 horses, which they took to Baltimore for sale.[23] Several members of the gang at least dabbled in mail robbery. Solomon Vickers, in his confession, said that he, along with Aaron Doane and George Sinclair, in July 1782 robbed a post "near the falls" and "sent the mail to New York with Caleb Paul."[24] In the summer of 1782, Congress ordered a troop of light horse "to be quartered" in Philadelphia to be used, at the discretion of the postmaster general, for the protection of post riders carrying "public dispatches."[25]

Jesse and Solomon Vickers, John Tomlinson, and Moses Winder were arrested. The two Vickers were convicted and condemned to die, on "general principles" since hard evidence was lacking, by a court of oyer and terminer, consisting of Pennsylvania Supreme Court justices Thomas Mc-Kean and George Bryan. By providing complete information on the Doane gang and their crimes in their confessions of August 1782, Jesse and Solomon Vickers received pardons. John Tomlinson was convicted and hanged. Moses Winder, tried for the Newtown robbery, was acquitted because of insufficient evidence. He afterward disappeared, but probably found refuge in New Jersey.[26]

Israel Doane, father of Abraham Doane, was tried and convicted in August 1782 and received six months in jail, later extended to one year.[27] The farms belonging to Joseph, Sr., and Israel Doane near Plumsteadville were confiscated and sold at public auction in September 1782. Both Doanes and their families, however, were allowed to continue to live on their estates as tenants.[28]

During the last half of 1782 and until spring 1783, the Doanes dropped out of sight in Bucks County. Posses relentlessly searched for the outlaws and probably discovered the main hideouts, including the ones in Towamencin Township, in present Montgomery County, and on Buckingham Mountain, in Bucks County.[29] The members of the gang kept on the move and probably joined other outlaws in raids at various places. Doane gang members were spotted in Lancaster County, and three of them may have been the ones who, on July 25, 1782, robbed the contents of two wagons, belonging to Archibald Henderson and John Johnson, on the Philadelphia-Lancaster road, near Valley Hill. Most of the property was destined for the American army—barrels of vinegar, clothing, blankets, and some provisions; the rest were a few items belonging to private citizens. One of the attackers wore a buttoned-down "quaker like coat" and a round hat. The bandits emptied the vinegar and burned most of the dry goods and came away with only a bundle of silk handkerchiefs, jeans, and some small nonmilitary articles.[30]

After returning to Bucks County, the Doane banditti repeatedly robbed tax collectors. Because of the robbery of several collectors in Bucks County during May 1783 alone, the Pennsylvania Supreme Executive Council, on June 30, 1783, proclaimed a £100 reward upon conviction to anyone apprehending Moses and Abraham Doane, Amos Dillon, and "other persons unknown" involved in the robbery of "money collected for the public use"; and any robber or anyone who assisted them who brought in any of their comrades would receive a pardon in addition to the reward upon conviction.[31] A similar proclamation of July 26, 1786, named Moses, Abraham, Levi, and Mahlon Doane and "other persons unknown."[32]

In a one-night crime spree on July 21, 1783, the Doanes committed robberies at the residences of six persons in the vicinity of Dublin, Bucks

County. One of the victims was John Shaw, a friend of Joseph Doane, Sr. Shaw had complained to the robbers' father that he thought the gang had stolen his horse. Joseph, Sr., subsequently questioned his sons regarding the accusation, which enraged the outlaws. Shaw was brutally beaten and would have been killed had not Moses Doane intervened. The gang also descended upon the house of Joseph Grier, a tax collector. Grier had declared in a newspaper that the Doanes were horse thieves. Warned of the impending raid, Grier hid himself and his money in the woods, and the Doanes came away with almost nothing; the gang did not harm Grier's family.

The residences of William Darragh (Darroch), a collector of taxes; Robert Darragh (Darroch), a collector of militia fines; Robert Gibson, and Robert Robinson were also raided on July 21. Robinson, a tavern keeper in Dublin and a local militia commander, had headed posses in search of the bandits. The outlaws broke into Robinson's establishment, badly beat Robinson, and roughed up his wife for refusing to reveal the hiding place of their money. Fortunately, a neighbor, Patrick Mechlin, discerning the presence of the robbers in the tavern, yelled out a warning for other neighbors, which, though going unheard, was sufficient to convince the Doanes to flee the robbery scene. Joseph Doane, Jr., however, stayed behind briefly to search the tavern's cellar. As Joseph, Jr., rode away, he was closely pursued by Mechlin, who managed to lodge a rifle bullet in Joseph, Jr.'s mouth. With his teeth splattering on the roadway, Joseph, sustaining much loss of blood, was soon apprehended near Montgomery Square (in present Montgomery County) and sent to Philadelphia's Walnut Street Gaol; six months later he was taken to the Bucks County jail. Joseph was tried and convicted for capital felony. Taking advantage of the jailor's son forgetting to fasten a lock, Joseph and three others escaped. Amazingly Joseph settled down across the Delaware River in New Jersey, where, under the surname of Grover, he taught school for about a year before again disappearing.[33]

The capture of Joseph and the hue and cry after them signaled to the remaining Doanes the danger of staying in Bucks County. For over a month after Joseph's arrest they did not venture far from their cave hideout near Tohickon Creek. Hunger finally drove them out into the open. On August 28, 1783, Moses, Abraham, and Levi went in search of flour. After arriving at the log cabin at the mouth of Tohickon Creek, which belonged to a former gang member, Nathaniel Halsey, they asked for flour. Halsey said he had none, and the Doanes offered to purchase some from nearby Wismer Mills, if Halsey's young son would go for it. The lad was sent on the errand, and at his destination let it slip that the Doanes were at the Halsey residence. Word quickly reached Colonel William Hart of the militia, who, with a posse including himself, Major William Kennedy, and seven others, reached Halsey's cabin unnoticed. Hart opened the door and called upon

Replica of the Halsey Cabin where Moses Doane was captured and killed. From John P. Rogers, *The New Doane Book*, rev. ed. by George McReynolds (Doylestown, Pa.: 1952), p. 461. Courtesy of the Bucks County Historical Society.

the three Doanes to surrender. Moses, with no time to reach for a weapon, was wrestled to the floor by Hart. Abraham and Levi managed to climb a ladder to the loft and jump out of a rear window. Abraham used Mrs. Halsey as a shield until he reached his horse and rode away. Levi paused, and, aiming his rifle at some of the attacking party, demanded Moses's release. At this moment, Captain Robert Gibson, a member of the posse, fearful that his comrades might accede to Levi's demand, shot Moses through the heart. Levi fired a shot before galloping off; the bullet struck Major Kennedy in the groin. Kennedy died two days later. Moses's body was dropped off in the yard of Joseph, Sr.'s house.[34]

A paper was found on the body of Moses Doane, which threatened the kidnapping and assassination of Frederick Muhlenberg, speaker of the Pennsylvania Assembly, who had signed a proclamation against the Doanes. At the time Joseph Doane, Jr., was in prison. The document declared,

These May inform Any That It May Concern that If Joseph Done prisner Now in philadelphia Is not Released And Acquitted Immediately That We Will put Muhlinburgh to Death In ten Days Without fail; and take another of your head Man and An other till Wee have taken ten for Every Refugee you put to Death Wee Will put ten to Death and for Every person you put in Jail on Our Accounts If you hang them Wee will hang five and Burn ten houses and Barns and We Will shew you Other Sort of Diversion than you have Ever Been Acquainted With yet for We Are Not your Subjects Neither Will Wee Ever Bee But If you Will Release Joseph Done And Acquit him Interely then We Will Release Muhlinburgh Directly Without harm As Soon as We know for Certain that Done Is Released But If you Dont think proper to Release him then Abide By the Consequence; for All you Can do Is hang him And if you Do Wee Will follow your Example to your Confusion So you and Us for It

[Signed] The Royal Refugees your Sworn Enemies

"They'll have to catch me before they hang me," wrote Frederick Muhlenberg to Reverend Christopher Emanuel Schultze. To be on the safe side, for Muhlenberg's journey from Philadelphia to his country home at Trappe (Collegeville), Pennsylvania, and back in early September 1783, the chief justice of the state provided him with a three-man bodyguard.[35]

It is not known how the ultimatum by the Doane gang was to be delivered, but it is revealing that the Doanes, with no definite ties with the British at the time, considered themselves as war combatants ("refugees"). Actually, the British command in New York had expressly denounced the gang. John Dickinson, the president of the Supreme Executive Council of Pennsylvania, who recently had heard that the outlaws had fled to New York City, wrote to the new British commander in chief, Sir Guy Carleton, requesting that, from "a Regard for Justice," if any of the Doane outlaws had appeared "within your lines" to turn them over to the custody of the person delivering Dickinson's letter. Dickinson also asked Governor Livingston of New Jersey to ensure delivery of the criminals to Philadelphia. General Carleton, in reply to Dickinson's letter, stated that after "diligent enquiry," there was no indication that the Doanes had come behind British lines but, if that should be the case, he would have them arrested and inform Dickinson to that effect.[36]

The Pennsylvania government was determined to put an end to the depredations of the Doane banditti. The state's supreme court, through a form of judicial attainder, declared outlawry against members of the gang, to be seized dead or alive. Following up on previous legislation and proclamations, the Pennsylvania General Assembly, only a week after Moses's death (September 8) passed "An Act to encourage the speedy apprehending and bringing to justice divers robbers, burglars and felons." The law was implemented by a proclamation by President Dickinson on September 13. Mentioned in the law and the proclamation were those persons who "have been duly attainted, by outlawry, in the Supreme Court of this State": Aaron, Mahlon, Abraham, and Levi Doane; Caleb and John Paul; Robert Steele; Edward and Henry Connard; Jeremiah Cooper; Amos White; and George Sinclair.

Also cited as "suspected and charged" were Gideon Vernon, Thomas Bulla, Amos Williams, Edward Richardson, and George Burns. A reward of £300 was offered for bringing in dead or alive any one of the above proscribed outlaws, and a reward was also promised of £50 for each person apprehended who had received stolen goods or had sheltered any of the fugitives. If one of the outlaws should bring in two of his comrades, he would receive a pardon and £100.[37]

After the murder of Moses Doane, the gang members distanced themselves from the posses who were combing Bucks County intensely. For several weeks in September 1783, the Doane outlaws showed up in Bedford County, where they stole horses, which they took to Baltimore for sale. Mahlon and Joseph Doane (presumably Joseph, Sr., the father of the Doane outlaws) were arrested in Maryland and extradited to Bedford County. Mahlon Doane was described as having "a Blemish on one of his Eyes and sort of a Scar under it," black hair, "Slender made, down looking," and five feet seven or eight inches tall. Other gang members broke into the Bedford jail and freed the two Doanes.[38]

Mahlon Doane was arrested again in Baltimore in January 1784 for horse thievery. He was placed in heavy irons while awaiting trial. Being slender, Mahlon was able to slip out of his shackles and escape. One version of the episode is that Mahlon cut off the fleshy part of his heels, which enabled him to be free of the leg irons. Pursuers tracked him from the trail of blood to Fells Point, "a Kind of Peninsula which runs out into the Harbour." It is speculated that Mahlon drowned himself to avoid further punishment. A nephew, late in life, however, asserted that Mahlon reached New York City and then went to England. In any event, Mahlon disappeared.[39]

To get farther away from the arm of the law in southeastern Pennsylvania, during spring and early summer 1784, the three remaining Doanes—Abraham, Aaron, and Levi—took their criminal talents to the southwestern counties of the state—Fayette, Westmoreland, and Washington. Ephraim Douglass of Uniontown informed John Armstrong, Jr., secretary of Pennsylvania, in May 1784, that "the banditti from Bucks county, or some others equally bad, or more probably both, have established themselves" in "the deserted part of Washington county." They "terrify the inhabitants, sometimes beat them unmercifully, and always rob them." Robberies occurred against tax collectors. The Doanes probably joined forces with others who acted more from motives of retaliation against excessive tax levies than from profit.[40]

Abraham and Levi reportedly joined with other outlaws to steal horses and other property. In this endeavor, Abraham Doane and Thomas Richardson were pursued by militia and captured. Abraham escaped from jail, but Richardson was convicted and hanged in Washington, Pennsylvania.[41]

Aaron headed eastward in midsummer 1784, and his brother and cousin probably did the same about this time. Aaron was captured by Captain Joseph McClellan and Amos Ogden in Baltimore County, Maryland, in August 1784. The captors received the £300 reward posted by the Pennsylvania government. Aaron was soon delivered to the Walnut Street jail in Philadelphia.

Since Aaron was under the process of outlawry enacted by the Pennsylvania legislature and similarly attainted by the supreme court, he could be executed without trial. Aaron had not surrendered; therefore he was automatically considered guilty. Three judges of the Pennsylvania Supreme Court—Thomas McKean, William Augustus Atlee, and Jacob Rush—met and simply ordered the execution of Aaron Doane. The judges evoked the legislative enactment of outlawry for robbery and burglary. Whereas a David Dawson of Chester County had been hanged in Philadelphia "upon attainder of Treason" on November 25, 1780, no one had been executed on grounds of outlawry in Pennsylvania. Outlawry, a common law practice, had rarely been used in America. From the view of the judges, Aaron could not claim immunity by virtue of the Treaty of Paris of 1783, which forbade prosecution of Loyalists for political offenses. In Aaron's case, the judges having confirmed the outlawry, it remained for the executive branch to set the date for the hanging. Aaron was to face the death penalty only for his alleged participation in the Newtown treasury robbery.[42]

Aaron Doane appealed to President Dickinson for reversal of the death sentence on grounds of innocence and denial of a jury trial. Aaron's plea struck to the core of his defense that his civil rights had been violated.

Innocent of the Crime laid to his Charge, Outlawed & being absent from the State, which hinder'd his knowledge thereof, He is now Condemned to Suffer an Ignominious death unheard or even Tried, to know if he was guilty of the Crime or not.[43]

The case was remanded to the council to set a date for execution on November 22, 1784. President Dickinson, on behalf of the council, sent a letter to the supreme court, with inquiries concerning the judicial process that led to Aaron's condemnation, citing technical errors and indicating that the assembly should nullify the outlawry. The council, having "attentively considered" the transcript of the judges' decision, viewed the case to be "of a novel and extraordinary nature, which being once established as a precedent, may greatly affect the lives, liberties and fortunes of the freemen of this commonwealth." The council, therefore, could not, "consistently with our ideas of duty," issue a warrant for Aaron's execution until "the doubts and difficulties" were removed. The letter questioned whether either in "modern" England or in Pennsylvania had there ever been a person "executed upon outlawry by judicial proceedings alone." It was suggested that the "outlawry in the present case" might be "legally reversed," and the defendant brought to a regular trial.

The president and council noted various technical errors, such as which court should give judgment—a court of oyer and terminer or the supreme court—involving outlawry, the sheriff not obtaining a Pennsylvania warrant in making the arrest, and confusion of language in the outlawry proclamation. It was also asked whether any effort had been made to find out whether the defendant was telling the truth when he stated he had been in New York City during the time of the Newtown robbery. The judges replied that they were not bound to assign reasons for their decision and that outlawry for a felony was itself a conviction; if this was improper, "it belongs to the legislature to alter the law." The judges maintained that outlawry was "a mode of attainder compatible with the letter and spirit of the constitution of the state." Not wishing to exercise judicial review, the judges further asserted that there was no mitigating error that would justify their reversing their order for the execution of Aaron Doane. Should there be any doubts about Aaron's case, it was pointed out that Aaron was known to have participated in other robberies, even if not charged with the crimes.[44]

Aaron Doane again petitioned the president and the council claiming his innocence. He said that the only knowledge he had of the Newtown robbery was that he had been told of Robert Steele's involvement. Steele had also been apprehended on the basis of outlawry, but, giving a complete confession, was pardoned. Aaron Doane cited the unfairness in the comparative treatment of himself and Steele.[45]

In his defense, Aaron Doane was able to make contact with seven British refugees in Halifax, Nova Scotia. These men sent a petition to the Pennsylvania president and council, declaring that Aaron had been in New York City for six weeks during the time that the Newtown robbery had occurred. Because of the difficulty in further verifying this alibi and on technical grounds, the Supreme Executive Council voted a pardon for Aaron Doane, on promise of future good behavior and that he leave the state. Aaron had been held in prison, shackled, for nearly three years.[46]

A year after being freed in Pennsylvania, in 1788, Aaron Doane was convicted for robbery in a court of oyer and terminer in Essex County, New Jersey, and sentenced to hang. He was reprieved (not pardoned) under the gallows in Newark. He apparently escaped from jail and eventually wound up in Upper Canada, where he received a land grant.[47]

The youngest members of the Doane gang, cousins Abraham and Levi, were not as fortunate as Aaron. Abraham and Levi had evaded capture by staying distant from Bucks County and Philadelphia, but by 1786 they were back in Bucks County. They may have participated in the robbery of the treasury at Newtown on May 5, 1786, although the actual culprits were not identified. For a while the two remaining Doane sons lived in Bucks County, sheltered by friends and relations. When authorities learned that Abraham and Levi were once again in Bucks County, intensive efforts were made to root them out, and the two bandits fled to Chester County, where they hid out in the woods near Kimberton. In the summer of 1788 a group of young men out hunting ran across Abraham and Levi, who tried to conceal themselves in the woods. Suspicious, the hunters apprehended the Doanes and brought them to West Chester for questioning before a magistrate. Abraham and Levi insisted that they were from New Jersey and were on their way to take up land in western Pennsylvania. Just as the prisoners were about to be released from custody, some persons from Bucks County arrived and made known the prisoners' true identities. Abraham and Levi were then sent to the Philadelphia jail.[48]

The outlawry against the members of the Doane gang still had force. Chief Justice Thomas McKean pronounced Abraham and Levi guilty of outlawry and ordered their execution. Their case was similar to that of their brother, Aaron, in that they were sentenced upon attainder for outlawry. The difference is that proper procedure was followed for Abraham and Levi, and there was no questioning of their having committed crimes. The outlawry was for robbery, although it was known that Levi had killed Major William Kennedy. Ironically, the two Doanes were sentenced to death for robbery, even though the death penalty for this crime had been repealed in Pennsylvania in 1786.[49]

Petitions from many citizens of Bucks and Philadelphia counties to the Supreme Executive Council asked for a remittance of the death sentence. Prominent figures, such as Robert Morris and Episcopalian Bishop William White, interceded on behalf of the two Doanes. The young men's fathers and others were able to secure a reprieve of one month. Meanwhile, the majority of the seventy-two-member Pennsylvania legislature also favored clemency, and they appointed a committee (William Lewis, Thomas Fitzsimmons, and David Rittenhouse) to confer with the council in the hopes of obtaining clemency. The majority of the twelve-man council, jealous of about the only privilege that it had under Pennsylvania's constitution of 1776, the power to pardon, refused to overturn the death sentence. If a pardon from the outlawry had been given, the Doanes would still have been liable for a trial by jury. The dispute between the council and the legislature over remitting the death sentence by outlawry for the Doanes had political overtones. Two parties, the Constitutionalists and the Republicans, differed over the constitution of 1776; the former favored the status quo, and the latter wanted a new constitution which provided for a single executive and a bicameral legislature. The Constitutionalists were drawn from men who,

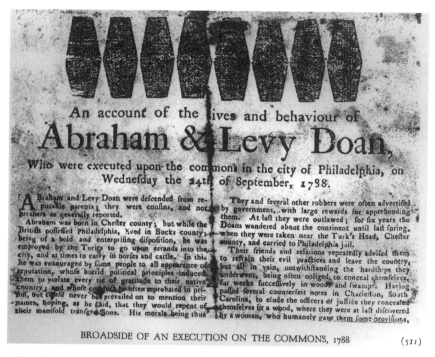

An account of the lives and behaviour of

Abraham & Levy Doan,

Who were executed upon the common in the city of Philadelphia, on Wednefday the 24th of September, 1788.

Abraham and Levy Doan were defcended from reputable parents; they were coufins, and not brothers as generally reported.

Abraham was born in Chefter county; but while the Britifh poffeffed Philadelphia, lived in Bucks county; being of a bold and enterpriling difpofition, he was employed by the Tories to go upon errands into the city, and at times to carry in horfes and cattle. In this he was encouraged by fome people to all appearance of reputation, whofe horrid political principles induced them to violate every tie of gratitude to their native country; and whofe conduct he often reprobated in prifon, but could never be prevailed on to mention their names, hoping, as he faid, that they would repent of their manifold tranfgreffions. His morals being thus

They and feveral other robbers were often advertifed by government, with large rewards for apprehending them. At laft they were outlawed; for fix years the Doans wandered about the continent until laft fpring, when they were taken near the Turk's Head, Chefter county, and carried to Philadelphia jail.

Their friends and relations repeatedly advifed them to reftrain their evil practices and leave the country, but all in vain, notwithftanding the hardfhips they underwent, being often obliged to conceal themfelves for weeks fucceffively in woods and fwamps. Having paffed feveral counterfeit notes in Charlefton, South Carolina, to elude the officers of juftice they concealed themfelves in a wood, where they were at laft difcovered by a woman, who humanely gave them fome provifions,

BROADSIDE OF AN EXECUTION ON THE COMMONS, 1788   (511)

Broadside of an execution on the Commons, 1788. From John P. Rogers, *The New Doane Book*, rev. ed. by George McReynolds (Doylestown, Pa.: 1952), p. 511. Courtesy of the Bucks County Historical Society.

at the start of the war, were chiefly outsiders, economically and politically, while the Republicans were representative of the elite. The Constitutionalists, in control during much of the war, had put into effect a harsh, repressive program against neutrals, pacifists, and Tories—a factor that might explain to some degree the reluctance of the Constitutionalist-dominated council to apply leniency toward the Doanes.[50]

Charles Biddle, a member of the minority in the council, which favored clemency, visited the two Doanes in jail. He was surprised to find that they "were surrounded by their relations and friends, among whom were several females, two of them very handsome girls that had lived with them in the woods." Both Doanes were "tall, handsome men." Biddle commented that "there hardly lived a more active man than the younger, Abraham. If he was seen by persons on horseback in pursuit of him, and he on foot, he would run like a deer, and no fence could stop him a moment."[51]

Mary ("Polly") Doane, sister of Levi who was "known to be fearless and reckless," tried to aid the prisoners in escaping. On one visit she brought a loaf of bread to the jail cell; the keeper, being suspicious, broke the loaf in half, whereupon a small saw and file fell out. At another time, Mary, dressed as a Quaker, with a long cloak, carried to the jail a basket of cakes, which she passed out to various persons, and coming to Levi, she dropped a small file down through her cloak to between his feet; this attempt was also defeated.[52]

After the council denied another request from the assembly for a reprieve, on September 24, 1788, Abraham and Levi were hanged before a large crowd on Smith's Island. Commented Charles Biddle, "[I]t was a very affecting sight. They died with great firmness." Mary Doane took the bodies to Plumsteadville. According to tradition the local Quakers debated for a while before denying use of their burying ground, and the two men were interred in the northeast corner of the woods opposite the meetinghouse.[53] According to Henry J. Young, the two Doanes were the last Loyalists to be hanged and "perhaps the only persons ever executed on outlawry in this country."[54]

Given their reputation for brutalizing victims and that evidence could be brought forward to implicate them in various robberies, the two Doanes could well have been convicted in a regular trial and sentenced to death. In Pennsylvania, from 1779 to 1789, twenty-six persons were executed for burglary, and twenty-three for robbery.[55] Indeed, Abraham's and Levi's offenses were more serious than those of a young Continental army veteran, who, in the fall of 1784, had been hanged in Philadelphia for stealing a handkerchief and nine dollars from a large bundle which he had graciously carried for a "lame countrywoman." The thief had taken the money in order to feed his sick wife.[56]

Most of those outlaws who associated with the Doanes presumably dispersed and went elsewhere, to Canada or to the Southern states, or met untimely ends. In 1788 George Sinclair was arrested. Although Sinclair had been attainted with high treason, for which he could not be punished according to provisions of the peace treaty, he had been under outlawry as had other Doane gang members. It was decided not to pursue outlawry condemnation since burglary was no longer a capital offense in Pennsylvania (which had been overlooked regarding Abraham and Levi Doane), and Sinclair was sentenced to a ten-year prison term.[57] Thomas Bulla, also a Doane bandit, returned to Pennsylvania. Though he, too, had been attainted for treason and under outlawry, he did not receive any punishment, although he was sued by one of the tax collectors.[58] Joseph Doane, Sr., and Nathaniel Halsey, both of whom were convicted for aiding the Doane gang, served six-month prison sentences and were branded on the hand.[59] Israel Doane earlier had been jailed for a year.

At war's end, the remaining Doanes went to Canada: Joseph, Sr., and his wife, Hester (Vickers), and their youngest son, Thomas, who had not been an outlaw, and three daughters—Mary, Hetty, and Betsey. Aaron was already there. Joseph, Jr., returned to his earlier profession and taught school at Humberstone, on Lake Erie in Ontario. In 1820 he and his family moved a short distance westward to Walpole. Joseph, Jr., Aaron, and Levi, Aaron's son, fought for the British during the War of 1812. Joseph was made a prisoner of war and sent to Green Bush, New York; he was later exchanged. About 1820 and 1839, Joseph, Jr., visited Pennsylvania, expecting to collect on an old debt and perhaps find stolen loot; no one bothered him. Joseph, Jr., died in Canada during the summer of 1847.[60]

It is difficult to gauge the extent of criminality on the part of the Doane gang. Certainly the Doanes themselves were an example of a peaceable and law-abiding family corrupted by the war. The persecution of the Quakers, particularly Joseph, Sr., and Israel Doane, led the sons to seek revenge. Three of the Doane sons exhibited a carefree nature by the time of the armed conflict, and, much like some of the "wild boys" who frequented Philadelphia's disreputable taverns, they may have well been propelled into a life in crime regardless of the circumstances of war. Moses, who lived with the Indians for a while, was a rebellious son.

What is significant is the public nature of many of the crimes attributed to the Doane banditti. Although committing indiscriminate assault and theft, their emphasis on robbing tax collectors indicates the desire both for avenging wrongs and for supporting the British cause. Of course, there was also simple larceny, going for the most money, in the custody of county tax collectors.

That the Doanes were outlaws first and only incidentally refugees is borne out by a lack of effort to collaborate with British military operatives or join in the larger refugee war, although at the very beginning of the war several of the Doanes allegedly had been present with the British army, a claim, however, without evidence. Yet, after the war, the Doanes seem to have been accorded refugee status, and they received minimal land grants in Canada.

Perhaps the fact that the Doanes did not link up with the British military effort had appeal to the pacifist Quakers in Bucks County; the Doanes were fighting against unfair treatment of a large number of citizens. The gang at times was quite large. The Doanes could not have persevered the many years that they did without substantial assistance from relations and friends. Even several tax collectors were implicated in the robberies of funds entrusted to them.

Although the two youngest Doanes at times exhibited sadistic cruelty toward victims, the gang committed no murders, other than when Levi killed a militia officer in self-defense at the very instance his brother was murdered in cold blood by a member of a posse.

The inconsistency in inflicting capital punishment on Doane gang members may be explained by several factors. Except for the execution of Abraham and Levi Doane and the long brutal imprisonment of Aaron, persons associated with the Doanes, after the war, received light or almost no punishment. For all but the worst offenders, it seems that authorities to some degree were willing to consider the Doane phenomenon a Loyalist one, concluded by the end of the war. There was also a growing revulsion toward the capriciousness in the administration of capital punishment in Pennsylvania (in the early 1790s the death penalty was reserved only for deliberate homicide). If the Doanes were not Robin Hoods, although evidently viewed as such by some members of the community, they loosely fit the mold of self-serving partisan guerrillas.

Chapter 9

Chesapeake Picaroons

The refugee war in Virginia and Maryland was not unlike its counterpart in the middle states. Raids were conducted against small craft, especially against rebel property along the extensive shorelines and inlets of Chesapeake Bay. The marauders were usually native to the areas of their depredations; while some were under military authority, others were freebooters passing as Loyalist refugees. The plunderers were often called picaroons (a term also used to the north). The word "picaroon" is derived from the Spanish *picarón*, meaning plunderer, pirate, or great rogue. In the American Revolution, "picaroon" usually meant "shore pirate."

Plundering in the Chesapeake Bay area by persons siding with the British was greatly abetted by two factors: the large number of Tories in the Eastern Shore and lower Tidewater regions of Virginia and Maryland and the almost constant presence of British royal ships in the coastal waters. Enemy vessels sustained the blockade and supported British expeditionary forces in the lower Chesapeake: the invasions of Dunmore, 1775–76; Collier-Mathew, May 1779; Leslie, October 1780; and Arnold-Phillips-Cornwallis, January to October 1781. Even after Yorktown, well into 1783, British naval vessels hovered off the Virginia and Maryland shores. The British permitted privateers operated by Loyalists to prowl between Capes Henry and Charles, the twenty-mile gap that formed the entrance into Chesapeake Bay, making it difficult for cargos belonging to patriots to reach the ocean without being taken.[1] Increasingly, in order to avoid the risks of Chesapeake Bay, new transportation routes were sought for ocean-going exports. Goods were carried by wagons to the Blackwater River in southeastern Virginia and then into the Chowan River in North Carolina; from Edenton, cargoes were sent along the Outer Banks and out to sea through Ocracoke Inlet. Although there was danger of running into British warships, at least vessels had more room to maneuver than in the Chesapeake capes.

Virginia had its own little civil war. Governor John Murray, earl of Dunmore, with his motley force of Tories, British marines, and slave recruits, supported by several British warships, fought to keep a toe-hold in the Norfolk area. After defeat at Great Bridge, on December 9, 1775, all of Dunmore's troops remained shipboard until they established a base, on May 27, 1776, at Gwynn's Island, opposite the mouth of the Piankatank. This position eventually became untenable owing to rebel bombardment from the mainland shore. The Dunmore fleet of fifty-five sail left Gwynn's Island, and on July 9 moved into the Potomac River, ascending as high as Saint Mary's River. Raiding parties from Dunmore's fleet, assisted by Tory picaroons, robbed plantations and warehouses along the Virginia and Maryland shores of the Potomac. Especially hard hit were properties in Stafford and Prince William counties of Virginia. The Stafford militia, whom Colonel Adam Stephen called "Blackguards" and "Poltroons," fled. A Virginia newspaper published on August 2, 1776, reported that Governor Dunmore "with his motley band of pirates and renegades, have burnt the elegant brick house of William Brent" in Stafford County and also "two other houses lower down Potomack river, the property of widow ladies."[2]

Neither Maryland nor Virginia could muster much of a naval defense. Virginia could obtain only sixteen small vessels along with a few private merchant ships.[3] Some Maryland militia rallied: 1,200 of them attacked Dunmore's temporary base on Saint George's Island. Lieutenant Colonel George Weedon of the Third Virginia Regiment, now in Continental service, was sent to police the shores of the Potomac. Weedon did not relish the duty, which covered both Virginia and Maryland coasts. On August 4 he moved his camp "from the Arse of the world" to Yeocomico Church in Virginia's Westmoreland County, where

nothing but racoon Oyshters, Crabs fattened on dead Negroes, and Lathefryed Beef can be had; for want of a Bird spit have never tryed a dish of rost Musketers, otherwise they are full large. Our business here was to Counteract Dunmore in his Motions. He lay Aposite us, near the mouth of St. Mary's on the Maryland side. . . . He has fill'd all the Wells with Desected Negroes, Leggs, Arms, hands, etc, etc, may be fished up [many of Dunmore's slave recruits had died of smallpox].

Experiencing a heavy death toll from disease among his force, and with no success in rallying more Americans to his standard, and with rebel troops taking to the field, Dunmore, on August 5, "after dividing his fleet, and burning ten or a dozen vessels, took leave of the capes of Virginia, where he has for more than a twelve month past perpetuated crimes that would even have disgraced the noted pirate BLACK BEARD."[4]

John Goodrich, Sr., with some involvement of four of his seven sons—John, Jr., William, Bartlett, and Bridger—caused great havoc in Chesapeake and even North Carolina waters by making raids on patriot shipping. One of Goodrich's sons, Edward, however, served in the Continental army. John Goodrich, Sr., had a lot to lose by going over to the British. He had acquired great wealth as a smuggler and a merchant sea captain. He had substantial land holdings in the Isle of Wight and Nansemond counties; he owned ten vessels, and, in Portsmouth, Virginia, he had a large wharf, a warehouse, a dry goods store, and other shops.[5]

John Goodrich, Sr., originally seemed to favor the rebel cause, but circumstances brought him to an alliance with Governor Dunmore. Goodrich had sent two of his sons to the West Indies to secure powder for the disposition of the Virginia Convention. The Goodriches, however, were under censure of the Convention for also bringing back dry goods in violation of the Continental Association, which required a boycott of all British imports. Meanwhile, Dunmore had John Goodrich, Sr., arrested, and what exactly transpired next is not clear, but Goodrich openly became a Loyalist in Dunmore's service, and he participated in various raids of patriot merchantmen and waterside plantations on the coastal rivers that empty into Chesapeake Bay.[6] Dunmore wrote to Lord George Germain in March 1776 that Goodrich and his sons were

now most zealously engaged in His Majesty's Service. Four of them are perfectly well acquainted with every River, Creek or Branch within this bay. I have now five of their Vessels employed constantly running up the Rivers, where they have orders to seize, burn or destroy every thing that is water born, that they can get at. They often land and take off what Provisions they can get, which keeps the Rebels in constant motion. . . . They land only where they are not likely to meet with opposition, and have orders to retire on Board so soon as they see any force coming against them.[7]

On April 7, 1776, John Goodrich, Sr., while engaged in privateering in North Carolina waters, was arrested by militia at Ocracoke Inlet and sent to Williamsburg, Virginia, as a prisoner. On June 11, 1776, the Fifth Virginia Convention adjudged him guilty of bearing arms against Virginia and of aiding the enemy. The Convention ordered all of Goodrich's estate seized and sent Goodrich to Charlottesville, Virginia, as a prisoner. His son, John, Jr., had also been apprehended, but he was discharged on the condition that he stay with William Harwood, who posted a £1,000 bond to this effect. John, Jr., later absconded, causing Harwood to lose the money he had put up as security. Meanwhile, John, Sr., escaped but was soon recaptured. Interned at various places, he was eventually released on terms not clear but probably on the promise to go to England.[8]

For the remainder of the war, the Goodriches appear here and there in Virginia and North Carolina waters, most often acting in conjunction with British naval operations. The Goodriches' bases were located in New York City and Bermuda. In June 1778 John Goodrich, Sr., and one of his sons were reported as having five vessels fully loaded with cargo at Ocracoke Inlet.[9] During the summer of 1778, "Privateers belonging to the infamous Goodrich" were active off Virginia's Eastern Shore, capturing vessels, and, at least on one occasion, they fought a heated engagement with Accomac County militia at the mouth of Metompkin Creek (oceanside) before being forced to flee.[10]

The Marine Committee of Congress noted in November 1778 that "at present we consider it an Object of importance to destroy the infamous Goodrich, who has much infested our Coast, cruising with a squadron of 4, 5, or 6 armed Vessels, from 16 guns downwards, from Egg Harbor to Cape Fear in North Carolina."[11] Congress, in January 1779, urged the governor of Virginia "to protect the trade of Chesapeake Bay," so that "a speedy end will be put to the depredations of Goodridge [Goodrich] and his associates."[12]

From May 8 to 24, 1779, a flotilla of twenty-eight warships and 1,800 troops from New York, under the joint command of General Edward Mathew and Commodore Sir George Collier, formed an incursionary force which visited the Portsmouth, Virginia, region, where they destroyed stored tobacco, military supplies, and provisions. Accompanying the expedition were at least four ships of the Goodrich "fleet," on which Bartlett and Bridger Goodrich were known to have been aboard. The Goodrich picaroons participated in the depredations and stayed on in the Chesapeake area for several months after the invaders had returned to New York. The Goodrich crews burned tobacco warehouses and took away slaves. On June 13–14, Goodrich picaroons plundered in Northumberland County and then moved onto the Wicomico River, on Maryland's Eastern Shore. They burned two well-stocked tobacco warehouses and residences, including those belonging to Samuel and George Blackwell, Charles Haynie, and Colonel Winder Kenner. Allegedly, the picaroons "killed several negroes, horses, and cattle." The body of Charles Haynie, who had tried to save some of his property, was found later floating in the river.[13]

Congressman Richard Henry Lee, who had joined a militia force to defend the Potomac shores, pestered Samuel Adams to persuade the Marine Committee of Congress to order Continental naval vessels into the Ches-

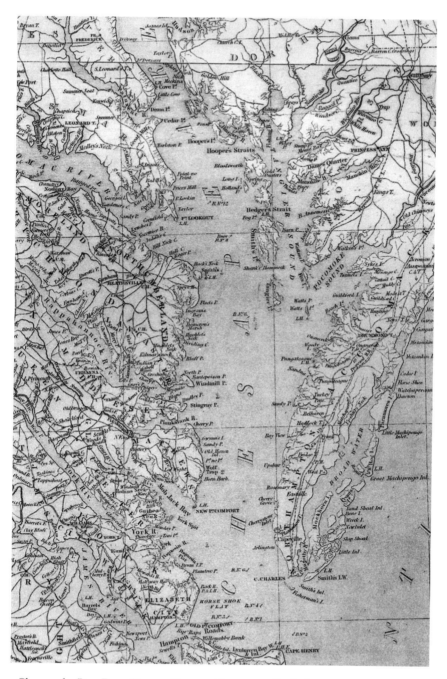

Chesapeake Bay. From Herman Boye and Lewis von Bucholtz, *A Map of the State of Virginia Reduced From the Nine Sheet Map of the State . . . 1828. Corrected by order of the Executive by L. v. Bucholtz, 1859.* Engr. Map, 68 × 120 cm. (BPW 7129[4]). Map Collection, Archives Research Services, The Library of Virginia, Richmond, VA.

apeake in order to get rid of "the whole collection of Banditti," including "tory miscreants from New York who have clubbed their force for the purpose of plunder and revenge."[14]

The Goodrich picaroons accompanied the expeditionary force of General Alexander Leslie, which duplicated the Mathew-Collier feat in October 1780 as it paused in Virginia on its way to join General Charles Cornwallis's army in the Carolinas.[15]

After the war, the Goodrichs settled in England. John Goodrich, Sr., wanted to take his family to Newport, Rhode Island, but he was denied entry because of his service to the enemy. John, Jr., sought to return to Virginia, but the government gave admittance only to his family and did not allow John, Jr., to land.[16]

With the many rivers and inlets along Chesapeake Bay, which was navigable all the way to near the Pennsylvania border, and inadequate shore defenses, Maryland planters and merchants sustained heavy losses from Tory picaroons and even British naval crews. Certainly Joseph Wheland, Jr., ranks as the leading marauder in the Maryland portion of Chesapeake Bay. He has been described as "one of the most notorious and feared Tory raiders of the Revolution."[17]

A resident of an island in Tangier Sound at the beginning of the war, Wheland was in the employ of a Somerset County merchant who delivered supplies to Dunmore's fleet. Wheland also served as a pilot before he himself commanded a raiding vessel.[18] By mid June 1776, Wheland had charge of five boats, including two ten-gun sloops and an armed schooner. On June 25, Wheland and his picaroon crew landed on Hopkin's Island in Hooper's Strait, carried off sixty cattle and "every thing else that was valuable," and then proceeded to the shores of Somerset County, where they robbed the plantation of William Roberts of substantial property, including slaves. On June 30 Wheland and his men landed at Nanticoke Point and burned the home of Samuel McChester. Meanwhile Wheland captured several merchantmen. In late July Wheland and three of his men, in a small schooner, returned to Hooper's Strait. While anchored at the mouth of a creek, they were attacked by thirty militiamen, commanded by Major Daniel Fallin. Weak from smallpox, Wheland and his comrades were easily captured.[19]

The Maryland Convention sentenced Wheland to jail in Frederick County until he made restitution for burning a sloop belonging to John White and posted bond for future good conduct. Eventually Wheland was transferred to the jail in Annapolis. While "a languishing prisoner" at Annapolis, Wheland petitioned the Maryland Council of Safety for the return of all his clothes, which had been taken from him when he had been captured by Major Fallin.[20] Wheland remained in confinement for more than four years. When he was finally released, he returned to marauding with greater intensity than ever before and continued his depredations for eighteen months after the British surrender at Yorktown.

Picaroons other than Goodrich and Wheland cruised the Virginia and Maryland waters. Picaroons came chiefly from the numerous refugee Loyalists of the lower Tidewater region and the Eastern Shore. Blacks constituted half or more of the crews. Some of the marauders came down from the New York vicinity.[21]

One young sailor aboard a French vessel headed for Baltimore in 1778 reported his encounter with local picaroons. When entering the bay one morning, the fog was so dense that "we were obliged to run into James River." When the fog lifted "we found ourselves within a couple of cannon shot of the *Isis*," a British warship anchored at the mouth of the James River. Under British fire, the French ship went aground. "All the shore pirates of the district at once embarked to pillage us, and a scene of terrible disorder ensued. These sea wolves, nearly all negroes or mulattoes, and numbering . . . about sixty came on board under the pretext of saving the vessel, but they cared more for pillage than salvage." The intruders opened up a cask of wine and brandy, and most of them were soon "very drunk." The young Frenchman and some of his comrades managed to jump into one of the boats belonging to the plunderers, and though "bullets whistled over our heads" they made it to shore. Soon the robbers came up, divided the booty, and drove away in wagons obtained from nearby Hampton. With all his belongings lost, the young Frenchman was destitute in a land where he could not even speak the language. Eventually he reached Valley Forge, Pennsylvania, where he joined the American army and served as an aide to General Lafayette.[22]

Picaroons in the Chesapeake operated mainly in small, open craft. Barges became used widely for attacks on ships and for shore raids. Barges resembled whaleboats, except that they had flat bottoms. A barge could carry thirty or more men. Like whaleboats, barges often had a sail, and, for combat, could mount a small cannon or swivel gun. By going out in small flotillas of four or five barges, picaroons had the advantage when attacking a merchantman. The barges, low in the water, could approach closely before being noticed and could assault a single vessel from all sides.[23]

Despite the inadequacies of the Virginia and Maryland naval forces and the frequent presence of British naval ships in the bay, there were brief spells of success in reducing picarooning. A French fleet in the Chesapeake Bay during February and March 1780 helped in "preventing the plundering expectations of the enemy."[24] By summer, however, picaroons were back in full force, making raids in Maryland along the Patuxent River on the Western Shore and along the Wicomico and Nanticoke rivers, which emptied into Tangier Sound off the Eastern Shore. Raids increased also at Virginia's

Eastern Shore. The "banditti" were "daily taking some of our Craft" and "plunder our Islands of Cattle and Sheep," wrote a Dorchester County resident in petitioning the Maryland government to step up defense measures.[25]

In August and early fall of 1780, the joint efforts of Virginia and Maryland naval units had some success in diminishing picaroon activity. The operations netted two big fish: Stephen Mister and James "Jemmy" Anderson. Mister had preyed mainly on vessels and plantations at the mouth of the Nanticoke River, taking his prizes to Smith Island, from which he made contact with British vessels for sales.[26] Anderson had formerly been a lieutenant in the Maryland navy. Commanding a Baltimore ship cleared for the West Indies, Anderson, after passing the Virginia capes, sailed the ship to New York where he sold the cargo to the British. Anderson and twenty-five crewmen returned to the Chesapeake, where they used a large barge and became among the most feared picaroons until they were captured in September 1780 at a place where "picaroons rendezvoused."[27]

The occasional crackdown, however, did little to discourage picarooning in the long run. In November 1780 it was reported that waterborne banditti had "visited several places on the eastern shore and the mouth of Patuxent where they have committed the greatest outrages. Not content with plundering the inhabitants of their negroes, cattle, and other property, they have savagely laid many of their habitations in ashes."[28]

In the summer of 1780, Joseph Wheland was out of confinement. He convinced the authorities that he had converted to the patriot cause, and he was freed on a £10,000 bond posted in Baltimore by Samuel Carrington and Thomas Holbrook. Wheland even offered to build a barge for Maryland's use. As evidence of his good faith, he moved his family from Tangier Island to a rented house on the Wicomico River and assured Colonel George Dashiell of Somerset County that "he never would live exposed to the enemies cruisers during the continuance of the war."[29] But Wheland was soon back to his old ways. According to Donald G. Shomette, Wheland "would soon become the undisputed king of the picaroons."[30]

Wheland entered upon a long series of depredations beginning in late fall 1780. He plundered plantations along Maryland's Western Shore for slaves, cattle, and other property.[31] In command of a small pilot boat, "manned with twelve men armed with Muskets, Cutlasses and Pistols," in early December 1780, Wheland captured a small schooner loaded with tobacco off Poplar Island, Maryland.[32] Witnesses gave depositions that Wheland had seized other patriot boats as well.[33]

At the end of 1780 Wheland was again captured and charged with high treason. Before going to trial, he escaped from the Baltimore jail by bribing the jailor with a "large sum of money." Not long afterward, it was reported that "Joseph Wheland that old offender is down in Somerset plundering again."[34] Throughout 1781 Wheland relentlessly plundered vessels and on-shore property on both sides of the bay. In February, in command of four barges, he raided Benedict, a commercial tobacco export town on the Pa-tuxent River. Wheland showed up in other rivers of the Western Shore—Saint Mary's, West, Potomac, and Wicomico. Presumably he joined other picaroons, backed up by British naval vessels. In June 1781 he plundered along the eastern Wicomico River "and all about the E. Shore."[35] Wheland and other picaroons had their main base on Saint George's Island in the Potomac, but when they were hard pressed they found easy refuge in the deep creeks among the marshes off Tangier Sound. By lowering the masts, the low-lying barges avoided detection.[36]

The Virginia and Maryland navies continued to be undersized, and shore defenses were also inadequate. The Maryland government unsuccessfully tried to persuade General Lafayette, when he was in the Baltimore vicinity briefly in 1781, to employ Continental troops for protection against the marauders.[37] Local Maryland citizens seemed incapable of providing suffi-cient defense measures on their own. Residents of Prince Georges and Cal-vert counties, however, formed a Board of Patuxent Associates for the purpose of establishing a post and stationing several armed vessels at the narrows in the Patuxent River. Although there was some success, a lack of funds led to the program's failure.[38]

Joseph Wheland frequently teamed up with other picaroon leaders, in-cluding John McMullen and Jonathan Robinson. McMullen could be ex-ceptionally brutal. In July he and his crew of four whites and nine blacks kidnapped Captain Henry Gale of Somerset County and took him to Clay Island, where they whipped and then hanged him. Gale was thought dead but revived, and McMullen wanted to string him up again, but a black crew member prevented this from happening. McMullen was captured in August 1781 but escaped.[39]

Robinson commanded a barge of mostly runaway slaves. In April 1781 these picaroons sailed up the Patuxent to Lower Marlborough, where they plundered the inhabitants and warehouses and took off vessels docked at the town's wharf.[40]

Picaroons—the likes of McMullen, Robinson, and Wheland—usually did not distinguish between Tories and patriots. The large number of ex-slaves in the picaroon crews posed an intimidating factor during raids. The pica-roons had as a primary objective the stealing of slaves as they became ready crewmen; many of the blacks in the area had nautical skills.[41]

Commodore George Grason set out with a flotilla of Maryland barges to confront the picaroons. On July 30, 1781, he engaged the combined forces of McMullen, Robinson, and Wheland. The picaroons were badly beaten, and about twenty-seven of them were killed. Wheland was wounded, but he and the other two picaroon leaders escaped.[42]

John Greenwood, a twenty-one-year-old captain of a freight schooner, heading out of the Piankatank River for a run to Baltimore, reported his encounter with Wheland and his picaroons, whom he described as a "set of gallows-marked rascals, fit for nothing but thieves; hell hounds and plunderers." Late one Sunday afternoon in August 1781, Greenwood dropped anchor before his ship had gone far. With his partner at the helm, Greenwood went down in the hold to sleep. Soon, however, he "heard a great noise on deck with swords and cutlasses; I first thought it was my [seven] passengers playing ... so I halloed out to them to be still." Forced up through the hatchway by one of the picaroons, Greenwood spoke with Joseph Wheland, who was on a boat nearby. Wheland impressed Greenwood as "a tall, slim, gallows looking fellow, in his shirt sleeves, with a gold-laced jacket on that he had robbed from some old trooper on the eastern shore." Greenwood and his passengers, upon capture, were placed on "a large galley," commanded by a mulatto, named George, formerly a Virginia slave. George's galley took Greenwood's ship in tow and headed for Gwynn's Island. Meanwhile, Wheland went off to rob the residents of the nearby Virginia mainland. Catching George off guard, Greenwood made him a prisoner, went aboard his own ship, cut the tow rope, and again set out for Baltimore. There was hardly any cargo left, as the picaroons had devoured all the provisions. George, on condition that his life be spared, served as Greenwood's helmsman. On resuming his course, Greenwood encountered only one other picaroon barge, which he was able to outsail. Greenwood considered himself lucky because, at the time, with Cornwallis's army at Yorktown, the Chesapeake Bay was "infested by innumerable pickaroons." Greenwood was convinced that had he remained in Wheland's custody he would have been killed "without mercy."[43]

During the summer of 1781, the picaroons had control of the bay and made Gwynn's Island their base of operations. General Cornwallis considered them "prejudicial to his Majesties service."[44]

Picaroon raids increasingly plagued Virginia's Eastern Shore in 1781 and persisted after the British surrender at Yorktown. The picaroon barges were manned by runaway slaves and refugee Loyalists.[45] Colonel George Corbin, commander of the militia of Accomac County on the Eastern Shore, wrote to Governor Thomas Jefferson, on May 31, 1781, that "several inhabitants of this county living near the water have been lately plundered even the clothes on their backs and their houses burnt to ashes."[46] A year later, Corbin complained to William Davies, the Virginia war commissioner, that "many plundering scenes" had been "exhibited in this County, honest families surprised in the night and robed of all their valuables, stripped naked of cloaths, turned into the open air men women and children, regarding neither age or sex, and their peaceful habitations burned to ashes."[47]

The picaroon raids throughout the lower Chesapeake continued unabated in 1782. Both the Virginia and Maryland governments were hard pressed to provide naval power. Calls for militia volunteers to serve aboard vessels went almost unheeded. "The annihilation of our paper money had so totally deranged our finances & resources," complained Governor Benjamin Harrison of Virginia, and merchants in both Virginia and Maryland gave "a deaf ear" to fitting out armed vessels; as a result "we must remain defenseless."[48] Maryland wanted to enlist Virginia in compelling the evacuation of certain islands in the Chesapeake to make it difficult for picaroons to obtain supplies. Because Governor Harrison said that he did not have the authority to issue such an order, the plan was abandoned. Harrison hoped to have some assistance from the French troops and naval vessels left at Yorktown after the battle there. He wrote to Lieutenant Colonel Chevalier de La Valette, commander of the French detachment who guarded artillery until it could be loaded on French ships, that "our bay and its shores" were "much infested with a Banditti of Pirates who take all the vessels navigating these Waters and plunder all our Inhabitants on their shores as we have no Naval Force of our own." Harrison noted that he had applied to the "French Commodore to send out some of the Vessels either to take or drive them away."[49] By midsummer 1782, however, the French were gone. The few American troops stationed on the Eastern Shore did not offer much protection.[50] From January 1781 to mid-July 1782, the Virginia government issued some sixty privateer commissions. These vessels, however, did not provide much deterrence against the picaroons because ships and brigs, which received 60 percent of the commissions, tended to engage in trade rather than seek out British vessels, and because they were heavily armed, they were avoided by the smaller picaroon craft.[51]

In May Maryland was determined to send out a barge flotilla against the picaroons. Even with some Maryland Continental troops pressed into service as sailors, not enough recruits were to be had, and the flagship barge, the *Revenge*, finally set out alone. On May 10 the Maryland vessel was attacked by picaroon barges. Commodore Thomas Grason of the Maryland navy, who commanded the expedition, and several other of his crew were killed. This tragedy led the Maryland Assembly, on May 22, to provide for the establishment of a squadron of four barges, which were to cooperate with any aid supplied by the Virginians and the French (who still had a presence on the York River). The Maryland Assembly, with funds from the sale of confiscated Loyalist estates, could now finance a renewed naval effort.[52]

Although interstate cooperative action against the picaroons met with delay, with the war ending, marauding in the Chesapeake was doomed to be extinguished. July 1782 represents the peak of picaroon success. During that month, Northumberland County, on the lower shores of the Potomac, alone experienced frequent visits by "the wretched barge-men," among whom were "as many negroes" as whites.[53]

An "obstinate engagement" occurred on July 5, 1782, off the mouth of Saint Mary's River on the Potomac. Two picaroon barges, carrying thirty men each, at 1:00 A.M. attacked the *Ranger*, a "flower [flour] loaded brig," which had come from Boston under the command of Captain Thomas Simmons and was on its return trip from Alexandria, Virginia. The *Ranger* had seven carriage guns but only a twenty-man crew. Reports differ as to who commanded the picaroon barges: John Anderson, a Royal navy deserter or Barret or Joseph Wheland. With the picaroons having come alongside stealthily, the crew of the *Ranger* could not use the ship's guns, but when the picaroons boarded the ship, the *Ranger*'s sailors "played them with cold shot," which had a most deadly effect. Sustaining a terrible loss, with at least sixteen killed and thirty-four wounded (one report says twenty-seven were killed), the surviving bargemen rowed off to Saint George's Island. Captain Simmons was wounded as were several of his crew, but only one of the *Ranger*'s sailors was killed. A black bargeman was captured. With no surgeon aboard, Simmons took his ship back to Alexandria. Word soon spread that Joseph Wheland had been in command of the bargemen and had been wounded and that one of the other picaroon leaders, Barret, had been killed.[54]

Joseph Wheland did not sustain a bad wound: three days after the fight with the *Ranger*, "the schooner Greyhound, a beautiful boat, laden with salt, peas, pork, bacon, and some dry goods" was taken in Hooper's Straits by "that notorious renegade-pirate Joe Wheland." The robbers sent their prize to New York after dumping the ship's skipper and crew on an island. A Mr. Furnival, one of the two owners of the cargo from Richmond, Virginia, had been aboard the ship. Furnival "was plundered of his money, watch, hat, and indeed every thing the thieves could lay their hands on." Furnival witnessed "several other Bay craft fall into the fangs of the same vultures" before he was released. One Michael Timmons (two of whose brothers had been executed on the Eastern Shore) was "Whelan's Lieutenant."[55]

For the rest of July, Wheland and another picaroon leader, a "Perrin, or Perry," teamed up to raid plantations along Virginia's rivers—Rappahannock, Potomac, Piankatank, and York. In Kingston Parish, Gloucester County, Virginia, they robbed "an innocent, worthy ancient Widow, Mrs. Matthews, of almost everything she was possessed of: Clothes, Furniture,

Money, Negroes; and what they could not bear off in Profit, they in Wantonness destroyed." One of the victims, a Mr. Thornton, was "severely whipt." As one report noted, "this Banditti are composed mostly of Negroes, there not being four Whites in Twenty."[56]

There was some welcome news in early September 1782. A Virginia newspaper reported,

> The noted Whaland, who has been cruising for some time past and taken several vessels in Chesapeake bay, was taken last week in Currituck inlet [North Carolina] by a galley from Maryland. He surrendered himself, it is said by capitulation, and restored the whole of the prizes that he then had in possession.[57]

This is the first mention that Wheland was entitled to prisoner-of-war status, indicating that he must have obtained a privateering commission from the British. In any case, it seems the report was erroneous, or the Maryland sailors or North Carolina authorities released him, or he escaped. He was soon back in the Chesapeake making raids.

After some delay, on September 28, the Maryland naval flotilla began its cruise of the Chesapeake in search of picaroons. Captain Zedekiah Walley, commander of the expedition, sailed in the largest of the four barges, the *Protector*, which carried sixty-five men and, at midship, an eighteen-pounder cannon. Captain Solomon Frazier had charge of the barge *Defence*; Captain Robert Dashiell, the *Terrible*; and Captain Levin Speeden, the *Fearnought*. For nearly two months, this little naval force kept a vigil in the Chesapeake and on the oceanside of the Eastern Shore, but it had only little success in apprehending enemy craft. Walley made his base at the village of Onancock on Virginia's Eastern Shore. Up Onancock Creek the Marylanders found an unmanned barge, the *Langodoc*, which they added to their naval force. Responding to a request from Walley, twenty-six-year-old Colonel John Cropper of the militia of Accomac County on Virginia's Eastern Shore brought up twenty-five "gentlemen volunteers" for service with the Marylanders and also a supply vessel, the *Flying Fish*, to be put into service.

On November 27 six picaroon barges and one galley were spotted in the Chesapeake bearing for the Tangier Islands. Walley went in pursuit and learned that six enemy barges (along with a row galley that was a prize) were on their way up Tangier Sound. Walley went full speed in chase of the enemy, believed to be in the command of Captain John Kidd. Later it was learned that none other than Joseph Wheland had the general command of the picaroon force. The six picaroon barges were heading for Fox Island, off Pocomoke Sound. Walley, who had a reputation for eagerness, pushed ahead from his other barges and caught sight of the picaroons in

Brigadier General John Cropper. By Charles
Wilson Peale. National Museum of American
History, Smithsonian Institution.

Kedges (or Cager's) Strait, between Smith and South Marsh islands, six
miles north of the Maryland-Virginia line in Tangier Sound.[58]

At the fierce Battle of Kedges Strait (or the Battle of the Barges), Walley
and his crew aboard the *Protector* carried the fight almost alone; the *Defence*
and *Terrible* fled "ingloriously without firing a shot," and the *Fearnought* and
Flying Fish were minimally engaged. Captain Walley was struck by a musket
ball and instantly killed. The picaroons trained their fire on the *Protector*,
which returned cannon fire and musketry. On the *Protector* a spark from
the firing pan of a musket ignited spilled cannon powder, which caused an
explosion of an ammunition chest; four crewmen were seared to death, and
others, who had become human torches, dove into the water. The picaroons
came forward and boarded the *Protector*. In the fierce hand-to-hand combat
of "cold steel against cold steel," Colonel Cropper, in command upon the
death of Walley, received a cutlass slash across his head, causing blood to
gush down into his eyes. He also was hit in the thigh by a boarding pike,
and another cutlass blow lacerated his shoulder. Cropper fell, whereupon a

picaroon, whose jaw had been shot away, in delirium struck Cropper's head with a cannon rammer, leaving Cropper unconscious.

Of the *Protector*'s sixty-five-man crew, twenty-five were killed or drowned, and twenty-nine were wounded. Twenty-three picaroons were killed. The survivors of the *Protector* were taken prisoner and allowed to go home on parole (after being exchanged in January 1783). Cropper recovered. The other Maryland vessels escaped up the bay. Cropper and the other survivors accused the crews of the other Maryland barges of cowardice. Captain Robert Dashiell of the *Terrible* and Lieutenant Zadock Botfield of the *Fearnought*, both naval officers, were court-martialed; Dashiell was cashiered, but Botfield was reinstated. Captain Frazier and Captain Speeden were cleared by a court of inquiry.[59] On the day of the Battle of Kedges Strait (November 30) negotiators in Paris signed a treaty of peace between Great Britain and the United States.

The defeat of the Maryland and Virginia crews at the Battle of Kedges Strait cleared the way for further picaroon depredations. A week after the battle, six or seven of the "enemy's barges" went into the Piankatank River "and landed about 100 plunderers," who marched about a mile into Gloucester County, Virginia, "distressing several worthy inhabitants," taking away their slaves, furniture, and clothes. The raiders then steered across to Gwynn's Island "from whence they proceeded on their pirational cruise."[60]

Maryland did not return a barge flotilla to Chesapeake Bay. The council, on January 2, 1783, cited reasons for the decision: the "Severity of the Season" made it difficult to cooperate with French "armed Vessels" then in the Chesapeake; crew enlistments expired on January 1; and the legislature was considering "an entire new System" for the "defence of the Bay."[61]

In February 1783 Governor William Paca of Maryland reported that "Depredations" were being "daily committed by the Enemy in the Bay. Not content with interrupting our Trade, they are guilty of the most wanton Destruction of Property on the Shores." Paca also noted that the arch villain Joseph Wheland had "taken Post with a considerable Force, and is building Barracks at Cage's [Cager's] Streights."[62] It was estimated that picaroon and British vessels in the bay amounted to thirteen barges, one sloop, and two schooners. In mid-February, Wheland, commanding crews on four barges, raided plantations and warehouses along the Patuxent River, including the sack and partial burning of the village of Benedict. During the wasting of Benedict, one resident, John Senior, who himself had previously been victimized by Wheland, approached the picaroon leader and asked if indeed Wheland was the "rogue" chief. Wheland went over to the house of Phillip Ferguson and wrote in red letters on a wall, "Joseph Wheland Commander of the Sloop Rover."[63]

Even though news had reached America of the signing of the preliminary treaty of peace in November 1782, picaroon depredations continued in the Chesapeake area. George Washington himself did not believe that the British commander in chief, Sir Guy Carleton, gave "any countenance to those dirty piccaroons that infest your River," as he wrote to John Augustine Washington on January 16, 1783. "If they are encouraged at all, it must be by the Admiral in whose Element they are; but I am rather inclined to think that they are Navigated by a Lawless Banditti who would rob both sides with equal facility, if they could do it with equal impunity."[64]

Congressman Arthur Lee informed Washington, in a letter of March 13, that "there are many complaints of the most atrocious depredations of the Refugees on the shoals of the Potomac." Lee wanted Washington to request General Carleton to put a definite stop to the plundering warfare in the Chesapeake.[65] As late as March 25, 1783, George Mason wrote to Arthur Lee about the revival of picaroon activity:

The refugee barges are lately returned; and again plundering on the shores of Potomac. One of their crews was lately pretty roughly handled by a small party of Northumberland militia. They lost two of their rascally officers and a few men, upon which they fled with the greatest precipation. It is a mortifying reflection on, and accords badly with the ideas of sovereignty and independence, that the power of two States is not sufficient to protect us from a band of robbers.[66]

Washington forwarded complaints of Chesapeake depredations received from Governor William Paca of Maryland to General Carleton,[67] and this undoubtedly influenced the British general to use his office to halt picaroon activity in the Chesapeake. In March, news arrived that King George III, on February 14, 1783, had declared an end to the hostilities.

At last the long spell of picarooning ceased. Washington himself punctuated this development. "The Picaroons in Chesapeake and the Waters of it, have now met their quietus," he wrote to Arthur Lee on March 29, 1783. Washington believed that Carleton had brought pressure to end the Chesapeake marauding.[68]

Joseph Wheland was probably one of the last picaroons to call it quits. One New York newspaper reported that a schooner (another newspaper said two schooners) "taken in Chesapeake by the *Victory*, privateer, Captain Wallen [Wheland]" arrived at New York on March 30, 1783.[69]

Wheland disappeared from history, although reputedly he settled on Tangier Island. He could not be tried on the old treason indictment by virtue of the peace treaty, and he had some immunity from prosecution because his deeds were committed under the Union Jack. Local legend has it that Wheland lived on to become a picaroon during the War of 1812, and when that conflict ceased and Chesapeake pirates and picaroons were rounded up, he took refuge on the marshes of Tangier Island. Subsisting on marsh grass and whatever else he could find, he finally went insane, and his groans and screams could be heard until he died.[70]

Chesapeake picarooning had flourished because of opportunity. Coastal sailors, fishermen, and runaway slaves discovered that, by banding together, obtaining a barge, and raising the Union Jack standard, they could enjoy a lucrative brigandage, sanctioned by the existence of war. In plundering vessels and shore properties, the picaroons often crossed the line from being privateersmen or Loyalist raiders to being simply robbers, with no distinction made as to the political loyalty of victims. Thus, for example, two wealthy Virginia Loyalists, Ralph Wormeley and Philip Grymes, suffered loss of property to the British-affiliated picaroons.[71] Stolen goods could be easily disposed of by being taken to British vessels in Virginia or Maryland waters or to New York. This meant, of course, that picarooning could prevail only so long as it was encouraged and supported by the British and also by the large numbers of persons disaffected from the American cause on the Eastern Shore and bay islands. The ineptitude of Virginia and Maryland to mount naval and shore protection contributed to the leeway in which the picaroons operated. Virginia and Maryland, like other states, had extreme difficulty in maintaining state navies. The U.S. Continental navy had its own limitations and priorities; fighting the enemy at sea was more important than policing the Chesapeake.

Since the picaroons were generally considered to have military status, it was difficult to prosecute them under regular law or special wartime treason statutes when they were made prisoners. A number of residents of Virginia's Eastern Shore and lower Tidewater region were arrested for treason during 1781 and 1782 for aiding the enemy, chiefly in relation to the British invasions of 1781, but they were eventually discharged, and none were executed, owing primarily to the war's coming to a close. No estimates have been formed as to the total cost of the picaroon depredations, but it was substantial resulting from both the pillaging and the destruction of property.

Chapter 10

Josiah Phillips

For three years the Josiah Phillips banditti terrorized citizens in the south-eastern corner of Virginia. Very little is known about Phillips himself or the actual misdeeds attributed to him. Josiah Phillips eluded capture by hiding out among numerous swamps and receiving protection from family, friends, and persons intimidated from fear.

There were probably several banditti groups operating, with Phillips, how-ever, being cited by the authorities as their ringleader. The Phillips phe-nomenon demonstrated to what lengths the government would go to scapegoat one person as the number-one public enemy, and it also created tension in the Virginia legal system, resulting in establishing a precedent, embarrassingly so, in defining the separation of powers in government and calling attention to the need for protected constitutional rights. The Phillips case had a direct bearing on the U.S. Constitution's prohibition of legisla-tive bills of attainder by either Congress or the states (Article 1, sections 9 and 10).

The Phillips banditti found easy prey among the patriot residents of Prin-cess Anne and Norfolk counties. Many Loyalists lived in the area, which contained the upper reaches of the Dismal Swamp. Both counties lay just below the seaport of Norfolk and bordered North Carolina. Neither county exists today; in 1963, Princess Anne County merged into the city of Virginia

Beach, and Norfolk County and South Norfolk joined to create a new city, Chesapeake.[1]

While Governor Lord Dunmore's motley force exerted military occupation in the region, citizens were required to take an oath of allegiance to the crown. An estimated 3,000 persons did. British soldiers and blacks looted the homes of the patriots. The defeat of Dunmore at Great Bridge led to the absence of British forces in the Norfolk area until late in the war. Even though many citizens renounced the oaths they had taken to support the British, claiming that their submission had been under duress, pro-Loyalist feeling was still substantial. Those who wanted to continue to resist the patriots could no longer count on war refugee status. They remained in their locales without any direct ties with the British military authorities. Although they concentrated on patriots as their victims, the banditti of southeastern Virginia were hardly more than freebooters. The Virginia government, nevertheless, feared that the likes of a Josiah Phillips had the potential to incite an insurrection—a crime of treason.

Before Josiah Phillips began his rampage, he was a landless laborer who lived in Lynnhaven Parish, along the Elizabeth River in Princess Anne County. In 1775 he received a commission from Lord Dunmore to recruit men for royal service.[2]

The first mention of Josiah Phillips as a leader of banditti comes in a letter of August 2, 1775, which was entered into the proceedings of the Third Virginia Convention. Officers of Virginia volunteer companies, commanded by Charles Scott, who were encamped on the outskirts of Williamsburg, were itching to be involved in some sort of action. They informed the convention delegates that "one Phillips commands an Ignorant disorderly mob, who are in direct opposition to our plan. It is our desire to crush these matters in Embryo." The officers wanted approval from the convention to go after the gang. The letter was taken under advisement and was referred to the committee on "the State of the Colony."[3] Scott's volunteers were soon occupied in ridding Virginia of Dunmore's invasion, and with that accomplished, serving as units in the Virginia Continental line, which went north to join George Washington's army. Thus a military effort against the Phillips gang did not materialize.

Until the Dunmore force pulled out of its ship stations in Norfolk Harbor and the Elizabeth River in May 1776, Loyalist banditti freely raided in Norfolk and Princess Anne counties. Citizens from both counties, in early January 1776, sought help from the Fourth Virginia Convention to put an end to this menace. The petitioners declared that

our Plantations have been ravaged, our Wives & Children stripped almost to Nakedness, our very Bed-Chamber invaded, at the silent Hour of Midnight, by Ruffians with drawn

Daggers & Bayonets; our Houses not only robbed of Plate, Specie & every Thing valuable, but wantonly reduced by Fire to Ashes.

Recognizing that the perpetrators were being aided and abetted by local Tories, the petitioners asked the convention to order the removal of "those who have been active in spiriting up the People, as well as those who have borne Arms against us" to "some distant Part of the Colony."[4] The Virginia Committee of Safety, acting for the convention, on April 10, 1776, responded by ordering the complete evacuation of all inhabitants residing in the triangle bounded by Norfolk, Kemp's Landing, and the ocean and for the removal thirty miles into the interior from Norfolk and Princess Anne counties those who had taken Dunmore's oath of allegiance. Funds were voted to assist poor families in their removal. On May 28 the order was rescinded except for those persons who were "inimical to the cause of America."[5] The evacuation program, which was only minimally enforced, was abandoned altogether when the theater of war moved away from Virginia.

By spring 1777 Josiah Phillips and his gang had stepped up their depredations, adding highway robbery to their raids on plantations in Norfolk and Princess Anne counties. The band, numbering at various times from ten to fifty, kept boats concealed at the edge of the Dismal Swamp in order to make quick getaways from their nighttime forays and find refuge in the jungle fastness during daytime.

Acting on a report from Colonel John Wilson, the county lieutenant for Norfolk County, in June 1777, Governor Patrick Henry proclaimed a £150 reward to anyone who apprehended Josiah Phillips and two of his henchmen, Levi Sykes and John Ashley, and brought them before a magistrate. The desperado leaders lay low for most of the remainder of 1777, staying close to their retreats. In late December 1777 Josiah Phillips was captured by militia under Lieutenant William Poythress and lodged in the Norfolk County jail. The governor authorized payment of £55 to be given to Colonel Wilson "for the purpose of rewarding sundry persons for apprehending Josiah Phillips who was outlawed by the Governor the 20th June as as a Traitor to the State." Ten pounds of the sum went to "a free Mulatto for informing where the said Phillips was." Phillips, however, soon escaped from jail, probably with the help of his associates.[6]

Again free, Josiah Phillips became more daring and conducted raids more frequently than before in Princess Anne County.[7] At a session of the Virginia Council of State on May 1, 1778, Governor Henry presented a letter from Colonel George Muter, commander of a regiment of state artillery, stating that "Phillips the noted Traitor has again made an Insurrection in Princess Anne County at the head of fifty men." Acting upon the advice of the council, Henry proclaimed a $500 reward, dead or alive, for Josiah

Phillips; any booty seized from him would be divided among the captors. The governor also called out 100 militia from Nansemond County to join "the party which Colonel Thomas R. Walker [of Princess Anne County] may raise for quelling these Insurgents."[8]

Colonel John Wilson, himself accutely aware of "the ravages by Phillips & his Notorious Gang," using his authority as county lieutenant, conscripted 200 men, 50 from each of Norfolk County's four militia companies, for the purpose of going after the Phillips banditti. Wilson was shocked that only ten persons appeared under his troop requisition, owing to the "Backwardness & even Disaffection of the people" and the preference to pay a 5s. fine for not showing up for duty. Wilson did manage to send out a small detachment under Captain Josiah Wilson, but it returned without success even in discovering Phillips's whereabouts. Colonel Wilson wrote Governor Henry to complain that "scarce a man, without being forced, can be raised to go after the outlaws." He recommended as the only solution the evacuation of all persons aiding the Phillips gang. On May 27, Governor Henry forwarded Wilson's letter to the House of Delegates, stating that as governor he did not have the authority to order the removal of citizens, but that he was dispatching a company of state troops, "drawn from the several stations," into the disturbed vicinity. Henry made it clear to the legislators that "no Effort to crush these Desperadoes should be spared."[9]

Meanwhile, Captain Josiah Wilson, shortly after he had returned from his futile mission, was killed by the outlaws. The Norfolk County officer had been visiting a neighbor concerning "some private business," only a mile from his own house. Four men allegedly belonging to the Phillips gang had concealed themselves in the neighbor's house and shot Wilson as he approached; Wilson died within a few hours.[10]

The Virginia House of Delegates acknowledged Colonel John Wilson's letters in its proceedings of May 28, 1778:

Information being received that a certain Phillips, with divers others, his associates and confederates, have levied war against the Commonwealth within the counties of Norfolk and Princess Anne, committing murders, burning houses, wasting farms, and doing other acts of enormity, in defiance of the officers of justice.

The House of Delegates resolved itself into a committee of the whole and, without any investigation, hearings, or debate, instantly voted to enact a bill of attainder against "Josiah Phillips, his associates, and confederates." A committee of three delegates—Thomas Jefferson, as chairman, John Tyler, and Meriwether Smith—was assigned to draw up a bill of attainder. The document was ready the same day, at which time it had its first reading.

Two days later the bill of attainder passed in the House of Delegates and was delivered to the Senate, which immediately gave its consent, thereby securing its enactment.[11]

Seldom has any legislation in Virginia received such light treatment, especially legislation pertaining to fundamental law and the rights of citizens based on unexamined evidence. Jefferson, who wrote the law, demonstrated his own cavalier attitude toward civil liberty during wartime.

The attainder law cited Phillips and other unnamed persons of Norfolk and Princess Anne counties for having "levied war" against Virginia and also for "committing murders, burning houses, wasting farms, and doing other acts of hostility." It, therefore, declared that Phillips and his associates must surrender by June 30, 1778, and stand trial for their crimes. If this did not occur, the culprits, without trial, "shall stand and be convicted and attainted of high treason, and suffer the pains of death, and incur all forfeitures, penalties and disabilities, prescribed by the law against those convicted and attainted of high treason." The sentence of attainder would be exacted simply by order of the general court upon notice that the offenders were in custody. If "an associate or confederate" of Phillips should be apprehended and declare that he had no connection with Phillips since July 1, 1777, "at which time the said murders and devastations were begun," then such person would be tried by a jury in a regular court, and if guilty receive the penalties stated in the attainder law. The attainder law stated that any one could "pursue and slay" Phillips or any of his "associates or confederates," who came under the attainder, providing that "the person so slain be in arms at the time, or endeavouring to escape being taken."[12]

Phillips had two no-win options. If he surrendered before June 30, 1778, he would stand trial and certainly be convicted and sentenced to death. If he were captured without voluntarily giving himself up, he was entitled to no judicial proceedings other than the judges of the general court, which would summarily order his execution. "Perhaps the most sinister aspect" of the attainder bill, according to Leonard W. Levy, "was its declaration of an open hunting season on the unnamed men whose guilt for treason and murder was legislatively assumed." Any person might be shot if he were merely deemed to be associated with Phillips.[13]

Meanwhile, the authorities sought out persons who had given assistance to the Phillips banditti. The Princess Anne County court, on May 21, 1778, issued a warrant for the arrest of Cornelius Land, a resident of the county, for the purpose of placing Land under a security bond pledging his "good behavior." Land was accused of having "harboured & entertained one William Wilbur thinking him one of Phillips's Gang, or what is commonly called the Green-Brier Company." Land informed the said Wilbur that in a short Time the Fleet would be in order to subdue the Rebels, and said that he knew where Philips's Company lodged for that they often came to his House and he had at times supplied them with Provision, and that those who join'd the said Philips were in the Right.

The Green-Brier Company, in reference to the Phillips banditti, probably had a local connotation rather than a link to the Greenbriar Company, which held land grants in what is now West Virginia; settlers viewed the purchase of land from the company as a form of extortion.[14]

On June 4, three days after the bill of attainder went into effect, Josiah Phillips and three of his cohorts—James and Robert Hodges and Henry McClellan—were seized in a nighttime encounter in Norfolk County by militia commanded by Colonel Amos Weeks. The prisoners were detained in Princess Anne County and a week or so later taken to the Williamsburg jail. Weeks and his "volunteer company" divided up the £150 reward then "offered by government for apprehending Josiah Philips."[15] In response to a petition from the inhabitants of Norfolk and Princess Anne counties, Governor Henry ordered four additional sentries placed at the Williamsburg jail.[16]

Rather than invoke the bill of attainder, it was decided that Phillips have a jury trial before the General Court. Since the General Court records of early Virginia were destroyed during the Civil War, it is difficult to determine the actual judicial proceedings. A newspaper account stated that Phillips was charged with "robbing the public waggons" and also "accused of murder, treason, and sundry other outrages." It seems that Phillips actually was charged only with robbing two wagons of a Continental army convoy. An indictment returned against him from an examiner's court of Princess Anne County on June 11, 1778, specified the charge of "Feloniously Robbing the Continent of America" on May 9, 1778, which involved robbing and assaulting James Hargrove, stealing goods, including twenty-eight men's felt hats, five pounds of twine, twelve pieces of linen, twelve gross of coat and waistcoat buttons, and seven muskets, and also robbing John Clarke of "50 weight of lead" and 1.5 pounds of powder.[17] Phillips and James Hodges were remanded to the General Court on only these charges, although the court and the jury undoubtedly kept in mind the general accusations cited by the bill of attainder.

Phillips himself did not face the charge of murdering Captain Josiah Wilson. Three of his gang were convicted of that crime.[18]

Josiah Phillips languished in jail for over four months before coming to trial. His case was one of the fourteen for capital crimes that came before the General Court during its October term. Phillips and three associates who had been captured with him—James and Robert Hodges and Henry

McClellan—were tried for highway robbery. Eleven other defendants from various Virginia counties stood trial for murder, burglary, grand larceny, or horse stealing.[19]

Phillips pleaded not guilty and claimed protection as a prisoner of war, a British citizen, and having acted under a commission from Governor Lord Dunmore. Indeed, one reason Edmund Randolph, the twenty-five-year-old attorney general who served as prosecutor in the Phillips case, pressed a robbery and not a treason charge was the expectation that Phillips would plead that he had prisoner-of-war status. Such a plea "was rejected by the court on the ground that a citizen's crimes cannot be justified by a commission from an enemy."[20]

Convicted on October 27, Phillips received the death sentence; the next day, the court fixed the execution date as December 4. Also condemned to die were Phillips's three associates; John Lowry, John Reizen, and Charles Bowman for murder; Joseph Turner for burglary; John Highwarden for grand larceny; and James Randolph for horse stealing. At a gallows erected on the outskirts of Williamsburg, on December 4, the sheriff of York County hanged Phillips, McClellan, Robert Hodges, Reizen, and Turner.[21] The fate of the other men condemned on October 27 is not known.

The Phillips case was considered, at the time, a regular trial for a capital crime, which resulted in conviction and execution; therefore, the application of a bill of attainder against him had no consequence. Other states during the war enacted bills of attainder, which may be defined as "a direct condemnation by the legislature without any judicial action" and which "inflicts punishment upon an individual by name."[22] State legislatures passed attainder laws from time to time, proscribing named individuals for the purpose of sequestering their estates. The cited individuals were declared forever banished. New York's law of 1779 named fifty-nine persons and ordered that they suffer death if they ever returned. Aaron Doane came close to execution under a Pennsylvania law that had attainted him for outlawry (see Chapter 8). Had Josiah Phillips been put to death by an attainder for treason, it would have been the only instance in the American states during the Revolution.

The attainder against Phillips violated Virginia's constitution of 1776. Athough there is no prohibition on legislative bills of attainder, the Declaration of Rights, incorporated into the constitution, guaranteed trial by jury and other due process "in all capital or criminal prosecutions."[23]

There is no evidence, however, that any Virginia legislators or judges were concerned about using a bill of attainder against Josiah Phillips, only the issue of trying a prisoner of war for treason. A primary reason for a regular trial of Phillips under the common law was because the Princess Anne County court inaugurated judicial proceedings that remanded Phillips for trial before the general court. Had Phillips been delivered, in the first instance, to the Williamsburg jail and placed under the custody of the General Court, the bill of attainder might have been implemented.

While the bill of attainder against Phillips may be regarded as a wartime aberration and of no consequence since it was not used, two important constitutional questions did arise. Could the court ignore the enforcement of a legislative act, or, for that matter, nullify it? Second, did the Virginia legislature abridge constitutional liberty?

The refusal of the General Court to abide by the Phillips attainder law presented the first small step in Virginia toward judicial review. The assertion of the judicial branch to determine the constitutionality of a law was minimally established concerning treason cases near the end of the war. In June 1782 the general court convicted and sentenced to death for treason three residents of Princess Anne County—John Caton, Joshua Hopkins, and James Lamb. While awaiting execution in Richmond, the condemned men petitioned the General Assembly, which under the Treason Act of 1776 had the sole authority to grant pardons in treason cases.

The prisoners' request for clemency provoked a constitutional crisis. While the treason act required the consent of the whole General Assembly (House of Delegates and the Senate) to issue pardons for treason, the Virginia Constitution stated that the governor, with advice of the Council of State, should have power to issue pardons, with one of two exceptions being if "the law shall otherwise Particularly direct; in which *cases*, no reprieve or Pardon shall be granted, *but by resolve of the House of Delegates.*"

The House of Delegates voted for a pardon, and the Senate rejected it. Under the constitutional provision, the prisoners were to be set free; according to the treason law, to be hanged. *Caton v. Commonwealth*, as the case became known, stirred the emotions of Virginia's leaders as well as the general public, the majority of whom demanded mercy. The petition of the prisoners came to the General Court, whose members were so divided that they passed the case on to the new Court of Appeals. Division also rankled the judges of the Court of Appeals over whether the judiciary could ever overturn a law. The Court of Appeals, by a vote of six to two on November 2, 1782, upheld the pardoning provision of the treason act. This meant that the three prisoners should hang. Another petition was submitted to the General Assembly on behalf of the condemned men; this time the two houses concurred in granting a pardon. John Caton was released from custody on condition that he join the Continental army; the other two, Hopkins and Lamb, that they leave the state and not return until after the war. Subsequent to the Court of Appeals decision upholding the pardoning power in the treason act, both houses of the legislature voted for pardon in several other treason cases.[24]

The bill of attainder against Josiah Phillips had been enacted during a state of absentmindedness among the legislators. Ironically, recovered memory many years later elicited regret and recrimination.

Josiah Phillips's case became enmeshed in heated debates at the Virginia Convention for the ratification of the federal constitution in June 1788. Edmund Randolph, who as attorney general had prosecuted the Phillips case, favored a strong national government as a check upon the recklessness of state legislators. Addressing the delegates on June 6, he declared,

> I ask you if your laws are reverenced. In every well-regulated community, the laws command respect. . . . We not only see violations of the constitution, but of national principles in repeated instances . . . violations of the constitution extends from the year 1776 to the present time—violations made by formal acts of the legislature: every thing has been drawn within the legislative vortex.
>
> There is one example of the violation in Virginia, of a most striking and shocking nature—an example so horrid. . . . A man, who was then a citizen, was deprived of his life thus: from a mere reliance on general reports, a gentleman in the House of Delegates informed the house, that a certain man [Josiah Phillips] had committed several crimes, and was running at large, perpetrating other crimes. He therefore moved for leave to attaint him; he obtained that leave instantly; no sooner did he obtain it, than he drew from his pocket a bill ready written for that effect; it was read three times in one day, and carried in the Senate. I will not say that it passed the same day through the Senate; but he was attainted very speedily and precipitately, without any proof better than vague reports. Without being confronted with his accusers and witnesses, without the privilege of calling for evidence in his behalf, he was sentenced to death, and afterwards actually executed. Was this arbitrary deprivation of life, the dearest gift of God to man, consistent with the genius of a republican government? Is this compatible with the spirit of freedom?[25]

Randolph had forgotten or was purposely misrepresenting the fact that Phillips had been tried and convicted in a court of law.

The vituperative remarks of Edmund Randolph were intended to cast aspersion on Patrick Henry,[26] who led the opposition in the convention against the constitution and who, therefore, defended Virginia's legislative past. Henry had actually initiated the bill of attainder by submitting Colonel John Wilson's letter reporting Phillips's outrages to the legislature rather than asking one of its members to do so. An angry Henry responded to Randolph's insinuations of legislative incompetence relative to the Phillips case. Like Randolph, Henry misconstrued the facts by asserting that Phillips had been executed under the attainder rather than by conviction in court by force of common law. What is alarming in Henry's rebuttal is that he justified the state's killing a citizen, albeit a notorious criminal, without judicial due process. Randolph, declared Henry, has given you an elaborate account of what he judges tyrannical legislation, and an *ex post facto law*, (in the case of Josiah Philips.) He has misrepresented the facts. That man was not executed by a tyrannical stroke of power. Nor was he a Socrates. He was a fugitive murderer and an outlaw—a man who commanded an infamous banditti, and at a time when the war was at the most perilous stage. He committed the most cruel and shocking barbarities. He was an enemy to the human name. Those who declare war against the human race may be struck out of existence as soon as they are apprehended. He was not executed according to those beautiful legal ceremonies which are pointed out by the laws in criminal cases. The enormity of his crimes did not entitle him to it. I am truly a friend to legal forms and methods; but, sir, the occasion warranted the measure. A pirate, an outlaw, or a common enemy to all mankind, may be put to death at any time. It is justified by the laws of nature and nations.[27]

Patrick Henry's argument damaged his cause. How could he support arbitrary government and still be a champion of liberty? In rebuttal, Randolph, offended by Henry's personal attack, slashed into the obvious flaw in Henry's reasoning:

I take the liberty of a freeman in exposing what appears to me to deserve censure. I shall take that liberty in reprehending the wicked act which attainted Josiah Phillips. Because he was not a Socrates, is he to be attainted at pleasure? Is he to be attainted because he is not among the high of reputation?

Henry, continued Randolph,

has expatiated on the turpitude of the character of Josiah Phillips. Has this any thing to do with the principle on which he was attainted? We all agree that he was an abandoned man. But if you can prepare a bill to attaint a man, and pass it through both houses in an instant, I ask you, who is safe? There is no man on whom a cloud may not hang some time or other, if a demagogue should think proper to take advantage of it to his destruction. Phillips had a commission in his pocket at that time. He was, therefore, only a prisoner of war. This precedent may destroy the best man in the community, when he was arbitrarily attainted merely because he was not a Socrates.[28]

In further discussion of the Phillips case in the Virginia ratifying convention, the views of several other delegates may be noted. John Marshall castigated Henry on the same grounds as Randolph. "What has become the worthy member's [Henry's] maxim?" Marshall asked. "Is this one of them? Should it be a maxim that a man shall be deprived of his life without the benefit of law?"[29]

Benjamin Harrison, who like Henry and Randolph had served as a governor of Virginia, sided with Henry; Phillips "was a man who, by the laws of nations, was entitled to no privilege of trial."[30] George Nicholas acknowledged that the bill of attainder against Phillips was wrong, but rights were better protected in the general provisions of the constitution rather than listed in a bill of rights.[31] Edmund Pendleton concurred, believing that a condemnation of a person by attainder or other violation of fundamental liberty was not likely to happen as long as "we preserve the representative character" of government.[32]

With the adoption of the U.S. Constitution, which absolutely forbade federal and state bills of attainder, the Phillips case faded from memory, but it resurfaced in 1803 when St. George Tucker, then a member of the Virginia Court of Appeals, published an edition of the *Commentaries* by an English jurist, Sir William Blackstone. In an appendix, Tucker emphasized a facet of the Phillips case other than that of fundamental rights. The General Court, said Tucker, had refused to deliver a "sentence of execution" upon Phillips in accordance with the attainder law. Instead, Phillips

was put upon his trial, according to the ordinary course of law. This is a decisive proof of the importance of the separation of powers of government, and of the independence of the judiciary; a dependant judiciary might have executed the law, whilst they execrated the principle upon which it was founded.[33]

Thomas Jefferson kept a long silence on the Phillips case, although he had been instrumental in the passage of the legislative bill of attainder. In France at the time of the Virginia ratifying convention, he was not privy to the discussions relating to the Phillips case. The proceedings of the convention were not published until 1836–45, and Jefferson probably had no knowledge of the speeches made by Randolph and the other delegates until about 1814, at which time he probably saw a record of Randolph's speech. St. George Tucker's reference to the Phillips case in 1803, however, had already refreshed his memory. On two occasions, in 1814 and 1815, Jefferson commented on Phillips's attainder. In reply to William Wirt, who was preparing a biography of Patrick Henry, Jefferson, in August 1814, simply said that Edmund Randolph's "censure" of Patrick Henry "was without foundation." Phillips, "a mere robber," who "collected a banditti," was such a threat that the best action for the government was to pass an attainder against him. Jefferson pointed out, however, that Phillips actually was tried by common law.[34]

In 1815 Louis Hue Girardin asked Jefferson to read the page proofs of his revised edition of John Daly Burk's *History of Virginia*. Girardin agreed to strike out the section that contained quotations from Henry, Randolph, and Tucker concerning the Phillips case and substitute Jefferson's own version. Jefferson depicted Phillips as a "man of daring and ferocious disposition." In Jefferson's view, Phillips and "his ruffian associates" engaged in murder and arson, retiring "with impunity to his secret haunts, reeking with blood, and loaded with plunder." Jefferson contended that the bill of attainder was fully justified. "No one doubted that society had a right to erase from the roll of its members any one who rendered his own existence inconsistent with theirs; to withdraw from him the protection of their laws, and to remove him from among them by exile, or even by death if necessary."[35] Obviously, thirty-seven years after the Phillips case, Jefferson had no remorse for his role in condemning a Virginia citizen to the gallows without trial.

Members of the Phillips gang and other banditti continued to terrorize the citizens in the lower Tidewater area, despite the capture and execution of Josiah Phillips and several of his cohorts. The outlaws saw no advantage in surrendering; no amnesty was offered, and the Phillips case had demonstrated how eager the authorities were to mete out extreme penalties with only a semblance of fair criminal procedure.

Even as early as July 1778, the Virginia Council of State had received a petition from the inhabitants of Norfolk County, with an endorsement from Colonel John Wilson, asking that Zadock Dailey and Caleb Powers, two deserters from Captain Thomas Bressie's state troops, be pardoned, discharged from service, and paid rewards for "taking & killing several of the noted Phillips's gang of Robbers." The council and Governor Henry considered that the executive could not oblige the request and referred the petition to the House of Delegates, which voted the recompense.[36] One of the Phillips banditti killed was a slave named Will, who, in "aiding and abetting Josiah Phillips and his accomplices in the perpetration of their wicked and traitorous actions," had "struck such terror into the inhabitants" of Norfolk and Princess Anne counties that Colonel Wilson himself offered a reward for his capture. Zadock Dailey had killed the slave, and the reward went to Colonel Wilson, who was out of pocket for having paid Dailey.[37] Another runaway slave, who presumably had associated with Phillips, known as "Negro Sandy" (alias Sanders) was convicted in a Norfolk County court of oyer and terminer in August 1778 for "Treason and Murder and sentenced to be hanged."[38]

If Negro Sandy was hanged it was for murder alone. No slave in Virginia was executed for treason, since, after what became a test case during the war, it was decided that a slave not being a citizen could not commit treason. A few slaves, however, were executed upon conviction of a compounded charge, with one of the accusations being treason.

About the time that their leader was captured in the summer of 1778, other members of the Phillips gang were arrested. Mason Miller, Thomas Thornton, and Wilson Pinkerton were arraigned before the Norfolk County court and sent to Williamsburg for trial on charges of high treason, robbery, and the murder of Captain Josiah Wilson. In late March 1779, all three, as well as Jesse Philpot, Luke Lenly, and Gilbert Pierce (also probably Phillips's associates), received the death sentence. Philpot was pardoned, and presumably the others were hanged.[39]

Two of "the great offenders" among the Phillips gang appear to have escaped justice. Nothing has been learned of the fate of Robert Stewart, who became the leader of the banditti after Phillips. James Sykes, who once had a £150 reward posted on him along with Phillips, also eluded capture. In 1782 Sykes's lands were confiscated, and at the end of the war he left the state.[40]

The banditti situation deteriorated in Norfolk and Princess Anne counties from 1781 to mid 1782. Loyalists were emboldened by the British invasion, and after the battle of Yorktown, Virginia and North Carolina refugees who had accompanied the British army found sanctuary in the two lower counties, hiding out in the swamps when necessary. Colonel Thomas Newton, the county lieutenant for Norfolk County, advised Governor Thomas Nelson in September 1781:

The County of Princess Anne has neither civil or military law in it. . . . Murder is committed & no notice is taken of it for want of some support up the Country. A few desperate fellows go about on the sea Coasts and large swamps and do mischief in the night, every one who appears active against them is an object of their fury.[41]

Newton, writing on November 10, 1781, had further woe for the governor. "The Tories & refugees," he complained, "are still unpunished to the great disatisfaction of the well Affected, many of them were in arms plundering & now live in affluence while those who were ingaged in their Country's service are ruin'd." Many of the banditti and refugees had become emboldened by the prospect of another British invasion in Virginia. Some justices of the courts were themselves friendly to the "delinquents." Newton mentioned that it was "horrid to think that a man (one of our best soldiers) should be taken out of a justices house & murder'd, the justice knowing the persons & they never call'd to any account for it." Such negligence "has caused several other murders as the friends revenge the death of their relations & acquaintances on both sides."[42]

As governmental authority asserted itself, it was found almost impossible to punish all those who had been involved in treasonable activities or outlawry. It was too troublesome and too costly to send persons charged with treason to Richmond, the state's capital, for trial, and the punishment of a large number of people would bring again a little civil war to the lower Tidewater area. At the end of the war, none of the Loyalist refugees, who were temporarily jailed, faced trials, and only a very few residents of the lower counties were sent to Richmond for trial for treason. These were subsequently released or inducted into the army.[43]

The British invasions and widespread discontent with the war effort distracted the attention of the Virginia government during the last years of the war from committing resources to confront the overall banditti problem. A series of draft and tax riots and a general uprising of Loyalists in the western part of the state broke out, all of which were nipped in the bud by the quick action of the patriot militia.

Besides the Chesapeake bargemen and the banditti in the lower Tidewater area, outlaw gangs briefly surfaced in Accomac County and central Virginia during 1781 and 1782. Vigilantism curtailed the outlaw rampages in Accomac, and in central Virginia the gang activity was so sudden and transient that, for the most part, the culprits eluded justice.

In the spring of 1781, during the British invasion, as George Corbin of Accomac County informed the Virginia war commissioner, "the disaffected amongst us believing that we should be soon reduced to british Government, and become an easy prey, began to rob privately." Levin Joynes, also of Accomac, reported that "there was another sett of Villains no less dangerous than the Bargers, inhabitants of this County—they would assemble six or eight together and Rob from house to house in remote places." The murder of "an active friend to the Commonwealth" proved to be the last straw. A posse formed and went in pursuit of "the supposed murderers." Upon information provided by "a negro, who was known to have been of the party, and had surrendered himself," the pursuers caught up with three suspects who, under severe intimidation, confessed. "A few nights afterwards," more than 100 citizens "marched out" to the gallows. Since the confessions were considered ample proof of guilt, the crowd voted unanimously that "the wretches should be immediately executed after giving them a few hours to settle their worldly affairs—which was at the expiration of the time given, cooly and deliberately done." As Joynes noted, "this act of Violence seems Justified by the necessity of the case, as it put an immediate stop to that kind of Mischief."[44]

Vigilantism took a tool also in Louisa County, situated above Richmond and east of Charlottesville, Virginia. In June 1781, while Cornwallis's army trekked down the Three Notched Road, returning from an advance into the southern edge of Virginia's piedmont, some local Tories engaged in pillaging along the army's line of march. A crowd greeted two captured marauders and summarily hanged them.[45]

If Cornwallis's invasion into central Virginia encouraged banditry, the surrender at Yorktown oddly had the same effect. As General Benjamin Lincoln informed George Washington, some 900 Yorktown prisoners of war, often unattended by their militia guards, on their way to prison camps in

Maryland and Pennsylvania, deserted and were "strolling through Virginia." An irritated citizenry frequently denied food to the escapees.[46] Not surprisingly, the delinquent prisoners joined runaway slaves as banditti.

In mid August 1782, "a gang of robbers" pillaged several houses in Fluvanna County, near Charlottesville, and "plundered sundry of the inhabitants, and set fire to, and wholly destroyed a small magazine of powder. This corps of banditti is composed of runaway blacks, headed it is thought, by some white emissaries of the enemy."[47]

The same banditti were probably responsible for the depredations committed a week later, a little farther down the James River, just above Richmond. Edmund Pendleton reported that, at the end of August, three or four "British deserters" and several slaves had stolen arms from the magazine in Goochland County and then set fire to the magazine.[48] About the same time, the Richmond newspaper reported apparently on the same gang:

a number of armed negroes, headed it is supposed, by some British vagabonds, set fire to a barn opposite Westham, about six miles from this city, and burnt it to the ground, together with about eleven bushels of wheat. They afterwards set fire to the dwelling house, but on being fired on they went off.[49]

Edmund Randolph wrote to Congressman James Madison on August 30:

The laxness and inefficacy of government really alarms me. A Notorious robber, who escaped from gaol about a twelve month ago, has associated in his villainies a formidable gang of blacks and whites, supposed to amount to fifty. They dispersed themselves, judiciously for the accomplishment of their work, and the elusion of punishment: and have perpetrated some of the most daring and horrid thefts. An attempt has been often made to arrest this prince of the banditti but it had hitherto miscarried. Nay I do not believe, that government can by any means in its power affect the seizure of this man. I live in the center [on Shockoe Hill overlooking the little state capital of Richmond] of the late depredations.[50]

There is no further report of a large banditti gang committing depredations in central Virginia. Obviously the members of the group, consisting of runaway slaves and prisoner-of-war deserters, were constantly on the move and probably quickly dispersed.

During the whole course of the war, landed banditti never posed much of a problem in Virginia. Like the situations elsewhere, wartime banditti thrived within a community that had a large Loyalist population and when proximity to British military forces offered both protection and opportunity to dispose of stolen goods. These factors existed much of the time in the lower Tidewater counties and also, to some extent, on the Eastern Shore. The Phillips banditti endured as long as they did because of the interde-

pendence of kin and friends; a Loyalist population that was at least a substantial minority; some access to British military forces, especially during
the Dunmore campaign of 1775–76 and other British incursions of 1779,
1780, and 1781; and ready means for refuge in nearby swamps.

The southeastern Tidewater region had never been committed to independence, owing largely to ties to British trade. For the most part, Tories
and patriots lived together in harmony, though at times it seemed a little
civil war prevailed. To avert further antipathy, courts and judges were reluctant to pursue repressive measures against Loyalists. The Phillips gang
brought law enforcement down upon them because of their outright criminal activity. There was also some fear that the Phillips banditti might
provoke an insurrection by Loyalists.

Loyalist-related banditti were almost nonexistent elsewhere in Virginia.
After 1776, the state, with repressive laws to the contrary, pursued mild
policies toward Loyalists. If one kept his political principles to himself, even
though refusing to take an oath of allegiance, he could expect no punishment beyond paying additional taxes and experiencing certain civil disabilities. Confiscation of property applied only to British firms having
property in Virginia and persons going over to the enemy. The treason act
had no widespread use until after the American victory at Yorktown. The
hysteria was short-lived, and accused persons were set free.

The Phillips case, however, blackened the reputation of the Virginia leadership during the war. Here was an individual rumored to have committed
numerous atrocious crimes, but he was convicted and executed for only one
robbery. Of course frustration had built up over a long period of time from
failure to apprehend Phillips. The bill of attainder against him became law
solely on uncorroborated reports of a single militia officer. It is of no special
credit to the commonwealth of Virginia that Phillips was executed under
the common law rather than under the attainder. Thomas Jefferson, in his
Notes on the State of Virginia, written at the end of 1781, bewailed the
tendency toward legislative tyranny in Virginia, but he himself had contributed to just that by being only too willing to exact condemnation on a
citizen without judicial due process.

In his *Notes,* Jefferson boasted that, in Virginia, "though this war has now
raged near seven years, not a single execution for treason has taken place."[51]
He preferred to ignore his hypocrisy. If Jefferson had his way in 1778, there
would have been an execution for treason, without the accused having a
jury trial or a right to confront his accusers.

Chapter 11

Maroons

Like the distant westward frontier, isolated terrain within or on the fringes of settled areas lured various outcasts from society. Runaway servants and slaves, fugitives from the law, and war refugees found sanctuary in forests, marshes, and swamps and on islands. Often to supplement their marginal living off the land they conducted sorties out of their makeshift communities to rob neighboring farmers and planters of livestock and provisions. These denizens of the out-of-way camps differed from the usual outlaw gangs who had hideouts in inhospitable environs because they developed at least temporary communities.

The secluded fugitive groups may be called maroons. The word "maroon" is derived from the Spanish *cimarrón*, meaning runaway or outlaw and also from the French *marron*. In its narrow definition, "maroon" designates a fugitive slave, particularly in the West Indies or Guinea, who, in the seventeenth and eighteenth centuries, hid out in mountain fastnesses and made raids against former oppressors.[1] In this chapter maroon is used in its broader sense to refer to any isolated group of fugitives living apart from the main society, somewhat self-sustaining, yet exhibiting hostility toward the regular communities nearest them. Maroonage was most common in the South, where the population in the plantation society was more spread out than in the North.

Areas that served as receptacles for Loyalist refugees had attributes of maroonage. Refugeetown on Sandy Hook, New Jersey, fits this category. Loyalists fleeing from patriot military successes in the Carolina interior during 1781 built a village of huts and shanties across from Charleston Neck, which they called Rawdon Town (after Lieutenant Colonel Lord Francis Rawdon, who at the time commanded the British army in the South). The Loyalist refugees at this enclave went out on maruauding expeditions. Loyalist refugees also stationed themselves on James Island, South Carolina, and in April 1782, 200 of them crossed at Wappoo Creek and "plundered all the inhabitants on Ashley River."[2]

In 1775 a large number of escaped slaves took refuge on Sullivan's Island near Charleston, South Carolina. "Lord William Campbell has gone great lengths in harbouring & protecting Negroes" on the island, "from whence these Villains made nightly Sallies and committed robberies & depredations on the Sea Coast at Christ Church [Parish]." The South Carolina Council of State dispatched 200 troops to attack the runaways in their camp. An early morning raid on December 18, 1775, succeeded in clearing out the "den of runaway slaves"; fifty of the defenders who would not be taken were killed, and the survivors were brought to Charleston.[3]

Fugitive slaves established camps on other islands along the South Carolina and Georgia coasts in expectation of being picked up by British naval vessels. Several hundred escaped slaves congregated on Tybee Island, at the mouth of the Savannah River, early in the war. Colonel Stephen Bull requested the South Carolina Council of Safety to send a force to the island to either capture or kill the "deserted Negroes." Bull proposed using Creek Indians for the mission, which would "deter other Negroes from deserting and will establish a hatred or Aversion between the Indians and the Negroes."[4] On March 25, 1776, Colonel Archibald Bullock led seventy troops "painted and dressed like Indians" and thirty Indians onto the island. The attackers were exposed to British ship weaponry while on the beaches. Since there is no mention of confronting the slave fugitives, it is assumed that all of them managed to board the British ships. The invaders, however, killed and scalped two British marines, killed one Tory, and burned houses.[5]

Loyalists encamping on coastal islands proved more aggressive than the slave fugitives. Refugee banditti living on Pace's Island in the Savannah River raided South Carolina and Georgia shores until routed by militia under Lieutenant Joel Calliham in 1780.[6] Several hundred refugees on James Island at Charleston's harbor in 1782 engaged in plundering patriot homes along the Ashley River.[7] Daufuskie Island, off the lower South Carolina coast, harbored fugitive Loyalists who went out on raids but were subdued by January 1782.[8]

In the Carolinas and Georgia, runaway slaves often congregated in woods or swamplands near their masters' plantations (*petit marronage*), while some found refuge on the frontier, where they linked up with white fugitives, or they made their way to the Floridas, where they were welcomed by Spanish authorities. The colonial and state governments, however, played a successful game in driving a wedge between Indians and fugitive slaves; black bondsmen fleeing to the protection of the Cherokees, Creeks, or other tribes generally were killed or returned to their white owners.[9]

Other than the hostility of Indians toward blacks, a major factor impeding the establishment of permanent maroon communities consisting of escaped slaves in North America, in contrast to Jamaica and elsewhere in the Caribbean, was the rapid spread of white pioneers into and across the mountains.[10] By mid-eighteenth century settlers, mostly Scotch-Irish and German, were occupying the western mountain valleys, which created a barrier to slave escapees. Earlier, the possibility of black maroonage in the mountains aroused fear among Virginians. In 1729 a dozen slaves from a plantation near present-day Richmond fled to the "Great Mountains" and set up camp near what is today Lexington, Virginia. The fugitives took with them arms, provisions, and tools. Alarmed that maroonage might spread in Virginia, the government dispatched militia who broke up the new maroon community. According to Virginia's governor, William Gooch, the capture of the slave maroons "prevented for this time a design which might have proved as dangerous to this Country, as is that of the Negroes in the Mountains of Jamaica to the inhabitants of that Island."[11]

The maroons who lived in the Dismal Swamp, which straddled the southeastern Virginia and northeastern North Carolina borders, formed the most permanent of the Southern fugitive communities. Nearly 2,000 people inhabited the swamp during the American Revolution. For nearly a century, the Dismal Swamp had harbored runaway white servants and black slaves and various rejects from society. Remnant Tuscarora Indians, who stayed behind when their brethren moved northward to join the Iroquois Confederacy, were added to the ethnic mix after the Tuscarora War of 1711–12. Living along the southern edge of the swamp were the Scratch Hall folk, tawny skinned and neither white nor black. While gaining some self-sufficiency by raising crops and livestock on dry patches of land, the "Swampers" occasionally raided plantations on the fringes of the swamp for provisions and livestock. They also carried on legal and illegal trade with outsiders.[12]

At the time of the war, the Dismal Swamp consisted of about 2,000 square miles (from sixty to seventy miles long and between twenty and thirty miles wide). As George Washington commented, it was "neither plain nor a hollow, but a hill side." On the high ground was a freshwater lake, Lake Drummond. The swamp encompassed parts of Norfolk, Nansemond, and Princess Anne counties in Virginia and Camden, Currituck, Gates, and

An armed swamper. Dismal Swamp. Nineteenth
century. From Harper's *New Monthly Magazine*, vol.
13 (September 1856), p. 452.

Pasquotank counties in North Carolina. The Dismal Swamp Company,
founded by George Washington and other speculators in 1763, for the purpose of draining the swamp, had made almost no progress. The swamp was
impassable, except for a footpath, which the Americans had hewed through
the wilderness when Lord Dunmore's military force was stationed just beyond the outskirts of the swamp in Virginia. As a German army surgeon,
during his travels at the end of the war, described the path, it consisted
mainly of trees "felled one before the other, over which the passenger must
spring and climb; whoever slipped his footing, sank up to the neck in water
and deep, fat mire."[13]

Governor Lord Dunmore, who issued a proclamation freeing any slaves
of rebel masters who joined his standard, recruited runaway slaves in the
swamp for his black "Ethiopian" regiment, as did banditti leader Josiah Phillips (see Chapter 10). White and black Loyalists retreated into the swamp
after Dunmore's departure.[14] Militiamen feared to pursue outlaws into the
swamp. The inhabitants "could not be approached with safety."[15]

Two travelers who approached the Dismal Swamp in 1784 left their impressions. Johann David Schoepf, the German army surgeon, reported that the dry spots in the swamp "have often been used as places of safety by runaway slaves." The fugitives "lived in security and plenty, building themselves cabins, planting corn, raising hogs and fowls which they stole from their neighbors, and naturally the hunting was free where they were."[16] J.F.D. Smyth, an Englishman, commented that "this astonishing and horrible place" was "in a great degree inaccessible" and harbored "prodigious multitudes of every kind of wild beasts peculiar to America, as well as runaway Negroes," who "are perfectly safe, and with the greatest facility elude the most diligent search of their pursuers."[17]

The Dismal Swamp continued as a haven for maroon banditti until well into the nineteenth century. Samuel H. Perkins, who skirted the Dismal Swamp on his way from Norfolk, Virginia, to Elizabeth City, North Carolina, to assume a job as a tutor, noted, "Traveling here without pistols is considered very dangerous owing to the great number of runaway Negroes. They conceal themselves in the woods, & swamps by day and frequently plunder by night." To Perkins, the Dismal Swamp was "inhabited almost exclusively by run away negroes, bears, wild cats & wild cattle."[18]

The whole North Carolina–South Carolina landscape had swamps and forests that attracted runaway slaves and Loyalists who went into hiding. In most instances, the locales to which the fugitives fled were fairly accessible to white settlers; therefore, maroon communities did not coalesce. To avoid capture, it was important to stay on the move.

The swamps and forests in the North Carolina counties of New Hanover, Bladen, and Brunswick near Wilmington in the Cape Fear coastal region offered places for temporary rendezvous for fugitive slaves. The lower Cape Fear region had the greatest concentration of slaves in North Carolina. Because slaves had a tendency to linger in "swamps, Woods and other Obscure Places, killing Cattle and Hogs, and committing other Injuries," the North Carolina legislature in 1741 had empowered justices of the peace to declare outlawry against fugitive slaves, who could be killed on sight if they did not surrender.[19] Despite this punitive measure, a slave insurrection almost occurred in the lower Cape Fear region, extending to counties northward, during July 1775. The British commander at Fort Johnston, at the mouth of the Cape Fear River, "basely encouraged Slaves" to desert their masters and made it known that he would support them in an insurrection. Janet Schaw, a Scottish gentlewoman visiting in the Cape Fear region, "hourly expected" an uprising, which reportedly aimed at killing all whites, with the perpetrators eventually taking flight to the mountains. Posses rounded up a large number of blacks in "the adjoining woods" of Wilmington, and quick action elsewhere ended the threat of a slave uprising.[20]

Although there appears to have been little trouble from menacing bands of slave fugitives in the area near Wilmington during the Revolution, runaways continued to find refuge in the swamps and woods. As late as 1795 a "number of runaway Negroes" during nighttime engaged in "various depredations on the neighboring plantations." Posses routed the fugitives, killing the "General of the Swamps" and four others; four captives were executed.[21]

Defeated Tory militia and those wanted by patriot authorities for disloyalty or activity friendly to the enemy faced long periods of incarceration. To escape this prospect, these wanted men hid out in forests and swamps. Colonel Robert Gray of a royal provincial regiment observed that the swamps were "filled with loyalists."[22]

Loyalist refugees individually lived like maroons, concealing themselves in wilderness environs ranging from the coastal plain to the "Indian ground" in the backcountry. Those Tory militia not captured at the patriot victory in the battle of Moores Creek, eight miles above Wilmington, scrambled for refuge in swamps and woods. In some cases, the fugitives stayed in the wilderness for months or even years.

Aaron Vardy, captured at Moores Creek, had the distinction of hiding out at widely separate locations. After escaping from jail in Frederick Town, Maryland, he kept to the "Woods & Mountains" of that vicinity before returning to North Carolina, hoping to board a British ship. The disappointment in that quest "obliged him to seek for protection & safety among Woods & Swamps." For eighteen months he led a precarious existence, with rebels "constantly in pursuit" and a reward posted for him dead or alive.[23] Donald McCrummen and his companion, Lieutenant Soirle McDonald, remained in the swamps for two years before managing to reach Philadelphia in 1778 to link up with the British army.[24] Other survivors of the Moores Creek defeat spent a long time in hiding. Among them was Donald Kary, who stayed out for four years before joining Major Archibald McArthur's 71st Regiment in June 1780.[25] Roderick McLenan "suffered beyond Expression thro' Desarts and Swamps"; he finally joined McArthur's troops at the siege of Charleston in 1780.[26] Ely Branson, from February through the summer of 1776, was "obliged to secret himself in the woods." He made it to the British at Head of Elk, Maryland, in September 1777. Back in North Carolina in 1778, he went in hiding until 1781 when he joined Cornwallis's army, only to be captured at Yorktown.[27]

Civilians persecuted by the patriots chose the safety afforded by the wilderness environs. William Fortune of North Carolina's Camden district, for example, made this decision. Treated "inhumanly" by the rebels, Fortune decided "to abandon all Society" and "secretly retire to the lonely Wilds," where he stayed for three years. Occasionally, "when in a starving condition" and "at the hazard of his life," he ventured "to an appointed place in some Swamp or Thicket to see his distressed & overgrieved Wife," who brought him "a bit of Victuals." Eventually Fortune joined up with Loyalist militia.[28] Angus Martin, driven from his plantation in Craven County, North Carolina, in 1779 endured the "necessity of Shifting in the Woods for two years."[29]

As the partisan war heated up in the Carolinas in 1780–82, Tory bands found cover in swamps and forests. Although these "outlyers" may not be considered maroons as such because their withdrawal was largely to gain tactical advantage and their stay in concealed areas had no degree of permanence, their isolated, wilderness camps protected them from retaliation from raids they conducted against patriot settlers and militia. David Fanning, a youthful leader of Tory partisans, spent various periods of time "outlying" in the North Carolina backwoods after escaping from imprisonment. He regrouped his followers. Fanning's band, according to his own estimate, fought thirty-six skirmishes in North Carolina and four in South Carolina. Fanning's "outlyers" were quartered deep in the forest and depended on plundering for subsistence.[30]

There were many small groups of "outlyers." One South Carolina assemblyman, Aedanus Burke, in May 1782 observed that

the Country is ravaged by small parties, who retiring in swamps, make cruel excursions on the inhabitants. They are called out-Lyers, and a petit War has been, & is now carried on between us, that no quarter is given on either side. The Out Lyers sally from their swamps, & destroy our people in Cold blood, and when taken they are killed in their turn.[31]

General Nathanael Greene informed the superintendent of finances, Robert Morris, in March 1782 that South Carolina and Georgia "are still torn to pieces by little parties of disaffected who elude all search and conceal themselves in the thickets and swamps from the most dilligent pursuit and issue fourth [sic] from these hidden recesses committing the most horrid Murders and plunder and lay waste the Country." Although "their collective force is not great, yet they do a world of mischief and keep the people in perpetual alarms and render traveling very unsafe and difficult."[32] Brutal attacks by patriots put an end to some of the outlying Tory bands.

Militia general Thomas Sumter went after the outlyers in their encampments. He used Catawba Indians to track them down.[33] Another method succeeded equally well in flushing out the hidden Tories. A report from Parker's Ferry in South Carolina in June 1782 observed that

the few tories that some time ago lurked among the bushes and swamps in several parts of this State, now find themselves unsafe, and wish either to make their peace with their

"David Fanning Losing the Bay Doe." Unattributed.
Courtesy of the North Carolina Division of Archives and
History, Raleigh.

injured countrymen, or retreat to places under American government, where they are not known. . . . A Colonel Black with six or eight tories, was the other day followed by means of a dog upwards of a 100 miles, himself and all his party would have been taken, had not the horses failed. About the same time a small party of noted villains, came out of the Indian grounds, burnt some houses and committed other irregularities in the vicinity of Ninety-Six, they were immediately by the same means followed and the whole killed and taken, except one who made his escape. . . . The late scheme of training dogs to follow human tracks, succeeded beyond our most raised expectations.[34]

Runaway slaves belonging to rebels secured protection from the British army during the war. Some of these gained their freedom; others found themselves re-enslaved and sent to the West Indies or elsewhere. There was little chance for freedom if they did not join the British. It was too risky to flee 250 miles from the coast to the Appalachian barrier, which was defended by antiblack Cherokee Indians. Spain had turned over the Floridas to Great Britain in 1763, and that area ceased to be a sanctuary for runaway American slaves. Gracia Real de Santa Teresa de Mose, a fortified town two miles above Saint Augustine, which was a haven for blacks, was abandoned in 1763, and the residents were shipped to Cuba.[35] From 1784 to 1790, the Floridas, again under Spanish control, admitted escaped American slaves; many of the former bondsmen went to live among the Seminole Indians.

Slaves fleeing their masters in South Carolina and Georgia found that about the only way to survive was to become maroons, which at best was a precarious existence because inevitably their communities would be attacked.

Swamp recesses in the vicinity of the Savannah River had long been used as refuge by fugitive slaves. In 1765 a maroon camp was discovered in a four-mile-wide swamp on the South Carolina side of the river. To reach the place one had to wade waist deep through mud and water. Armed planters succeeded in forcing their way to the maroon base, but the occupants, being forewarned, had fled; the attackers destroyed four houses, provisions, and equipment. During 1772 and 1773 small bands of maroons from swamps and islands above Savannah went on plundering raids. Maroon camps at Beach-Hill and Black Swamp, each having a half dozen or so escaped slaves, were broken up, and most of the captives were executed.[36]

At the end of the Revolutionary War, when the British evacuated Savannah and Charleston, some of the black irregular troops, who had been trained in arms in British service and who called themselves the King of England's Soldiers, preferred to stay behind. After establishing themselves in the swamps, they plundered on both sides of the Savannah River. Residents feared that these banditti might incite a slave insurrection.

On May 6, 1786, Colonel James Gunn, leading about forty South Carolina militia and fifteen Catawba Indians, attacked the maroon camp on Bear Creek. The enclave, situated on an island in the swamp, one-half mile long and 400 yards wide, was protected by a four-foot-high breastwork made of log and cane pilings. Access into the camp was through an opening that permitted the entrance of only one person at a time. Half of the militia advanced frontally, and the other militia came on from the right; the Catawbas, from the left. The black maroons were pursued for several miles. Although most escaped, a number of the maroons were killed or wounded. There was no loss to the attacking force. Gunn's men burned the twenty-one houses in the maroon camp and destroyed the crops.[37]

Georgia and South Carolina authorities continued the campaign to root out the maroons from along the Savannah River. The next objective was about 100 "runaway Negroes" who "sheltered themselves" on Bellisle Island, seventeen miles up the Savannah River, who had "for some time" been committing "robberies on the neighboring Planters." On October 11, 1786, a small party of Georgia militia attacked the maroons, killing three or four; four of the militia were wounded. After running out of ammunition, the Georgians withdrew, but at sunset the same day fifteen Savannah light infantrymen and a few others "drove in one of their guards, but the Negroes came down in such numbers" that the attackers had to retreat to their boats. The maroons attempted to cut off the Georgians, only to find that they were on the receiving end of three volleys of grapeshot fired from a field-piece on one of the invader's boats. The blacks fled; "a good deal of blood was afterwards seen about the place to which the shot was directed." Two days later, on October 13, General James Jackson and the Georgia militia advanced into the maroon encampment, destroying "the houses and huts," four acres of "green rice," stores of corn and rice, and fifteen boats and canoes. Though the enemy had escaped, General Jackson reported that they were dispersed, and it was simply a matter of time before they would be captured.[38]

Jackson's prediction rang true, but further action was needed to remove the maroon threat conclusively along the Savannah. Refugees from the Bear Creek maroon camp appeared in Harleston Swamp and then at Patton's Swamp, on the Savannah near Purysburg, South Carolina, thirty miles from the ocean. In March 1787 Georgia and South Carolina militia and some Catawba Indians assaulted the fugitives' hideout in Patton's Swamp, killing six maroons and taking captive several women and children; presumably other maroons were wounded as blankets covered with blood were left behind. The next day another fight occurred, involving a maroon chieftain, Sharper, and eighteen of his followers. Sharper and his men escaped and eventually found refuge in Spanish East Florida; nine more women and children were taken into custody during the second attack. The invading troops destroyed some twenty dwellings in the maroon camp and went away with seven of the fugitives' boats. The South Carolina government was now offering a reward for the killing or capture of escaped slaves. At £10 per head, the Catawba Indians participating in the attack collected £40, and two white militiamen each received £10.[39]

The maroon problem was related to an incessant fear of slave rebellion. Any group of escaped slaves had the potential of winning over other slaves to rebellion, which would lead to the killing of whites. With any success, the fugitives would fight their way to sanctuary in the Floridas, which happened during the South Carolina slave insurrections of 1739–40. In August 1787 the South Carolina government ordered up militia into the field in the Stono River area near Charleston to apprehend those fugitive slaves who were "too numerous to be quelled by the armed parties of patrol."[40] Militia were still rounding up fugitives until spring 1788.[41]

None of the maroons in the Carolinas and Georgia succeeded in establishing any degree of permanence. With vulnerability to attack, they did not have time to develop a sustaining agriculture or to achieve a balance in sex ratios.[42] Slaves, nevertheless, continued to escape into the wilderness environs and commit depredations. In the 1790s tighter slave controls and prohibition on immigration of blacks from the West Indies, where insurrection was rife, particularly in Haiti and Santo Domingo, lessened the prospect of maroonage. Slave rebelliousness, however, sprouted in North Carolina counties along the Roanoke River and Albemarle Sound regions and in central Virginia from 1794 to 1802.[43] In the 1790s several maroon camps were located briefly along the Combahee and Ashepoo rivers in southeastern South Carolina, from which the fugitives raided nearby plantations. The Revolution left some imprint on the pattern of slave resistance—of black bondsmen perceiving that collective action within society was more viable than withdrawing from it.[44]

One interesting episode during the war demonstrated the maroon skills of a band of slaves, who were not actually maroons. After the surrender of Fort Cornwallis (Augusta, Georgia) on June 5, 1781, John Burnet, serving with the Georgia militia despite his Tory leanings, was entrusted with the safekeeping of some of the captured stores until they could be divided among the victorious militiamen. Meanwhile, he carried out indiscriminate raids on property belonging to both rebels and Loyalists, and in doing so acquired some sixty slaves. Burnet persuaded his militia comrades to allow him to take the slaves into the mountains to prevent their seizure by the enemy. Burnet and his slave band, however, kept on going, remarkably making the hazardous trek across the Appalachians into Kentucky and down the Ohio River, in Indian country, and the Mississippi to Natchez, which was in territory claimed by both Britain and Spain. Burnet settled among the illegal immigrants, many of them ruffians from Kentucky, and divided the slaves among himself and several white companions.[45]

Maroonage during the Revolutionary period developed most extensively in Spanish Louisiana, amid the widespread swamps, bayous, and forests around New Orleans and at the rear of the lower Mississippi River plantations. Unlike the maroons in the Chesapeake region and the low country of the Carolinas and Georgia, maroon communities here kept open ties with plantation slaves, who provided food to the maroons and warned them about impending punitive efforts. In return, the maroons assisted slaves in their work, such as planting corn and gathering firewood. At the market in New Orleans, slaves from nearby plantations sold stolen goods and handicrafts, such as baskets and other articles made of willow, obtained from maroons. According to historian Ira Berlin, "maroon colonies thus became both an alternative to and an extension of the slave quarter, and maroon settlements or *pasaje* were literally passages that connected the lives of maroons and plantation slaves."[46]

A census of 1777 revealed 9,009 slaves, 8,383 whites, and 536 free blacks in Louisiana; a count in 1775 indicated 4,387 slaves in Lower Louisiana (the New Orleans District). When the Spaniards officially assumed control over Louisiana in 1766 they retained most of the harsh provisions of the French *Code Noir* (Black Code). Runaway slaves who were absent for a month or more were subject to having their ears cropped and being branded on one shoulder; a second offense called for being hamstrung and branded on the other shoulder; and a third brought the death penalty. The planters, however, were limited in exacting control over their slaves. Instructions from Charles III of Spain gave only civil and church officials the authority to punish slaves. Slaves resisting their masters were to be executed under government authority. The centralization of police power and the absence of a patrol system made it difficult to prevent slaves from running away and to apprehend the delinquents. To compound the problem, free blacks rather than soldiers were relied upon for enforcement. From 1777 to 1783 a company of free blacks stationed in New Orleans had the duty of apprehending maroons, a task that yielded little success.[47]

Fugitives from different plantations entrenched themselves in a maroon community, Gaillardland (*Gaillard Terre*), a vast area (now Saint Bernard's Parish) consisting of marshes and swamplands bordering Lake Borgne, several miles east of New Orleans. *Gaillard*, in translation, means the combined quality of being strong, healthy, free, adept, and clever. The maroons built cabins, which were held in common, and grew crops. By raiding plantations along the Mississippi River and Lake Borgne they acquired large quantities of rice, corn, and flour. Several of the leaders were carpenters and made tubs for indigo processing. The maroons fished in the bayous and the lake. Various commodities found their way to the New Orleans market or were sold to slaves in return for guns and ammunition. The maroons supplemented their diet with fowl, roots, and herbs.[48]

Juan Malò, who renamed himself San (Saint) Malò, became the undisputed leader of the Gaillardland maroons, having at his command over 100 banditti. San Malò had been a slave belonging to the commandant of the Saint Charles post on the German Coast on the Mississippi north of New Orleans. Courageous and daring, San Malò had an ability to win cooperation from plantation slaves. He was known to be cruel: he killed his mistress who wanted to return to her master, and he also murdered one of his men who refused to slaughter a calf as ordered. From 1780 to 1784, San Malò and his followers terrorized planters, pillaging their storehouses and stealing their cattle. Fear mounted that a general maroon war was imminent, similar to the one in Jamaica.[49] With the Revolutionary War in progress, the Spaniards pitted against the British for control of the lower Mississippi and the Gulf Coast, the government for the New Orleans District neglected taking punitive actions against the maroons. The planters soon exhausted funds raised from a levy they placed on themselves by paying recompense to owners whose slaves had been killed and the costs of sending the ineffective black militia against the maroons.

During 1782 and 1783, the maroons split Gaillardland into two sections. San Maló, though retaining a cabin for a subheadquarters at the original site, established a new settlement, called Chef Monteur, nearby. Juan Pedro and his son, Jolie Coeur, also known as El Caballero de la Hacha for having cleaved the head of a white man with an axe, took charge of those who remained behind.[50]

In March 1783, Lieutenant Guido Dufossat, a Frenchman in Spanish service and a plantation owner, conducted troops along with other whites and free blacks, aboard seven pirogues, into the swamps. At Gaillardland the invaders, formed into two detachments, captured forty-three maroons. It was a surprise to learn of the family networks among the slave fugitives. San Maló and some of his followers, who had been absent during the attack, tried unsuccesfully to rescue the captives. The destruction of the maroon village led San Maló and his band to find other campsites and to escalate the scale of depredations.[51]

The San Maló maroons became more deadly. Hitherto they had avoided killing whites. While traveling by boat to the Bay of Saint Louis, San Maló and his companions were enticed by a party of Americans to go ashore to exchange guns. The Americans shot one maroon dead and seized others of the fugitives. San Maló escaped, only to return with several of his followers. The maroons killed the four Americans; it was on this occasion that Jolie Coeur performed his hatchet head-splitting. Shortly afterward, the maroons killed four Englishmen.[52]

These killings and the increase in the number of runaway slaves, which underscored the possibility of a general slave insurrection, frightened the planters and the government into making a more determined effort to wipe out the maroons. Esteban Rodríguez Miró, the Spanish governor of Louisiana, in the spring of 1784, proclaimed tightened measures for slave control: any white person catching a slave away from his plantation was to administer twenty-five lashes on the spot and return the culprit to his master; trade with slaves was forbidden; and masters were to imprison any slave found providing food or shelter to fugitives.[53]

The Dufossat expedition of 1783 had delivered a hard blow to the San Maló maroons, who subsequently set up camp behind the Prévost planta-

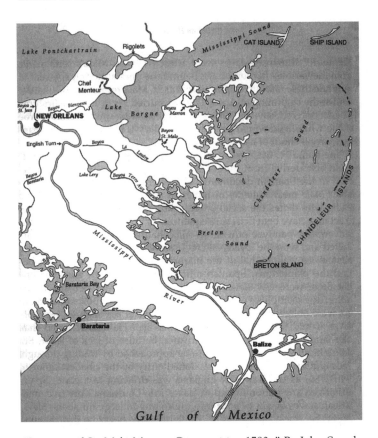

"Location of St. Maló Maroon Communities, 1780s." By John Snead.
Reprinted by permission of Louisiana State University Press from *Afri-cans in Colonial Louisiana: The Development of Afro-Creole Culture in the Eighteenth Century*, by Gwendolyn Midlo Hall. Copyright © 1992 by Louisiana State University Press.

tion. There they had a close relationship with the Prévost slaves, who turned over cattle to the maroons; in return, members of the San Maló band joined in the work chores of the slaves. Slaves and maroons daily ate together in the woods, and some of San Malo's men had wives on the plantation. A quarrel over the affections of a woman, however, spoiled the alliance, and a Prévost bondsman revealed to his master the arrangement between the slaves and the maroons. A crackdown on the Prévost slaves deprived San Maló and his band of supplies and information.[54]

While Miró and the Spanish intendant, Martin Navarro, journeyed to Pensacola to attend an Indian congress, the New Orleans Cabildo (town council) pressed upon Lieutenant Colonel Francis Domingo Joseph Bouligny, acting governor and military commandant, to undertake an expedition against the maroons. A captured runaway slave, who had lived with the maroons for six months, informed the authorities that the Maló band, last known to be lying out in the bayous, had returned to their former hideouts in Gaillardland. Bouligny organized a large force, divided into separate probing units, to sweep through the area suspected of being the haunts of the fugitives. Captain Gilberto Guillemard, an army engineer, was placed in charge of the field operations; his force consisted of regular and militia troops and a detachment of free and enslaved Africans. Blacks had been an important component of Spanish forces in the Floridas and Louisiana during the Revolution.

San Maló's band, at the time, had dwindled to thirty-eight persons, including at least twelve women. Lieutenant Pierre de Marigny, who was leading a party, found San Maló's camp, but he fired prematurely, allowing the maroons to escape. Marigny destroyed the huts of the makeshift village. Eventually San Maló and fifty runaways were caught in Guillemard's net. San Maló was shot in one arm, which soon developed gangrene. Guillemard and his prisoners sailed in pirogues up the Mississippi. Local planters lined the riverside to hail the event. The procession reached New Orleans on June 12, 1784.[55]

San Maló did not receive a trial, only a hearing before Francisco de Reggio, the chief magistrate (*alcalde ordinario*) in New Orleans. Dying from gangrene, San Maló confessed to his crimes and prevailed upon several of his companions to do the same. Reggio gave death sentences to San Maló, Jolie Coeur, two henchmen known only as Michel and Henry, and San Maló's woman friend, Cecilia Canoy. Other captured maroons received punishment that included up to 300 lashes, the branding of an "M" on the cheek, wearing irons for three months, and banishment. Although the condemnations met criticism for denial of regular trials and not waiting for the return of Governor Miró to Louisiana, the swift justice was considered necessary to deter a slave rebellion.

San Maló and his three male cohorts went to their deaths on a gallows in the Plaza de Armas (later Jackson Square) in New Orleans on June 19, 1784. Cecilia Canoy, pleading pregnancy, was reprieved; her ultimate fate is unknown. Four more of the San Maló gang were hanged the following August.[56]

According to legend, San Maló's body was left hanging to rot and have its flesh plucked by birds. In memory, he was revered as a folk hero. A Creole slave song, popular among New Orleans blacks after the Civil War, mourns his death.

The Dirge of San Malo (translation)
Alas! young men, come, make lament
For poor St. Malo in distress!
They chased, they hunted him with dogs.
They fired at him with a gun.
    . . . . [portion not extant]
They hauled him from the cypress swamp,
His arms they tied behind his back,
They tied his hands in front of him;
They tied him to a horse's tail,
They dragged him up into the town,
Before those grand Cabildo men.
They charged that he had made a plot
To cut the throats of all the whites.
They asked him who his comrades were;
Poor St. Malo said not a word;
The judge his sentence read to him,
And then they raised the gallows-tree.
They drew the horse—the cart moved off—
And left St. Malo hanging there.
The sun was up an hour high
When on the levee he was hung;
They left his body swinging there,
For carrion crows to feed upon.[57]

The roundup of the San Maló band and other slave fugitives yielded 103 captives. Besides those otherwise punished, fifty maroons were imprisoned. Maroonage hereafter came to be only a minor irritant. The more stringent slave controls and the difficulties of subsisting in the swamps worked against the formation of maroon communities. After 1786 the Spaniards began restricting slave importations from the West Indies, and by 1796, because of the slave revolts in the Caribbean, prohibited entry of all slaves. This measure was somewhat abridged by the granting of exemptions, smuggling, and, from 1795 on, slavers taking advantage of the United States gaining free navigation of the Mississippi.[58]

Poor whites learned how to survive in the swamps, largely through hunting and fishing, from fugitive slaves. Speaking Louisiana Creole, the white denizens of the swamps today refer to themselves as coon-asses, signifying the defiance, craftiness, and self-sufficiency of the raccoon.[59]

During the Revolutionary War period, the cutting loose of a large number of slaves from their masters in the south Atlantic states and the initial laxity in slave supervision in Louisiana encouraged maroonage. In time, stiffened regulations and enforcement curtailing mobility and the interconnection between fugitives and plantation slaves diminished opportunity for survival as maroons.

While slave runaways forming bands remained a problem for the slav-ocracy on through the Civil War, such groups had to keep on the run, and they lacked the capacity for secure defense, a self-sustaining economy, and replenishment of their numbers.

What maroon success there was during the Revolutionary War period resulted from the slowness of authorities to discover hideaways and to meet the challenge with adequate funds and manpower. Persistent depredations, especially the killing of whites, brought about effective punitive measures.

Maroonage gained some momentum when whites and slaves migrated into Tennessee and the Gulf states, but even then slave fugitives found it very difficult to establish communities. New African slaves did not tend to join maroon bands, and Creole bondsmen had forfeited much of their native African ability to live in the wilds.[60]

During the Revolutionary War, the broad frontier, west and south, af-forded no safety valve for fugitive slaves, with the Indian barrier and British-controlled Florida. Runaways could expect to find refuge almost exclusively within small interior "frontiers"—pockets of marshes, swamps, and forests enclosed by white settlements. Lacking in numbers and the mountainous terrain that made some of the West Indian maroon communities a lasting success, the American fugitives were never in a position to bargain, or even make treaties (as did the maroons in Jamaica), with their former masters. At best the North American maroons were outlyers, who, for a time, robbed provisions and livestock from neighboring farms and plantations. Even the maroons of the Dismal Swamp in Virginia and North Carolina never evolved into an organized and stable society capable of confronting the full power of the whites.

Chapter 12

Scopholites

"The Scopholites were some of the tories who were led by one Col. Scophol, Col. of militia, an illiterate, stupid, noisy blockhead," wrote William Moultrie.[1] The South Carolina general was referring to Joseph Coffell (variations in name include Coffel, Scovil, Scoffel, and Scophol). As the war progressed, Scopholite (or Scofellite) became a derisive term applied to Tory partisans of the South Carolina backcountry who made raids against the rebels and who trekked to East Florida, from where, as refugees, they assisted British forces in the invasion of Georgia and the Carolinas.

The Scopholites coalesced as a self-conscious minority out of the troubled times of the late 1760s. Scotch-Irish and German pioneers from Pennsylvania, Virginia, and North Carolina had migrated down the western valleys into the South Carolina backcountry, taking up parcels of 100 acres of farmland offered free by the South Carolina government. The newcomers settled amid a frontier mix of rootless folk—hunters, thieves, escaped slaves, and other discards of society. The western settlers lived a kind of maroon-like existence, cut off entirely from the 100-mile westward stretch of the low country. The rivers in the backcountry were unnavigable. At the fall line, the Sand Hills, the middle country, a pine belt from twenty to forty miles in width, formed a barrier between backcountry and low country. The South Carolina backcountry extended for some 100 miles through the Piedmont and hills. The Scopholites came principally from the region between the Broad and Saluda rivers.[2]

Without a governmental system in the backcountry, anarchy prevailed. To attend court, one had to travel a great distance to Charleston, South Carolina. Living side by side with the small planters and farmers in the backcountry, as Richard M. Brown noted, were "hunters and squatters, absconded debtors, idlers, gamblers, and unsavory refugees from the northern colonies . . . deserters from the military forces, and, often, mulattoes, Negroes, or people of mixed white, Indian, and Negro blood."[3] By the mid-1760s outlaw groups pounded the backcountry with robberies and depredations against the more respectable settlers of the area. An Anglican missionary in the region was shocked at "the Number of Idle, profligate, audacious Vagabonds! Lewd, impudent, abandon'd Prostitutes Gamblers Gamesters of all Sorts—Horse Thieves Cattle Stealers, Hog Stealers," especially "pernicious" when "United in Gangs and Combinations."[4]

Among the occupants of the South Carolina backcountry were "crackers," a breed of ruffians living at the farthest edge of the southern frontier, although later in history "crackers" referred to those listless, poor whites existing in squalor primarily in upper Georgia. Crackers, at the time of the Revolution, were usually of Scotch-Irish extraction. In Scottish parlance, "crack" meant to talk boastingly, and a "cracker" was a "noisy boasting fellow."[5] Reverend Charles Woodmason warned travelers to avoid "the Virginia Crackers—for they'l bluster and make a Noise about a Turd."[6] Gavin Cochrane, a British army captain on a tour of inspection in June 1766, wrote to Lord Dartmouth, explaining "what is meant by Crackers, a name they have got from being great boasters; they are a lawless set of rascals on the frontiers of Virginia, Maryland, the Carolinas, and Georgia, who often change their places of abode."[7] James Habersham, in 1772, referred to "Crackers" living above Augusta, Georgia, as having "no settled Habitations" and subsisting "by hunting and plundering."[8] General Archibald Campbell reported in March 1779 that a large number of "irregulars from the upper country" of South Carolina, known as "Crackers," had joined British troops in Augusta.[9] "Cracker" may also in small part be derived from "Creeker." A German officer serving in the South in 1782 referred to the high rate of desertion in "a detachment of 'Creekers,' people who live along the little rivers and creeks and who, in return for provisions, have taken up arms in behalf of the [royal] government."[10]

Criminal activity ran amok in the backcountry. Some of the culprits were arrested and convicted, but the new South Carolina governor, Lord Charles Greville Montague, to inaugurate his administration in 1766 with a gesture of good will, pardoned the malefactors. Outraged property holders in the backcountry protested and demanded protection and a fair share in government for their region, which now had 75 percent of the colony's population. In response, the legislature established circuit courts and allowed six representatives in the Commons House of Assembly for the backcountry; two ranger companies were to be raised to get rid of the outlaws.[11] The rangers and their supporters styled themselves Regulators.

The Regulators wasted no time in taking on the outlaws. Bandit leaders, such as Govee Black, were summarily executed, and others fled. The Regulators scoured both the South Carolina and North Carolina backcountry. Sixteen members of a maroon-like outlaw community in Mount Airy, North Carolina, were hanged, and stolen horses and kidnapped young girls were brought away from the camp. By March 1768, the Regulators had largely achieved their goal. Unfortunately, they turned their attention to punishing persons thought to have aided and abetted the outlaws and to disciplining "worthless, vagrant People." The Regulators "pull'd down the Houses of all who had entertain'd secreted, abetted, and supported these Gangs of Thieves Whipped the Magistrates Who went Snacks with them in their Plunder, and protected them."[12]

Many property holders came under the excessive vengeance of the Regulators. Soon those who were oppressed, calling themselves "Moderators," rallied against the Regulators. The backcountry had two "parties," according to a biased Charleston newspaper:

the *first* (called the *Honest Party*) consists, in general, of People of good Principles, and Property, who have assembled . . . professedly with the View of driving all Horse-Thieves, with their Harbourers, Abettors, and other Vagabonds, from amongst them; and that the *other* (called the *Rogues Party*) are a Gang of Banditti, or numerous Collection of outcast Mulattoes, Mustees, free Negroes, all Horse-Thieves, etc., from the Borders of Virginia and other Northern Colonies . . . and have taken up Arms to carry on their Villainy with Impunity.[13]

The South Carolina government was unwilling to intervene in the backcountry to avert civil war. An assistant judge, however, took it upon himself to issue a bench warrant for the arrest of the twenty-five persons most responsible for "Riots and Tumults in the Back Country" and any others who might have committed "Outrages or Misdemeanors."

Joseph Coffell, "one of the Greatest Villains and Scoundrels in the Creation," was assigned to execute the warrant. Nothing is known of the early life of Coffell. He was probably the son of Philip and Rachel Scofield of Prince Frederick Parish. In his youth he allegedly was a "roamer" in the backcountry, where he mingled with both settlers and outlaws. From 1758 to 1772, he was a constable for the Broad-Saluda fork area. In 1771 a 250-acre tract of land was surveyed for him near Orangeburg.[14]

Coffell falsely claimed that he had a colonel's commission from the crown and that he was "cloathed with an authority superior to all the Country Magistrates and Militia Officers." He enlisted men into his service at £20 per month and "a bottle of rum." Coffell collected "all the Rogues whom the two Troops of Rangers had dispers'd—and with his Band of Ruffians, enters ev'ry House around, carrying off Horses, Meal, Corn, and Provisions, of all Kinds." For several weeks Coffell and his followers continued the rampage, in the meantime taking Regulator leaders into custody.[15]

Bands of Coffell's Moderators, some 600 in all, skirmished with Regulators. Learning of Coffell's violation of his trust, the South Carolina government disowned him and stripped him of authority to make arrests and sent out three emissaries—Richard Richardson, Daniel McGirth, and William Thompson—with orders to disband Coffell's troops. On March 26, 1769, as the Moderators and Regulators prepared to do battle at the junction of the Bush and Saluda rivers, the three delegates persuaded the opposing forces to lay down their arms and to abide by South Carolina law.[16]

Although the South Carolina backcountry quieted down, supporters of the Moderator movement substantially filled the ranks of the Loyalists when the war came. Harboring resentment against the South Carolina government, dominated by low-country grandees, the former Moderators were not unlike the backcountry protesters in North Carolina, who, styling themselves Regulators, had actually rebelled, but were crushed in battle in 1771. The Moderators versus the Regulators (not to be confused with the North Carolina Regulators) in the South Carolina backcountry was a local struggle between two social elements, tinged with revenge and vigilantism.

Joseph Coffell's influence seems to have waned. He does not appear to have been engaged as a particular leader during the events that led up to the Revolution or the war itself, although evidently he did serve as a Loyalist militia officer. He had the dubious distinction of the rebels conferring his name on backcountry Loyalists. A reason for Coffell's obscurity probably was a result of his reputation falling into disrepute. In April 1772 a Charleston court found Coffell, "Constable in the District between the Waters of Saluda and Broad River," guilty "of evil Practices in the Execution of his Office, as well as in assuming greater Authority than a Constable had a Right to do," and ordered his dismissal as a constable.[17] The next year the Orangeburg circuit court convicted Coffell of cattle stealing and petit larceny and sentenced him to twenty lashes for the former and nineteen for the latter. Coffell had been charged with petit larceny for stealing thirty-eight chickens. Coffell swore this was "a dom'd lie, there were only six and thirty, for I eat the guzzards."[18]

Tories in the South Carolina backcountry became militarily active at the start of the war. A "great proportion of them," wrote David Ramsay not long after the Revolution, "was an ignorant unprincipled banditti, to whom idleness, licentiousness and deeds of violence were familiar. Horse-thieves and others whose crimes had exiled them from society, attached themselves to parties of the British."[19]

Fort Charlotte, on the Savannah River opposite Augusta, a post that the South Carolina Council of State said was defended by "one Coffell" and his followers, fell to patriot militia in June 1775; there is no record whether Coffell was actually there or was captured. Two hundred backcountry Loyalists, commanded by Major Joseph Robinson and Captains Robert and Patrick Cunningham, however, intercepted ammunition sent by the patriot force at Fort Charlotte destined for Ninety-Six Courthouse.[20]

Not all backcountry people who took up arms were poor people or border ruffians. Some prominent and wealthy inhabitants embraced the British cause. Richard Pearis, who served as a Scopholite captain, had long been a successful Indian trader and speculator, and at the start of the war he owned 20,000 acres of land and twenty-six slaves. Colonel Thomas Fletchall, who received a colonel's commission from Governor Montague, had the overall command of the backcountry Loyalist militia. He had a large plantation in the upper Saluda District, near the Broad River; made a prisoner of war in late 1775, he left South Carolina for the West Indies after his release in the summer of 1776. Patrick and Robert Cunningham, members of a Scottish family who migrated from Virginia in 1769, settled in the Ninety-Six District, near the Saluda River, and became substantial landowners. Robert Cunningham rose to the rank of brigadier general of Loyalist militia serving with Cornwallis's army.[21]

With the threatened disaffection of the whole South Carolina backcountry, the Council of Safety sent a five-man commission to the area, including William H. Drayton, Reverend William Tennent (Presbyterian), Joseph Kershaw, Colonel Richard Richardson, and Reverend Oliver Hart (Baptist). Despite the delegates' visiting separately many places, assiduously trying to win support for the rebel cause, they were unsuccessful in their mission. Learning that the Loyalist leaders assembled troops, Drayton, who had authorization from the Council of Safety to do the same, gathered patriot militia. In early September 1775, the two forces encamped near each other on opposite sides of the Saluda River. Bloodshed was avoided by an agreement to a treaty, whereby backcountry people did not have to swear acceptance of the Association (sanctions imposed by the Continental Congress) and in return promised not to aid British troops in South Carolina.[22]

Many backcountry Loyalists, however, were dissatisfied with the terms of the truce agreement. In early November 1775, the patriot authorities in Charleston learned that "the Scoffel lights were coming down from the back

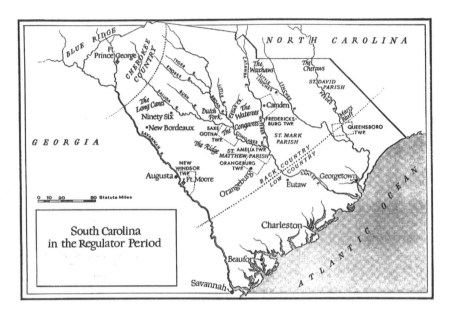

"South Carolina in the Regulator Period." From Richard M. Brown, *The South Caro-lina Regulators* (Cambridge: Harvard University Press, 1963). Reproduced by permission of Richard M. Brown.

country in great force." It was feared that their first objective would be an ammunition depot at Dorchester, thirty-five miles northwest of Charleston.[23]

From November 19 to 22, backcountry Loyalists invested a temporary fort constructed by patriots out of fence rails, straw, and cattle hides at the courthouse village in the Ninety-Six District. After an almost continuous exchange of fire for three days, again both sides arranged a truce: the patriots would destroy the fortifications, and the Loyalist troops would withdraw to beyond the Saluda River.[24]

The revolutionary South Carolina government, who viewed the Loyalist retreat as a show of weakness and a lack of resolution, quickly violated the truce and ordered Colonel Richard Richardson, a seventy-year-old commander, and several thousand troops to sweep through the backcountry. Richardson, who took instantly to the field, issued a declaration on December 8, 1775:

To satisfy public justice in the just punishment of all which crimes and offences, as far as the nature of the same will admit, I am now come into these parts, in the name and behalf of the Colonies to demand of the inhabitants, the delivery up of the bodies of all the principal offenders herein, together with the said ammunition and full restitution for the ravages committed, and also the arms and ammunition of all the aiders and abettors of these robbers, murderers, and disturbers of the peace and good order as afore-said; and, in case of refusal or neglect, for the space of five days, I shall be under a necessity of taking such steps as will be found disagreeable, but which I shall certainly put in execution for the public good.[25]

Many "insurgents" abided by the declaration, giving up their arms, and were treated with "soft words, and kind admonitions." Nevertheless, about 200 of those Loyalists who had formed a military force refused to surrender and "constantly retreated," keeping twenty miles distant from Richardson's troops. Pursuit extended deep into the interior, with prisoners taken along the way, including Colonel Thomas Fetchall, who was "unkennelled" from a cave. The Loyalists finally settled into a camp at Great Cane Brake, on the Reedy River, four miles within the borders of Cherokee territory. On December 22, Richardson attacked the Loyalist camp in the battle of the Canebrakes. There were only a few casualties on each side. Being fore-warned, many of the Loyalists had fled; the others were made prisoners. With the "insurrection" now crushed and his men not having tents and proper winter clothing, Richardson marched his army "downwards" and dis-banded his troops upon reaching "their old camp on the Congarees" on January 1, 1776. Because of the heavy snowfall encountered on the return, Richardson's expedition became known as the Snow Campaign.[26]

Captain Thomas Sumter conveyed the 136 prisoners down the Congaree and Santee rivers to Nelson Ferry, from where a detachment of South Car-olina rangers escorted them to Charleston. Six of the prisoners were listed as "scopholite" officers, five of them as "scopholite Captain." Like the ear-lier Scopholites, the captives represented an ethnic and racial diversity. Two of the Scopholite captains were not white: a Captain Jones was a "colored Powder Man," and Captain William Hunt, a "Mulatto." Most of the prisoners were Germans or Scotch-Irish, along with a few Scots, who had arrived in South Carolina after the Cherokee War of 1759–61 to take up 100-acre bounty lands. Seven of the prisoners had appended after their names "a very bad man." All but about a dozen of the captives soon gained release. Eventually all were amnestied in the summer of 1776 largely be-cause the British naval force that had entered Charleston harbor had left, and a war erupting on the frontier with the Cherokee Indians temporarily presented South Carolinians with a common cause.[27] Even then, several groups of Loyalists trekked through the South Carolina and Georgia back-country into East Florida to join British military forces in Saint Augus-tine.[28]

Militia campaigns conducted by South Carolinians, North Carolinians, and Virginians deep into the Cherokee country brought widespread destruc-tion of native villages and crops. The Indian treaties of Dewitt's Corner

(May 20, 1777) with South Carolina, and Georgia, and of Long Island, on the Holston River (July 20, 1777) with Virginia and North Carolina, concluded the war, providing for the Indian cession of all lands east of the Blue Ridge and territory at South Carolina's northwest border, adjoining the Ninety-Six District. The Cherokees were disappointed in not having received British military assistance.

White renegades from the Carolina backcountry joined the Indians during the Cherokee War. Colonel Andrew Williamson's campaign was viewed as a punitive expedition against "Indians and Scovilites." The South Carolina troops captured whites "painted like Indians." Some of the more respectable backcountry Loyalists also aided the Indians. Richard Pearis's house on his large plantation, within Cherokee country on the Reedy River, was used as a "rendezvous for the Indians and Scopholites." At the start of the Indian war, in July 1776, David Fanning, who himself had once been an Indian trader, and twenty-five other men joined other whites to form "a Junction with the Indians" at the Pearis estate. The combined party of about ninety Indians and 120 white men "Sarrounded" Lyndley's Fort, defended by 450 rebels. After "a smart firing on both sides," the attackers retreated; in pursuit, the rebels captured thirteen white men, nine of whom were painted and dressed as Indians.[29] According to historian Rachel N. Klein, the "evidence of close cooperation between scoffelites and Indians is a further indication of continuity between hunters and bandits of the 1760s and tories during the Revolution."[30]

Backcountry Loyalists hesitated to renew the war with the rebels, in view of having been beaten each time they had taken up arms. Settlers feared for their property and families. The undesirable element of the backcountry, the true "Scopholities," however, were anxious to link up with British troops and thereby, under protective cover, be able to carry on plundering raids. A Loyalist military response depended upon whether the British would stage invasions of Georgia and the Carolinas.

When British troops were sent to East Florida in 1778 to conduct a Southern offensive, backcountry Loyalists again were inspired to resort to arms. Lieutenant Colonel Thomas Brown, who commanded Tory rangers in East Florida, made contacts with the Loyalists of the South Carolina backcountry; in spring 1778, he reported that 2,500 men from between the forks of the Broad and Saluda rivers were pledged to join him "on any Service whenever orders are sent for that purpose" and that 3,000 more from the South Carolina and North Carolina backcountry were ready to fight.[31] Instead of igniting an independent uprising in the backcountry, which would cause immediate punitive action from rebel militia and Continental army troops then in the South, it made sense that militarily embodied Loyalists strike out southward to connect with British forces in East Florida, counting on the element of surprise to keep patriot forces at bay.

In late March 1778, some 400 Loyalists from the Ninety-Six District, led by Benjamin Gregory and John Murphy, headed for East Florida. Captain John York, one of the "white Indians," was recruited by Brown to conduct another party on the same mission, but York's delay in appearing at the rendezvous afforded time for rebel militia to be alerted, and therefore, the march of this second group was canceled.[32]

All but a few of the Gregory and Murphy party were mounted on horseback. These "Scopholites" traveled swiftly, pausing only briefly to find "Shelter in the woods"; bringing few provisions with them, they made "prize of all as they march along." On April 3, 1778, after commandeering "trading boats," they crossed the Savannah River about forty miles below Augusta. A "number of insurgents" from the Georgia backcountry, including Loyalists led by Colonel John Thomas, and even some deserters from a rebel force "stationed beyond the Ogeechee" joined the trekkers, increasing the Scopholite group to about 600 men. Hoisting "the King's Standard as they passed," the fleeing Loyalists continued to commit "outrages and many Robberies particularly of Horses, Provisions Arms & Ammunition." They "made little Halt" until they reached the Satilla River, in the southeast corner of Georgia, where they encamped for several days.[33]

The Scopholite traverse of South Carolina and Georgia caused panic among patriot authorities. The plundering did not matter so much as the fact that the episode signaled the reinforcement of British forces in East Florida, that more disaffected inhabitants probably would try to link up with the enemy, and that the backcountry itself was seething with Loyalist insurgency.

Colonel Andrew Williamson and the South Carolina militia, on one occasion, ran across the trekkers and managed to capture "30 Scopholites in arms." But the Loyalists kept ahead of any sizeable body of pursuers. General Robert Howe, commander of Continental troops in the South, from his headquarters in Savannah, sent a detachment under Colonel Samuel Elbert after the fleeing Loyalists. Elbert planned to intercept the enemy at the Satilla River, but this was prevented by "unfortunate heavy rains" which forced Elbert to halt for two days.[34]

The Georgia Executive Council reacted to the crisis:

Whereas there is great reason to apprehend some dangerous attempt is meditated against this State—many of the back inhabitants of South Carolina having passed over the River with a manifest intention of joining the Enemy in East Florida It is Therefore Ordered that the Militia throughout the State be immediately embodied—that a Draft of two thirds of each Battalion be immediately made and marched into Barracks or in pursuit of the Enemy as the Commanding Officer of the County from Circumstances shall judge advisable until further orders or if such Commanding Officer shall deem it necessary that he call out the whole of the said County Militia and that every measure be embraced to quell the present insurrection.[35]

The Scopholites crossed Saint Marys River into East Florida and pitched camp on Trout Creek, ten miles from its junction with Saint Johns River. A few weeks later they stationed themselves near the British-held Fort Tonyn on Saint Marys River. The newcomers became "extremely discontented," and they talked of returning "back again from whence they came." General Augustine Prevost visited their camp and "pacified them for the Present."[36] Still some returned home, carrying their booty with them. Providing for the Scopholites was a burden since 2,500 refugees (1,500 whites and 1,000 blacks), over a three-year period, had already arrived in East Florida.[37]

Some of the Scopholites, whose number had dwindled to 350 by June, joined Lieutenant Colonel Thomas Brown's King's (or East Florida) Rangers; others waited to be organized into a Loyalist regiment of their own. Brown's Rangers had already struck terror into Georgia. Brown had immigrated from England at the age of twenty-four and acquired 5,600 acres of ceded Creek Indian lands. Because of his steadfast refusal to support the Revolution, he was tarred and feathered on August 1, 1775; thereafter, he joined armed Loyalists of the South Carolina backcountry and received a commission to command mounted rangers in 1776. In March 1778, rebel governor John Houstoun of Georgia commented that Brown's "Banditti" had "robbed, plundered and insulted" some of "our most worthy Inhabitants." Houstoun estimated that the "effective men" in East Florida were "chiefly Renegades" from South Carolina and Georgia.[38] Four months later, a Charleston newspaper described Brown's Rangers as composed of

about 40 vagabond savages (out-casts of the Creek nation) about 150 of the most infamous horse thieves and other banditti (worse than savages) that have fled from the frontier parts of this state and Georgia, during the last three years, and run-away debtors; together with a number of those poor, deluded, ignorant people, who have been seduced, or terrified, by a variety of arts, to abandon their families and settlements, under promise of vast encouragement . . . and clap on them, in a little while, the soldiers garb, and compel them to rob, murder, scalp, and spread desolation, with as little remorse as the rest of the gang.[39]

General Prevost, not knowing what else to do with the refugees from South Carolina who had not returned home or had joined Brown's Rangers, in May 1778 formed them into a provincial corps—the South Carolina

Royalists—consisting of four infantry companies of forty-five men each and two rifle dragoon companies of forty each. Three months later, the corps was reestablished with eight companies of fifty rank and file each. The enlistees were provided with arms and uniformed with red coats faced with yellow. The South Carolina Royalists, who served until the end of the war, participated in many military actions; the strength of the corps was eventually raised to 660 men.

General Henry Clinton, the British commander in chief in America, named the officers: Alexander Innes, colonel and commander; Joseph Robinson and Evan McLaurin, majors. Both Robinson and McLaurin had been Loyalist militia officers at the siege of Ninety-Six in November 1775 and had lived in the Broad-Saluda river area of South Carolina. With Innes preferring to stay in Savannah, Robinson had "almost the Sole Command" of the South Carolina Royalists.

Clinton objected to the pay of 1s. per day afforded the soldiers of the South Carolina Royalists and other provincial units based in East Florida; the compensation was higher than that given to regular British troops and northern Loyalists in military service. Nevertheless, Governor Patrick Tonyn of East Florida and General Prevost prevailed in maintaining the higher pay, the reasoning being that the Loyalist refugee troops in East Florida received no bounties for enlisting, did not have any provision for barracks, supplied their own horses, and engaged in continual service in the field.[40]

The Loyalist refugee forces in East Florida posed a double threat: the continuance of raids into Georgia and the enhancement of British military capability to invade the Deep South. Already the British had an advantage on the Georgia–East Florida frontier. In early 1777 William Moultrie, commanding Continentals and militia, set out to invade East Florida. The expedition, however, was abandoned in progress because of disease among the troops and insufficient equipment. Meanwhile the enemy crossed the border and captured the American garrison at Fort McIntosh on the Satilla River. In May 1778 Brigadier General Robert Howe gathered a mix of 2,250 Continentals and South Carolina and Georgia militia at Fort Howe on the Altamaha River for the purpose of securing the area between the Saint Marys and Saint Johns rivers and capturing Saint Augustine. To resist the invasion, General Augustine Prevost readied his force of 800 regulars and 600 other troops, composed of provincial militia, South Carolina and Georgia refugee Loyalists, and some Creek Indians.[41]

With the American advance, the British forward post, Fort Tonyn, manned by Brown's Rangers and South Carolina Royalists, was abandoned. Confusion as to command—which Howe and John Houstoun both claimed—lack of provisions, disease, desertion, and dilatoriness in getting militia into the field all hindered the American advance. On June 29 Houstoun and his militia attacked a Ranger and South Carolina Royalist force at Alligator Creek Bridge, fourteen miles below Fort Tonyn on Saint Marys River. After a heated engagement, the Georgians beat a retreat. Fifteen Scopholites deserted and showed up at Houstoun's camp; the Georgians had been able to take a few prisoners, including "Ensign Gigilighter of the South Carolina Royalists who wore yellow breeches." General Prevost did not order the pursuit of the withdrawing Georgians.[42]

The American expedition against East Florida had ended without any penetration into enemy territory; the only achievement was the enemy's evacuation of Fort Tonyn. The British retreated to Saint Johns River, forgoing any counteroffensive for the time being. During late summer of 1778, however, "a number of men inimical to the measures of America" who had "joined the enemy in East Florida" were "daily coming in Scouts or parties and robbing and plundering the inhabitants" of Georgia.[43]

Late 1778 British war strategy shifted from northern operations to an invasion of the Southern states, initially aimed at securing Georgia and then capturing Charleston. In November, General Henry Clinton dispatched 4,000 troops under Lieutenant Colonel Archibald Campbell to capture Savannah and to coordinate operations with General Prevost's army from East Florida. Preliminary to the assault on Savannah, Major Mark Prevost, with 750 men, including the South Carolina Royalists, marched northward in the expectation of capturing Sunbury, a port town south of Savannah. Major Prevost, on November 24, skirmished with a small force of Continental troops and Georgia militia, commanded by Colonel John White and militia general James Screven, in thick woods near Midway Meetinghouse. Screven was mortally wounded, and the Americans made a hasty retreat. Prevost and the British forces returned to East Florida, scouring the Georgia countryside on the way, taking 2,000 head of cattle and 200 slaves. In East Florida, Prevost sold the plunder at public auction for £8,000.[44]

The South Carolina Royalists were among the troops at Savannah who thwarted the Franco-American siege of September–October 1779. During 1780 the South Carolina Royalists had duty in the area of their former homes, in the Ninety-Six District. On August 18, 1780, about half of the unit fought with other provincial troops against rebel militia commanded by Isaac Shelby and Elijah Clarke at Musgrove's Mill on the Enoree River; the Loyalists suffered heavy casualties—sixty-three killed, ninety wounded, and seventy captured—while their opponents had only four killed and eight wounded. The South Carolina Royalists were at the battle of Hobkirk's Hill on April 24, 1781, and they retreated with Lieutenant Colonel Francis Lord Rawdon's army to the seacoast. They established their base at the Quarter House, near Charleston. When Lieutenant Colonel Innes left for New York in May 1781, Major Thomas Fraser replaced him in charge of the South Carolina Royalists, which then consisted of five cavalry units totaling 209 men and one infantry company of fifty-five troops. In 1782 John Harrison's South Carolina Rangers were incorporated as a company in Fraser's corps. The last major battle for the South Carolina Royalists occurred at Eutaw Springs, on September 8, 1781; afterward, they had a few skirmishes with Francis Marion's rebel militia and went on raids into the interior to procure cattle and slaves.[45]

In October 1782 the South Carolina Royalists sailed from Charleston to Saint Augustine; the group consisted of 242 troops, 52 women and children, and 31 servants. The Loyalist refugee soldiers helped maintain the garrison at Saint Augustine until the spring of 1783, when their numbers had dwindled to 200 people. Most of the Scopholite riffraff had been weeded out by then. Captain Patrick Murray of Prevost's Royal American Regiment said a few years before that the South Carolina Royalists were the "remains and descendants of the Palatines." In October 1783 those who wanted to return to their homes or stay in the soon-to-be Spanish-controlled East Florida were discharged. Sixty-four others, commanded by Captain George Dawkins, who previously had recruited 100 men in South Carolina for the corps, sailed for Nova Scotia, where they were discharged upon arrival. These immigrants received lands granted by the British government: 200 acres for each noncommissioned officer and 100 acres for each private; no quitrents or fees were required until after ten years. The remnant South Carolina Royalists settled around Stormont at Country Harbor, Guysborough, Nova Scotia. Those who elected to remain in East Florida became part of the lawless element that plagued the East Florida–Georgia border.[46]

The Carolina and Georgia backcountry refugees who fled to East Florida and formed the ranks of Loyalist military units, such as the South Carolina Royalists (initially drawn from the Scopholites), South Carolina Rangers, King's Rangers, and Royal North Carolina Regiment, provided valuable service to the British during the war. During the British southern campaigns of 1779–82, a large number of backcountry inhabitants rose to fight under the royal standard: among their leaders were Brigadier General Robert Cunningham, who commanded all the Loyalist militia in the Ninety-Six District, James Boyd, David Fanning, and William "Bloody Bill" Cunningham. The internecine war in the backcountry incurred a heavy toll in lives and atrocities. Of 137 battles fought in South Carolina, 40 occurred in the Ninety-Six District. Count Francisco de Miranda, the Latin American revolutionary, commented during his American tour that "in District No. 96" there were "twelve hundred widows. Whoever wants to choose a wife, therefore, should come to this land of abundance."[47]

The South Carolina backcountry seemed ready to revert to the anarchy and outlawry of the 1760s. Governor Thomas Burke of North Carolina, in March 1782, inquired of Governor John Mathews of South Carolina what should be done in the backcountry where "predatory habits" persisted; the people, who, "being originally outlaws," during the war had become "remorseless plunderers and murderers."[48] Aedanus Burke, a Charleston lawyer who was a backcountry judge, in 1784 observed that settlers in the Ninety-Six District were "worried and half ruined by a sett of horse thieves and outlying Banditti that constantly beset the roads, rob the inhabitants and plunder their dwellings." Trade had all but ceased in the district; as soon as wagoners from Charleston crossed the Saluda River they were set upon by robbers.[49]

Criminals from the low country reappeared in the Ninety-Six District, and if hard pressed by pursuers sought refuge on the frontier. Three malefactors—John Black, Zekial Maulfers, and Lark Loudon—"plundered and murdered" in the low country and also crossed over into Georgia doing the same. After committing a murder at Cherry Hill, Georgia, John Black and an accomplice were caught and hanged. Maulfers and Loudon stole horses and five slaves belonging to Judge Thomas Heyward, a signer of the Declaration of Independence, and others who resided in southeastern South Carolina and "started for the Western country." A foursome of Tarleton Brown, Benjamin Brown, Richard Simmons, and Gill Thomas trailed the two fugitives through the northwestern part of the state and up beyond the Watauga River in eastern Tennessee. The bandits were captured, although one was soon killed while trying to escape. With the other robber and the stolen horses and slaves in tow, the posse wound their way back across the mountains in two feet of snow and extreme cold. The prisoner was lodged for a while in the Ninety-Six District jail, before being taken to Beaufort, South Carolina, for trial and execution.[50]

There was danger that vigilantism might surface again, this time aimed at both outlaws and former Loyalists known for the cruelties they inflicted on rebels. Matthew Love, a former Loyalist, in 1784 returned to the Ninety-Six District, thinking he was protected under the terms of the peace treaty. Brought before a circuit court then sitting at Cambridge, he was tried for wanton murder of rebel soldiers and also for horse thievery. Judge Aedanus Burke discharged Love for insufficient evidence and because the defendant had treaty protection. No sooner had Judge Burke given his decision, than General William Butler, whose father and uncles had been slaughtered by Love, entered into the courtroom with friends and relatives, seized the prisoner, carried him to the courtyard, and hanged him from a tree. Judge Burke, who commented that he himself might have been hanged had he tried to interfere with this extreme contempt of court, hightailed his way back to Charleston.[51]

Various factors reduced the lawlessness in the South Carolina backcountry after the war. More settlers moved into the area, taking up lands confiscated from Loyalist exiles and available in the ceded Indian territory, where 100-acre parcels were offered for $10, with a maximum purchase of 640 acres. By 1788, 1,600 persons had moved onto the old Indian lands. Former Loyalists were left unmolested by the state government. The legislature, however, provided for three ranger companies to hunt down "notorious offenders" and bandits. The opening of inland courts, which had been discontinued during the war, helped bring about order. The circuit court, which visited seven districts to hold sessions, renewed proceedings in the backcountry in 1783, and two years later the legislature established a county court system. Provision was made for more secure jails. Horse stealing again carried the death penalty. Of the eight persons sentenced to be hanged in the Ninety-Six District from November 1783 to November 1784, six were executed.[52]

Some newcomers to the backcountry were dissolute and poor, adding to the mix of idlers and the lawless element that had long been prevalent in the region. In 1785 petitioners from the Little River district, part of the region between the Saluda and Broad rivers, complained that "the late war" had "given some people habits of idleness and vice"; therefore, "some mode of a vagrant law" was desired. The petitioners also requested the legislature to place bounties on the "Heads" of "a desperate set of Outlaws." An Edgefield grand jury noted as a "great Grievance" that many "Strolling persons are allowed to pass unnoticed often to the great Injury of the peaceable Inhabitants."[53]

South Carolina enacted its first vagrancy law in 1787. Vagrants were defined as "all idle, lewd, disorderly men" who had no fixed place of dwelling, persons lacking means of supporting themselves or their families, "sturdy beggars, and all strolling or straggling persons," suspicious travelers not possessing certificates attesting to their good behavior, "unlicensed peddlers," and such ne'er-do-wells as gamblers, horse racers, and fortune-tellers. Persons cited as vagrants, who could not put up one year's security for good behavior, were subject to one year's labor. If no one bought their services, they were to be whipped as many as thirty-nine lashes and banished.[54]

Many of the backcountry people had no education and had grown up with little moral training. In 1782 Governor Thomas Burke of North Carolina advised South Carolina Congressman Arthur Middleton that "spreading of knowledge thro' the land" would enable "the Youth in our Back Country" to "become valuable useful men, instead of being, as they are at present, brought up deer-hunters & horse thieves, for want of education."[55]

The war had disrupted the lives of a people, the majority of whom lived a marginal existence and were accustomed to near anarchy. The situation was much like that of the 1760s in the aftermath of the Cherokee War of 1759–61. During the Revolution, Loyalists of the South Carolina backcountry fled to East Florida, where the menfolk served in British-sponsored military units. Others stayed in the backcountry and became involved in partisan warfare. All the while lawlessness flourished. With extended peace and the enhancement of institutional controls, the backcountry became more civilized.

Chapter 13

Daniel McGirth

In October 1795 a Georgia militia captain alerted the Spanish commandant of the northern frontier of Florida that Daniel McGirth, "a man notoriously infamous" and an "old offender against the State of Georgia," was again on the loose, plundering with his "desperate ruffians."[1] Indeed, by this time, McGirth had proved to be the most durable of the Southern banditti; his marauding career extended nearly two decades. A Loyalist refugee from South Carolina, McGirth became a wanted man in Georgia and in British and Spanish East Florida. Fittingly, his last escapades involved a conspiracy in rebellion.

Born and raised in the vicinity of Camden, in the Kershaw District of South Carolina, McGirth hailed from a respected and well-established family. His parents were James McGirth and Priscilla Davison. The father was a prosperous merchant and a small landowner who served as a militia officer and court justice.[2]

The coming of the war excited young Daniel McGirth. Already an accomplished woodsman and horseman, he scouted for patriot forces, and then joined a mounted militia unit. McGirth's enthusiasm for the rebel cause, however, was soon dampened by the cruel treatment he received from his comrades. The problem started when an officer coveted McGirth's prized mare, Gray Goose, iron-gray with a snow blaze on the forehead, regarded as the fleetest horse in South Carolina. The officer persisted in his desire to purchase the horse, but McGirth refused to sell. Tempers flared, and McGirth struck or verbally abused the militia captain. For the offense, a court-martial sentenced McGirth to three whippings of ten lashes each on consecutive days. After receiving the first punishment, McGirth was remanded to the guardhouse to await the further lashings. Finding a broken trowel in his cell, McGirth used it to break away the masonry around the prison bars. Escaping, he spotted Gray Goose nearby, leaped on her, and rode away, shouting damnation to the startled sentries. From that day, McGirth resigned himself to vengeance against all patriots. He and his brother, James, linked up with a mounted company of Georgia militia, commanded by Captain John Baker. At an unsuspecting moment, Daniel and James rode off with all the company's horses and headed for British-held East Florida.[3]

After arriving in East Florida in January 1776, the McGirth brothers enlisted in the newly formed Loyalist corps, later named the King's Rangers, headed by Lieutenant Colonel Thomas Brown; Daniel received a lieutenant colonel's commission, and James, a captaincy. The Rangers conducted raids into southern Georgia, and soon Daniel McGirth had charge of his own band, operating in conjunction with Brown's and other East Florida Tory units. Given a free hand, "McGirth's people" increasingly became more independent and inclined toward marauding.[4]

On February 2–4, 1777, McGirth's men, along with Loyalist provincials led by Brown and William Cunningham, a few regular soldiers, and eighty Indians, forced the surrender of Fort McIntosh, a small rebel post on the Satilla River in southeastern Georgia. On May 17 McGirth's mounted troops and Brown's Rangers lured into an ambush and routed a patriot force under Colonel (formerly captain) John Baker at Thomas's Swamp, near the Nassau River in Florida; one-half of Baker's men were killed or captured. McGirth then joined Loyalist troops and British regulars led by Colonel Mark Prevost in making raids on Georgia settlements in 1778, skirmishing with the enemy at Bulltown Swamp on November 19 and forcing the retreat of Georgia rebel militia at Midway Meeting House on November 24.[5] After the latter battle, "300 Horsemen composed of Brown's and McGirt's Rangers" and British regulars, on their retreat to East Florida, "gave loose to their savage disposition, burning, destroying and plundering every house and all the effects and property of the distressed inhabitants and driving off "a large number" of livestock.[6]

Meanwhile the property that Daniel and James McGirth had acquired in southeastern Georgia, in what became Camden County in 1778, was confiscated by the Georgia legislature by an act of March 1, 1778. The two brothers were also "attainted and adjudged guilty of treason."[7]

Despite the growing awareness that McGirth's band cared more for plundering than military duty, the British command, during 1779 and most of 1780, employed these irregulars to cover the Georgia backcountry between the Ogeechee and Savannah rivers and also to join with the British army invasion from East Florida. Although close by, having just withdrawn from Augusta with the British force commanded by Lieutenant Colonel Archibald Campbell, McGirth and his men failed to come to the aid of Georgia and South Carolina backcountry militia, commanded by Colonel James Boyd, at the battle of Kettle Creek on February 14, 1779. The rebel militia, led by Colonel Andrew Pickens and Colonel John Dooly, crushed their opponents, and Boyd was killed.[8]

McGirth accompanied General Augustine Prevost's army during its excursion into lower South Carolina during the summer of 1779. According to a Charleston newspaper, Prevost had with him "a large body of the most infamous banditti and horsethieves that perhaps ever were collected together anywhere, under the direction of McGirt." McGirth's men stole "plate, horses, or negroes"; McGirth boasted that "his own share of what was stolen" amounted "to his weight in gold."[9] Blacks served in McGirth's band, despite a main objective of stealing slaves, who were sold by the banditti.[10]

McGirth's banditti occasionally met patriot militia patrols. In late summer, while pillaging in western Georgia, the McGirth gang was pursued by Colonel John Twiggs and 150 men. At Buckhead Creek, on August 3, 1779, Twiggs's rebel militia routed McGirth's force. McGirth, wounded in the thigh, escaped on his speedy horse.[11] Not long afterward, while patrolling the frontier, Colonel Elijah Clarke and Colonel John Dooly came across McGirth and his men plundering and burning houses along the Ogeechee River; in a brief fight, several of the marauders were killed.[12] Still retaining some approval from General Prevost, McGirth, with his force now diminished to about thirty men, continued depredations in Georgia. On March 20, 1780, while marauding in Liberty County, McGirth's band was attacked by the militia of Colonels Pickens and Twiggs; some of the banditti were killed or captured, but McGirth escaped.[13]

During May 1780, the McGirth gang scoured an area thirty miles long and ten miles wide along the Georgia side of the Savannah River. One Hollingsworth, a McGirth captain, led a detachment following the river from Summerline Ferry and murdered seventeen men on their farms in two days, ostensibly because the victims refused to take an oath to the king. In trying to learn the whereabouts of a Georgia militia captain named McKay, the banditti tortured his wife by removing flint from the lock of a musket and putting her thumb in its place, then tightening the screw until her thumb was about to burst.[14] Members of the gang often went out in small groups, sometimes five or six men, and, although McGirth himself may not have been involved in the wanton cruelty, by not holding his men to account, he condoned the behavior.

McGirth was now a major cattle rustler. During the summer of 1780, he was reported to have stolen and driven to East Florida some 1,000 head of cattle. McGirth's official ties to the British military campaigns had now ended. The excesses beyond conventional warfare and the depredations for personal profit prejudiced citizens against the British cause. The situation tried the patience of Georgia's royal governor, Sir James Wright, who had resumed his office after the British capture of Savannah (December 29, 1778). Citing "McGirth's people, for robbing, murdering, distressing, and breaking up the Settlements of this Province," Wright issued a proclamation entreating "the Country to seize upon and bring to Justice these people so offending." The council posted a £50 reward for the capture of the gang. Wright had royal arrest warrants drawn up for the banditti. The warrants went unserved, however, because no mounted troops could be spared to go after the McGirth gang. Wright's request to General Cornwallis for fifty cavalry to make the arrests was rejected on the grounds that the local militia, rather than regular military personnel, should be so employed.[15]

The British military command, however, had not fully repudiated the McGirth band. A commissioned officer, leading the "remains" of a duly constituted cavalry unit, McGirth still considered himself in the service of the crown. With the British occupying Charleston, McGirth staged raids nearby on the lower South Carolina coast.

Eliza (Yonge) Wilkinson, a young widow who resided on a plantation on Yonges Island, south of Charleston, reported encounters with McGirth's gang, an experience that revealed some chivalry on the part of McGirth. On June 2, 1780, "two men rode up to the house, one had a green leaf, the other a red string in his hat; this made us suspect them as spies (for we heard M'Girth's men wore such things in their hats)." The two made inquiries and said that McGirth and 200 men would arrive in an hour or two. Eliza reflected that "I'd far rather (if I must see one) see old Beelzebub, but here are some of his imps—the forerunners of his approach." One of the women with Mrs. Wilkinson, a Miss Samuels, told the intruders that "if Col. McGirth should come, I hope he wont act ungenteel, as he'll find none but helpless women here." One of the visitors replied, "O! He'll only take your clothes and negroes from you."

Then came "the day of terror—the 3d of June." Eliza "heard the horses of the inhuman Britons coming in such a furious manner that they seemed to tear up the earth" and the riders were "bellowing out the most horrid curses imaginable." The newcomers were soon in the house "with drawn swords and pistols in their hands," plundering "every thing they thought valuable or worth taking," including shoe buckles, earrings, and a wedding ring. "After bundling up all their booty, they mounted their horses. . . . Each wretch's bosom stuffed so full, they appeared to be all afflicted with some dropsical disorder." These robbers called themselves "British dragoons." One of the robbers was an officer, and another had what looked like a sergeant's "patch" on his shoulders.

Only several hours after the intruders rode off, another mounted party of "banditti" arrived. "These were a large party of M'Girth's men," but surprisingly "they did not behave in that outrageous manner the others had done." One of the band said that they had no intention of robbery, and to prove himself he went over to his horse and took off "a great quantity of yard [piece goods], (which I dare say he had plundered)," and gave it to Mrs. Wilkinson's sister. Actually the McGirth gang wanted directions to another plantation. In their party, however, was one of the dragoons who had robbed the Wilkinson plantation earlier. McGirth himself promised the offending dragoon would be punished with 500 lashes. Mrs. Wilkinson learned later that McGirth was as good as his word. "So here was 'the devil correcting sin.' " McGirth's men appropriated several horses which Mrs. Wilkinson said did not belong to her or the other ladies of the household.

While McGirth and his comrades were still on the Wilkinson plantation, "a poor, meagre looking mortal, with a wound in his shoulder, went into the kitchen, and fell to upon some rice. He told the negroes that he wished he had some meat; and, if he was not afraid of distressing the ladies, he would ask them for some." Mrs. Wilkinson thought "such trifling circumstances" showed "how much more humanity M'Girth's men treated us, to what the Britons did"; yet "to tell the truth, they behaved to us more like friends than enemies, when they saw our distress." After the McGirth banditti left the Wilkinson plantation without doing any harm, they went down the road to Mrs. Wilkinson's parents' house, which they robbed of about everything they could carry away. Eliza Wilkinson and her two sisters had experienced enough terror, and they quickly left for a more safe residence in Charleston.[16]

By the fall of 1780, McGirth's mounted troop unit had disintegrated, and he was now merely the leader of a small group of banditti. In mid May 1781 McGirth, however, had the audacity to request Governor Wright, who at Savannah still presided over the remnant royal government of Georgia, for authorization to raise a "Troop of Horse" to go to the relief of Thomas Brown's Rangers at Augusta, provided that arms, ammunition, and provisions be furnished. Wright was not about to deal with someone he regarded as a criminal, and, besides, Brown surrendered Augusta on June 5, 1781.[17]

The sweeping victories of the rebels in the Carolina-Georgia backcountry, beginning with King's Mountain in October 1780 and ending with driving the enemy from all their interior posts by summer 1781, made it extremely difficult for Tory raiders to be active in the backcountry; indeed, as one writer noted, they had to play "the game of 'the least in sight' and 'shut-mouth.' "[18] McGirth stayed out of the Georgia backcountry and limited his range of depredations to the lower Georgia seacoast, from which he could conduct a hasty retreat back across Saint Marys River into East Florida. In September 1781, Governor Wright received a report that McGirth's men "made a Practice of going up the Country" into St. John's (Midway) and St. Andrew's (Darien) parishes, where "they have committed, indiscriminately, an infinite number of Robberies, as well as other Enormities." Rustling cattle was still McGirth's main goal.[19]

In the spring of 1782, Governor John Martin, the rebel governor of Georgia, assigned a "volunteer Corps" of militia to the command of General Anthony Wayne, whose Continental troops were on cleanup operations in Georgia. Martin told Wayne to be on the lookout for McGirth "and a number of Tories," who "have collected a large property belonging to this State consisting of negroes, horses, cattle, etc." Along with McGirth, other partisan leaders, namely William "Bloody Bill" Cunningham, Belay Cheney, John Linder, Sr., and Jr., and Stephen Mayfield, had formed outlaw gangs and were based in an area bordered by the Saint Marys and upper Saint Johns rivers, in present Nassau County, Florida. Nothing was accomplished in reducing the banditti activity in Georgia. Governor Martin, in September 1782, noted that "there is a set of banditti" in Georgia and "on the other side of St. Marys that make a point of plundering both sides indiscriminately." Martin made an arrangement with Governor Patrick Tonyn of East Florida to issue whatever orders were necessary to suppress the outlawry, but it brought no resolution of the problem.[20]

With the war coming to a close, McGirth turned his attention to robbing Floridians. The situation in East Florida was chaotic, to say the least, with the province undergoing a transition from British to Spanish rule. According to the treaty of retrocession (ratified on September 19, 1783), British citizens not transferring their allegiance to Spain had until March 19, 1785 (the deadline later extended to July 19, 1785) to depart from East Florida.[21] Governor Tonyn stayed on until November 1785, and, even out of office, while acting as the protector of the Loyalist refugees in Florida, often was at cross-purposes with the new Spanish regime.

Just before relinquishing his office, Governor Tonyn, angered by McGirth's continual "defiance against the Laws and Government of the Country," declared McGirth an outlaw whereby McGirth's property was to be forfeited to the crown.[22] In fact, any legal recourse against McGirth was left up to the Spaniards.

McGirth's robberies, some aimed at British officials, from late 1783 to mid 1784, had especially tried Governor Tonyn's patience. McGirth stole

"Georgia–East Florida Frontier" (1779 map).
From J. Leitch Wright, Jr., *Florida in the Ameri-can Revolution* (Gainesville: University Press of
Florida, 1975). Reproduced by permission of the
University Press of Florida.

horses in Saint Augustine belonging to Francis Levett, the former provost
marshall; horses near Saint Johns bluff owned by Captain Peter Edwards,
the clerk of the British East Florida legislature; and slaves from Saint Marys
beach, the property of John Fox, a public accountant. In March 1784, "a
Banditti under the command of MacGirth" stole two coach horses from the
servants of James Hume, the chief justice of East Florida, as they were
driving a carriage on the Saint Johns road, twenty-five miles from Saint
Augustine.[23]

McGirth was implicated in other robberies in East Florida. Along with
John Linder and nine others, he accosted Thomas Clarke and took away a
mare, a saddle and bridle, five bushels of corn, two bushels of clean rice,

two "Osnaburg bags," a white shirt, a "pair of Boots and Spurs," a knife, twenty pounds of bacon, and one gun. Clarke recalled that, during the incident, McGirth used "very abusive language" and exclaimed, "Damn you I'll have your Ears for it" and that he "had taken nothing" but "what he ought."[24]

A chief abettor of the McGirth gang was Francisco Sanchez, a Spanish native of East Florida. Tonyn referred to Sanchez as one who "owed every thing he possesses to the indulgence of the British government, under which he rose from a State of obscure poverty to a degree of affluence seldom attained." Sanchez became a major supplier of the Spanish garrison in Saint Augustine. He secretly turned over to McGirth arms and ammunition and provisions from his plantation, about eighteen miles from Saint Augustine, and gave McGirth dummy bills of sale in receipt for stolen property. Sanchez's "Cow pen" was "one of the principal places of rendezvous" for the McGirth banditti.[25]

Before being named an outlaw by Tonyn, McGirth occasionally visited Saint Augustine, confident that the authorities had insufficient evidence to arrest him. He was easily recognized; he usually wore a blue coat with large silver buttons and a frilled linen scarf about his neck. One day in May 1784, "not knowing that any information had been made against him by his accomplices in robberies," he was arrested and "put in the Castle." From his cell, McGirth executed a bill of sale with Sanchez for a large number of slaves and other property to prevent them from being seized under the law. With money probably given him by Sanchez, who visited him in jail, McGirth bribed one of the guards and escaped along with several other banditti who had been jailed. The escapees were soon "lurking in the Swamps and other Places of concealment."[26]

A few days after his escape, McGirth wrote a letter to Governor Tonyn asking for "Royal mercy." Tonyn met with his council, and it was agreed to grant McGirth a pardon on the condition that he surrender and bring in his accomplices; furthermore, all stolen property was to be recovered and restored to the "proper owners," and McGirth and his followers must immediately leave East Florida. But "instead of accepting this merciful offer," McGirth demonstrated that he had written his letter "merely to gain time and amuse and throw [the] Government off their guard." McGirth

collected his friends in the Country, stripped plantations robbed Houses, collected numbers of Horses, in one instance it appeared he sent thirty over St Johns, he now formed a plan to defeat two Troops of Light Horse in the pay and commission of His Britannic Majesty and to plunder the Country.

Concealed in a swamp along the "King's high way," McGirth, along with John Linder, Jr., James McGirth, Joseph Bradley, and several others, ambushed Captain John Hood and a few of his troops, part of a small force Governor Tonyn had dispatched to apprehend the outlaws. In the exchange of fire, Hood and one of his men were killed. The McGirth gang robbed the remaining soldiers. The outlaws then ran across Colonel William Young, who commanded a troop of horse also sent out by Tonyn. But "being well mounted," Young safely reached his army post on the banks of the Saint Johns. This action was the primary factor in the British governor's declaration of outlawry against McGirth and ordering the confiscation of his property.[27]

After the changeover to Spanish governance in East Florida, two troops of mounted horse kept in the field to ferret out the banditti and arrest them. The soldiers, commanded by Colonel William Young, a refugee from Georgia, and Captain Alexander Stuart, a Loyalist from South Carolina, were paid by the British but served supposedly under Spanish authority. Young established a new post on the Moore plantation at the mouth of Julanton Creek. Learning that the McGirth banditti were assembling at the house of Daniel Melyards, on the Nassau River, for the purpose of conducting a plundering raid along the west side of the Saint Johns River, on July 27, 1784, Young and his men surrounded the Melyards' house. Among the outlaws present were James McGirth and John Linder, Jr. The "villains" had with them "some Negroes all armed." The outlaws managed to break out of the house, although Linder's "waiting man" was killed, and a fifteen-year-old lad, named Whaley, was captured. The boy was tied to a post and unsuccessful attempts were made to get him to reveal the whereabouts of Daniel McGirth. The fleeing outlaws found refuge in "a very large Swamp." Young took away property belonging to James McGirth: eight slaves, a horse, a cow and calf, and "various articles of household furniture."[28]

Daniel McGirth had a score to settle with Samuel Farley, a friend of Governor Tonyn. Presumably Farley had possession of slaves belonging to the McGirths. While nearly everyone in Saint Augustine, including Farley, was attending a ball at the Spanish garrison, celebrating the assumption of office by Vicente Manuel de Zéspedes as governor under Spanish rule, on the evening of July 14, 1784, McGirth slipped into Saint Augustine. He entered Farley's house and took away eight slaves. Farley brought suit under the new Spanish judicial system for the recovery of his slaves from McGirth. Unfortunately for Farley, about the same time he refused to subscribe to the required oath as an arbitrator, a position to which he had been appointed, on the grounds that he was still a British citizen. Francis Philip Fatio, the justice of the peace who was to hear the case, cited Farley for contempt and dismissed the suit.[29]

For the time being, McGirth kept a low profile. The Spanish government did not take any action against him, and he was allowed to retain his stolen property. Colonel Young's mounted troops, without any support from the Spanish government, kept up its patrol, guarding plantations against banditry. For the remainder of 1784, the only misdoing attributed to McGirth was his having two of his slaves, in December, slaughter four hogs that belonged to Nathaniel Ashley on Neilly's Island.[30] A South Carolina newspaper published an erroneous report from Saint Augustine that "a party of McGirt's followers" were preparing "to visit the Wateree and Congaree rivers, to steal horses."[31]

Tonyn pressed the Spanish governor to proceed aggressively against McGirth and his banditti. Tonyn reminded Zéspedes that the Spanish government considered "Colonel Young's Troop but as people hired," whom, "out of compliment to me," were permitted "to act upon the defensive, covering my Plantation and those in the neighbourhood." The former British governor insisted that "two notorious Men," Daniel McGirth and John Linder, Jr., should be apprehended and "sent out of the Province" for "the common safety, and security" of the Spanish government and the "british Inhabitants." Both McGirth and Linder were "murderers and assassins, and the former is an outlaw, Head and support of a desperate Gang of high Way Robbers." The two miscreants "headed a party of Desperadoes who had committed every outrage, murder and treason" in "the catalogue."[32]

Zéspedes had good reason to delay in taking forcible action against the East Florida banditti, who were among a large group of "exiled Americans" who refused to leave the province. Zéspedes feared that hasty measures might lead to a revolt and endanger an Indian alliance in the making. The Spaniards controlled only a small part of East Florida, an area twenty-five miles wide between the Saint Johns River and the coast and ninety miles below the Saint Marys River; Creek Indians (in Florida called Seminoles by the British) held sway in the rest of East Florida. Englishmen dominated the trade with the Seminoles, who formed part of the 45,000-member Creek Confederacy which stretched as far north as the Tennessee River.[33]

Zéspedes wrote to Bernardo de Gálvez, captain-general of Louisiana, the Floridas, and Cuba, to explain his caution toward the banditti.

The great number of rogues, including those openly and secretly such, who infested the outlying areas of this densely wooded and swampy country, particularly the banks of the St. Johns and Nassau rivers and as far as the St. Marys River, when I took over this government caused me to decide that it would be best to temporize with them. I was without horses for my dragoons, without armed boats to patrol the rivers in question, and without the money necessary to equip myself to operate with the energy so desirable and so necessary in dealing with people who acknowledge neither law nor king. These powerful and obvious motives obliged me to resist the repeated insinuations and moves of the British Governor Tonyn, directed . . . rather toward protecting his own and five other fine plantations under his charge than, as he pretends, to looking out for the public tranquillity. . . . If I had attempted to suppress and punish a few excesses with armed force greater harm and scandal would have resulted in this country which, as the result of the civil war between England and America, is overrun with desperate men capable of all kinds of wickedness. Major General Patrick Tonyn said in one of his letters that this province contained sixteen thousand British subjects, but of this number at least twelve thousand were exiled Americans. . . .

In view of all these circumstances, I judged that it was for the highest good of the royal service and decorum of the Spanish government to go on dissimulating in order to give this large number of desperate and abandoned people time to quit the country, using moderation until I saw myself in a position to act vigorously.[34]

Eventually, Zéspedes, being "fully impressed with a due knowledge of the perverse dispositions, and incorrigible actions" of McGirth and "his declared associates," decided to have the leading banditti arrested. Zéspedes noted that Tonyn, desiring to finish his administration with clemency, did not proceed "with capital punishment against Daniel McGirtt and sundry others his adherents." Zéspedes similarly wished to begin his administration "using clemency with some unhappy persons, altho' noted villains." The best way to deal with McGirth and John Linder, Jr., was to dispatch "both of those evil doers out of the province by Sea."[35]

Zéspedes offered to any person accused of crimes by the British the opportunity to leave Florida. McGirth accepted the proposal, but then he refused to surrender. Upon learning that McGirth, William Cunningham, John Linder, Jr., and other banditti intended to raid plantations, attack the station held by Colonel Young's mounted troops, and then "drive all the Country before them to the Gates of Augustine and take the Town if possible," Zéspedes ordered the arrest of McGirth, "the ostensible chief of the highwaymen of this country," and his associates.[36] On January 20, 1785, Daniel McGirth, James McGirth, William Cunningham ("a worse man than the preceding"), and Stephen Mayfield, "who always harbored in his inn every thief who presented himself there," were taken into custody and lodged in separate cells in the dungeon at the Saint Augustine fort. Zéspedes informed Gálvez that he would send the prisoners to Havana and let Gálvez determine the judgment; "even if the evidence is not conclusive" against the prisoners, "it would be in the interest of the royal service and the public tranquillity" to banish them forever from Spanish territory.[37]

Confined to one of the cells underground on the river side of the Saint Augustine fort, McGirth endured a harsh ordeal. Once every day he received dry bread and a pitcher of water thrust through a small hole in the wall. McGirth's wife, Mary, appealed to Tonyn to persuade Zéspedes to grant relief to McGirth from "the most deplorable situation for want of the common necessaries of life," which "certainly must in a short time prove fatal to him."[38]

Zéspedes's belated get-tough policy frightened other East Florida banditti to cross the Saint Marys River into Georgia. In February 1785 Colonel John Baker of the Georgia militia asked Governor Samuel Elbert to "take the most effectual means to secure the villains who are at this time assembled between St. Illa [in Camden County, Georgia] and St. Marys Rivers, with a number of negroes, horses & other property supposed to have been stolen from the citizens of these States." The "number of the banditti assembled" amounted to about twenty-five men, and "a few more will join them, as the Spaniards in East Florida are making severe example of all such who fall into their hands."[39] About the same time, it was learned that "offenders who have committed Robberies in East Florida, and are well known to be persons that have been guilty of violent outrages" against Georgia citizens had gathered together on the Satilla River. The outlaws had with them slaves, horses, and other stolen property and were about to leave for West Florida.[40]

In May 1785 McGirth was released from confinement and, along with five others, including William Cunningham and Stephen Mayfield, was sent to Havana, where Gálvez would pass sentence. Like Zéspedes, former governor Tonyn also advised leniency: "If these unhappy men were transplanted into another country," there was "yet a ray of hope, that upon proper reflection of their past wicked courses, a reformation might be effectuated."[41]

Gálvez liberated McGirth, Cunningham, and Mayfield on the condition that they proceed "to any English colony they might choose," but under no circumstance were they to go "to any of our possessions." McGirth and Cunningham purchased a boat, which "they manned with four foreign seaman and one Negro slave belonging to Cunningham." On the last day of September 1785, McGirth and Cunningham ostensibly set out for New Providence Island in the Bahamas. All four crewmen abandoned ship before it left Cuba. In depositions, several of them claimed that the ex-prisoners' plan "was to sail to the coast of East Florida, and, going ashore, remain in hiding among the Indians until McGirtt could manage to penetrate" into Saint Augustine "by night and acquaint himself with the state of the province." Apparently McGirth hoped that a rebellion might be forming against Spanish rule. McGirth lingered for a while in the area of the Saint Marys and Nassau rivers, probably with the intent of settling back on his farm, which had not actually been confiscated. Local residents, however, petitioned against his remaining. Zéspedes's border agent, Henry O'Neill, arrested McGirth, whose excuse for appearing in East Florida was that he had been shipwrecked off the mouth of the Saint Marys River. McGirth was imprisoned until January 1786, when, with his family, he sailed for New Providence.[42]

None of the banditti associates of Daniel McGirth fared badly. William Cunningham, the Loyalist militia leader during the war whose cruelties earned him the nickname of "Bloody Bill," went to the Bahamas. In London in 1786 he was granted a half-pay pension of a major, and early the next year, being allowed to visit South Carolina, he died in Charleston.[43] Stephen Mayfield lived the rest of his life in the Bahamas. On the theory that former bandit ruffians make good frontier settlers, the Spanish government gave Belay Cheney, John Linder, Sr., and John Linder, Jr., land grants in the Tensaw District of West Florida, about thirty miles northeast of Mobile. The two Linders became cattlemen. Probably both men had headed west with a large number of cattle and horses. The younger Linder must have greatly mended his ways, for he served as a district lieutenant and a justice of the peace. James McGirth, although initially imprisoned and sent to Cuba, was allowed to return to East Florida, where reputedly he became a model citizen. He received several land grants and eventually settled near the St. Marys River. In 1786 Saint Augustine census records show James as fifty years old and of the Lutheran religion, living with his wife, Ysabela Sanders, a native of East Florida, and their six children, age ten through twenty: Jayme, Juan, Esacarias, Daniel, Reveto, and Maria. Several of the children converted to Catholicism. James McGirth died in about 1800.[44]

Daniel McGirth's incarcerations by the Spaniards and his brief sojourns in the Bahamas merely interrupted his banditti course in the southeastern borderlands. He also became an incidental figure in filbustering efforts for the conquest of East Florida.

In February 1788, McGirth arrived in Saint Augustine with a note from the Earl of Dunmore, the new governor of the Bahamas, to Zéspedes, stating that McGirth was traveling from Nassau, in the Bahamas, to Florida, aboard the sloop *Mayflower*, to "settle his private affairs—he is a British subject, and as such, I beg leave to recommend him to Your Excellency's protection."[45] Zéspedes suspected that Dunmore was employing McGirth as a spy. The Spanish government kept McGirth under close scrutiny. McGirth was allowed to meet Francisco Sanchez but then was sent back to the Bahamas, accompanied by his wife and family.

Zéspedes had good reason to be suspicious. Dunmore and several wealthy Bahamian merchants, particularly John Miller, planned to incite a rebellion against the Spaniards in Florida. The project aimed not so much to replace Spanish with British rule, but to secure for the Bahamians domination of the Florida and southeastern Indian trade. The Spaniards had awarded a trade monopoly to a firm headed by two Englishmen, William Panton and John Leslie, who had stayed in Florida and taken the oath of allegiance to Spain.

In the summer of 1788, Dunmore and his allies dispatched an expedition to Florida aboard two vessels, carrying sixty men recruited from among jailbirds and Royal Navy deserters, arms, ammunition, and provisions. William

William Augustus Bowles. By Thomas Hardy.
From J. Leitch Wright, Jr., *William Augustus Bowles:
Director General of the Creek Nation* (Athens:
University of Georgia Press, 1967). Courtesy of the
University of Georgia Press.

Augustus Bowles, a former Maryland refugee who had lived among the
Creek Indians, was given the command of the expedition. With the assistance of the Indians, who preferred a British- rather than a Spanish-
sponsored Indian trade, and disgruntled whites of northeastern Florida, the
Bahamian interlopers expected an easy victory. The Spaniards had only a
small, scattered military force, located in undermanned garrisons at Saint
Augustine, Saint Marks, Mobile, and Pensacola. Daniel McGirth seems to
have been with Bowles's freelance troops as they landed on the coast at the
mouth of the Indian River.[46]

Bowles selected as his immediate objective Panton's and Leslie's company
stores at Lake George on the Saint Marys River and Saint Marks, across
the peninsula at the head of Apalachee Bay. The filibusterers had success
at Lake George, but then everything went awry. Indian support did not

materialize, rations ran low, Spanish soldiers from Saint Augustine were marching to intercept the expedition, and most of Bowles's followers deserted. Bowles found refuge in Indian country, first residing at the Creek town of Cuscowilla, in present-day Alachua County, Florida, and then at Mucosukie Old Town in central Florida. Over the years, Daniel McGirth must have been a regular visitor to Cuscowilla, not far from his own home. The inhabitants of the Indian village lived in thirty wood-frame houses and kept large herds of cattle and horses. Bowles tried to establish the "Creek and Cherokee Nation," of which he was elected director of affairs. He again schemed to drive the Spaniards out of Florida using an army enlisted from Indians and American frontiersmen. Duped by the governor of Louisiana, Baron de Carondolet, to visit New Orleans to negotiate, Bowles was seized in August 1791 and spent the next several years in Spanish prisons as far away as the Philippines. Eventually he escaped while being conveyed off the coast of Africa. He returned to America for further adventure.[47]

With Bowles's fiasco of 1788, McGirth showed up in custody in Saint Augustine. He may have accompanied other defectors of the Bowles expedition who surrendered to the Spaniards. McGirth was sent to Havana under arrest and may have spent some time there in prison. His whereabouts are unknown until a few years later when he surfaced as a leader of banditti on the Georgia side of the Saint Marys River.[48]

By 1794 McGirth was involved in full-scale banditry in Liberty and Camden counties, Georgia. He made his base of operations at Colerain, a small village in westernmost Camden County, on the Saint Marys River, fifty-four miles from the coast. McGirth's band of whites and Indians raided plantations, keeping to the Georgia side. He was indicted for stealing slaves in Liberty County.[49]

McGirth once again engaged himself in a design to oust the Spaniards from Florida. The new French minister to the United States, Edmond Charles Genet, after arriving in Charleston on April 8, 1793, set about engineering a three-pronged invasion of Spanish territory. While George Rogers Clark would lead an expedition into Louisiana, Colonels Samuel Hammond of Georgia and William Tate of South Carolina, as commanders of "Revolutionary Legions" in America, would attack Saint Augustine and Pensacola, in West Florida, respectively. These projects, considered a violation of President George Washington's declaration of neutrality, were terminated by Genet's replacement, Jean Antoine Joseph Fauchet.[50]

Meanwhile, Elijah Clarke resigned as major general of the Georgia militia to accept a similar commission from the French to lead troops in conjunction with Colonel Hammond's invasion of East Florida. Clark brought 300 men to the Georgia-Florida border, only to find that the French had backed off from sponsoring any expeditions against the Spaniards, and the Georgia and the federal governments were also opposed to the projects. Subsequently, some of Clarke's followers joined him in an unsuccessful attempt to establish the Trans-Oconee Republic in Indian territory in west Georgia. The abortive East Florida venture enlisted Daniel McGirth and other banditti, who expected cover for plundering along the Saint Marys and Saint Johns rivers.[51]

When Clarke's men were encamped at Temple, Georgia, about seven miles southeast of Colerain and one and a half miles north of the Saint Marys River, McGirth with "desperate ruffians," joined by "a gang of Indians," lingered at the border.[52]

On guard against any filibuster incursion into East Florida, Georgia militia Captain Jonas Fauche and Spanish Captain Carlos Howard patrolled their respective sides of the Saint Marys. Fauche seized four "armed rebels," including McGirth. Fauche remanded McGirth for a hearing before magistrates in Saint Mary's (in Camden County, Georgia) and then had him jailed until orders came from Georgia authorities. Howard wrote to Fauche that McGirth was the leader of a group that had been raiding plantations on both sides of the river and requested that McGirth be turned over to the Spaniards. Although acknowledging that Howard had referred to enough evidence to convict McGirth of crimes in East Florida, the Saint Marys magistrates refused to surrender their prisoner, unaware that McGirth had been under indictment elsewhere in Georgia, on the grounds that McGirth claimed American citizenship. McGirth was set free. Fauche explained that the major reason for not surrendering McGirth was that Georgia had sent back two deserters from the Saint Augustine garrison on condition that they not be executed; the Spaniards hanged them anyway.

Governor George Mathews of Georgia was unhappy with McGirth's release. The Georgia governor ordered Fauche, "if that nefarious villain McGirth is still lurking" in Camden County, to send him to Augusta for arraignment. Mathews was certain that there was enough evidence of McGirth's crimes to get a conviction. McGirth was never tried in a Georgia court.[53]

Now about fifty years of age, Daniel McGirth returned to the neighborhood of his birth, the vicinity of Camden, South Carolina. His wife, Mary, after leaving the Bahamas in 1788, had gone to live with her Cantey family relatives in the region. The McGirths lived for a while in a "secluded cottage" in the yard of the home of Zachariah Cantey, son of McGirth's sister, Mary, and then eventually resided with McGirth's brother-in-law, Colonel John James. For his own safety, Daniel McGirth kept a very low profile and had protection from two nephews, Zachariah and James Cantey.[54]

A Camden resident recalled that years after the Revolutionary War, Anthony Hampton visited Colonel James Chesnut, a neighbor of the Canteys. During conversation, Hampton told how Daniel McGirth had once saved his life. While Hampton was being carried a prisoner to Charleston, McGirth "secretly cut the cords that bound his limbs," thus allowing him to escape. When the guest asked about the "ultimate fate" of McGirth, Chesnut replied that he would take him to McGirth's little house on Zachariah Cantey's estate. Hampton was astonished at meeting McGirth.

The two men had been friends as boys, and, despite the fact that both were bent with age, the meeting was cordial and pleasant. Among the many reminiscences . . . was that of the escape of Hampton above related. "Well, come now, Anthony," said McGirtt, "suppose we had been in each other's shoes that night, what would you have done?" "Let you go on and be hanged, by George," said Hampton; "it would have been a great pity, I know now, since you have turned out such a clever fellow, but the truth must be told."[55]

Easy pickings might be one way to style the motivation for Daniel McGirth's bandit excursions. During the war and afterward, he plundered isolated plantations and farms in Georgia and South Carolina, retiring to the safety of northeastern East Florida, an area itself not immune to pillaging. Disorder caused by partisan warfare and then the shaky transition from British to Spanish rule in the Floridas allowed McGirth to operate with relative impunity. The Spaniards, with limited military resources, hesitated to exercise any stringent jurisdiction over British Loyalists in East Florida, despite the outrages committed by some of them. The massive exodus of Loyalists from East Florida to the Bahamas, West Indies, and Nova Scotia finally enabled the Spanish government to instill a measure of law and order in the province.

Daniel McGirth had the advantage of living on a frontier amid sparse settlement, bounded by an expansive Creek Indian reserve, where he could find refuge if need be and dispose of surplus stolen livestock. Banditti could readily obtain cattle and other livestock in Georgia, where the animals ranged widely. Roundups by owners occurred only annually. It was an easy matter for robbers themselves to gather free-roaming cattle or simply overpower one or several "cow cap boys" tending the cowpens and drive the animals to a destination.[56]

McGirth's role as a leader of banditti is difficult to assess. Almost instantly and in different situations he was able to enlist followers. There is no evidence that McGirth exacted tight organization or discipline in his nonmilitary bands. It seems that the cruelties attributed to the McGirth banditti resulted from the actions of individuals or small groups from the outlaw association rather than the actions of McGirth himself. The McGirth banditti may best be described as freebooters combining in the pursuit of common goals. There is some indication, even after the war, those persons who had embraced the American rebel cause were most likely to be victims of the East Florida marauders.

Chapter 14

"A Perfect Desert"

Destruction, pillage, and the horrors of murderous partisan warfare transformed regions of the Carolinas and Georgia into virtual wastelands. A large number of slaves departed, especially after General Henry Clinton's proclamation of 1779 offering protection and freedom for bondsmen (belonging to rebels) who sought refuge behind British lines. Many whites fled, and others endured homelessness. Those who stayed on their homesteads experienced abject fear and deprivation.

General Nathanael Greene, writing from his camp near the North Carolina border in the Cheraws district of South Carolina, in December 1780, told General Robert Howe that "the Whigs and Tories pursue one another with the most relentless Fury killing and destroying each other wherever they meet. Indeed a great Part of this Country is already laid Waste & in the utmost Danger of becoming a Desert."[1] Lewis Morris, Jr., Greene's aide-de-camp, expressed a similar view, while Cornwallis's army was encamped at the junction of the Broad and Congaree rivers. "The country is so thinly inhabited," declared Lewis, "and has been so much stripped by the militia and the Enemy that there is no moving through it."[2]

Captain Walter Finney, a Pennsylvanian serving in the Southern army, in 1782, was shocked in viewing Camden, South Carolina: "At present there is not more than Half a Duzen of Houses can be ocquepid, the remaindor being either Totally Demolished, or so much Racked by the British, that they are abandoned by thire oaners."[3] General Anthony Wayne, writing to Greene from Ebenezer, Georgia, in January 1782, reported that he found "this Country a perfect desert below Bryer [Briar] Creek, and between the Great Ogechee & Savannah rivers, except that Included in the Enemies lines from Mulberry Grove & Mr. Gibbons's to Savannah."[4]

A traveler going from Salem, North Carolina, to Rugeley's Mills (Clement, South Carolina) commented in June 1782 that "most of the plantations that we passed were either abandoned or burned, now and then one was inhabited, but they had nothing."[5]

Even stretches of coastal South Carolina were devastated. General William Moultrie reported on his journey from near Georgetown, South Carolina, to Greene's camp on the Ashley River, fifteen miles from Charleston, in September 1782:

It was the most dull, melancholy, dreary ride that any one could possibly take, of about one hundred miles through the woods of the country, which I had been accustomed to see abound with live-stock and wild fowl of every kind, was now destitute of all. It had been so completely checquered by the different parties, that not one part of it had been left unexplored; consequently, not the vestiges of horses, cattle, hogs, or deer, &c. was to be found. The squirrels and birds of every kind were totally destroyed. The dragoons told me, that on their scouts, no living creature was seen, except now and then a few camp scavengers [turkey buzzards], picking the bones of some unfortunate fellows, who had been shot or cut down, and left in the woods above ground.[6]

As late as November 1783, a Presbyterian minister, John Simpson, traveling near the Combahee River in southeastern South Carolina, found that "all was desolation, and indeed all the way there was a gloomy Solitariness. Every field, every plantation, showed marks of ruin and devastation. Not a person was to be met in the roads."[7]

Many citizens left their homes because of wartime conditions. Banishment, intimidation, and military service contributed to population fluctuation. Persons vulnerable to cruel treatment and wanting subsistence became fugitives.

Groups of upper-class women and children whose menfolk were in military service went off to other plantations for better protection. Others wound up at places where they paid excessive rents.[8] One American officer commented that many persons were "leaving their property behind them and as Surely causing a famine where they go."[9]

When the property of Nicholas Welsh, of Tryon County, North Carolina, was seized, his wife and nine children were banished from the state and sent to Georgia.[10] John Ross, of the Cape Fear region of North Carolina, and his wife and children were forced to move 100 miles "up the Country to a place called Campbelltown," where the family was "often obliged to

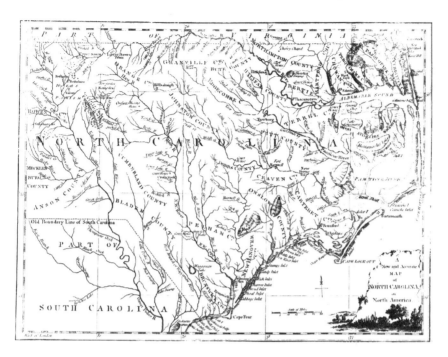

"A New and Accurate Map of North Carolina," 1779. Courtesy of the North Carolina Division of Archives and History, Raleigh.

take shelter in the Woods and Swamps" for fear of the rebels.[11] In November 1781, North Carolina militia "kidnapped" children of Loyalists and took them to Wilmington, recently evacuated by the British.[12]

During Cornwallis's march through the Carolinas in 1781, many settlers sought "to find safety and repose in flight." Refugees from the Pee Dee River country fled northeastward to the Neuse River area. "The resources of the Carolinas are either exhausted, or are denied" the British, wrote a young aide in General Rochambeau's army. "The inhabitants leave their firesides" at Cornwallis's approach, and "what they cannot carry away, they hide or destroy." Another observer noted that patriots "generally fled from their plantations into North Carolina," and "their crops of course were neglected, and the little that was harvested was consumed by the enemy, and when the American detachments became possessed of any part of this intermediate Country, or marched thro' it, the Tories suffered in their turn." General Andrew Pickens informed Greene in July 1781 that "people who have removed their families to the Remote parts" of North Carolina and Virginia "seem to make a Trade of Carrying off Every thing Valluable," either "the property of friend or enemy." A Moravian settler in Salem, North Carolina, was surprised that so "many people who to save their lives had placed them-selves, their wives and children under the protection" of the British army.[13]

Except for the backcountry, Georgia's population decreased during the war. The colony had 18,000 white and 15,000 black residents in 1773. By July 1782, 4,000 Georgians had gone to East Florida and others to the West Indies and elsewhere. Because families along the Ogeechee River kept "so easy a communication with their husbands" who had gone to East Florida and afforded them "great assistance and help in their plundering schemes," the state of Georgia ordered that the wives and children be removed to "some of the forfeited estates where reasonable provision will be made for them, and where they cannot hold any intercourse with their husbands"; if the refugees became dissatisfied, they were to be sent to Saint Augustine.[14] Some destitute families in Georgia roamed into South Carolina. General Moultrie, in going from Charleston to Purysburg, saw "poor women and children and negroes of Georgia (a spectacle that even moved the hearts of soldiers) traveling to they knew not where."[15]

Patriot resistance in Georgia collapsed after the fall of Augusta in June 1780. Colonel Thomas Brown's Rangers and other Loyalist bands raided the Georgia upcountry, particularly in Wilkes County, seeking out families of rebel militiamen, destroying their homes and farms, and inflicting cruelties on the defenseless victims. Colonel Elijah Clarke and his Georgia militia unsuccessfully attempted to capture Augusta in September 1780. On his withdrawal, he and his remnant troops ran across a gathering of 400 women and children who were trying to find a place of refuge. Loyalist troops and Indians blocked most avenues for escape. Clarke and his small militia force took charge of the refugees and conducted them some 200 miles across the mountains to the Watauga Valley, between the Holston and Nolichucky rivers in northwestern North Carolina. The intrepid band, many of whom were barefoot, trekked through three feet of snow, and after exhausting the food supply, existed on acorns, roots, and nuts from the woods. Loyalist militia, Indians, and robbers harassed the band on their eleven-day journey. Those who fell behind were killed and scalped. The refugees stayed in their newfound homes until the rebels secured Georgia.[16]

Rebels drove Loyalists from their homes. Private James Collins, a South Carolina militiaman, described a favorite method:

Wherever we found any Tories, we would surround the house, one party would force the doors and enter sword in hand, extinguish all the lights . . . commence hacking the man or men that were found in the house, threatening them with instant death, and occasionally making a furious stroke as if to dispatch them at once, but taking care to strike the wall or some object that was in the way, they generally being found crouched up in some corner, or about the beds. Another party would mount the roof of the house and commence pulling it down. . . . The poor fellows, perhaps expecting instant death, would beg hard for life, and make any promise on condition of being spared, while their wives or friends would join in their entreaties; on the condition that they would leave the country, within a specified time, and never return, they would suffer him to live, and I never knew an instance of one that failed to comply. . . . There were none of the poor fellows much hurt, only they were hacked about their heads and arms enough to bleed freely.[17]

Other than scaring people from aiding the enemy or joining up with them, the most common factor in bringing on cruelties of the partisan war in the South was revenge. As one writer noted, "The principle seems to have been that one atrocity deserved another."[18] Patriots and Loyalists dispatched their victims in cold blood. The hanging of a Loyalist militia captain, Francis Tidwell, who was apprehended near Camden, South Carolina, was unduly cruel.

As his murderers never took the trouble of pinioning his arms, in his struggles, while dying, he attempted several times to take hold of the limbs of the tree on which he was hanged; and it afforded them high amusement to beat down his hands with their whips and sticks. His body remained hanging for three days.[19]

Some military commanders set the pace for brutality. Prisoners were executed summarily or at best under sentence of drumhead courts-martial for alleged offenses, such as having committed depredations, wanton killings, violations of parole, or activity tantamount to treason. On the patriot side, two leading examples of prisoner hangings are the execution of nine captives from the battle of King's Mountain (October 1780) and Lieutenant Colonel "Lighthorse" Henry Lee's ordering the hanging of four prisoners from the fence belonging to Rebecca Motte (May 1781). In the second instance the victims were stripped naked before being hanged.[20] It was always the practice to steal the clothing from hanged persons, but to do so before the execution prevented the likelihood of soiled garments.

Colonel Benjamin "Bull Dog" Cleveland reputedly hanged more Tories than anyone else. On one occasion, after he had hanged a prisoner, he enjoined the dead man's companion to choose either the same fate or "take this knife and cut off your own ears and leave the country." Needless to say, there was soon a trail of blood down the road. Once when Cleveland was absent from his home, his men brought a prisoner before Cleveland's wife and asked what should be done. Mrs. Cleveland simply replied to do what the colonel would do, and the captive was hanged from the gate to the Cleveland estate.[21]

General Griffith Rutherford "butchered in cold blood" Loyalists taken in Mecklenburg County, North Carolina, in early 1782. "This villainous ruffian" made "his men wound with their swords every loyalist they met." This was called "General Rutherford's mark."[22]

Both Patriot and Loyalist troops committed wholesale slaughter. The most egregious was Pyle's Massacre, also known as Pyle's Hacking Match, which occurred on February 25, 1781. Henry Lee's Partisan Corps (Lee's Legion) was patrolling in the Haw River region to prevent Tory militia from linking up with Cornwallis's army at Hillsborough. At the same time, Dr. John Pyle, a Tory militia colonel, with 300 recruits, mostly teenagers, were on the march to join Cornwallis. Pyle had been informed that the British general had sent out Lieutenant Colonel Banastre Tarleton and his dragoons to provide a safe escort to the British army. Two of Pyle's scouts ran across Lee's troops, who sported green jackets similar to those worn by Tarleton's men, and, mistaking them for Tarleton's dragoons, told Lee of Pyle's location. Lee, posing as Tarleton, ordered the scouts to go back and have their militia ready to stand review. As Lee approached Pyle's band, the Loyalist troops formed a column at the side of a road, standing at attention with weapons slung over their shoulders. Pyle was at the far end of the formation. Lee, still acting the part of Tarleton, rode down the line, with the intent of asking Pyle to surrender; on the way, Lee complimented the Tory militiamen on their sharp appearance. Just as Lee reached Pyle, firing broke out, probably initiated by one of the rebel militiamen who had accompanied Lee's Legion. What ensued was a massacre, execution style. Lee's men sabered and shot at point blank the astonished Tories, who, still believing that Lee was Tarleton, pleaded for a halt to the proceedings. After fifteen minutes, the butchery left ninety-three Loyalists dead. Most of the rest were captured; many were severely wounded. Lee later denied that he himself had ordered the massacre. Although the barbarity was unjustified, it at least cowed would-be enlistees for the British cause, and to the patriots it seemed a fitting retaliation for Tarleton's having given no quarter to Virginia Continental troops led by Colonel Abraham Buford at the Waxhaws, South Carolina, on May 29, 1780.[23]

Another instance when the rebels killed prisoners en masse was the Orangeburg Massacre of May 15, 1781, when Captain John McCord's militia shot fourteen chained British prisoners, captured from their fort on the North Edisto River, as they were being marched toward General Greene's encampment.[24] Captain Patrick (Paddy) Carr's militia "inhumanely butchered in cold blood" captives at Darien, Georgia, and elsewhere along the Altamaha River in February 1782.[25]

Tory partisans matched the excessive bloodletting of their counterparts. Three Tory leaders in particular earned infamy for their cruelties: David Fanning, Thomas Brown, and William Cunningham. During early 1782, David Fanning, normally a merciful person during his impressive career as a partisan raider, went on a spree of desolation and murder to avenge the cruelty and hangings inflicted on some of his men when captured by the rebels. Fanning personally hacked to death some of his prisoners.[26] Thomas Brown of the King's Rangers, mostly Tory refugees in East Florida, was not accustomed to give quarter. After the failure of the American siege of Augusta, on September 14–18, 1780. Brown allegedly hanged thirty captives (most accounts, however, say thirteen) and let the Indians behead four others. Brown denied responsibility for the Augusta atrocities. His biographer suggests the probability that Lieutenant Colonel John Harris Cruger, "who rescued Brown and superceded him carried out Cornwallis's standing order to hang all relapsed parolees."[27] William "Bloody Bill" Cunningham and his band, known as the "Bloody Scout," dispensed terror throughout the Carolinas and Georgia. Cunningham even had sick persons taken from their beds "into the yard" and put to death "in cold blood." In November 1781 alone, Cunningham's Tory militia, in South Carolina's Ninety-Six District, slaughtered fourteen captives seized from a rebel post and shortly afterward "most cruelly murdered and mangled" Captain Sterling Turner and twenty other prisoners. Turner was decapitated, and one of his men had both hands cut off before he was killed.[28]

In the backcountry, if the cruelties of the internecine war were not enough, depredations by bandit gangs and Indians from the mountains added to the terror. Sometimes Indians and Tories combined in making raids.

Moravians living in settlements in the Wachovia tract (Friedberg, Friedland, Bethania, Bethabara, Hope, and Salem), near the Yadkin River in northern North Carolina, regularly endured robberies of their homes and storehouses. The peaceful brethren were not above strong-arming and shooting at the "villains" within their towns, and they served as guides for local militia in pursuit into the mountains.[29]

Governor Thomas Burke of North Carolina referred to the "remorseless plunderers and murderers" who combed the backcountry.[30] After the war, one writer commented that "there were in the upper country a great many plundering renegades," who "belonged to no party" and "were a great terror to the inhabitants. They were always prowling about in small companies and never living in one place. In fact their habits were as migratory as the wandering Arabs."[31] General Greene, while encamped at Ninety-Six in June 1781, advised Colonel Elijah Clarke that there were "parties living over the mountains who are carrying away Negroes and committing other enormities which want checking."[32] This came as no surprise to Clarke, whose own militia troops "consisted of men whose restless dispositions or crimes prevented them living in any country wherever the resemblance of government was maintained" and who, therefore, had "betaken themselves to the vacant lands on the western frontier."[33]

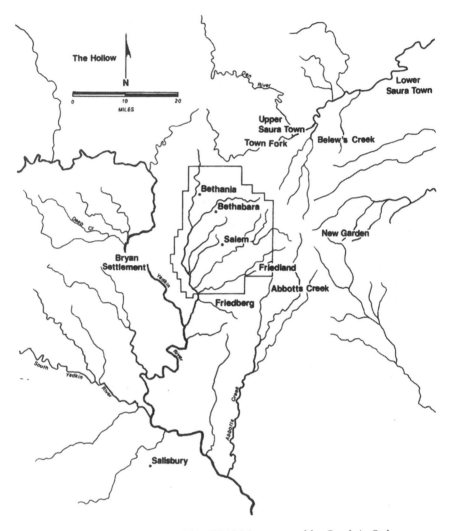

"Wachovia and Its Environs, 1753–1774." Map prepared by Carol A. Sielemann. From Daniel B. Thorp, *The Moravian Community in Colonial North Carolina: Pluralism on the Southern Frontier* (Knoxville: University of Tennessee Press, 1989). Reproduced by permission of the University of Tennessee Press.

Indians and mixed bands of renegade whites and Indians harassed back-country settlements. William Bates ("Bloody Bates") led a band of Indians and Tories who terrorized western settlements in the Carolinas. Operating mainly in Spartanburg and present Greenville counties of South Carolina, the desperados usually limited their raids to farms and families of men who were away with Andrew Pickens's militia or Greene's army. Among the dastardly deeds of the Bates banditti was a raid at the farm of a Mr. Motley in Spartanburg County. The gang promptly killed Motley and several others. Intending also to murder Motley's son, Bates first asked him to remove his clothes and buckles, so that these articles would not be bloodied. When Bates leaned forward to grab a buckle, young Motley sprang forward, knocking down several of his oppressors, and escaped.[34] In late 1780, Bates's men captured two small forts and massacred all persons within them. Pursued by patriot militia, Bates fled into Cherokee Indian territory for safety. After the war, Bates turned to horse thievery, was arrested, and was incarcerated in the Greenville log jail. Young Motley, whose father had been killed by Bates, took the keys to the jail from the sheriff, gained custody of Bates, and shot him dead.[35]

Indian marauding plagued Carolina and Georgia settlers. Despite the quelling of the Cherokee uprising of 1776, warrior bands reappeared in the backcountry, killing and scalping settlers. Punitive expeditions led by Andrew Pickens and Elijah Clarke, penetrating into the Cherokee country in 1782, put a stop to the Indian raids, and a new treaty secured more of the Cherokee lands.[36] The Creeks, although proclaiming neutrality during the war, gave some aid to the British, and occasionally tribesmen made raids against rebel settlements. Seventy warriors served with General Augustine Prevost's invasion of South Carolina in 1779, and other Creeks assisted Thomas Brown's Rangers. In April 1779 it was reported that "a party of 30 savages either Indians or British painted as Indians" crossed the Savannah River below Purysburg and "proceeded to the house of Capt. Hartston, set fire to the buildings on the plantation, murdered and scalped an old negro woman." The family managed to escape.[37]

Blacks serving with the British army as forward units to skirmish with the enemy outside the lines and as foragers, despite measures to keep them in check, often engaged in pillaging. General Alexander Leslie's Black Dragoons, in the summer of 1782, were "daily committing the most horrible depredations."[38]

The depletion of livestock made regions in the South appear all the more as wastelands. At the start of the war it was not unusual for North Carolina and Georgia planters to have herds of a thousand or more head of cattle, but war demands and cattle rustling exacted a heavy toll. "Cattle are every where very poor and scarce," commented an American army captain in February 1782.[39] Banditti from East Florida drove away sizeable numbers of livestock. Cornwallis's army in its invasion of the Carolinas lived largely off the land, and Greene's force obtained 50 percent of its food from impressment. Cattle thieves posed as army impressment agents. Cornwallis complained in July 1780 that "evil-disposed persons" seized cattle, "falsely asserting that they were properly authorized to do so."[40]

Military forces were the most responsible in depriving families of necessary subsistence by taking their cattle, along with hogs and horses. "The Enemy are no more than a small party come over to plunder & drive off cattle," Colonel Bernard Beekman, a South Carolina officer, reported to General Benjamin Lincoln. The American general himself was concerned that patriot militia were doing the same. He asked Governor John Rutledge of South Carolina to order militia not to clean out homesteads. For those residents "who are between the lines of the two armies," it was only humane to leave some cattle, horses, and provisions for "the Support of the distressed families."[41]

From time to time, Loyalist bands of rustlers were captured. In August 1779 patriot troops in South Carolina "made prisoners of 16 men, who were driving 400 cattle to Georgia, and brought off the cattle."[42] Loyalist militia also became exasperated with cattle rustling at their expense. On one occasion William Cunningham's partisans ran across Oliver Towles, well known for stealing cattle from Tories. Towles was hanged, fittingly "with a thong cut from the rawhide of a Tory cow."[43]

Upland Georgians stole from each other's range herds. In March 1782 Governor John Martin notified Colonel Elijah Clarke that some "inhabitants" of Wilkes County "drove several gangs of cattle" from Burke County into their own county, and "forty others are daily expected there on the same horrid business." Martin requested Clarke order the "field officers" of the Wilkes County militia "to be vigilant in apprehending & securing all such parties of men."[44]

The prevalence of horse stealing called for exemplary justice. At the start of the war, South Carolina did not have the death penalty for horse thievery. It was felt that without a capital penalty a horse thief would less likely commit murder to cover up his tracks. A person might even innocently pick up a horse he thought was a stray. As the war became an increasingly bitter one and banditti were everywhere, the harsh penalty was restored in South Carolina, largely as a protection for farmers whose livelihood was threatened by the theft of a horse.[45]

During the war, North Carolina courts sentenced horse thieves to be hanged.[46] James Iredell, a North Carolina judge, wrote in July 1782 that his court was "altogether taken up with Criminals, mostly for horse stealing." In the fall 1779 session of Iredell's court, five persons were condemned to die for the crime.[47]

Partisan militia rooted out horse thieves. Culprits either were killed during a fight or often afterward were summarily dispatched.[48]

A South Carolina gang headed by Tobias and Ambrosius Sikes had a long record of stealing horses. In early 1784, however, a militia company under Captain Jacob Rumpf accosted the bandits, killed two of them (William Jones and Ambrosius Sikes), and mortally wounded another member of the gang. Tobias Sikes and Thomas M'Dowell were captured, convicted in a court, and hanged in Charleston on March 5, 1784.[49]

Horse thievery continued to be a major problem in the backcountry. Aedanus Burke lamented in 1784 that the "poor people" of the Ninety-Six District were "harassed by a set of horsethieves and an outlying Banditti that constantly beset the roads, rob the inhabitants and plunder dwellings." Burke, a circuit judge who tried criminal cases at Ninety-Six, resulting in a number of capital convictions, announced that "for however averse I ever was to the taking away of life, I have seen so much of distress in the country on my circuit that I am resolved never again to recommend a horse thief for mercy 'til the Crime be less frequent."[50]

In the war-devastated South, bandits roamed the countryside, posing as supporters of one side or the other as convenience suited them or not bothering at all with any pretence of loyalty, indiscriminately plundering. Colonel Wade Hampton found that, in the area around his station at Friday's Ferry in upper South Carolina, "almost every person that remain'd" after military forces passed through in 1781 "seems to have combin'd in committing Robberies the most base & inhuman that ever disgraced man kind."[51] General Griffith Rutherford of North Carolina reported that "our frontiers are greatly distressed with Tories and Robbers."[52] A grand jury of Richmond County, Georgia, meeting in Augusta in March 1780, cited "the infamous and execrable custom of Plundering pursued by Persons lost to all Sense of Virtue & Shame, by which the property of the friendly and unfriendly, the Widow & the Orphan is indiscriminately Subject to the Lawless hands of Violence & rapine."[53]

While most militia bands, Tory and rebel, were guilty of plundering and committing cruelties, some were hardly more than groups of outlaws. In spring 1781 "a numerous rebel banditti," some of them from South Carolina, "who skulk about in the Woods & Swamps," raided in Georgia, murdering three dozen Loyalists in their homes.[54] Ned Williams and a Captain Barton led Tory gangs in the Beaufort district of South Carolina; "they are desperate fellows, killing, plundering and robbing the inhabitants without mercy or feeling."[55]

Captain Bill Young and a Tory band went on a murderous rampage in upper South Carolina during 1781. Young's men gained easy admission into patriot homes by wearing a piece of paper in their hats, imprinted with large capital letters, "Liberty or Death," an insignia sported by patriot militia.[56] In early 1779 "a villainous tribe of plunderers, under the celebrated horse thief, Capt. Few," ravaged a thirty-mile stretch above Augusta, "without regard to age or sex, the widow or the orphan's cries," and "worse than the heathen savages of the wilderness," murdered in cold blood. "Every man that had a ride pushed instantly in quest of the robbers," but Few and his followers, except one, escaped across the Savannah into South Carolina.[57]

Some Loyalist military units sanctioned by the British command were viewed more as banditti than as soldiers. John Harrison recruited ne'er-do-wells to form the South Carolina Rangers in June 1780. He was commissioned a major, and his brother, Robert, a captain. A biographer of General Francis Marion claims that the two brothers were "two of the greatest banditti that ever invested this country [South Carolina]." Although alloted 500 men, the South Carolina Rangers seldom had more than sixty. Harrison's troops joined with Major James Wemyss's 63d British Regiment in August 1780 in cutting a swath in the Williamsburg district, from Georgetown to Cheraw, plundering and burning fifty plantations, and then in patrolling the area between the Santee and Pee Dee rivers. Wemyss wrote to General Cornwallis about his disgust with Harrison's Rangers: "They are if possible worse than militia, their sole desire being to plunder and steal, and when they have got as much as their horses will carry" return home. During eighteen months 42 percent of the Rangers were lost through casualties and desertion. When enlistments expired on December 24, 1781, few reenlisted. John Harrison and the remaining men then did service with the South Carolina Royalists, based in East Florida.[58]

Small outlaw gangs took advantage of the anarchy caused by the war and the vulnerability of a scattered citizenry living in the countryside. Perhaps the most legendary of this breed was "Plundering Sam" Brown. Sam, along with his sister, Charity, performed many thieveries in the Catawba-Yadkin river area of western North Carolina and northwestern South Carolina. The main loot consisted of horses, wearing apparel, pewter ware, and money. Samuel Brown hailed from Tryon (now Lincoln) County, North Carolina. For a while he served as a Loyalist militia captain, and, in 1778, hid out in the woods for six weeks with partisan leader David Fanning. Brown was once married. His wife, finding him increasingly repulsive, returned to her father's farm; Brown, in a rage, killed all of his father-in-law's livestock. Sam Brown had a perfect hideaway: a cave on a 300-foot bluff above the Catawba River, at Look-out Shoals, fifteen miles northwest of Stateville, North Carolina. A large rock partially concealed the entrance to the cave.

One time, while in the Spartanburg area, Brown and an accomplice, one Butler, visited the home of Josiah Culbertson, who was absent at the time. Culbertson's wife refused to disclose her husband's whereabouts, and Brown became abusive, promising to return and burn the house and kill Josiah Culbertson. Brown later kidnapped John Thomas, the father of Mrs. Culbertson, and took him, his two sons, his slaves, and his horses to the British at Ninety-Six. To avenge Brown's deeds, Josiah Culbertson, accompanied by Charles Holloway, went in search of Brown and Butler, finally tracing the outlaws to a house near the Tyger River, where they had paused to rest. While the two outlaws left the house heading toward a roadside stable to get their horses, Culbertson shot Brown dead; Butler escaped. A visit to Brown's cave revealed the outlaw's mistress, who denied any complicity in robberies. Chastity Brown fled westward into the mountains. No hidden treasure was discovered in the area of Brown's hideout, except some pewter ware in a felled hollow tree.[59]

William Lee, who had been sentenced to death in 1763 for cattle and horse stealing but pardoned owing to insanity, was associated with William Cunningham's Tory raiders during the war, and then went out on his own. In 1785 the South Carolina legislature designated Lee the "most noted of the banditti who have so long infested the district of Ninety-Six."[60] In August 1781 Colonel Wade Hampton sent "all those plunderers which have been apprehended" to General Greene's camp, with a list of their names and crimes; unfortunately, the list has not been found. Eluding Hampton's net, however, was Francis Goodwyn, who had been "at the Bottom" of most of the robberies. Goodwyn made the practice of committing robberies in northeastern South Carolina and then retreating back into North Carolina.[61]

The Georgia Council, on October 22, 1782, proscribed twenty-two outlaws:

WHEREAS, there are a number of notorious characters, who infest the roads and other parts of the State, and are continually murdering and plundering the virtuous inhabitants of the same, and in order to the more effectually expelling and totally annihilating those enemies to mankind (those hellish and diabolical fiends) from the face of the earth. Therefore,

ORDERED That any person either employed in the public service or otherways, shall not only be released from his term of enlistment, but shall also receive the sum of ten guineas as a reward on his producing to the Governor and Council in Savannah the body, or good and sufficient proof that such of the under mentioned persons are absolutely and bona fide killed—

Samuel Moore	John Jarvis
George Cooke	John Webster
Henry Cooper Jun[r]	Joseph Adams
William Cooper	Swearing Jones
Samuel Cooper	Philip Thomas
Henry Cooper Sen[r]	James Altman
Noah Harrill	Thomas Altman
Cudd Mobly	Elias Bonnell
Ludd Mobly	Owen Harrigall
Capt. Marler	Clark Johnson
William Langham	Jack Hague[62]

Travelers went on their way at great peril in the Revolutionary South. There was always a prospect of confronting partisan militia. A Moravian group, near the end of their journey to Camden, in June 1782, had to turn back when they learned there was "not a chance for us to get through the Swamp, as there were more than three hundred Tories in it, and while they would probably not kill us, they would rob us of everything we possessed."[63] Colonel Samuel Hammond noted that, near Augusta in 1781, "both roads were closely watched and guarded by some Seventy or Eighty men. Each party lay concealed in the bushes, impatiently waiting, like vultures, for their prey."[64]

Even more feared than armed military bands were the highwaymen, unconnected with any party, who waylaid roads, popping out from forests and thickets to rob unwary travelers of valuables and horses, and even commit murder. The topography of the eighteenth-century South encouraged highway robbery. Except in some areas of the low country, roads were cut through dense forests and swamps, which provided quick refuge and concealment for road thieves. Unwisely, the Georgia government required trees within ten feet of a roadway to remain uncut, upon penalty of a fine.[65] In America, as in England, the incidence of highway robbery diminished in proportion to an increased rate of area settlement and development. Highway robbery had been a problem during the colonial period, but during the Revolution, with the vast numbers of persons suddenly displaced and impoverished, it became an even more fearsome reality.

Road conditions that impeded or slowed traffic made travelers all the more easy victims of highwaymen. The longest thoroughfare was the Philadelphia Great Wagon Road which traced a course in western Virginia and in the Carolinas passed through Salem, Bethania, Salisbury, Charlotte, and Camden before terminating at Augusta, Georgia. No routes had hard surfaces; most were barely more than Indian and bridle paths, cattle trails, and private roadways connecting plantations to river fronts. Maintenance was provided by local citizens, and in sparsely settled areas upkeep was practically nil. Heavy freight wagons, with narrow wheels, cut up the roadways. Floods, mud, sand, and unreliable corduroy bridges (made with thin logs covered with earth for use in swampy areas) were obstacles to travel, as were the steep hills and slippery, sticky red clay (when wet) in the piedmont region.[66]

Upper-class travelers could normally expect a hearty welcome from the owners of plantations. Hosts relished entertaining company and catching up on the news. The war, however, diminished such receptions. One North Carolina traveler in 1782 reported that "we saw nothing but burned houses and open fields; now and then houses still standing but completely ruined."[67] Lieutenant Anthony Allaire and three other officers of the Loyal American

Roadside scene, western Carolina: "The Cherokees are coming!" From *Harper's Magazine*, vol. 71 (June 1885), p. 74.

Regiment, in November 1780, stopped overnight at the Sheppard plantation in upper South Carolina: "this poor family were so completely stripped of everything they had, by the Rebels, that they could give us nothing but a hoe cake, and some dried beef."[68]

As well as despoiled plantations along the roadways, one could find hovels of the very poor. William Drayton (cousin of William Henry Drayton), traveling near the Saluda River in 1784, observed that "the Huts along the Road in general are miserable dwellings, built with Logs open to the Wind & Rain, & inhabited by a Parcel of half naked Beings, almost every one with out shoe or stocking."[69]

With few options for decent accommodations, respectable travelers had little choice but to lodge in one of many ordinaries, which were filthy log huts that catered to riffraff. Even before the war, such establishments were abominable. Wrightstill Avery, a lawyer, recalled staying at a one-room roadside ordinary in North Carolina in 1769. He spent a sleepless night among several inebriated men, "who all blunder'd brawl'd, spew'd and cursed, broke one another's heads, and their own shins with stools and bruised their Hips and Ribs with Sticks of the Couch Pens, pulled hair, lugg'd hallo'd, swore, fought and kept up the Roar-Rororum till Morning."[70]

Horse thieves and other delinquents gathered at the roadside ordinaries. At one such place, between Augusta and Savannah in 1775, a traveler lamented that "to a very bad dinner, was added the oaths and execrations of as detestable a crew as horse thieves in general are."[71] One may presume that the Southern highwaymen, much like their counterparts in Elizabethan England, learned from an innkeeper or his servants a traveler's intended route and what might be the contents of his baggage. Although hosts were in collusion with thieves, they were not party to robbery occurring several miles farther along the road.[72]

Highway robbery carried less risk than most thievery. One could waylay one or several victims and then quickly disappear into the wilderness. Those highwaymen who were most persistent, however, inevitably met their match or were hunted down and killed.

The war offered expanded motivation for becoming a highway robber. To some malefactors it was simply a matter of survival. General William Henry Harrington of the South Carolina militia, on a journey from visiting his family in Richmond County to his command station at Cross Creek (Fayetteville, North Carolina), within two miles of McKay's ordinary directed his aides to go there, while he alone took a side road to spend the night at a friend's home. The next morning, upon resuming his journey, he was suddenly hailed by a young man behind a tree, pointing his gun and ordering Harrington to dismount. The assailant entered the road and demanded Harrington hand over his money. The victim complied, delivering all that he had, five guineas. To Harrington's surprise, the robber returned three guineas, saying that Harrington looked like he needed the money. Later when Harrington and his troops encamped near Wilmington, a captive was brought in, tried, and condemned to death. Harrington recognized the doomed man as the one who had robbed him. Thinking that the prisoner could not be all bad, having not taken all his money, Harrington interviewed his former assailant, and asked him why he had turned to high-way robbery. The reason was extreme poverty. Harrington countermanded the death sentence on condition that the prisoner sign up with his troops, which he gladly did. The new recruit faithfully served out his enlistment.[73] A Moravian diarist cited another factor why persons became highwaymen: "Fear of being called into the militia has driven many to hide in the woods, and as they have nothing on which to live they resort to highway robbery."[74]

Military escorts accompanied army supply wagons as protection against robbers as well as the enemy.[75] Soldiers away from their units had to be careful. In August 1780 thirteen-year-old Lewis Ayer, on an errand to warn a Whig militia detachment, was greeted on a road near Cheraw, South Carolina, by a decrepit old man, wielding a long-barreled fowling piece. Ayer asked for directions and was told to keep on going, past where two dead British soldiers were lying in the road. The old man himself had killed the two redcoats for plundering the home of an elderly woman who lived nearby.[76]

Bands of highwaymen made traveling the roads out of Savannah unsafe. In 1780 the McKay gang of twenty horsemen frequently robbed travelers on the Savannah-Augusta thoroughfare. Two years later, Samuel Moore and "his infernal set of outlaws" were doing the same. Persons were "obliged to travel through the woods and avoid all roads."[77] General Lachlan McIntosh, a Georgia planter and a Continental Army general, complained in October 1782 that robbery "has grown to such a Highth by a Lawless Savage & unprincipled Banditti" that "traveling a Mile upon the Roads" was unsafe.[78] About the same time John Martin, the rebel governor of Georgia, advised that the "people on the Carolina side" of the Savannah River should be aware that "the roads are waylaid."[79]

Traversing Carolina roads entailed similar hazards. General Greene, from "Camp Cheraws" on the Pee Dee River, just below the South Carolina–North Carolina border, observed that "people between this and the Santee are frequently murdered as they ride along the road, also between this and Cross Creek, Guilford Court House and Hillsborough"; in this "extent of Country great numbers of tories are way laying the roads."[80]

A North Carolina widow, Mrs. Martha Bell, showed her mettle when confronted by a highwayman. Upon the death of her husband, William Bell, Mrs. Bell assumed direction of his farming and merchandizing concerns, which required making various trips. On a journey from her plantation on Deep River in Randolph County, to Petersburg, Virginia, passing through a sparsely settled area, she was accosted on the road by Stephen Lewis, an outlaw who had once served with David Fanning's Tory raiders. Lewis had spotted Mrs. Bell coming down the road and figured that he did not need to take any precaution. Lewis dismounted, hitched his horse to a tree, and rested his gun next to the tree. Sauntering out, unarmed, to the middle of the road, he blocked Mrs. Bell's passage. The highwayman found himself staring into a barrel of a pistol that Mrs. Bell had drawn. She warned Lewis that if he took another step she would shoot him. Proceeding down the road, Mrs. Bell kept her prisoner in front, expecting to deliver him to some local authority. The captive, however, escaped, only later to be killed by his own brother.[81]

The Moravians experienced major problems with highwaymen during the war. The brethren conducted trade over a wide area, extending from the mountains of Virginia to Charleston, South Carolina. They were often on the road to the Quaker settlement of New Garden, the Cape Fear towns of Cross Creek, Brunswick, and Wilmington, and Hillsborough, Salisbury, and Pine Tree (Camden). From their industrial and marketing town, Bethabara, they shipped commodities including butter, flour, provisions, saddles, shoes, pottery, clothing, blankets, tinware, and axes. Deerskins were a substantial trade staple. Each year some 400 visitors arrived to exchange goods.[82]

Moravian diarists frequently referred to highwaymen and robbers who lurked in the woods and attacked travelers and residents, calling them *spitz-buben* (rascals/thieves): "a band of horse-thieves and robbers prepared to rob and plunder everything that came their way" (April 1770); "at present there are many highwaymen about, who steal and even murder" (November 1780); "robbers swarming in the woods" around Bethania (February 1781). Robberies on the roads were reported from time to time. In one instance (in June 1777),

when our negro Jacob, from the tavern, went for the cows and was one mile out on the Friedland road, he was murderously attacked by a man who wanted his clothes and who struck him over the head with a club. Jacob jerked the club away from him and hit him in the face, bringing the blood; the man cried for help and the negro let him go, fearing there might be other rascals in the woods.

The Moravians preferred backing off from apprehending highwaymen, thinking that sooner or later the militia or other local authorities would catch up with them. The brethren were not overjoyed when Colonel William Campbell and his western Virginia militia hanged "a well known high-wayman" next to the brewery in Salem, although the culprit "himself admitted that he deserved death."[83]

Several years passed after the war before inland roads became relatively safe for travel. Colonel William Bratton of North Carolina declared, in February 1784, that persons were being robbed "in open daylight upon the highway" and that it was "out of the power of the law to suppress" the robbers.[84] In March 1784, when the president and other members of the

Executive Council of Georgia, journeyed from Savannah to Augusta to establish a new land court, each county, as the group passed through its borders, was required to furnish an escort of from six to twelve horsemen in order to guarantee safety.[85]

The destruction and pillaging committed by partisan raiders and unconnected banditti turned much of the inland South into wasteland. Poverty increased. J.F.D. Smyth could have been referring to other sections as well when he said in 1784 that the settlements along the Cape Fear River "and its branches are greatly depopulated, or decreased in the number of inhabitants since the general war."[86] Law and order, however, soon returned, and the justice systems once again functioned fully and new counties and courts were established.

Yet the psychological effects of the anarchy and excessive brutality of citizens against citizens during the war could not be easily erased. Judge Aedanus Burke, presiding over the Court of General Sessions in Charleston, on June 10, 1783, in his charge to the grand jury, expressed his fear that citizens "from the habit of putting their enemies to death, have reconciled their minds to the killing of each other" and that "man by custom may be so brutalized as to relish human blood."[87] Ralph Izard, a South Carolina congressman, wrote to Thomas Jefferson in April 1784 that the "inconveniences" resulting from "conflagrations" and robberies committed by the British would "in a little time be forgotten." But "the animosity, and hatred planted by them in the breasts of our Citizens against each other, is the most serious injury they have done us."[88] The uncivil war in the South created a legacy of proneness toward violence, vigilantism, extremism, and class hatred that was to last many generations.

Epilogue

In certain respects, the War for Independence was not unique to the American experience. Rebellion and resistance had been a regular occurrence, including, in the seventeenth century, the civil wars in Maryland, Bacon's Rebellion, and the repercussions of the Glorious Revolution in New England, New York, and Maryland; and in the eighteenth century, the rebellions in North Carolina (1711 and 1771) and South Carolina (1719) and the land riots in New Jersey (1740s) and New York (1760s). The colonies had formed a confederation (New England, 1643–1690) without consulting the mother country and had combined resources and manpower to wage war against a foreign enemy. The decade before the Revolution witnessed an accelerating protest movement against Parliamentary authority. Of course, the American Revolution attained singular accomplishments in establishing independence and a federal republic. The savagery exhibited between whites and Native Americans during the Revolution and its immediate aftermath represented but another bloody chapter in the ethnic conflict along a moving frontier.

Uniquely the Revolutionary War itself was a successful, prolonged revolt against the mother country, involving peoples of North America east of the Mississippi and having a global dimension. Significantly it also brought on a vicious predation of neighbors against neighbors.

The Revolutionary War may be viewed as a major episode in the con-

tinuum of violence that has shaped American identity and character. According to Richard Slotkin, from a literary perspective, "The myth of
regeneration through violence became the structuring metaphor of the
American experience."[1] Charles Royster has called attention to America's
being founded "not just on principles but also on the passions of bloodshed."[2]

As a civil war, the Revolution created a milieu that encouraged brutality
and depredations. Areas most prone to disorder were those with opposing
military forces nearby. While neither the American nor the British military
commands sanctioned marauding, it was a common practice. Military capabilities were lacking on both sides during most of the campaigns to effect
a decisive conclusion to the war. At the subsurface, a struggle, motivated
by revenge mixed with greed, emerged as a kind of guerrilla warfare that
could wear down an enemy. The British seldom held refugee bands and
Loyalist militia accountable for excessive violence and depredations. Although regular soldiers faced severe punishment for plundering citizens, violations were often overlooked. Members of the outright banditti gangs had
short careers, falling victims to an enraged populace, and the perpetrators
were killed legally or extralegally or scared off permanently.

Outside of army depredations, the banditti phenomenon was much of a
one-sided affair; perpetrators often had Loyalist affiliation. Of course, in the
South, the worst depredations and atrocities were committed by both rebels
and Tories; the rebels were perhaps the more brutal. But, by and large, with
the British unable to secure territory, the Tories, confronted with dire
threats to their lives, families, and property, had little choice but to flee to
near or within the British lines. When there was an opportunity, the refugees returned to wreak vengeance upon their oppressors, aiming at destruction or appropriation of property. As one historian has observed, "By openly
advocating a war of depredation and revenge the Refugees willingly burned
their bridges behind them."[3]

The banditti of Westchester County, New York; Long Island Sound; New
York Highlands; and the coastal and pine barrens areas and the Hackensack
Valley in New Jersey; and the Southern maroons operated within confines.
The Doane gang, however, moved freely throughout eastern and western
Pennsylvania and in Maryland. Picaroons had full range of the coasts of
Virginia and Maryland, and Southern bandits and marauders covered large
regions of the Carolinas and Georgia, reaching from the far backcountry to
Spanish East Florida. Most banditti leaders were young, in their mid to late
twenties, and were the sons of small farmers, who at the start of the war
were regarded as persons disaffected to the American cause.

Success of British arms in the South, especially the securing of Georgia
in 1779, the capture of Charleston, and the defeat of the Southern Con-

tinental army under General Gates in 1780, accentuated the internecine aspects of warfare. A premium was placed on allegiance, with Whigs and Tories employing extreme measures to induce inhabitants to disavow any attachment to the opposite side. Brutality met with retribution in kind. In the Southern backcountry, much of the struggle had the semblance of class war. Riffraff and wanderers, some of whom had joined the South Carolina Regulator movement in the 1760s, "infested" the backcountry as freebooters and members of Tory militia bands. The backcountry offered ample refuge in the mountains and Indian territory. Many went off to East Florida, where they enlisted in the Loyalist provincial units that raided in Georgia and the Carolinas. Similar to their Northern counterparts, Southern "refugee" banditti were assisted by sympathizers, who were soon disllusioned by the indiscriminate raiding.

Scotch-Irish settlers in the backcountry from Pennsylvania to South Carolina had long been accustomed to violence as a remedy for societal or personal wrongs, real or imagined. Such a propensity was evident in western Pennsylvania before the war in the murder of the peaceful Conestoga Indians and, after the war, in the events that culminated in the Whiskey Rebellion. The American backwoods honed a sense of deprivation and a contempt for government and law. According to Terry G. Jordan and Matti Kaups, "The massive genetic contribution of the Ulster immigrants to the American backwoods population convincingly supports a claim of detrimental societal influence." These immigrants reverted to "medieval Scottish methods of suppressing violence and depredation."[4]

The slowness in establishing sufficient government institutions in the backcountry contributed to the social instability. One principle of "backcountry order ways," according to David Hackett Fischer, was "the idea that order was a system of retributive violence and that each individual was the guardian of his own interests in that respect."[5]

The war was viewed as having a debilitating effect on character. "The spirit of men became more and more debased," wrote Traugott Bagge, a Moravian leader in North Carolina. "Many a lad, in his native simplicity, went into the field with the Militia, and a few months later came back a thorough scamp. This made life harder and harder, for men became more and more brutal."[6] Benjamin F. Perry, a politician of antebellum South Carolina, noted that "the idleness of habits, the laxness of morals, and general improvidence of almost all classes of persons, were perhaps the most serious and permanent evils which the country sustained during the Revolutionary War."[7]

More evident after the war than before, backcountry and frontier rowdies delighted in sadistic violence. "Knock-down and drag-out" contests often resulted in the severance of body parts, such as noses, lips, ears, and eyes. A traveler in the western country was horrified at the savagery of the "backwoodsmen, as the first emigrants from the eastward of the Allegheny mountains are called." The ruffians fought each other over the slightest provocation. "Their hands, teeth, knees, head and feet are their weapons." The combatants engaged not only in fisticuffs but also in "tearing, kicking, scratching, biting, gouging each others eyes out by a dexterous use of a thumb and finger, and doing their utmost to kill each other." If a victor continued to harm an opponent who had given up, "he is generally attacked by a fresh man, and a pitched battle between a single pair often ends in a battle royal, where all present are engaged." Reportedly an observer

who had kept aloof during a fray of this kind, when it was over, seeing a man with the top of his nose bit off . . . approached him and commiserated his misfortune. "Don't pity me," said the noseless hero, "pity that fellow there," pointing with one hand to another who had lost an eye, and shewing the eye he held triumphantly in the other.[8]

Davy Crockett, in Tennessee, boasted about a rough-and-tumble that he had been in: "I kept my thumb in his eye, and was just going to give it a twist and bring the peeper out, like taking up a gooseberry in a spoon."[9]

Judge Aedanus Burke mentioned that at a trial over which he presided in the South Carolina upcountry the plaintiff, a juror, and two witnesses all had a missing eye.[10] In 1786 South Carolina enacted a law that made severing another person's body parts a capital offense, with the exception of the removal of ears and noses, which involved no other harm than disfigurement.[11]

While many backwoodsmen were outcasts or fugitives from eastern communities, one may wonder what happened generally to the banditti who had surfaced under wartime conditions. Some met justice during the war; others kept to their criminal ways on familiar turf. Highway robbery and cattle rustling in the South persisted into the antebellum period. Frequently, in South Carolina, criminals were "sent packing" to leave the state.[12] Many of the Tory banditti joined in the mass exodus to other British territories in the Western Hemisphere. Others went with the westward migration, leaving their pasts behind to begin life anew, by and large being accepted by pioneer neighbors who themselves were seeking a clean slate. A very few of former Tory banditti were fortunate in being able to remain in their original home areas, in accordance with a spirit of toleration agreed upon in the peace treaty of 1783, and with time healing old wounds.

Various travelers after the war had the impression that the backcountry and frontier had become receptacles for the lawless and indolent. It is impossible to determine the numbers of actual criminals and other troublemakers in the original states who, at war's end, felt the necessity to push westward, although a few can be identified.

Western Pennsylvania attracted the very poor. While population in the area increased, from 3,300 to 9,500 from the end of the war to 1800, 60 percent of the inhabitants were landless.[13] Among the newcomers were criminals who sought an environment of less secure law and order than in the East.[14] Border ruffians had already pretty much ruled the roost in the Pittsburgh–upper Ohio Valley region, priding themselves on killing Indians, such as the peaceful tribesmen slaughtered at Yellow Creek (1774), Beaver Creek (1780), and Gnadenhutten (1782).[15] The territorial dispute between Virginia and Pennsylvania, from 1774 to 1781, which led to establishing rival, duplicate governments for western Pennsylvania, hindered law enforcement.

David Lewis (the "Robin Hood of Pennsylvania") became the best-known outlaw in the region west of the Juniata River. Born in 1790 at Carlisle, Lewis entered the army at the age of seventeen. Imprisoned for desertion, he escaped and then turned to a life in crime, leading a band of counterfeiters and thieves. A menace to drovers and stagecoach travelers, the Lewis bandits had as their main hideout a cave at the foot of Kittanning Mountain. Lewis's career came to an end when, in June 1820, after waylaying a wagon driver he was wounded and captured by a posse. He died shortly afterward of gangrene.[16]

Some fugitives settled among mixed blood groups (whites–blacks–Native Americans) in the Appalachian Mountains at the borders of Virginia and the Carolinas and in eastern Tennessee. These "Tri-Racial Isolates," who had mysterious origins, included the Melungeons, allegedly descended from the Indians of early Virginia, and the Lumbee Indians, in and around Robeson County, North Carolina, said to be in direct lineage with the natives present at Sir Walter Raleigh's lost colony of the 1580s.[17]

While traveling in South Carolina in 1786, Luigi Castiglioni, an Italian botanist, noted that "delinquents" who had departed North Carolina, Virginia, and Pennsylvania had fled into the mountains, where they "hid away in the woods to escape pursuit by the law, and there they continue a vagabond life."[18] A Charleston newspaper commented in the same year that "many there are who depend wholly on hunting for a subsistence, and have supported nature's calls out of the forest without attending to civilization."[19]

The Creek Indian country now began to receive an influx of blacks and whites, some of whom were illegal squatters, while others mingled with tribesmen. General Andrew Pickens of South Carolina decried that "disorderly persons" were moving on to Creek lands, and the Georgia Executive Council expressed alarm that "banditti and thieves" were taking cover on Creek hunting grounds.[20]

One gang that preyed on travelers and traders in the Creek country consisted of John Catt, a slave named Bob, Catt's wife, an Indian woman, and
an Indian man nicknamed "the Murderer." In 1789 the band crept into the
camp of a trading party, whose members were Colonel Kirkland, his son,
John Linder, "another white man," and a black boy. Bob picked up a gun
leaning against a tree and "put it to the head of the old man, and blowed
his brains out." Catt slit the throat of Kirkland's son with a knife. Linder
"had a tomahawk stuck in his head; he after set on his hams, and throwing
his head back, Catt stuck him in the throat." The "Murderer" killed the
other white man with a hatchet. The robbers "took everything except the
clothes on the ded [*sic*] bodies"; the black boy was made a prisoner. The
Indians caught Catt, and the Creek chieftain, Alexander McGillivray, had
him executed.[21]

After the war, a floodtide of emigrants entered the Trans-Appalachian
West. Veterans exchanged military warrants for free land. Others purchased
lots from speculators or at public auction, while the very poor became squatters, claiming land by "cabin rights." Many settlers had been farmers or even
planters in the East, but among the immigrants were outcasts, adventurers,
and felons. Kentucky in 1790 had a population of 220,955.[22]

Moses Austin, while traveling on the Wilderness Road, from the southwestern corner of Virginia to central Kentucky in December 1796, noticed
that he passed "many Distressed families"; women and children made their
way through "Ice and Snow" across "large rivers and Creeks with out Shoe
or Stocking, and barely as maney raggs as covers their Nakedness, with out
money or provisions except what the Wilderness affords," all unrealistically
expecting to receive free land.[23]

From visiting Kentucky in about 1820, one traveler came away with the
impression that "the west has the scum of all the earth."[24] A historian of
the Kentucky frontier observed that "Transappalachia attracted not only
the congenitally reckless backwoodsmen . . . but also assorted incorrigibles,
for whom the older settlements held out the prospect of a life behind bars."[25]

An adequate criminal justice system was slow to come to Kentucky. Before 1782 criminals had to be transported several hundred miles to Richmond, Virginia, for trial. Subsequently a court for the district of Kentucky
and county courts alleviated the situation, but it was not until ten years
after statehood, in 1802, that circuit courts for trying criminal cases were
established, embracing thirty-three jurisdictions.[26] In some locales, the prevalence of large numbers of criminals intimidated law enforcement.

Horse stealing was a major problem in Kentucky. Judge Harry Innes reported in 1790 that from the end of the war the Indians had made off with
20,000 horses.[27] During the 1790s, in the Green River region of southwestern Kentucky, a large gang repeatedly collected rewards for recovering

horses they themselves stole, blaming the thefts on Indians.[28] In fact, during the mid 1790s, Logan County, constituting about one-half of southwestern Kentucky, including the Green River country, had the reputation of containing the "greatest concentration" of criminals on the frontier—murderers, horse thieves, counterfeiters, and highway robbers. When young Peter Cartwright moved to Logan County with his father in 1793, the county was referred to as "Rogues' Harbor" or "Satan's Stronghold." Cartwright reported how the criminal element was vanquished.

The honest and civil part of the citizens would prosecute these wretched banditti, but they would swear each other clear; and they really put all law at defiance, and carried on such desperate violence and outrage that the honest part of the citizens seemed to be driven to the necessity of uniting and combining together, and taking the law into their own hands, under the name of Regulators. This was a very desperate state of things.

Shortly after the Regulators organized,

a general battle ensued between the rogues and the Regulators, and they fought with guns, pistols, dirks, knives, and clubs. Some were actually killed, many wounded, the rogues proved victors, kept the ground, and drove the Regulators out of town. The Regulators rallied again, hunted, killed, and lynched many of the rogues, until several of them fled, and left for parts unknown.[29]

Before the war Virginians and North Carolinians crossed the Appalachian divide to settle in the river valleys of the Watauga, Holston, Clinch, and upper Tennessee, territory then part of North Carolina. These pioneers created the Watauga Association in 1772; after the North Carolina cession of Tennessee, the Wataugans, in 1785, formed the state of Franklin, which lasted until Congress established the Southwest Territory in 1790. Eastern Tennessee was not an area where former Tories and banditti were welcomed, considering that many of the inhabitants were the "overmountain men," who had exacted terrible vengeance on Tories after the battle of King's Mountain in 1780. Tories who did come into the area were denied protection of the forts, and lashings from "fine hickory whips" convinced them to keep on moving westward.[30]

The settlement along the Cumberland River in middle Tennessee, founded in 1779–80, flourished, and became Davidson County in 1783. Horse thieves plagued the community. Governor William Blount of the Southwest Territory reported that, from January through November 1792, 500 horses had been stolen in middle Tennessee. Both Indians and whites stole horses, sometimes in collaboration, and drove the animals away for sale as far as New Orleans, Georgia, Spanish Florida, and eastern Tennessee. Stern punishment awaited horse thieves, occasionally a hanging, but more often nailing a culprit's ears to a board and then cutting them off and also branding a "T" on one cheek and an "H" on the other. Those thieves who had been Tories had to sever their own ears with a dull knife.[31] A group of Tories during the war was allowed to settle along an "out of the way" branch of the Cumberland River.[32]

West Tennessee, between the Tennessee and Mississippi rivers, including Chickasaw Bluffs (Memphis area), did not fully open for settlement until after a treaty with the Chickasaw Indians in 1818. Drifters and squatters from the southeastern states and Alabama arrived along with Revolutionary War veterans taking up military lands. Samuel Cole Williams has identified only one Tory (from North Carolina) who settled in West Tennessee.[33]

By the time the Spanish government had ceded territory north of 31° latitude, the area along the Tombigbee River, just north of the new boundary line, had attracted diverse settlers: French planters, refugee Tories from the Carolinas and Georgia, numerous fugitives from both American and Spanish justice, and other outcasts. Cattle rustlers and other banditti plied both sides of the boundary. The Tombigbee settlement was isolated, separated from the territorial capital at Natchez by a great distance and by Indian country. In 1800, of the five local justices of the peace, three were fugitives—two were murderers and one had broken a condemned prisoner out of jail.[34]

Ephraim Kirby found the inhabitants of the Tombigbee region a dissolute sort. A notable lawyer from Connecticut, Kirby became a judge of the newly created Washington County (southwestern Alabama). He informed President Thomas Jefferson that "this section of the United States has long afforded an asylum to those who prefer voluntary exile to the punishments ordained by law for heinous offences." The administration of justice was "imbecile and corrupt." There were "emigrants from the Carolina's and Georgia who were attainted and proscribed for treasonable practices during the revolution." Since they had "long lived without any restraint, committing many enormities against society," they "are now hostile to all law and to every government."[35] As settlements spread in western Alabama, lawlessness was rampant. To instill order, extralegal groups punished criminals; these law enforcers, however, became so abusive and brutal that, as happened during the South Carolina Regulation movement of the 1760s, citizens resorted to further vigilantism to check the vigilantes.[36]

During the war Loyalists driven out of the Carolinas and Georgia appeared in the Spanish-controlled Natchez district, along the Mississippi River. Criminals were among the newcomers. An observer in 1778 commented that the Mississippi River was filled with "vagabonds & rascalls."[37] Even after the United States acquired the region, pirates and robbers preyed on the boats and barges conveying provisions and livestock from Kentucky and the Ohio country and raided the riverside plantations.[38] Kentuckians and others who had delivered cargoes to New Orleans, upon returning by land, were robbed of their hard-earned cash. The Natchez Trace, a 450-mile path from Natchez to Nashville, was beset with highwaymen.

Until General Anthony Wayne's victory at Fallen Timbers in August 1794, banditti in the Ohio Valley consisted almost exclusively of Indians who waylaid river travelers and stole horses on both sides of the Ohio River. The orderly settlement in the Northwest Territory precluded any major outlaw problem. Some of the newcomers, however, turned out to be horse thieves. In Princeton, Indiana, a traveler who inquired what was done with such offenders, received the reply, "O, shoot them off the horses."[39] Regulator associations in southern Illinois formed from time to time to catch horse thieves and counterfeiters.[40]

Outlaws positioned themselves along or near the Ohio River. In the early nineteenth century, "a gang of brigands" on the Little Blue River, just above its confluence with the Ohio, "lived by passing forged notes, stealing horses &c and hunting." The group had their headquarters at "a strong rock house among the hills."[41] River pirates from Diamond and Hurricane islands in the lower Ohio River robbed passing boats.[42]

From 1797 to 1808, robbers, murderers, and counterfeiters congregated at Cave-in-Rock, twenty miles below Shawneetown, Illinois. The cavern (160 feet deep, 40 feet wide, and 25 feet high) penetrated a limestone bluff overlooking the river. Denizens of the cave robbed boats passing by. A favorite snare was to have a woman stand on the bank and call for help, thereby enticing unsuspecting boatmen to approach land. The crews were killed and the cargoes were seized; the boats were either sunk or steered down the Mississippi by the outlaws, who then sold both the vessel and its contents. To better attract boatmen, a sign graced the entrance for a while: "Liquor Vault and House of Entertainment." Bodies of murder victims were weighted down in the river or disposed of in other ways. Sixty skeletons were eventually discovered in an out-of-the-way recess of the cave.[43]

Legend places a variety of vile characters at Cave-in-Rock. The most infamous of the outlaws on the Trans-Appalachian frontier, Samuel Mason and Micajah and Wiley Harpe, reportedly stayed for a while before moving on to less conspicuous haunts.

Samuel Mason, who was born in western Virginia in 1750, enlisted in the militia in 1777, rose to the rank of captain, and performed heroic service fighting Indians in the Ohio Valley. He accompanied George Rogers Clark's western expedition of 1778–79. Mason ran a tavern for a while near Wheeling, West Virginia. Settling down at Red Banks (Henderson, Kentucky) with his wife and five children, Mason lived as a respectable citizen and even served as a justice of the peace, while clandestinely leading a gang of robbers. After being implicated in thefts and several murders, Mason fell under suspicion and, in 1797, crossed the Ohio to Cave-in-Rock, where he stayed for about a year, allegedly joining other criminals in plundering and murdering boat crews. Mason then became the leader of "a daring banditti," consisting of two of his sons and about ten others; the gang "infested the wilderness from Natchez to Tennessee and the river Mississippi." Evading increased efforts to apprehend him on the eastern side of the Mississippi, Mason made his headquarters at Little Prairie, Missouri. Arrested by the Spaniards in July 1803, Mason and several members of his gang were sent to New Orleans. Spanish authorities, however, could not gather enough evidence for conviction, and the captives were sent upriver to Natchez for trial. On the way, they escaped, killing their chief guard, Captain Roberto McKay. The governor of Mississippi Territory offered a $2,000 reward for the capture of Mason dead or alive. Wiley Harpe and James May, who had joined Mason's gang, could not resist the temptation. They tomahawked the bandit leader and cut off his head. Placing the head in a sack, "rolled up in blue clay to prevent putrification," the treacherous killers carried their trophy to Greenville, just north of Natchez, where they presented it to a circuit court then in session. Instead of collecting the reward, Harpe and May were recognized by members of the community who had been victimized by them on the Natchez Trace. Tried for armed robbery, not murder, Harpe and May were convicted and hanged on February 4, 1804.[44]

If the Harpe brothers, sons of a North Carolina Tory, were too young to be numbered among banditti during the Revolution, they surpassed any outlaws in sheer horrific deeds. Leaving North Carolina in 1795, Micajah ("Big Harpe," born c. 1768) and Wiley ("Little Harpe," born c. 1770) with Betsey and Susan Roberts, who were sisters, struck out for the mountains of Tennessee. After living with outcast Cherokees for two years, the group rented a place eight miles from Knoxville. There they were joined by another woman, Sally Rice. The three mistresses each gave birth; later Big Harpe, annoyed by the crying of his own nine-month-old baby, dashed its brains out against a tree. Suspected of robberies and murders, the Harpes fled from eastern Tennessee into Kentucky. On the Wilderness Road the outlaws robbed travelers, leaving their badly mangled bodies behind. A posse caught up with the Harpes in December 1797, but, while lodged in the Lincoln County jail, awaiting trial, they escaped. The Harpe womenfolk with their babies remained but were eventually released, whereupon they managed to rejoin their hideous masters. Fearful citizens all over Kentucky were now on the lookout for the Harpes. Allegedly the Harpes found refuge at Cave-in-Rock, but there they were so cruel with their victims that they became persona non grata even among the other hardened criminals. Much has been written about the crimes of the Harpes. One fairly credible list cites thirty-nine murders committed by the Harpes. Chased by a posse in Muhlenberg County, Kentucky, Big Harpe was shot and killed; his severed head adorned a limb of an oak tree for many years, along "Harpe's Head Road," near the future town of Dixon. Wiley escaped the posse, but, as already noted, met his own end on the gallows. All three of the Harpe mistresses were tried as accessories to several of the Harpe murders in a district court in Russellville, Kentucky, but were acquitted. The women went their own ways and lived respectable lives for many years afterward.[45]

A primary figure among the Trans-Appalachian outlaws was a South Carolinian, James Ford (born c. 1782), who settled at Tolu (later Kirksville), on the Kentucky side of the Ohio, five miles below Cave-in-Rock. Ford passed as a reputable citizen—farmer, ferry operator, banker, and Livingston County sheriff—while all the time in league with and supervising the activities of a network of bandits. Ford became a large landholder by financing his acquisitions through ill-gotten gain. He kept an aloofness between himself and the criminals with whom he was associated. Although he was never arrested, Ford had a hand in several murders committed along a thoroughfare he established on the Illinois bank of the Ohio, Ford High Water Road (on which was a tavern kept by multiple murderer Billy Potts), and the Red Banks Trace, a branch of the Natchez Trace, which passed near his home. One murder too many finally led to revenge: Ford was assassinated in July 1833.[46]

Highwaymen appeared along the Federal Road (established by Congress in 1805), which traversed mainly Indian country from Athens, Georgia, by way of the Tombigbee settlement in Alabama on to New Orleans; northward the road followed the eastern piedmont, connecting with Washington, D.C., Baltimore, and Philadelphia. Foremost of the road bandits was a gang led by Joseph Thompson Hare, whose headquarters was Turk's Cave in Conecuh County, Alabama. Hare, born in Chester County, Pennsylvania, lived in Baltimore and Philadelphia before going west. For a while Hare's gang robbed travelers on the Natchez Trace from a hideaway just under the Tennessee line in Chickasaw County. The outlaws often disguised themselves as Indians, painting their faces with berry juices and bark stains. Hare was captured and imprisoned from 1813 to 1818. Immediately upon his release he headed for Baltimore, where, for robbing a mail coach (a federal capital crime), he was hanged on September 11, 1818.[47]

The outlaws of Trans-Appalachia represent a transition, from the banditti of the Revolutionary War to criminals exploiting frontier conditions. Of the miscreants of the Revolutionary period who drifted toward the frontier, some kept to a life of crime. But the frontier produced its own variety of cutthroats. There were marked contrasts between Revolutionary War banditti and the villains of the Ohio Valley and the old Southwest. The later villains had a greater propensity for killing to leave no witnesses; the banditti were more likely to commit murders out of revenge or to punish victims who resisted or failed to cooperate with demands during a robbery. The war banditti were more the marauders, often bent on destroying as well as seizing property on farms and plantations. Much of the eastern despoilation came from fairly well-organized bands; felons on the open frontier were more individualistic and set their sights on robbing the possessions of unsuspecting travelers.

A common denominator was the highwayman. Some of these criminals lingered in the former war zones to practice their frightful vocation, as happened in certain areas after the American Civil War.[48] The war banditti and the frontier outlaws both relied upon physical mobility and profited from the instability of society—whether war disorder or the newness of settlements—and competing governmental jurisdictions, such as "neutral ground" or territory straddling Indian or Spanish borders.

It would be interesting to quantify and describe precisely the peoples living a marginal existence, former Tories, and outright fugitives from the law who, during the generation after the war, migrated westward. What is impressive is that the incidence of crime in most frontier sections was not unduly high, not much more than could be expected in any locale. It is true that some of the frontier outlaws exhibited a degeneracy surpassing their Eastern counterparts, but their numbers were very few. Most communities in the West quickly coalesced, and criminality of any kind was not tolerated. As one traveler wrote in 1811, "In Kentucky, and, indeed, in the western country, there are a vast majority of civil, discreet, well-disposed people, who will hold the lawless and disobedient in check, and in time correct the morals of the whole."[49]

What made for the widespread plundering, robbery, and violence upon citizens during the war was the context of divided loyalty. Bands of Tories, rebels, and those who were simply outlaws could depend upon a network of friends, relatives, and sympathizers for assistance and, at least in some cases, military approval and support. The loss in property and lives inflicted by banditti proved a heavy price for a war that seemed to be fought on the surface only by engaging armies. James Iredell, a North Carolina lawyer and later a justice of the U.S. Supreme Court, expressed a view that was all too foreboding. Writing in June 1771, a month after the Regulators of backcountry North Carolina had been crushed at the battle of Alamance by a force commanded by the royal governor, Iredell stated, "How horrid are the miseries of civil war, but how much more horrid, to have Property insecure, and lives held at the will of a parcel of Banditti."[50]

Abbreviations

AHR	*American Historical Review*
AWP	W. W. Abbot et al., eds., *The Papers of George Washington, Revolutionary War Series* (Charlottesville: University Press of Virginia, 1983–2001), 11 vols. to date
Draper Coll.	Lyman C. Draper Collection, Wisconsin State Historical Society
FWW	John C. Fitspatrick, ed., *The Writings of George Washington* (Washington, D.C.: U.S. Government Printing Office, 1931–44), 39 vols.
GHQ	*Georgia Historical Quarterly*
GHSC	*Collections of the Georgia Historical Society*
JCC	C. Ford Worthington, ed., *Journals of the Continental Congress, 1774–1789* (Washington, D.C.: U.S. Government Printing Office, 1904–37), 34 vols.
JP	Julian P. Boyd, ed., *The Papers of Thomas Jefferson* (Princeton: Princeton University Press, 1950–58), vols. 1–14
LD	Paul H. Smith, ed., *Letters of Delegates to Congress, 1774–1789* (Washington, D.C.: Library of Congress, 1976–2000), 26 vols.
LT	Transcripts of the Manuscript Books and Papers of the Commission of Enquiry into the Losses and Services of the American Loyalists . . . 1783–1790, New York Public Library, 60 vols.

Md. Archives	William H. Browne et al., eds., *Archives of Maryland* (Baltimore, 1883–1971), 71 vols. to date
Md. Gaz.	*Maryland Gazette*
MHS	Massachusetts Historical Society
NCHR	*North Carolina Historical Review*
NCR	William L. Saunders, ed., *The Colonial Records of North Carolina*, vols. 1–10; and Walter Clark, ed., *The State Records of North Carolina*, vols 11–26 (Raleigh: P. M. Hale, 1886–1907), 26 vols.
NDB	John P. Rogers, *The New Doane Book*, ed. George McReynolds (Doylestown, rev. ed. 1952, orig. publ. 1897)
NG	Richard K. Showman et al., eds. *The Papers of Nathanael Greene* (Chapel Hill: University of North Carolina Press, 1976–2000), 11 vols. to date
N.J. Gaz.	*New Jersey Gazette*
NJA	William S. Stryker et al., eds., *Archives of the State of New Jersey*, 2d ser., (1901–17), 5 vols.
NJH	*New Jersey History*
NJHS	New Jersey Historical Society
NYHS	New York Historical Society
PA	Samuel Hazard, ed., *Pennsylvania Archives*, 1st ser. (Philadelphia, 1853–56), 12 vols.
Pa. Evening Post	*Pennsylvania Evening Post*
Pa. Gaz.	*Pennsylvania Gazette*
Pa. Gaz. and WA	*Pennsylvania Gazette and Weekly Advertiser*
Pa. Journal and WA	*Pennsylvania Journal and Weekly Advertiser*
PCC	Papers of the Continental Congress, National Archives
PCR	Samuel Hazard, ed., *Colonial Records of Pennsylvania* (Harrisburg, 1838–53), 16 vols.
PMHB	*Pennsylvania Magazine of History and Biography*
Royal Gaz. (R)	*Royal Gazette* (James Rivington)
Royal Gaz. (S.C.)	*Royal Gazette* (Charleston, S.C.)
RRG	Allen D. Candler, ed., *The Revolutionary Records of the State of Georgia* (Atlanta, 1908), 3 vols.
RV	William J. Van Schreevan et al., eds., *Revolutionary Virginia: The Road to Independence* (Charlottesville: University Press of Virginia, 1973–1983), 7 vols.
S.C. Gaz.	*South Carolina Gazette*
SCAG Gaz.	*South-Carolina and American General Gazette*
SCHGM	*South Carolina Historical and Genealogical Magazine*

SCHM	*South Carolina Historical Magazine* (succeeds *SCHGM*)
Va. Gaz.	*Virginia Gazette*
Va. Gaz. and WA	*Virginia Gazette and Weekly Advertiser*
VHS	Virginia Historical Society
VMHB	*Virginia Magazine of History and Biography*
WA	*Weekly Advertiser*
WL	Carl E. Prince, ed., *The Papers of William Livingston* (Trenton and New Brunswick: New Jersey Historical Commission and Rutgers University Press, 1979–1988), 5 vols.
WMQ	*William and Mary Quarterly*
WP-LC	George Washington Papers, Library of Congress

Notes

PREFACE

1. John Shy, *A People Numerous & Armed: Reflections on the Military for American Independence* (New York: Oxford University Press, 1976), 18–19.

2. David J. Fowler, "Egregious Villains, Wood Rangers, and London Traders: The Pine Robber Phenomenon in New Jersey During the Revolutionary War" (Ph.D. diss., Rutgers University, 1987); Susan B. Shenstone, *Obstinately Loyal: James Moody, 1744–1809* (Montreal: McGill–Queens University Press, 2000); Wilbur H. Siebert, *Loyalists in East Florida, 1774 to 1785*, 2 vols. (Deland: Florida State Historical Society, 1929).

3. *Oxford English Dictionary* (Oxford, England: Oxford University Press, 1989), 2d ed., 1: 924.

4. Eric Hobsbawm, *Bandits* (1969; reprint, New York: The New Press, 2000), 19.

5. Kent L. Steckmesser, "Robin Hood and the American Outlaw: A Note on History and Folklore," *Journal of American Folklore* 79 (1966): 353–54.

6. Hobsbawm, *Bandits*, 34, 45.

CHAPTER 1

1. *Va. Gaz.* (Dixon and Nicolson), May 22, 1779.

2. For example, in the British army, "recompense," Cornwallis Proclamation, July 18, 1780, in Banastre Tarleton, *A History of the Campaigns of 1780 and 1781 in the Southern Provinces of North America* (1787; reprint, New York: Arno Press, 1968), 121–22.

3. Mark E. Lender, "The Social Structure of the New Jersey Brigade: The Continental Line as an American Standing Army," in Peter Karston, ed., *The Military in America: From the Colonial Era to the Present* (New York: The Free Press, 1986), 73.

4. Ira D. Gruber, ed., *John Peebles' American War: The Diary of a Scottish Grenadier, 1776–1782* (Mechanicsburg, Pa.: Stackpole Books, 1998), 191; Charles C. Pinckney, *Life of General Thomas Pinckney* (Boston, 1895), 57.

5. Steuben to Greene, Jan. 8, 1781, NG 7: 78; Joseph P. Tustin, ed., *Diary of the American War: A Hessian Journal, Captain Johann Ewald* (New Haven, Conn.: Yale University Press, 1978), Jan. 6, 1781, 268–69; Harry M. Ward and Harold E. Greer, Jr., *Richmond During the Revolution, 1775–83* (Charlottesville: University Press of Virginia, 1977), 90.

6. Washington to Brig. Gen. John Lacey, Jr., Feb. 18, 1778, FWW 10: 478.

7. John Lacey to Greene, April 27, 1778, NG 2: 365.

8. Berry Fleming, comp. *Autobiography of a Colony: The First Half-Century of Augusta, Georgia* (Athens: University of Georgia Press, 1957), Mar. 9, 1778, 124.

9. Francis Marion to Isaac Huger, Feb. 6, 1781, NG 7: 230; Greene to Joseph Reed, May 4, 1781, NG 8: 200.

10. Major John Armstrong to Greene, July 10, 1781, NG 7: 515.

11. Residents of Salem, N.C., to Greene, Feb. 8, 1781, NG 7: 260.

12. Col. Henry Lee to Greene, June 22, 1781, NG 7: 443.

13. John M. Roberts, ed., *A Revolutionary Soldier* [Autobiography of James P. Collins] (1859; reprint, New York: Arno Press, 1979), 54.

14. Thomas Smith letter to Francis Marion, quoted in NG 8: 67n–68n.

15. *Journals of the House of Representatives [South Carolina], 1783–84* (Columbia, S.C.: University of South Carolina Press, 1977), Jan. 22, 1783, 11.

16. John André, *Major André's Journal . . . June 1777 to November 1778* (1904; reprint, New York: Arno Press, 1968), June 14, 1777, 27–28.

17. Md. Gaz., Nov. 21, 1776, letter from a gentleman at Haarlem, New York, Oct. 8, 1776; Sylvia R. Frey, *The British Soldier in America: A Social History of Military Life in the Revolutionary Period* (Austin: University of Texas Press, 1981), 75–76; Rodney Atwood, *The Hessians: Mercenaries from Hesse-Kassel in the American Revolution* (Cambridge, England: Cambridge University Press, 1980), 177.

18. Gruber, *Peebles' War*, May 26, 1780, 378.

19. Edward H. Tatum, ed., *The American Journal of Ambrose Serle* (San Marino, Calif.: Huntington Library, 1940), Sept. 1 and Oct. 7, 1776, 86–87 and 120.

20. Buettner quote in John H. Stutesman, Jr., "New Jersey's Foreign Legion," NJH 85 (1967): 69.

21. Aaron Burr to General McDougall, Jan 13, 1777, in Matthew L. Davis, ed., *Memoirs of Aaron Burr with Miscellaneous Selections from His Correspondence* (New York, 1838), vol. 1: 142.

22. General Orders, Jan 21, 1777, AWP 8: 119.

23. N.J. Gaz. and Weekly Mercury, July 7, 1777, in NJA, 2d ser., 1: 420.

24. Greene to Washington, Aug. 26, 1780, NG 6: 233–34 and 234n.

25. Extract of a letter from Col. Francis Wade to Greene, Jan. 7, 1779, NG 3: 192.

26. Gruber, *Peebles' War*, Oct. 8, 1778, 225.

27. Lewis Nicola to Washington, April 12, 1778, WP-LC; Washington to Col. Lewis

Nicola, April 14, 1778, *FWW* 11: 258; Washington to the Board of War, May 18, 1778, *FWW* 11: 417.

28. Washington to Brig. Gen. Charles Scott, Oct. 31, 1778, *FWW* 13: 187; Harry M. Ward, *Charles Scott and the "Spirit of '76"* (Charlottesville: University Press of Virginia, 1988), 63–64.

29. Lee Kennett, *Marching Through Georgia: The Story of Soldiers and Civilians During Sherman's Campaign* (New York: HarperCollins, 1995), 95.

30. Extract of a letter of Frederick Marschall to a member of the Unity's Elder Conference, June 21, 1781, in Adelaide L. Fries, ed., *Records of the Moravians in North Carolina* (Raleigh: North Carolina Department of Archives and History, 1968), vol. 4: 1910.

31. Theodore G. Tappert and John W. Doberstein, eds., *The Journals of Henry Melchior Muhlenberg* (Camden, Maine: Picton Press, 1982), vol. 3: 78–80 and III; Paul A. W. Wallace, *The Muhlenbergs of Pennsylvania* (Philadelphia: University of Pennsylvania Press, 1950), 26, 154.

32. James O. Carr, ed., *The Dickson Letters* (Raleigh, N.C.: Edwards and Broughton, 1906), 15.

33. *The Kemble Papers: British Army Orders, Collections of the NYHS* 16 (1883): July 18, 1778, 601; Colin Campbell, ed., *Journal of an Expedition Against the Rebels of Georgia in North America under the Orders of Archibald Campbell* (Darien, Ga.: The Ashantilly Press, 1981), General Orders, Dec. 22, 1778, 15; Brigade Morning Orders, March 2, 1781, in A. R. Newsome, ed., "A British Orderly Book, 1780–1781," *NCHR* 9 (1932): 379; "The Kemble Papers; British Army Orders," *Collections of the NYHS* 16 (1883): 601, July 3, 1778.

34. Extract of a letter from Stamford, Conn., Nov. 12, 1776, *Freeman's Journal or New-Hampshire Gazette*, Dec. 3, 1776; LT, Richard Cockran, 38: 229–30; Holly A. Mayer, *Belonging to the Army: Camp Followers and Community during the American Revolution* (Columbia: University of South Carolina Press, 1996), 8–10; Cynthia A. Kierner, *Southern Women in Revolution, 1776–1800: Personal and Political Narratives* (Columbia: University of South Carolina Press, 1998), 18.

35. Quotes in Jeffrey J. Crow, *The Black Experience in Revolutionary North Carolina* (Raleigh: North Carolina Department of Archives and History, 1977), 75.

36. Robert M. Hatch, *Major John André: A Gallant in Spy's Clothing* (Boston: Houghton Mifflin Company, 1986), 137.

37. Tatum, *Journal of Serle*, Aug. 29–31, 1777, 246.

38. Report of a Court of Inquiry, Nov. 1, 1777, *NG* 2: 188–89: General Orders, Nov. 29, 1777, *FWW* 10: 89.

39. Brigade Orders, Feb. 22, 1781, in Newsome, "British Orderly Book," 373.

40. *The Journal of Lieut. William Feltman of the First Pennsylvania Regiment, 1781–82* (Philadelphia, 1853), Jan. 22, 1782, 37.

41. Robert Bray and Paul Bushnell, eds., *Diary of a Common Soldier [Jeremiah Greenman] in the American Revolution, 1775–1783* (De Kalb: Northern Illinois University Press, 1978), Jan. 18–28, 1780, 168; Leonard Lundin, *Cockpit of the Revolution: The War for Independence in New Jersey* (1940; reprint, New York: Octagon Books, 1972), 422; Samuel S. Smith, *Winter at Morristown, 1779–80* (Monmouth Beach, N.J.: Philip Freneau Press, 1979), 14–15; *Morristown: A History and Guide* (Washington, D.C.: National Park Service, 1983), 55–63.

42. Washington to the President of Congress, Jan. 5, 1780, FWW 17: 357–58.

43. Washington to the Magistrates of New Jersey, Jan. 8, 1780, FWW 17: 363.

44. General Orders, Jan. 28, 1780, FWW 17: 459–60; S. Sydney Bradford, "Discipline in the Morristown Encampments," *Proceedings of the NJHS* 80 (1962): 15.

45. General Orders, June 11, 1780, FWW 18: 503–4; Nov. 6, 1780, FWW 20: 303; June 27, 1781, FWW 22: 269.

46. After Orders, June 11, 1780, FWW 18: 503.

47. General Orders, Dec. 25 and 26, 1777, FWW 10: 206–7; June 30, 1778, FWW 12: 132; Dec. 29, 1779, FWW 17: 331–32; After Orders, Aug. 29, 1781, and Orders, Sept. 19, 1781, NG 9: 270 and 311n.; "Order Book of Samuel Elbert, Oct. 1776 to Nov. 1778," GHSC 5 (1901), May 20, 1778, 148; James H. Edmonson, "Desertion in the American Army During the Revolutionary War" (Ph.D. diss., Louisiana State University, 1971), 303.

48. Harold C. Syrett and James E. Cooke, eds., *The Papers of Alexander Hamilton* (New York: Columbia University Press, 1961), vol. 1: 420n.; Robert W. Coakley and Stetson Conn, *The War of the Revolution: Narrative, Chronology, and Biography* (Washington, D.C.: Center for Military History, 1945), 112.

49. Instructions to Capt. Bartholomew Von Heer, Oct. 11, 1778, FWW 13: 68–70; Howard L. Applegate, "Constitutions Like Iron: The Life of the American Revolutionary Soldiers in the Middle Department, 1775–1783" (Ph.D. diss., Syracuse University, 1966), 131–32; Henry F. et al., *Major Bartholomew Von Heer* (Steuben Society of America, copy State Library of Pennsylvania, Harrisburg, n.d.), 7; Charles H. Lesser, *The Sinews of Independence: Monthly Strength Reports of the Continental Army* (Chicago: University of Chicago Press, 1976), Oct. 1778, 79.

50. General Orders, Nov. 19, 1782, FWW 25: 355; General Orders, Nov. 28, 1781, NG 9: 633; General Orders, Nov. 2, 1777, in Worthington C. Ford, ed., *General Orders Issued by Major-General Israel Putnam When in Command of the Highlands . . . 1777* (Brooklyn, N.Y., 1893), 86; "Orderly Book of the Company of Captain George Stubblefield," *Collections of the VHS*, new series, 6 (1887): 187–88.

51. Applegate, "Constitutions Like Iron," 131.

52. Edmonson, "Desertion in the American Army," 212–14.

53. Fries, *Records of Moravians in North Carolina*, Salem Diary, June 22–23, 1776, 3: 1066–67; Hunter James, *The Quiet People of the Land: A Story of the North Carolina Moravians in Revolutionary Times* (Chapel Hill: University of North Carolina Press, 1976), 52–53.

54. *Pa. Evening Post*, Dec. 28, 1776, in NJA, 2d ser., 1: 244–45.

55. SCAG Gaz., Mar. 4, 1779.

56. *Pa. Gaz. and WA*, Sept. 5 and Oct. 3, 1781.

57. Md. Gaz., Supplement, Dec. 13, 1781.

58. Edmonson, "Desertion in the American Army," 269–70; John D. McBride, "The Virginia War Effort, 1775–1783: Manpower, Politics, and Practice" (Ph.D. diss., University of Virginia, 1977), 249; Arthur J. Alexander, "A Footnote on Deserters from the Virginia Forces During the American Revolution," VMHB 55 (1947): 142, 146.

59. *Pa. Gaz.*, May 26, 1779.

60. Richard Sampson, *Escape in America: The British Convention Prisoners, 1777–1783* (Wiltshire, England: Picton Publishing, 1995), 151–53.

61. Harry M. Ward, *General William Maxwell and the New Jersey Continentals* (Westport, Conn.: Greenwood Press, 1997), 145–46.

62. Stephen Conway, "To Subdue America: British Army Officers and the Conduct of the Revolutionary War," *WMQ*, 3d ser., 43 (1986): 384–86, 393, 397.

63. Quoted in Hatch, *André*, 137.

64. Ford, *General Orders*, Sept. 24, 1777, 78–79.

65. General Orders, Nov. 19, 1782, *FWW* 25: 355.

66. Ford, *General Orders*, Nov. 2, 1777, 85.

67. General Orders, Feb. 18, 1780, *FWW* 18: 22; Feb. 24, 1780, *FWW* 18: 48; Nov. 23, 1782, *FWW* 25: 368–69; Greene to Capt. Faunt le Roy, Dec. 25, 1780, *NG* 6: 612, General Orders, Dec. 10, 1781, *NG* 10: 25; Dec. 11, 1781, *NG* 10: 34; Feb. 11, 1782, *NG* 10: 355.

68. Joseph C. Neagles, *Summer Soldiers: A Survey and Index of Revolutionary War Courts-Martial* (Salt Lake City: Ancestry Inc., 1986), 34.

69. General Orders, Jan. 21, 1777, *AWP* 8: 119.

70. General Orders, July 12, 1778, *FWW* 12: 172, Feb. 19, 1780, *FWW* 18: 34; General Court Martial, July 12, 1778, *NCR* 12: 502.

71. Brigade Court-Martial, Oct. 6, 1779, Benjamin Lincoln Papers, MHS.

72. Brigade Orderly Book, Gen. Alexander McDougall, Sept. 20, 1776, McDougall Papers, NYHS; General Orders, July 25, 1777, *FWW* 8: 465–66, May 16, 1779, *FWW* 15: 100–101, Feb. 18, 1780, *FWW* 18: 22, Feb. 20, 1780, *FWW* 18: 48, July 27, 1781, *FWW* 22: 423; Ford, *General Orders*, July 31, 1777; Mark E. Lender, "The Enlisted Line: The Continental Soldiers of New Jersey" (Ph.D. diss., Rutgers University, 1975), 183; Bradford, "Discipline in the Morristown Encampments," 17–18.

73. James Thacher, *Military Journal of the American Revolution* (Hartford, 1862), April 20, 1779, 161–62.

74. William B. Weeden, ed., "Diary of Rev. Dr. Enos Hitchcock," *Publications of the Rhode Island Hist. Soc.*, no. 7 (1900), Aug. 26, 1780, 221, and Sept. 12, 1780, 223.

75. Ibid., Sept. 12, 1780, 223.

76. "Extracts from the Journal of Lieutenant John Bell Tilden," *PMHB* 19 (1895): 222, Mar. 1, 1782; General Orders, Feb. 28, 1782, *NG* 10: 417, Mar. 2, 1782, *NG* 10: 432, Mar. 5, 1782, *NG* 10: 443.

77. *Journal of Feltman*, 8; "Journal of Ebenezer Wild, 1776–1781," in *Proceedings of the MHS*, 2d ser., 6 (1890–91): 145, July 22, 178; "Journal of Captain John Davis of the Pennsylvania Line," *PMHB* 5 (1881): 296, July 22, 1781; Francis E. Lutz, *Chesterfield: An Old Virginia County* (Richmond, Va.: William Byrd Press, 1954), 125.

78. After Orders, Entry Books, Jan. 27, 1775, Public Record Office War Office 36/1; Gruber, *Peebles' War*, Sept. 15–16, 1777, 134; André, *Journal*, Sept. 15, 1777, 47; Tatum, *Journal of Serle*, Aug. 25, 1777, 245.

79. Gruber, *Peebles' War*, Nov. 24, 1779, 310; "Kemble Papers," June 18, 1778, 595.

80. Thomas Jones, *History of New York during the Revolutionary War*, ed. Edward P. DeLancey (1879; reprint, New York: Arno Press, 1968), vol. 2: 72–74; Joseph S. Tiedemann, "Response to Revolution: Queen's County, New York, During the Era of the American Revolution" (Ph.D. diss., City University of New York, 1977), 155–56, includes quote; Conway, "To Subdue America," 385–86.

81. Jones, *History of New York*, 2: 93–94.

82. Greene to James McCormick, Nov. 8, 1781, *NG* 9: 548, 552n.

83. Greene to Col. Alexander Stewart, Nov. 3, 1781, *NG* 9: 613.

84. Frey, *British Soldier*, 75.

85. D. Doyle to General Marion, Nov. 9, 1781, in Robert W. Gibbes, *Documentary History of the American Revolution* (1853; reprint, New York: Arno Press, 1971), vol. 3: 208–9.

CHAPTER 2

1. Loammi Baldwin to his wife, July 14, 1776, Loammi Baldwin Papers, Harvard University Library.

2. Lewis Morris to Gen. McDougall,—1782, Alexander McDougall Papers, NYHS.

3. Otto Hufeland, *Westchester County During the American Revolution, 1775–1783* (White Plains, N.Y., 1926), 4–7 and *passim*; Frederic Shonnard and W. W. Spooner, *History of Westchester County, New York* (New York, 1900), 416; Stephen Jenkins, *The Story of the Bronx* (New York, 1912), 152; Catherine S. Crary, ed., *The Price of Loyalty: Tory Writings from the Revolutionary Era* (New York: McGraw-Hill Book Company, 1973), 173n.

4. William S. Hadaway, ed., *The McDonald Papers* (White Plains, N.Y., 1926–27), Part 2, vol. 5: 3.

5. Abbé Robin, *New Travels Through North America* (1783; reprint, Arno Press, New York: 1969), 31.

6. Timothy Dwight, *Travels in New England and New York*, ed. Barbara M. Solomon (Cambridge, Mass.: Harvard University Press, 1969), vol. 3: 345–46.

7. Henry B. Dawson, *Westchester County, New York During the American Revolution* (New York, 1886), vol. 3: 129–31, 345–46.

8. Lewis Morris to Gen. Lewis Morris, Sept. 6, 1776, "Letters to General Lewis Morris," *Collections of the NYHS* 8 (1875): 442.

9. *Diary of Samuel Richards, Captain of the Continental Line . . . 1775–1781* (Philadelphia, 1909), June 1777, 77–78; Diana Reische, *Of Colonists and Commuters: A History of Scarsdale* (Scarsdale, N.Y.: Junior League of Scarsdale, 1976), 43–45.

10. Extract of a letter from Stamford, Conn., Nov. 12, 1776, in *Freeman's Journal or New-Hampshire Gazette*, Dec. 3, 1776.

11. Otto Hufeland, "The Burning of the Village of White Plains on November 5th, 1776," *Publications of the Westchester Historical Society* (1929), 30–41; Kent Forster, "Westchester: A House Divided," *Proceedings of the New York State Historical Association* 45 (1947), 406.

12. Catherine S. Crary, "Guerrilla Activities of James DeLancey's Cowboys in Westchester County: Conventional Warfare or Self-Interested Freebooting," in Robert A. East and Jacob Judd, eds., *The Loyalist Americans: A Focus on Greater New York* (Tarrytown, N.Y.: Sleepy Hollow Restorations, 1975), 16–17.

13. Gen. Heath to George Clinton, Aug. 30, 1777, in Hugh Hastings, comp., *Public Papers of George Clinton* (Albany, 1899–1914), vol. 5: 243; Memorial of Philip Landerback, LT, 45: 313–16; Job Smith, LT, 6: 20, 45: 332; Milton M. Klein and Ronald W. Howard, eds., *The Twilight of British Rule in Revolutionary America: The New York Letter Book of General James Robertson, 1780–83* (Cooperstown: New York State Historical

Association, 1983), 207n.; Gruber, *Peebles' War*, July 31, 1781, 277; Jones, *History of New York*, 1: 301; Hugh E. Egerton, ed., *The Royal Commission on the Losses and Services of American Loyalists, 1783 to 1785* (1915; reprint, New York: B. Franklin, 1971), 139; Robert A. East, *Connecticut's Loyalists* (Chester, Conn.: Pequot Press, 1974), 291.

14. *Pa. Gaz.*, Nov. 17, 1779.

15. Hufeland, *Westchester County*, 313.

16. Quote in James H. Pickering, "The Oral Tradition of the Neutral Ground," *Westchester Historian* 43 (1967): 5.

17. LT, James DeLancey, 41: 253–59: Crary, "Guerrilla Activities," 18–19; Philip Ranlet, "James DeLancey," *American National Biography*, 9: 371–72.

18. LT, Memorial of James Holmes, 23: 5–14 and James DeLancey, 41: 255–57; *N.Y. Packet*, Dec. 4, 1777; *Royal Gaz. (R)*, Mar. 9, 1782; Frederic G. Mather, *The Refugees of 1776 from Long Island to Connecticut* (Albany, 1913), 196; Crary, *Price of Loyalty*, 173–74; Fred A. Berg, *Encyclopedia of Continental Army Units* (Harrisburg, Pa.: Stackpole Books, 1972), 85. DeLancey was attainted with treason by the New York act of Oct. 22, 1779, and his property was confiscated.

19. John L. Romer, *Historical Sketches of the Romer, Van Tassel and Allied Families and Tales of the Neutral Ground* (Buffalo, 1917), 94–95.

20. Christopher Ward, *War of the Revolution* (New York: MacMillan Company, 1953), vol. 2: 620. The *Royal Gaz. (R)*, Feb. 5, 1780, reported rebel casualties as 40–50 killed and 97 prisoners; the attacking force, 5 killed and 18 wounded.

21. *Pa. Gaz.*, July 14, 1779.

22. Bernhard A. Uhlendorf, ed., *Revolution in America: Confidential Letters and Journals, 1776–1784 of Adjutant General Major Baurmeister of the Hessian Forces* (New Brunswick, N.J.: Rutgers University Press, 1957), Jan. 11, 1779, 248.

23. *Royal Gaz. (R)*, Nov. 29, 1780.

24. Ibid., May 13, 1780, and Dec. 16, 1780.

25. For example, see Ibid., Dec. 27, 1779, and Address of the Loyal Refugees to Maj. Gen. Mathews, April 19, 1780; *N.J. Gaz.*, Aug. 8 and 25, 1779, and Mar. 13, 1782; *Pa. Journal and WA*, Dec. 27, 1780, Jan. 3 and Feb. 7, 1781; *Connecticut Courant*, Jan. 22 and April 9, 1782; Washington to Rochambeau, Jan. 29, 1781, *FWW* 21: 152, General Orders, Jan. 30, 1781, *FWW* 21: 160, Washington to President of Congress, Jan. 31, 1781, *FWW* 21: 166, Instructions to Benjamin Lincoln, July 1, 1781, *FWW* 22: 303, Washington to De Lauzun, July 1, 1781, *FWW* 22: 318–19; Maria Campbell, *Revolutionary Services and Civil Life of General William Hull* (New York, 1848), 182–90; Rufus R. Wilson, ed., *Heath's Memoirs of the American War* (New York, 1904), Mar. 4 and 14, 1782, 345–46; Jenkins, *Story of the Bronx*, 166–179; Hufeland, *Westchester County*, 417; Robert Bolton, *The History of the Several Towns . . . County of Westchester*, 3d ed. (New York, 1905), vol. 2: 428–29; Robert B. Roberts, *New York's Forts in the Revolution* (Rutherford, N.J.: Fairleigh Dickinson University Press, 1980), 398; North Callahan, *Royal Raiders: The Tories of the American Revolution* (Indianapolis: Bobbs-Merrill Company, 1963), 72–73.

26. Joseph Plumb Martin, *Private Yankee Doodle: Being a Narrative of Some of the Adventures, Dangers and Sufferings of a Revolutionary Soldier*, ed. George F. Scheer (Boston: Little, Brown and Company, 1962), 138–48.

27. Ibid., 218–21.

28. *Diary of Samuel Richards*, 78–79; Crary, "Guerrilla Activities," 18, q. on 21–22.

29. Report of Chief Justice Richard Morris, June 15, 1785, in Crary, *Price of Loyalty*, 444–46; Ranlet, "James DeLancey," 372.

30. George Clinton to Justice Hobart, July 24, 1779, in Hastings, *Papers of Clinton*, vol. 5: 158–59.

31. Heath to Gov. Clinton, Aug. 30, 1779, in Hastings, *Papers of Clinton*, vol. 5: 243–44.

32. *Pa. Journal and WA*, July 11, 1781.

33. Frederick Jay to John Jay, Nov. 18, 1781, in Richard B. Morris, ed., *John Jay: The Winning of the Peace, Unpublished Papers, 1780–1784* (New York: Harper and Row, 1980), vol. 2: 201–2, also pp. 10 and 182n.

34. *New Hampshire Gazette*, Nov. 15, 1781, Fishkill notice of Sept. 6, 1781.

35. Pickering, "Oral Tradition of the Neutral Ground," 5; Romer, *Romer, Van Tassel and Allied Families, passim*; Crary, "Guerrilla Activities," 24.

36. James H. Pickering, "Shube Merritt: Freebooter of the Neutral Ground," *New York Folklore Quarterly* (Mar. 1965): 32–38; *Pa. Gaz. and WA*, Aug. 22, 1781; Robin, *New Travels*, Sept. 1, 1781, 40.

37. Forster, "Westchester: A House Divided," 408.

38. Pierre Van Cortlandt to Meshech Weare, July 27, 1777, in Jacob Judd, ed., *Correspondence of the Van Cortlandt Family of Cortlandt Manor, 1748–1800* (Tarrytown, N.Y.: Sleepy Hollow Restorations, 1977), vol. 2: 218.

39. Burr to Gen. McDougall, Jan. 13, 1779, and Samuel Youngs to Valentine Morris, Jan. 25, 1814, in Davis, ed., *Memoirs of Aaron Burr*, 142–43, 158–166, resp.

40. *Royal Gaz. (R)*, July 7, 1779; Carl Van Doren, *Secret History of the American Revolution* (1941; reprint, New York: Viking Press, 1968), 237; Adrian C. Leiby, *The Revolutionary War in the Hackensack Valley: The Jersey Dutch and the Neutral Ground* (New Brunswick, N.J.: Rutgers University Press, 1980), 184.

41. *Royal Gaz. (R)*, Feb. 9, 1782.

42. Memorial of Lorenda Holmes, LT, 46: 538–45; Forster, "Westchester: A House Divided," 408–9.

43. Pickering, "Oral Tradition of the Neutral Ground," 7; Bolton, *History of Several Towns*, 2: 305–7; Benjamin J. Lossing, *The Pictorial Field Book of the Revolution* (1857; reprint, Freeport, N.Y.: Books for Libraries, 1969), 185n.

44. William Heath to George Clinton, Nov. 1, 1780, in Hastings, *Papers of Clinton*, 6: 366.

45. John Jameson to William Heath, Oct. 18, 1780, in Winthrop Sargent, *The Life and Career of Major John André*, ed. William Abbatt (New York, 1902), 347.

46. Washington to Philip Van Cortlandt and Elias Dayton, July 3, 1782, in Judd, *Correspondence of the Van Cortlandt Family*, 2: 472.

47. James Fenimore Cooper, *The Spy: A Tale of the Neutral Ground*, ed. James H. Pickering (New Haven, Conn.: College and University Press, 1971), 405. For Enoch Crosby as the model for Cooper's Harvey Birch, see Tremaine McDowell, "The Identity of Harvey Birch," *American Folklore* 2 (1930–31): 111–20, and James H. Pickering, "Enoch Crosby, Secret Agent of the Neutral Ground: His Own Story," *New York History* 47 (1966): 61–73.

48. *Pa. Journal and WA*, Oct. 11, 1780; Alexander Hamilton to Lt. Col. John Laurens, Oct. 11, 1780, in Syrett and Cooke, *Papers of Hamilton*, 2: 463–70; William Abbatt, *The Crisis of the Revolution: Being the Story of Arnold and André* (1899; reprint, Harrison,

N.Y.: Harbour-Hill Books, 1976), 27–35; Hatch, *André*, 243–47; Romer, *Romer, Van Tassel and Allied Families*, *passim*; Bolton, *History of Several Towns*, 2: 308–10; Hufeland, *Westchester County*, 27–35.

49. JCC, Nov. 3, 1780, 18: 1009–10; Emma L. Patterson, *Peekskill in the American Revolution* (Peekskill, N.Y.: The Friendly Town Association, 1944), 137–40; Egbert Benson, *Vindication of the Captors of Major André* (1865; reprint, Boston: Gregg Press, 1972), 17–23, 59, 76–84.

50. For Tallmadge's remark and rebuttal, see Shonnard and Spooner, *History of Westchester County*, 486–87.

51. Gen. James Robertson to Lord Amherst, May 12, 1782, in Klein and Howard, *Letter Book of Robertson*, 251.

52. Roberts, *New York's Forts*, 299; Jenkins, *Story of the Bronx*, 173.

53. JCC, April 11 and 15, 1783, 24: 238–51; Guy Carleton to Gov. Clinton, May 13, 1783, in Hastings, *Papers of Clinton*, 8: 175–76; Substance of Conference between Washington and Carleton, May 6, 1783, FWW 26: 405; Josiah Quincy, ed., *The Journals of Major Samuel Shaw* (1847; reprint, New York: Paragon Book Gallery, 1968), April 12, 1783, 108–9; Douglas S. Freeman, *George Washington* (New York: Charles Scribner's Sons, 1953), 5: 440; Hufeland, *Westchester County*, 431, 434; Roberts, *New York's Forts*, 299.

54. Carleton to President Elias Boudinot, Aug. 17, 1783, in K. B. Davies, ed., *Documents of the American Revolution, 1770–1783* (Dublin, Ireland: Irish Academic Press, 1972), vol. 21: 208–9; Harry B. Yoshpe, *The Disposition of Loyalist Estates in the Southern District of the State of New York* (1939; reprint, New York: 1967), 14–18; Alexander C. Flick, *Loyalism in New York During the American Revolution* (1901; reprint, New York: Arno Press, 1969), 136–42.

55. David Colden to Mrs. Henrietta Maria Colden, Sept. 15, 1783, in E. A. Jones, "Letter of David Colden, Loyalist, 1783," AHR 25 (1919–20): 83–85; Philip Ranlet, *The New York Loyalists* (Knoxville: University of Tennessee Press, 1986), 149, 166.

56. Quote from depositions of John Orser and Joseph Orser, May 20 and 21, 1783, in Ranlet, *New York Loyalists*, 165–66; Carleton to Clinton, June 18, Clinton to Carleton, July 1, and Carleton to Clinton, July 25, 1783, in Hastings, *Papers of Clinton*, 8: 209, 213, and 239–42, resp.

57. Washington to Commanding Officer of Troops in Westchester County, May 21, 1783, FWW 26: 447, General Orders, June 20, 1783, FWW 27: 26, Washington to Col. Hull, July 8, 1783, FWW 27: 46–47; Mark V. Kwasny, *Washington's Partisan War, 1775–1783* (Kent, Ohio: Kent State University Press, 1996), 326; Ranlet, *New York Loyalists*, 166.

58. Gov. Clinton to Carleton, May 23, 1783, in Hastings, *Papers of Clinton*, 8: 186.

59. Washington to Ralph Izard, June 14, 1783, FWW 27: 10.

60. William Hull to Washington, July 7, 1783, WP-LC; Roberts, *New York's Forts*, 299; Uhlendorf, *Letters and Journals of Baurmeister*, Aug. 30, 1783, 587.

CHAPTER 3

1. Uhlendorf, *Letters and Journals of Baurmeister*, Sept. 24, 1776, 45.

2. J.D.F. Smyth, *A Tour of the United States of America* (1784; reprint, New York: Arno Press, 1968), vol. 2: 378–79.

3. Quote in Thomas J. Wertenbaker, *Father Knickerbock Rebels: New York City During*

the American Revolution (New York: Charles Scribner's Sons, 1948), 103; Gerald F. De Jong, *The Dutch in America, 1609–1974* (Boston: Twayne Publishers, 1975), 118–19.

4. Uhlendorf, *Letters and Journals of Baurmeister*, July 20, Aug. 14, and Nov. 9, 1778, Aug. 27, and Nov. 8, 1779, and April 26, 1781, pp. 189, 197, 229, 296, 319–20, and 431, resp.; Tustin, *A Hessian Journal*, 158; Joseph S. Tiedemann, "Patriots by Default: Queens County, New York, and the British Army, 1776–1783," *WMQ* 43 (1986): 46–47; Tiedemann, "Response to Revolution," table 36, 153.

5. Gen. Samuel Holden Parsons to Washington, May 25, 1777, in Charles S. Hall, ed., *Life and Letters of Samuel Holden Parsons* (1905; reprint, New York: James Pugliese, 1968), 97–98; Roberts, *New York's Forts*, 247–50.

6. *Memoir of Col. Benjamin Tallmadge* (1858; reprint, New York: Arno Press 1968), 32.

7. Ibid., 39; *Royal Gaz. (R)*, Dec. 2, 1780; Hermon D. Smith, ed., *Revolutionary War Journals of Henry Dearborn* (1939; reprint, New York: Da Capo Press, 1971), Dec. 1, 1780, 209; Jones, *History of New York*, 2: 32–34; Mark M. Boatner, *Encyclopedia of the American Revolution* (New York: David McKay Company, 1966), 376.

8. Narrative of William Patchin, in John C. Dann, ed., *The Revolution Remembered: Eyewitness Accounts of the War of Independence* (Chicago: University of Chicago Press, 1980), 77; *Memoir of Tallmadge*, 46; Roberts, *New York's Forts*, 250–55.

9. Hall, *Life and Letters of Parsons*, 110; Charles B. Todd, "Whale-Boat Privateersmen of the Revolution," *Magazine of American History* 8, part 1 (1882), 169; Fred J. Cook, *What Manner of Men: Forgotten Heroes of the American Revolution* (New York: William Morrow and Company, 1959), 276–77; Benjamin F. Thompson, *History of Long Island*, 3d ed. (New York, 1918), vol. 1: 316.

10. Louis F. Middlebrook, *History of Maritime Connecticut During the American Revolution, 1775–1783* (Salem, Mass., 1925), vol. 2: 258; Wallace E. Davies, "Privateering Around Long Island During the Revolution," *New York History* (1939) 20: 291; W. Q. Maxwell, *A Portrait of William Floyd, Long Islander* (Setauket, N.Y.: Society for the Preservation of Long Island Antiquities, 1956), 262; At a meeting of the Governor and Council of Safety, May 22, 1779, in Charles J. Hoadley, ed., *The Public Records of the State of Connecticut* (Hartford, Conn., 1895 and 1927), vol. 2: 346, and rejected by the Assembly, May 1780, 3: 34. During the war, Connecticut mariners captured about 500 boats of various kinds.

11. Davies, "Privateering Around Long Island," 291–93.

12. Benjamin Tallmadge to Abraham Woodhull, April 21, 1779, in Morton Pennypacker, *General Washington's Spies on Long Island and in New York* (Brooklyn, N.Y., 1939), 240–41.

13. Council of Safety Resolution and Letter of Trumbull to Rogers and Vail, Aug. 11, 1778, in Hoadley, *Records of Connecticut*, 2: 110.

14. Washington to Tallmadge, Nov. 2, 1779, *FWW* 17: 62–63.

15. *Royal Gaz. (R)*, Mar. 10, 1779.

16. Quote in Henry Onderdonk, Jr., *Revolutionary Incidents of Suffolk and Kings Counties* (1849; reprint, Port Washington, N.Y.: Kennikat Press, 1970), 83–84.

17. *Royal Gaz. (R)*, June 26, 1779.

18. Letter of Samuel Culper, Sr. (Abraham Woodhull), Sept. 19, 1779, in Pennypacker, *Washington's Spies*, 62–63.

19. Samuel Culper, Sr. (Abraham Woodhull) to Tallmadge, Oct. 29, 1779, in Morton Pennypacker, *The Two Spies: Nathan Hale and Robert Townshend* (Boston, 1930), 37.

20. *New York Gaz.*, Feb. 16, 1778, in Thompson, *History of Long Island*, 1: 309.

21. Lt. Caleb Brewster to Gov. Clinton, Aug. 20, 1781, in Hastings, *Papers of Clinton*, 7: 233–34; Pennypacker, *Washington's Spies*, 285.

22. Memorial from Inhabitants of Southold and Shelter Island to Gov. Clinton, Sept. 21, 1781, in Hastings, *Papers of Clinton*, 7:343–46.

23. For example, *Royal Gaz. (R)*, July 12, 1780, and *NY Journal and General Advertiser*, Sept. 20, 1779.

24. For example, *Royal Gaz. (R)*, June 30, 1779, and *Pa. Journal and WA*, June 13, 1781.

25. Gov. Clinton to Gov. Trumbull, Aug. 20, 1781, in Hastings, *Papers of Clinton*, 7: 234–35.

26. JCC, Aug. 7, 1781, 21: 835–36.

27. At a meeting of the Governor and Council of Safety, Nov. 23, 1781, in Hoadley, *Records of Connecticut*, 3: 553.

28. *Connecticut Courant and WA*, Sept. 24, 1782.

29. *Royal Gaz. (R)*, Oct. 26, 1782.

30. Richard J. Koke, "War, Profit, and Privateers along the New Jersey Coast: Letters of 1782 Relating to an Obscure War Front of the American Revolution," *NYHS Quarterly* 41 (1957): 293–94, 300.

31. *Pa. Journal and WA*, June 27, 1781.

32. Excerpt from an account in the *Naval Magazine* by Gen. Jeremiah Johnson, in Todd, "Whale-Boat Privateersmen," 177. For a narrative on the life and exploits of Hyler, see Cook, *What Manner of Men*, 127–48.

33. John Taylor to William Livingston, June 19, 1781, WL 4: 223–24.

34. Proclamation, June 12, 1782, WL 4: 428–29; JCC, May 21, 1782, 22: 280–81.

35. Inhabitants of Norwalk to the Connecticut General Assembly, Oct. 4, 1777, in Michael J. Crawford, ed., *Naval Documents of the American Revolution* (Washington, D.C.: Naval Historical Center, 1996), vol. 10: 161.

36. *Royal Gaz. (R)*, June 23, 1779.

37. *NY Journal and General Advertiser*, June 5, 1779.

38. *Royal Gaz. (R)*, July 3, 1779, in Thompson, *History of Long Island*, 1: 310.

39. John Bell and Nathaniel Slason to John Reed, Aug. 30, 1780, in *The Trumbull Papers, Collections of the MHS*, 7th ser., 3 (1902): 118–19; Uhlendorf, *Letters and Journals of Baurmeister*, July 26, 1781, 455; Richard J. Buel, Jr., *Dear Liberty: Connecticut's Mobilization for the Revolutionary War* (Middletown, Conn.: Wesleyan University Press, 1980), 252.

40. Todd, "Whale-Boat Privateersmen," 176–77.

41. Gov. Tryon to Sir Henry Clinton, June 30, 1779, with enclosure "concerning the Embodying Loyalists," in E. B. O'Callaghan, ed., *Documents Relative to the Colonial History of the State of New York* (Albany, 1853), vol. 8: 769–70; Oscar T. Barck, *New York City During the War for Independence* (New York, 1931), 203–4.

42. Jones, *History of New York*, 1: 303.

43. Gruber, *Peebles' War*, July 24 and Aug. 8, 1781, 461 and 464; Hall, *Life and Letters of Parsons*, 401.

44. *Pa. Gaz. and WA*, Aug. 22, 1781.

45. Journal of Mrs. Silliman, quoted in Todd, "Whale-Boat Privateersmen," 171–72; Joy D. Buel and Richard J. Buel, *The Way of Duty: A Woman and Her Family in Revolutionary America* (New York: W.W. Norton and Company, 1984), ch. 6.

46. Todd, "Whale-Boat Privateersmen," 173–74; Buel and Buel, *Way of Duty*, 162–64; Thompson, *History of Long Island*, 1: 311–13.

47. Buel, *Dear Liberty*, 252; David H. Villers, "King Mob and the Rule of Law: Revolutionary Justice and the Suppression of Loyalism in Connecticut, 1774–1783," in Robert M. Calhoon, et al., eds., *Loyalists and Community in North America* (Westport, Conn.: Greenwood Press, 1994), 22–24.

48. Jones, *History of New York*, 1: 302–4.

49. An Act to Prevent Robberies and Plunder . . . Nov. 29, 1780, in Hoadley, *Records of Connecticut*, 3: 235–36.

50. At a Meeting of the Governor and Council of Safety, Dec. 29, 1780, in Hoadley, *Records of Connecticut*, 3: 283–84.

51. *Royal Gaz. (R)*, Oct. 23, 1779, in Onderdonk, *Revolutionary Incidents*, 186.

52. *Royal Gaz. (R)*, April 21, 1779.

53. Ibid., Oct. 20, 1779.

54. Thompson, *History of Long Island*, 1: 286–87.

55. "Journal of Wild," Oct. 5, 1778, 118; Edward Peterson, *History of Rhode Island and Newport* (New York, 1853), 222–23; Lorenzo Sabine, *Biographical Sketches of Loyalists of the American Revolution* (1864; reprint, Baltimore: Genealogical Publishing Company, 1979), 1: 343, vol. 2: 428.

56. "The Life and Dying Confession of Richard Barrick, Highway Robber," from the *American Bloody Register* (Boston, 1784), in Daniel E. Williams, *Pillars of Salt: An Anthology of Early American Criminal Narratives* (Madison, Wisc.: Madison House, 1993), 233–37.

57. Lydia M. Post, *Personal Recollections of the American Revolution*, ed. Sidney Barclay (1859; reprint, Port Washington, N.Y.: Kennikat Press, 1970), Jan. 1777, 75–76.

58. Ibid., Jan. 1778 and Oct. et seq. 1780, 106–7, 153–66.

59. Ibid., Aug. 1778, 125–26.

60. Ibid., May 3, 1777, 84–85.

61. Barck, *New York City*, 206.

62. *Royal Gaz. (R)*, Mar. 12, 1783, quoted in Onderdonk, *Revolutionary Incidents*, 198.

63. Ibid., Oct. 25, 1783, quoted in ibid., 200.

64. Maxwell, *William Floyd*, 22, 28; Mather, *Refugees of 1776*, 187, 193, 888–965.

65. Onderdonk, *Revolutionary Incidents*, Dec. 2, 1783, 203–4.

CHAPTER 4

1. Michael P. Riccards, "Patriots and Plunderers: Confiscation of Loyalist Lands in New Jersey, 1776–1786," *NJH* 86 (1968): 16, 24; Smith, *Winter at Morristown*, 16; *WL* 2:227n.

2. *Pa. Journal and WA*, Dec. 22, 1779.

3. Proclamation Concerning Persons Swearing British Allegiance, Jan. 25, 1777, *AWP* 8: 152–53.

4. Larry R. Gerlach, *Prologue to Independence: New Jersey in the Coming of the American Revolution* (New Brunswick, N.J.: Rutgers University Press, 1976), 354.

5. LT, Abraham Buskirk, 15: 269, and Cortlandt Skinner, 38: 49–68; W. O. Raymond, ed., *Winslow Papers, 1776–1826* (Saint John, N.B., 1901), 20n.; David A. Bernstein, "New Jersey in the American Revolution: The Establishment of a Government and Military Disorder, 1770–1781" (Ph.D. diss., Rutgers University, 1970), 266–67; William S. Stryker, *The New Jersey Volunteers (Loyalists) in the Revolutionary War* (Trenton, N.J., 1887), 4–11; Lender, "The Enlisted Line," 46.

6. *Pa. Gaz. and WA*, April 18, 1782.

7. Edward H. Tebbenhoff, "The Associated Loyalists: An Aspect of Militant Loyalism," *NYHS Quarterly* 63 (1979): 138.

8. Ibid., 115–19, 126–37; William H. Mariboe, "The Life of William Franklin, 1730–1813: 'PRO REGE ET PATRIA' " (Ph.D. diss., University of Pennsylvania, 1962), 490–96; Sheila L. Skemp, *William Franklin, Son of a Patriot/Servant of a King* (New York: Oxford University Press, 1990), 248.

9. NG, 5: 330n.; E. A. Benians, ed., *A Journal by Thos. Hughes, 1778–1779* (Cambridge, England, 1947), 59; Kenneth T. Jackson, ed., *The Encyclopedia of New York City* (New Haven, Conn.: Yale University Press, 1995), 1112.

10. *Pa. Gaz.*, Aug. 22, 1781; *Royal Gaz. (R)*, Dec. 9, 1780, Skemp, *William Franklin*, 241.

11. Klein and Howard, *Letter Book of Robertson*, July 25, 1980, 138, 141; Charles H. Winfield, "The Affair at Block-House Point 1780," *Magazine of American History* 5 (1880): 161–63.

12. John G. Simcoe, *A History of the Operations of a Partisan Corps Called the Queen's Rangers* (1787; reprint, New York: Arno Press, 1968), 73; *The Diary of Frederick Mackenzie . . . 1775–1781* (Cambridge, Mass., 1930), June 19, 1781, vol. 2: 548–49; Gustav Kobbé, *The Jersey Coast and Pines* (1889; reprint, Baltimore: Gateway Press, 1970), 1–2; William S. Horner, *This Old Monmouth of Ours* (Freehold, N.J., 1932), 403; Edwin Salter and George C. Beekman, *Old Times in Old Monmouth: Historical Reminiscences of Old Monmouth County* (1887; reprint, Baltimore: Genealogical Publishing Company 1994), 71; Henry C. Beck, *The Jersey Midlands* (1939; reprint, New Brunswick, N.J.: Rutgers University Press, 1962), 350.

13. For example, see *Pa. Evening Post*, April 30, 1779, in NJA, 2d ser., 3:300–301, and *N.J. Gaz.*, June 23, 1779; Franklin Ellis, *History of Monmouth County, New Jersey* (1885; reprint, Cottonport, La.: Polyanthos, 1974), 204–11.

14. *Pa. Journal and WA*, Nov. 22, 1780.

15. Leiby, *Revolutionary War in the Hackensack Valley*, 270.

16. Ibid., 207–9; *Royal Gaz. (R)*, May 12, 1779; *N.J. Gaz.*, May 12, 1779, in NJA, 2d ser., 3: 359; Mary A. Demarest and William H. S. Demarest, comps., *The Demarest Family* (New Brunswick, N.J., 1938), 67.

17. Petition of Peter Wilson, Sept. 8, 1781, WL 4: 289. For the refugee war in Bergen County, see Leiby, *Revolutionary War in the Hackensack Valley, passim*.

18. For example, Rahway and Woodbridge, *Pa. Gaz.*, July 14, 1779; Kenneth Scott, comp., *Rivington's New York Newspaper: Excerpts from a Loyalist Press, 1773–1783* (New York: New-York Historical Society, 1973), 211–13; George A. Boyd, *Elias Boudinot: Patriot and Statesman* (Princeton, N.J.: Princeton University Press, 1952), 83; Robert V. Hoffman, *The Revolutionary Scene in New Jersey* (New York: The American Historical Company, 1942), 43–45; Richard M. Bayles ed., *History of Richmond County, Staten Island, New York* (New York, 1887), 175.

19. Stirling to Washington, Jan. 16, 1780, WP-LC; Melvin J. Weig and Vera B. Craig, *Morristown National Historical Park, New Jersey: Military Capital of the American Revolution* (Washington, D.C.: U.S. Government Printing Office, 1955), 19; Smith, *Winter at Morristown*, 26.

20. *Royal Gaz. (R)*, Feb. 2, 1780.

21. Simcoe, *History of Operations of Queen's Rangers*, 130–34; Smith, *Winter at Morristown*, 27.

22. *Royal Gaz. (R)*, July 22 and 26, 1780; Wayne to President Joseph Reed, July 26, 1780, in Charles J. Stillé, *Major-General Anthony Wayne and the Pennsylvania Line in the Continental Army* (Philadelphia, 1893), 219; Wayne to Washington and Return of the Killed and Wounded, July 21, 1780, and Wayne to Washington, July 22, 1780, in Winfield, "Affair at Block-House Point," 44–47, 161–86; James Robertson to Lord Amherst, July 25, 1780, Klein and Howard, *Letter Book of Robertson*, 138–42; Henry Clinton, *The American Rebellion: Sir Henry Clinton's Narrative of His Campaigns, 1775–1782*, ed. William B. Willcox (1954; reprint, Hamden, Conn.: Archon Books, 1971), 200; Paul D. Nelson, *Anthony Wayne: Soldier of the Early Republic* (Bloomington: Indiana University Press, 1985), 108–9; John B. B. Trussell, Jr., *The Pennsylvania Line: Regimental Organization and Operations, 1776–1783* (Harrisburg: Pennsylvania Historical and Museum Commission, 1977), 36–37, 218–19.

23. Extract of a letter of Lord George Germain to Sir Henry Clinton, Oct. 4, 1780, in Winfield, "Affair at Block-House Point," 184.

24. Harry E. Wildes, *Anthony Wayne: Trouble Shooter of the American Revolution* (New York: Harcourt, Brace and Company, 1941), 213–14; Sargent, *André*, 264–78. The poem is printed in Winfield, "Affair at Block-House Point," 264–68.

25. *Royal Gaz. (R)*, Oct. 11, and Nov. 25, 1782, and Feb. 9, and Mar. 20, 1782; Winfield, "Affair at Block-House Point," 170.

26. *Royal Gaz. (R)*, Jan. 29, 1780, in *NJA*, 2d ser., 4: 182–83.

27. Ibid., Feb. 9, 1780, in Ibid., 178–79; *Pa. Journal*, Jan. 29, 1780; Theodore Thayer, *As We Were: The Story of Old Elizabethtown* (Elizabeth, N.J.: Grassman Publishing Company, 1964), 133–34; Boyd, *Boudinot*, 83; Thomas Fleming, *The Forgotten Victory: The Battle for New Jersey—1780* (New York: Reader's Digest Press, 1973), 80–83.

28. *Royal Gaz. (R)*, Nov. 25, 1780, and Feb. 6, 1782; *Md. Gaz.*, Oct. 10, 1782; Bayles, *Richmond County*, 212–14, 243–44; E. Alfred Jones, *The Loyalists of New Jersey: Their Memorials, Petitions, Claims, Etc. from English Records* (1926; reprint, Bowie, Md.: Heritage Books, 1988), 90–92; Sabine, *Biographical Sketches of Loyalists*, 1: 524, Thayer, *As We Were*, 130.

29. Martin, *Private Yankee Doodle*, 177–80.

30. John W. Barber and Henry Howe, *Historical Collections of New Jersey* (1868; reprint, Spartanburg, S.C.: The Reprint Company, 1975), 371.

31. Ibid., 371–74.

32. For example, *N.J. Gaz.*, Oct. 24, 1781, and Feb. 13, and Mar. 13, 1782; *Pa. Gaz. and WA*, Oct. 31, 1781, and Feb. 20, 1782.

33. Samuel Ferguson to William Livingston, Nov. 7, 1781, *WL* 4: 326.

34. Petition of the Inhabitants of Little Egg Harbor, Nov. 12, 1781, *WL* 4: 328.

35. From the *N.J. Gaz.*, in Horner, *Old Monmouth*, 416–17.

36. Gregory E. Dowd, "Declarations of Dependence: War and Inequity in Revolutionary New Jersey, 1776–1815," *NJH* 103 (1985): 49.

37. Francis D. Pingeon, *Blacks in the Revolutionary Era: New Jersey's Revolutionary Experience* (Trenton: New Jersey Historical Commission, 1975), 21.

38. Quote from Asher Holmes Papers, Rutgers University, in Dennis P. Ryan, "Six Towns: Continuity and Change in Revolutionary New Jersey, 1770–1792" (Ph.D. diss., New York University, 1974), 135.

39. *Royal Gaz. (R)*, Supplement, Nov. 13, 1779.

40. Graham R. Hodges, "Black Revolt in New York City and the Neutral Zone, 1775–1783," in Paul A. Gilje and William Penack, eds., *New York in the Age of the Constitution* (Rutherford, N.J.: Fairleigh Dickinson University Press, 1992), 34–35. The sketch of Tye is the same in Graham R. Hodges, *Slavery and Freedom in the Rural North: African Americans in Monmouth County, New Jersey* (Madison, Wisc.: Madison House, 1997).

41. *Pa. Gaz.*, Nov. 22, 1775.

42. Charles W. Carey, Jr., "Lord Dunmore's Ethiopian Regiment" (master's thesis, Virginia Polytechnic Institute and State University, 1995), 89. Includes the roster of the Ethiopian Regiment for May 1776.

43. Graham R. Hodges, *African-Americans in Monmouth County During the Age of the American Revolution* (Lincroft, N.J.: Monmouth County Park System, 1990), 17.

44. *NJA*, 2d ser., 3: 504.

45. Hodges, "Black Revolt," 35.

46. *N.J. Gaz.*, April 12, 1780, in *NJA*, 2d ser., 4: 297; Extracts of Letters from Monmouth County, June 12 and 22, 1780, *NJA*, 2d ser., 4: 434, 456–57; David Forman to William Livingston, June 9, 1780, *WL* 3: 523, also 423n.; George C. Beekman, *Early Dutch Settlers of Monmouth County, New Jersey* (Freehold, N.J., 1901), 77–78; Hodges, *African-Americans in Monmouth County*, 19–20.

47. Quote in Hodges, *African-Americans in Monmouth County*, 21.

48. Samuel Forman to William Livingston, Aug. 6, 1780, *WL* 4: 28–29.

49. Hodges, *African-Americans in Monmouth County*, 19–20.

50. Skemp, *William Franklin*, 257 and 343n.

51. Kobbé, *Jersey Coast and Pines*, 24.

52. James W. St. G. Walker, *The Black Loyalists* (New York: African Publishing Company, 1976), 34n.–35n.; Hodges, *Slavery and Freedom*, 104.

53. *Pa. Gaz. and WA*, Feb. 13, 1782.

54. *N.J. Gaz.*, June 5, 1782.

55. *Pa. Gaz.*, Dec. 24, 1782.

56. *Royal Gaz. (R)*, Mar. 27, 1782; Samuel Forman to Livingston, Mar. 25, 1782, *WL* 4: 388–89; William H. Fischer, "Toms River Block House Fight, March 24, 1782," *Proceedings of the NJHS*, new series, 14 (1929), 424 and 428; Andrew D. Mellick, Jr., *The Story of an Old Farm* (Somerville, N.J., 1889), 542–43; Kobbé, *Jersey Coast and Pines*, 68–70.

57. *N.J. Gaz.*, April 24, 1782, in *NJA* 2d ser., 5: 424–25; Katherine Mayo, *General Washington's Dilemma* (New York, 1938), 79–83; L. Kinvin Wroth, "Vengeance: The Court Martial of Captain Richard Lippincott, 1782," in Howard H. Peckham, ed., *Sources of American Independence: Selected Manuscripts from the Collections of the William L. Clements Library* (Chicago: University of Chicago Press, 1978), 2: 499, 502–3; Alfred M. Heston, *South Jersey: A History, 1664–1924* (New York, 1924), vol. 1: 235–36; Ellis, *History of Monmouth County*, 215–18; Mellick, *Story of an Old Farm*, 543.

58. The full document is in Ellis, *History of Monmouth County*, 219–20; Koke, "War, Profit and Privateers," 335–36.

59. Washington to General and Field Officers, April 19, 1782, and to President of Congress, April 20, 1782, *FWW* 24: 136–37, 145–56; Wilson, *Heath's Memoirs*, 309; Ellis, *History of Monmouth County*, 220.

60. Quoted in Mayo, *Washington's Dilemma*, 103.

61. Stryker, *New Jersey Volunteers*, 64.

62. Clinton, *American Rebellion*, 360; Wroth, "Vengeance: Court Martial of Lippincott," 511–517, 601; Skemp, *William Franklin*, 262; Klein and Howard, *Letter Book of Robertson*, 244; Larry Bowman, "The Court-Martial of Captain Richard Lippincott," *NJH* 89 (1971): 23–36; Frederick B. Wiener, *Civilians under Military Justice: The British Practice since 1689 Especially in North America* (Chicago: University of Chicago Press, 1967), 115–21.

63. JCC April 29, 1782, 22: 217–18.

64. Washington to Moses Hazen, May 3, 1782, *FWW* 24: 217–18.

65. Washington to Vergennes, Nov. 21, 1782, *FWW* 25: 359, Washington to Brig. Gen. Forman, Dec. 3, 1782, *FWW* 25: 388; Lady Asgill to Comte Vergennes, July 18, 1782, Vergennes to Washington, July 29, 1782, and Reminiscence of Elias Boudinot, in Henry S. Commager and Richard B. Morris, eds., *The Spirit of 'Seventy-Six': The Story of the American Revolution as Told by Contemporaries* (Indianapolis: Bobbs-Merrill Company 1958), vol. 2: 888–91; JCC, Oct. 17 and 28 and Nov. 7, 1782, 23: 662–66, 689–91, and 844–47, resp.; *WL* 4: 363–64; Boyd, *Boudinot*, 104, 108; Mellick, *Story of an Old Farm*, 544–45.

66. Washington to Brig. Gen. Forman, Dec. 3, 1782, *FWW* 25: 389; Carleton to Washington, Dec. 11, 1782, WP-LC; Mayo, *Washington's Dilemma*, 102–3; Gerald O. Haffner, "Captain Charles Asgill: An Anglo-American Incident, 1782," *History Today* 7 (May 1957), 333–34.

67. Washington to Carleton, April 9, 1783, *FWW* 26: 307, Washington to General Officers, April 17, 1783, *FWW* 26: 328.

68. *Pa. Gaz.*, Oct. 16, 1782, and June 11, 1783; Dennis Ryan, *New Jersey in the American Revolution, 1763–1783: A Chronology* (Trenton: New Jersey Historical Commission, 1974), 75.

69. Leiby, *Revolutionary War in the Hackensack Valley*, 304n.–5n.; Firth H. Fabend, *A Dutch Family in the Middle Colonies, 1660–1800* (New Brunswick, N.J.: Rutgers University Press, 1991), 220.

70. Tebbenhoff, "Associated Loyalists," 118–19.

CHAPTER 5

1. Patrick M'Robert. *A Tour Through Part of the North Provinces of America, 1774–1775*, ed. Carl Bridenbaugh (1776; reprint, Philadelphia, 1936), Aug. 18, 1774, 7; Thacher, *Military Journal*, 103; Michael Kammen, *Colonial New York* (1975; reprint, White Plains, N.Y.: KTO Press, 1987), 4; Thomas F. Gordon, *Gazeteer of the State of New York: Comprehending Its Colonial History* (Philadelphia, 1836), 596–97; Ruth M. Keesey, "Loyalty and Reprisal: The Loyalists of Bergen County, New Jersey and Their Estates" (Ph.D. diss., Columbia University, 1957), 28.

2. Josephine Emerson, "The Jackson Whites," in Soluitur Ambulando, ed., *In the Hudson Highlands* (New York, 1945), 45–47.

3. "Diary of Captain John Chilton," *Tyler's Quarterly* 12 (1931): 284–85; Jeremiah Wadsworth to S. B. Webb, June 17, 1779, in Worthington C. Ford, ed., *Correspondence and Journals of Samuel Blachley Webb* (New York, 1893), vol. 2: 172; A. Edward Corning, *Washington at Temple Hill* (Newburgh, N.Y., 1932), 4; Mark M. Boatner, *Landmarks of the American Revolution* (Harrisburg, Pa.: Stackpole Books, 1992), 294.

4. Willard L. De Yoe, "A Celebrated Revolutionary Highway," *De Halve Maen* 34 (Jan. 1960): 7, 35 (April 1960): 7.

5. Claire K. Tholl, "The Career of Claudius Smith," *North Jersey Highlander* 4, no. 3 (1968): 3. For regional literature in reference to Claudius Smith, see Henry C. Beck, *Tales and Towns of Northern New Jersey* (1964; reprint, New Brunswick, N.J.: Rutgers University Press, 1988), 112–13.

6. Samuel W. Eager, *An Outline History of Orange County* (Newburgh, N.Y., 1846–47), 550; Albert B. Brushaber, "Claudius Smith," in Ambulando, *In the Hudson Highlands*, 76.

7. Eager, *Orange County*, 551; Tholl, "Claudius Smith," 3–5.

8. Eager, *Orange County*, 552.

9. Ibid., 556–57.

10. Ibid., 553–54; George Clinton to Washington, Oct.—and to the Committee of Safety, Oct. 12, 1777, and Return of Prisoners taken by the British, Oct. 6, 1777, in Hastings, *Papers of Clinton*, 2: 404, 424, and 623, resp.; E. Wilder Spaulding, *His Excellency George Clinton* (New York, 1938), 7.

11. Tholl, "Claudius Smith," 4; Eager, *Orange County*, 563; Robert M. Burns, "Schunemunk Mountain," in Ambulando, *In the Hudson Highlands*, 97.

12. Verdict of Coroner's Inquest, Oct. 7 and 8, 1778, in Hastings, *Papers of Clinton*, 4: 145–49; Eager, *Orange County*, 555; Russel Headley, *The History of Orange County, New York* (Middletown, N.Y., 1908), 87.

13. James Tusten to Victor M. Watkins, Nov. 6, 1833, in Eager, *Orange County*, 557–58.

14. Ibid., 558; Gov. Clinton's Answer, Nov. 1778, and Clinton to Gen. Heath, Sept. 22, 1781, in Hastings, *Papers of Clinton*, 4: 278–79 and 7: 348. Major Brush was later captured by the British and for two years was "confined in Dungeon with the most vigorous Treatment," supposedly because of his role in apprehending Claudius Smith.

15. *N.Y. Journal and General Advertiser*, Jan. 18, 1779; *Pa. Journal and WA*, Feb. 17, 1779; At a Court of Oyer and Terminer and General Delivery, Goshen, Jan. 13, 1779, in Eager, *Orange County*, 559; Sheriff Isaac Nicoll to Gov. Clinton, Jan. 17, 1779, and Clinton to Nicoll, Jan. 19, 1779, in Hastings, *Papers of Clinton*, 4: 497–98; Tholl, "Claudius Smith," 5.

16. From the *True Sun*, Feb. 12, 1846, under signature of A.B.C., in Eager, *Orange County*, 556–57; Tholl, "Claudius Smith," 5.

17. Elizabeth Sharts, *Land O' Goshen: Then and Now* (Goshen, N.Y.: The Bookmill, 1960), 13; Daniel N. Freeland, *Chronicles of Monroe in the Olden Time: Town and Village, Orange County, New York* (New York, 1898), 60; Tholl, "Claudius Smith," 3.

18. NJA, 2d ser., 3: 81.

19. "Confession of William Cole," Mar. 29, 1779, McDougall Papers, NYHS, also printed in Claire K. Tholl, "The Confession of William Cole," *North Jersey Highlander* 4, no. 4 (1968): 8–20.

20. *Pa. Packet*, April 17, 1779, in NJA, 2d ser., 3: 291; Leiby, *Revolutionary War in*

the Hackensack Valley, 197. The sheriff was paid £200 for the imprisonment and execution of Cole and Welcher. *Minutes of the Justices and Freeholders of Bergen County (Hackensack, 1924)*, 135.

21. *Pa. Gaz.*, June 23, 1779; *Pa. Journal and WA*, June 23, 1779.

22. *Pa. Packet*, April 17, 1779 in *NJA*, 2d ser., 3: 251.

23. "The Examination of William Cole," Mar. 23, 1779, McDougall Papers, NYHS; also in Tholl, "Confession of William Cole"; John Barr's Diary, July 5, 1782, in Almon W. Lauber, ed., *Orderly Books of 4th . . . 2d New York Regiment* (Albany, N.Y., 1932), 852; Washington to Clinton, Aug. 10, 1781, in Hastings, *Papers of Clinton*, 2: 634n.

24. "Diary of Ebenezer Erskine, 1778," *North Jersey Highlander* 3 (spring 1967): 16–21; Tholl, "Confession of William Cole," 18–19; Robert Erskine to Philip Schuyler, May 7, 1780, in Albert H. Heusser, *George Washington's Mapmaker: A Biography of Robert Erskine* (New Brunswick, N.J.: Rutgers University Press, 1966), 211, also pp. 154–55; Alice R. Allan, "Robert Erskine of Ringwood," in Ambulando, *In the Hudson Highlands*, 64–65; Leiby, *Revolutionary War in the Hackensack Valley*, 194, 195.

25. *N.J. Gaz.*, Dec. 2, 1778; "Examination of William Cole," Mar. 23, 177, in Tholl, "Confession of Cole," 9, 10; LT, Weart Banta, 15: 295–97; Jones, *Loyalists of New Jersey*, 17–18; Leiby, *Revolutionary War in the Hackensack Valley*, 186–90, 194–95, and 201.

26. "A Warning to Rebels" (Mason), in Carl Van Doren, *Mutiny in January* (New York: Viking Press, 1943), 87–90, also pp. 91–93; "Confession of William [Thomas] Welcher," in Tholl, "Confession of Cole," 11; William B. Reed, *Life and Correspondence of Joseph Reed* (Philadelphia, 1847), 2: 325; Leiby, *Revolutionary War in the Hackensack Valley*, 198; Klein and Howard, *Letter Book of Robertson*, 172n.

27. Keesey, "Loyalty and Reprisal," 22; Leiby, *Revolutionary War in the Hackensack Valley*, 253–54 and 291n.

28. Headley, *History of Orange County*, 389; Hall, *Life and Letters of Parsons*, 249.

29. *N.J. Gaz.*, June 23, 1779; *Pa. Gaz.*, June 23, 1779; *Md. Gaz.*, July 2, 1779.

30. *Pa. Gaz. and WA*, June 21, 1780.

31. By Zephanah Platt et al. . . . for the Committee, April 26, 1779, McDougall Papers, NYHS.

32. *Pa. Gaz. and WA*, Jan. 10, 1781.

33. Major Villefranche to Gov. Clinton, Feb. 27, 1782, McDougall Papers, NYHS.

34. "A Quaker's Daughter in a Night of Terror (from an Old Newspaper Record)," in Tholl, "Claudius Smith," 8–13; E. M. Ruttenberger and L. H. Clark, *History of Orange County, New York* (Philadelphia, 1881), 72.

35. Gordon, *Gazeteer of New York*, 423–24.

36. Tholl, "Confession of William Cole," 11.

37. Victor H. Paltsits, ed., *Minutes of the Commissioners for Detecting and Defecting Conspiracies in the State of New York* (Albany, 1909), July 27, 1778, vol. 1: 181.

38. Cynthia A. Kierner, *Traders and Gentlefolk: The Livingstons of New York, 1675–1790* (Ithaca, N.Y.: Cornell University Press, 1992), 232–33.

39. Col. Livingston to Gov. Clinton, July 29, 1778, and Petition from the Northern Towns of Dutchess County and the Southern Manor Towns . . . , 1778, in Hastings, *Papers of Clinton*, 3: 593–94 and 674–75, resp. There had also been a banditti problem above Peekskill in early 1777, robberies involving "atrocious Acts of Violence." James Livingston to Brig. Gen. McDougall, Jan. 27, 1777, McDougall Papers, NYHS.

40. Paltsits, *Minutes of the Commissioners*, 1: 53–54.

41. Ibid., June 12 and 13, 1778, 143–44.

42. McDougall to Maj. Gen. Heath, Dec. 10, 1781, McDougall Papers, NYHS.

43. *N.Y. Packet*, April 26, 1781.

44. *N.J. Gaz.*, Sept. 19, 1781; *New Hampshire Gazette and General Advertiser*, Sept. 29, 1781.

45. *Connecticut Courant and Weekly Intelligencer*, July 2, 1782.

46. Paltsits, *Minutes of the Commissioners*, 1: 55.

47. *Pa. Journal and WA*, Aug. 3, 1782.

CHAPTER 6

1. "James Moody, the Notorious Tory Spy Terrorized Warren/Sussex County," *Oak Leaves* (Warren County Historical Society Newsletter) 15, no. 2 (1999): 3.

2. Wallace Brown, *The King's Friends: The Composition and Motives of the American Loyalist Claimants* (Providence, R.I.: Brown University Press, 1965), 114. See Emmuska Orczy, *The Scarlet Pimpernel* (1905; reprint, New York; Bantam Books, 1992).

3. James Moody, *Lieut. James Moody's Narrative of His Exertions and Sufferings* (1783; reprint, New York: Arno Press, 1968), 2; Neil MacKinnon, "James Moody," *American National Biography* 15: 723. For a thorough biography of Moody, which makes use of a private collection of family papers and vividly describes Moody's life in New York City when he was not on his missions, see Shenstone, *James Moody*.

4. Moody, *Narrative*, 3, 6; "Minutes of the Sussex County Committee, Aug. 10–11, 1775," in Larry R. Gerlach, ed., *New Jersey in the American Revolution, 1763–1783: A Documentary History* (Trenton: New Jersey Historical Commission: 1976), 158–59; Benjamin B. Edsall and J. F. Tuttle, *The First Sussex Centenary* (Newark, N.J., 1854), 56–57; Thomas B. Wilson, "Notes on Some Loyalists of Sussex County, New Jersey," *Ontario Register* 2 (1969): 39.

5. LT, Joseph Barton, 15: 399, 409; Moody, *Narrative*, 7–9; WL 2: 36n.: George E. McCracken, "Lieut. Colonel Joseph Barton, Loyalist of Sussex County, New Jersey," *Proceedings of the NJHS* 69 (1951): 287, 296–302.

6. Robert Morris et al. to Livingston, Nov. 12, 1777, WL 2: 111–12, 115n.; James Robertson to Livingston, Jan. 4, 1778, WL 2: 159–60; Livingston to James Robertson, Jan. 7, 1778, WL 2: 161; WL, 2: 71n.; Proclamation of William Livingston, Feb. 5, 1777, *Pa. Packet*, Feb. 11, 1777, in NJA, 2d ser., 1: 283–84.

7. Moody, *Narrative*, 9.

8. Ibid., 10; James R. Williamson and Linda A. Fossler, *Zebulon Butler: Hero of the Revolutionary Frontier* (Westport, Conn.: Greenwood Press, 1995), 59.

9. Beck, *Tales and Towns of Northern New Jersey*, 194–97; "James Moody," *Oak Leaves* 15: 3; James P. Snell, *History of Sussex County, New Jersey* (1881; reprint, Washington, N.J.: Genealogical Researches, 1981).

10. Moody, *Narrative*, 10; John Bakeless, *Turncoats, Traitors and Heroes* (Philadelphia: J. B. Lippincott Company, 1959), 158.

11. Malcolm G. Sausser, "An American Loyalist—Moody of New Jersey," *Magazine of History* 12 (1910): 167; Stryker, *New Jersey Volunteers*, 15.

12. Washington to Livingston, Jan. 12 [13], 1782, FWW 23: 445; "James Moody," *Oak Leaves* 15: 4; Philip R. N. Katcher, *Encyclopedia of British, Provisional, and German Army Units, 1775–1783* (Harrisburg, Pa.: Stackpole Books, 1973), 93.

13. Moody, *Narrative*, 10–12; *Royal Gaz. (R)*, June 15, 1779, in NJA, 2d ser., 3: 456–57; Beekman, *Early Dutch Settlers of Monmouth County*, 126–27; Horner, *Old Monmouth*, 403–5; Sausser, "Moody," 167–68.

14. Moody, *Narrative*, 13; Washington to Greene, Nov. 30, 1779, NG 5: 134; McDougall to Greene, Feb. 18, 1780, NG 5: 399–400n.; "Journal of Lieut. Erkuries Beatty," Oct. 15, 1779, and "Journal of Lieut. William McKendry," Oct. 20, 1779, in Frederick Cook, ed., *Journals of the Military Expedition of Major General John Sullivan Against the Six Nations of Indians in 1779* (1887; reprint, Freeport, N.Y.: Books for Libraries, 1972), 36 and 210, resp.

15. George Beckwith to Moody, May 10, 1780, NJA, 2d. ser., 4: 552.

16. Moody, *Narrative*, 14; Extract of a letter . . . from Friend in Sussex County (May–June, 1780), NJA, 2d. ser., 4: 435–36; "James Moody," *Oak Leaves* 15: 4.

17. Moody, *Narrative*, 14–15.

18. David A. Bernstein, ed., *Minutes of the Governor's Privy Council, 1777–1789*, NJA, 3d ser., 4: 158–59, June 16, 1780.

19. *N.J. Journal*, May 17, 1780, NJA, 2d. ser., 4: 380–81. For a full account of the John McCoy and Robert Maxwell case, see Ward, *William Maxwell*.

20. Moody, *Narrative*, 15–21; WL, 3: 400n.; Joseph R. Fischer, *A Well Executed Failure: The Sullivan Campaign Against the Iroquois, July–September 1779* (Columbia: University of South Carolina Press, 1997), 182–85; Sausser, "Moody," 220.

21. Moody, *Narrative*, 20–21.

22. Ibid., 21–22; Fleming, *Forgotten Victory*, 198–99; Sausser, "Moody," 223.

23. Lewis Morris, Jr., to Lewis Morris, July 15, 1780, "Letters to General Lewis Morris," 461; At a Council Held at Preakness, July 17, 1780, in Bernstein, *Minutes of the Governor's Privy Council*, 160–61.

24. Moody, *Narrative*, 22–29; *N.J. Gaz.*, Aug. 9, 1780; William A. Livingston to William Livingston, Aug. 17, 1780, WL 4: 37; Leiby, *Revolutionary War in the Hackensack Valley*, 279; James T. Flexner, *The Traitor and the Spy: Benedict Arnold and John André* (New York: Harcourt, Brace and Company, 1953), 320.

25. Pennypacker, *General Washington's Spies*, 126–27, 215.

26. Benedict Arnold to Col. John Lamb, Aug. 11, 1780, and Lamb to Arnold, Aug. 12, 1780, in Isaac Q. Leake, *Memoir of the Life and Times of General John Lamb* (Albany, N.Y.: J. Munsell, 185), 217–18; Washington to Livingston, Aug. 17, 1780, WL 4: 39; Livingston to Washington, Aug. 21, 1780, WL 4: 49, also 3 and 49n.–50n.; Moody, *Narrative*, 29–31; Leiby, *Revolutionary War in the Hackensack Valley*, 280; Freeman, *George Washington*, 5: 180, 188.

27. Moody, *Narrative*, 31–34.

28. Ibid., 37; Stryker, *New Jersey Volunteers*, 22.

29. Moody, *Narrative*, 36–40; Sausser, "Moody," 225.

30. Washington to Rochambeau, June 3, 1781, FWW 22: 155; Washington to Lafayette, June 4, 1781, FWW 22: 161; Washington to the President of Congress, June 6, 1781, FWW 22: 169; Paul L. Ford, ed., *The Journals of Hugh Gaine, Printer* (New York, 1902), June 5, 1781, 2: 119; Donald Jackson, ed., *The Diaries of George Washington* (Charlottesville: University Press of Virginia, 1978), vol. 3: 375n.; *Diary of Mackenzie*, June 5, 1781, 2: 536. Susan B. Shenstone argues that Mackenzie incorrectly credited John Moody instead of James Moody for this mail robbery. (Shenstone, *Moody*, 116–17 & 120n.

31. John Witherspoon to Livingston, April 5, 1781, LD 17: 134; Freeman, *George*

Washington, 5: 288–93. For a good story, allegedly gleaned from an old-timer's reminiscences, but probably more fiction than fact, regarding Pvt. James Montanie carrying dispatches along a road in the Highlands selected by Washington, who was expecting a robbery, see "Preacher Jim's Failure," *Relics* 3 (Jan. 1958): 2–4.

32. For example, *Md. Gaz.*, Aug. 2, 1781, and June 20 and July 11, 1782; *Pa. Gaz. and General Advertiser*, Oct. 3, 1781; *Royal Gaz. (R)*, June 26, 1782, and Nov. 8, 1783; JCC, June 20, 1781, 20: 678; Moody, *Narrative*, 42; *Diary of Mackenzie*, June 5, 1781, 2: 537.

33. Moody, *Narrative*, 42; Shenstone, *Moody*, 118.

34. Silas Condict to Livingston, July 20, 1781, WL 4: 242; Proclamation of Aug. 25, 1781, WL 4: 248; Proclamation of Livingston, Aug. 8, 1781, and James Moody "HUE AND CRY," Aug. 25, 1781, WL 4: 258–59.

35. LT, Memorial of Jonathan Clawson, Sr., 39: 146–47, 151; *N.J. Gaz.*, Oct. 28 and Dec. 2, 1778, Oct. 20, 1779, and Dec. 13, 1780; *Pa. Journal and WA*, Dec. 20, 1780; David Brearley to Livingston, Feb. 6, 1781, WL 4: 139–40; Theodore Brush, "Lt. James Moody, 'the Most Distinguished Partisan,'" *North Jersey Highlander* 14 (fall 1978): 19; Sabine, *Biographical Sketches of Loyalists*, 1: 317; Harry M. Weiss and Grace M. Weiss, *An Introduction to Crime and Punishment in Colonial New Jersey* (Trenton, N.J.: The Old Times Press, 1960), 32–33, 35, and 37.

36. Thacher, *Military Journal*, 200; Jones, *Loyalists of New Jersey*, 44; Ward, *William Maxwell*, 147–48; Callahan, *Royal Raiders*, 240.

37. Moody, *Narrative*, 43; *Diary of Mackenzie*, Nov. 20, 1781, 2: 698; William T. Hutchinson and William M. E. Rachal, eds., *The Papers of James Madison* (Chicago: University of Chicago Press, 1963), vol. 3: 321n.–322n.; E. James Ferguson, ed., *The Papers of Robert Morris* (Pittsburgh: University of Pittsburgh Press, 1977), vol. 3: 317n.–318n.; Boyd S. Schlenther, *Charles Thomson: A Patriot's Pursuit* (Newark: University of Delaware Press, 1990), 195.

38. Moody, *Narrative*, 46–50; Richard Peters to Livingston, Nov. 9, 1781, WL 4: 327; *Diary of Mackenzie*, Nov. 20, 1781, 2: 699; Jacob Parsons, ed., *Extracts from the Diary of Jacob Hiltzheimer of Philadelphia* (Philadelphia, 1893), Nov. 13, 1781, 47.

39. Richard Peters to Livingston, Nov. 11, 1781, WL 4: 329; John Hanson to Philip Thomas, Nov. 16, 1781, LD 18: 201; Parsons, *Diary of Hiltzheimer*, Nov. 13, 1781, 47: JCC Nov. 8, 1781, 21: 1109; Moody, *Narrative*, 51–52; Thomas Scharf and Thompson Westcott, *History of Philadelphia, 1609–1884* (Philadelphia, 1884), vol. 1: 419; *Pa. Gaz. and WA*, Nov. 14, 1781.

40. JCC Dec. 5, 1781, 21: 1160, April 23, 1782, 22: 209, June 25, 1782, 22: 349, Sept. 3, 1782, 23: 542, and Oct. 1, 1782, 23: 629; Hutchinson and Rachal, *Papers of Madison*, 3: 322n.; Ferguson, *Papers of Robert Morris*, 3: 318n.; Bakeless, *Turncoats*, 275–76.

41. Livingston to Washington, Jan. 1, 1782, WL 4: 357; Washington to Livingston, Jan. 12 [13], 1782, FWW 23: 445.

42. *Pa. Gaz. and WA*, Nov. 14, 1781; *N.J. Gaz.*, April 10, 1782; Richard Peters to Livingston, Nov. 9, 1781, WL 4: 327.

43. Shenstone, *Moody*, 139–43.

44. Ibid., 157–58, 163–64, 193; MacKinnon, "James Moody," 724.

45. Moody, *Narrative*, 56; Jones, *Loyalists of New Jersey*, 145; Shenstone, *Moody*, section 3, *passim*; Sabine, *Biographical Sketches of Loyalists*, 2: 96–97.

46. Sausser, "Moody," 230.

47. Shenstone, *Moody*, 101–2, 189, 292.

48. Extract of a letter from Rev. Dr. Charles Inglis to Rev. Dr. Thomas Bradbury Chandler, May 11, 1782, in Moody, *Narrative*, appendix.

CHAPTER 7

1. Fowler, "Egregious Villains," 180, 300. For a critical appraisal of fictional works on the Pine Barrens robbers, see Oral S. Coad, "Pine Barrens and Robber Barons," *Proceedings of the NJHS* 82 (1964): 185–99.

2. John McPhee, *The Pine Barrens* (New York: Farrar, Straus and Giroux, 1968), 36–37; Lundin, *Cockpit of the Revolution*, 30–31; Herbert Bernstein, "Privateers and Pine Robbers Linked by Find at Martha," *Batsto Citizens Gazette* 6 (winter 1972): 3; Lida Newberry, ed., *New Jersey: A Guide to Its Present and Past* (1939; reprint, New York: Hastings House, 1977), 598, 645.

3. Philip Vickers Fithian, *Journal, 1775–1776*, ed. Robert G. Albion and Leonidas Dodson (Princeton, 1934), Feb. 5, 1775, 249–50.

4. *N.J. Gaz.*, May 5, 1779, in *NJA*, 2d ser., 3: 324; Fowler, "Egregious Villains," 54–56, 59–60, 63, 68–73, 76, 82–86, 108; Sabine, *Biographical Sketches of Loyalists*, 2: 421, 455; John E. Stillwell, *Historical and Genealogical Miscellany: Early Settlers of New Jersey and Their Descendants* (1932; reprint, Baltimore: Genealogical Publishing Company, 1970), 5: 420–24.

5. *N.J. Gaz.*, July 22, 1778, and Sept. 30, 1778, in *NJA*, 2d ser., 2: 453; *Royal Gaz.* (R), Aug. 1, 1778; Fowler, "Egregious Villains," 166–67; Salter and Beekman, *Old Monmouth*, 68.

6. *Pa. Gaz.*, May 22, 1776, in *NJA*, 2d ser., 1: 104; Fowler, "Egregious Villains," 144–49.

7. Newberry, *New Jersey: A Guide*, 631–32; Horner, *Old Monmouth*, 406.

8. A. H. Smith, "The Outlaw of the Pines: A Tale of the Revolution," *Atkinson's Casket* 8 (1833): 54.

9. Account of Amelia Coryel, death of Benjamin Dennis, in Salter and Beekman, *Old Monmouth*, 36; Fowler, "Egregious Villains," 151.

10. *N.J. Gaz.*, Oct. 14, 1778; *WL*, 5: 512; Coad, "Pine Barrens and Robber Barons," 189; Sabine, *Biographical Sketches of Loyalists*, 1: 408; Smith, "Outlaw of the Pines," 55.

11. At a Council held at Princeton, Oct. 1, 1778, in Bernstein, *Minutes of the Governor's Privy Council*, 91–92.

12. Letter supposedly by Dr. Thomas Henderson, from *N.J. Gaz.*, Jan. 29, 1779, and deposition of William Courlis, in Ellis, *History of Monmouth County*, 197–98; Livingston to Moore Furman, Feb. 7, 1779, *WL* 3: 30 and 31n.; Fowler, "Egregious Villains," 159–60.

13. Beekman, *Early Dutch Settlers*, 74; Barber and Howe, *Historical Collections of New Jersey*, 351.

14. *Royal Gaz.* (R), July 17, 1779: *N.J. Gaz.*, Aug. 11, 1779, in *NJA*, 2d ser., 3: 549; Proclamation of William Livingston, Aug. 18, 1779, *WL* 3: 161–62 and n.; Salter and Beekman, *Old Monmouth*, 35; Ellis, *History of Monmouth County*, 198; Fowler, "Egregious Villains," 161–62; Beekman, *Early Dutch Settlers*, 74.

15. *N.J. Gaz.*, Sept. 22, 1779, in *NJA*, 2d ser., 3: 641; Fowler, "Egregious Villains," 164–65; Beekman, *Early Dutch Settlers*, 74–75.

16. Fowler, "Egregious Villains," 238.

17. Ellis, *History of Monmouth County*, 211.

18. Fowler, "Egregious Villains," 239–41.

19. Richard P. McCormick, *Experiment in Independence: New Jersey in the Critical Period, 1781–1789* (New Brunswick, N.J.: Rutgers University Press, 1950), 7; Horner, *Old Monmouth*, 88; Coad, "Pine Barrens and Robber Barons," 193; Salter and Beekman, *Old Monmouth*, 45.

20. Salter and Beekman, *Old Monmouth*, 45.

21. Ibid., 43–44, 69; *N.J. Gaz.*, Dec. 20, 1780; Fowler, "Egregious Villains," 243.

22. Salter and Beekman, *Old Monmouth*, 44–45; Ellis, *History of Monmouth County*, 211; Heston, *South Jersey*, 239.

23. Fowler, "Egregious Villains," 252–55. A £50 reward was offered for the capture of Bacon and £25 for each of two accomplices, Icabod Johnson and Job Atkinson. At a Council at Trenton, Dec. 26, 1782, in Bernstein, *Minutes of the Governor's Privy Council*, 240–41.

24. *N.J. Gaz.*, Sept. 25, 1782; *Md. Gaz.*, Oct. 20, 1782.

25. Fowler, "Egregious Villains," 258.

26. Ibid., 252; Horner, *Old Monmouth*, 80; Arthur D. Pierce, *Smugglers' Woods: Jaunts and Journeys in Colonial and Revolutionary New Jersey* (New Brunswick, N.J.: Rutgers University Press, 1960), 41.

27. *N.J. Gaz.*, Jan. 8, 1783; E. M. Woodward, *History of Burlington County, New Jersey* (1883; reprint, Burlington, N.J.: Burlington County Historical Society, 1980), 29.

28. Fowler, "Egregious Villains," 204–5, 262–68, 272.

29. Ibid., 274–75; George F. Fort, "An Account of the Capture and Death of the Refugee John Bacon," letter of George F. Fort, April 8, 1846, *Proceedings of the NJHS* 1 (1845–46): 151–52; Salter and Beekman, *Old Monmouth*, 69; Pierce, *Smugglers' Woods*, 42.

30. Fowler, "Egregious Villains," 213; Arthur D. Pierce, *Iron in the Pines: The Story of New Jersey's Ghost Towns and Bog Iron* (New Brunswick, N.J.: Rutgers University Press, 1957), 190; Alfred Heston, *Absegami: Annals of Evren Haven and Atlantic City, 1609–1904* (Camden, N.J., 1904), vol. 1: 153–54.

31. Fowler, "Egregious Villains," 213, 220–21, 233–34; Henry C. Beck, *Forgotten Towns of Southern New Jersey* (New York, 1936), 167–68; Livingston to Thomas Sim Lee, Oct. 29, 1781, *WL* 4: 323; Pierce, *Iron in the Pines*, 190; Heston, *Absegami*, 1: 153.

32. Beck, *Forgotten Towns of Southern New Jersey*, 169; Charles F. Green, *Pleasant Mills, N.J.: Lake Nescohague, a Place in Olden Days*, 3d ed. (Hammonton, N.J., 1926), 14–15.

33. Beck, *Forgotten Towns of Southern New Jersey*, 170–73; McPhee, *Pine Barrens*, 33, 35.

34. *N.J. Gaz.*, Aug. 15, 1781; *Pa. Gaz. and WA*, Aug. 15, 1781; Fowler, "Egregious Villains," 222–23; Beck, *Forgotten Towns of Southern New Jersey*, 173–74.

35. Fowler, "Egregious Villains," 181–83; George A. Raybold, *Reminiscences of Methodism in West Jersey* (New York, 1849), 181–83; Watson Buck, "The Refugee Chieftain Joseph Mulliner," *Batsto Citizens Gazette* (spring 1970): 1, 4; Henry C. Beck, "Hanged in Three Places, Buried in Two," *New York Folklore Quarterly* 3 (1947): 243–46; Newberry, *New Jersey: A Guide*, 644.

36. Fowler, "Egregious Villains," 169; Salter and Beekman, *Old Monmouth*, 38; Sabine, *Biographical Sketches of Loyalists*, 2: 413–14.

37. *N.J. Gaz.*, Jan. 3, 1781, in *NJA*, 2d ser., 5: 167; Pardon of Henry Sellers, *WL* 4: 115–16; Bernstein, *Minutes of the Governor's Privy Council*, Jan. 1, 1781, 191.

38. Proclamation of William Livingston, Aug. 3, 1781, *WL* 4: 248, and Oct. 9. 1781, *WL* 4: 309; Fowler, "Egregious Villains," 125, 132, 134, 139; Coad, "Pine Barrens and Robber Barons," 194; Pierce, *Iron in the Pines*, 192–93; Heston, *South Jersey*, 243–44.

39. Fowler, "Egregious Villains," 169–70; McPhee, *Pine Barrens*, 36; Kobbé, *Jersey Coast and Pines*, 70.

40. *N.J. Gaz.*, Feb. 7 and 14, 1781; Horner, *Old Monmouth*, 161, 220; Salter and Beekman, *Old Monmouth*, 38.

41. "Associators of Monmouth," *NJA*, 2d ser., 4: 544–45; David A. Bernstein, "New Jersey in the American Revolution: The Establishment of a Government and Military Disorder, 1770–1781" (Ph.D. diss., Rutgers University, 1970), 366–69; Horner, *Old Monmouth*, 220.

42. Order of Committee for Retaliation, Jan. 19, 1782, *NJA*, 2d ser., 5: 365–66; David J. Fowler, "David Forman," *American National Biography*, 8: 257–58; Fowler, "Egregious Villains," 194–96.

43. Horner, *Old Monmouth*, 219.

44. Ibid., 220.

45. Fowler, "Egregious Villains," 314, 323, 329–31.

CHAPTER 8

1. John Adams to Abigail Adams, Mar. 7, 1777, in L. H. Butterfield, ed., *Adams Family Correspondence* (Cambridge, Mass.: Harvard University Press, 1963), vol. 2: 169–70.

2. Col. Andrew Boyd to President Wharton, April 22, 1778, *PA* 6: 432; Arthur J. Mekeel, *The Relation of the Quakers to the American Revolution* (Lanham, Md.: University Press of America, 1979), 161, 189.

3. Kirke Bryan, *A Christmas Story* (Norristown, Pa., 1948), 6–15. For literature on the Doanes, see John P. Rogers, *The New Doane Book* (1897; rev. ed. George McReynolds, Doylestown, Pa.: Bucks County Historical Society, 1952), hereafter referred to as *NDB*, chapters 10–12. The new edition of the *NDB* contains a long introduction, Rogers's work on the Doanes, and various articles and documents. Rogers relied substantially on Henry K. Brooke, *Annals of the Revolution, or History of the Doans* (Philadelphia, 1848). Rogers mixed fact and material that was plainly specious.

4. John F. Reed, "Rogues of the Revolution: The Story of the Doane Renegades," *Historical Society of Montgomery County, Pennsylvania Bulletin* 18 (1968), 6.

5. *NDB*, 435.

6. Reed, "Rogues," 8.

7. *Pa. Gaz.*, Aug. 20, 1777.

8. Brooke, *Annals*, 30–34.

9. Reed, "Rogues," 10–11.

10. Ibid., 8; *NDB*, 311; Carl Bridenbaugh, *Cities in Revolt: Urban Life in America, 1743–1776* (1955; reprint New York: Capricorn Books, 1964), 102, 106; Rosemary S. Warden, "Chester County," in John B. Frantz and William Pencak, eds., *Beyond Phila-*

delphia: The American Revolution in the Pennsylvania Hinterland (University Park: Pennsylvania State University Press, 1998), 19, 210n.

11. Col. Andrew Boyd to President George Bryan, June 6, 1778, *PA* 6: 582; Reed, "Rogues," 11 and 27.

12. Reed, "Rogues," 10–11; Brooke, *Annals*, 34–42.

13. Reed, "Rogues," 11–12; Brooke, *Annals*, 22.

14. Reed, "Rogues," 13–14.

15. *N.J. Gaz.*, May 31, 1780, in *NJA*, 2d ser., 4: 401; Ellis, *History of Monmouth County*, 387; Anne M. Ousterhout, *A State Divided: Opposition in Pennsylvania to the American Revolution* (Westport, Conn.: Greenwood Press, 1987), 292.

16. *Pa. Journal and WA*, Aug. 7, 1782; Confession of Jesse Vickars, Aug. 7, 1782, *PA* 9: 609–13; Reed, "Rogues," 15–16; Henry C. Mercer, "The Doans and Their Times," *Bucks County Historical Society Collections* 1 (1885): 276–81.

17. In Council, Nov. 26, 1781, *PCR* 13: 129; July 27, 1782, *PCR* 13: 338; Proclamation, Oct. 5, 1781, *NDB*, 412–13.

18. In Council, Dec. 5, 1781, *PCR* 13: 138–39.

19. Joseph Hart to President Moore, Mar. 3, 1782, *PA* 9: 507.

20. Sarah Keith Deposition, *NDB*, 414–17; *PA* 9: 501–2.

21. Confession of Solomon Vickers, Aug. 7, 1782, *PA* 9: 615–16; Hart to Moore, Mar. 3, 1782, *PA* 9: 508; *NDB*, 418, 424.

22. Ousterhout, *State Divided*, 213.

23. Reed, "Rogues," 17.

24. Confession of Solomon Vickers, Aug. 7, 1782, *PA* 9: 614.

25. *JCC*, June 19 and July 12, 15, and 19, 1782, 22: 337, 385–86, 399, and 416.

26. *NDB*, 419–20; Reed, "Rogues," 18–19.

27. Petition of Israel Doane, discussed in Council, Feb. 26, 1783, *PA* 9: 759.

28. Reed, "Rogues," 19–20. Joseph Thomas purchased the confiscated estate of Joseph Doane. Joseph Thomas to President Mifflin, Aug. 26, 1790, *PA* 11: 725.

29. Reed, "Rogues," 8–9, 19.

30. Depositions of Archibald Henderson, Jacob Miller, and John Johnson, July 28–29, 1782, *PA* 9: 597–606.

31. Proclamation of John Dickinson, June 30, 1783, *PCR* 13: 616.

32. Proclamation of John Dickinson, July 26, 1783, *PCR* 13: 630.

33. Ibid., 630–31; Relation of Captors of Joseph Doane, April—, 1784, *PA* 16: 565; *NDB*, 432–33; Reed, "Rogues," 17–18, 20–22.

34. *Pa. Journal and WA*, Sept. 3, 1783; Resolution of General Assembly, Sept.—, 1783, *PA* 10: 178; Samuel Hart to John McAllister, Sept. 5, 1830, in Helen S. Spruance, "The Doane 'Outlaws' in Bucks County," *Old York Road Historical Society Bulletin* 26 (1965): 13–14.

35. *Pa. Gaz.*, Sept. 3, 1783; Paul A. W. Wallace, *The Muhlenbergs of Pennsylvania* (Philadelphia: University of Pennsylvania Press, 1950), 249–50; Paul A. W. Wallace, *Pennsylvania: Seed of a Nation* (New York: Harper and Row, 1962), 133–34; Ousterhout, *State Divided*, 214–15.

36. President Dickinson to Gen. Carleton, Sept. 5, 1783, *PA* 10: 101–2; Dickinson to Gov. Livingston, Sept. 5, 1783, *PA* 10: 103; Sir Guy Carleton to President Dickinson, Sept. 27, 1783, *PA* 10: 131.

37. Proclamation of John Dickinson, Sept. 13, 1783, *PCR* 13: 687–90; "Act to en-

courage . . . apprehending . . ." Sept. 8, 1783, in *NDB*, 332, also 426–29; John M. Coleman, *Thomas McKean: Forgotten Leader of the Revolution* (Rockaway, N.J.: American Faculty Press, 1975), 229.

38. Depositions Respecting Arrest of Joseph Doane, Sept. 25, 1783, and Mahlon Doane, Sept. 27, 1783, and Deposition of Thomas Hart, Jailor, Bedford, Oct. 28, 1783, *PA* 10: 110–13; Barnard Dougherty and David Espy to President Dickinson,—1783, *PA* 10: 114; Joseph Wilson to Council, Frederick County, Maryland, Dec. 15, 1783, *PA* 10: 152.

39. Reed, "Rogues," 25; *NDB*, 332; quote of John Adams in Arthur P. Middleton, "Ships and Shipbuilding in the Chesapeake and Tributaries," in Ernest M. Eller, *Chesapeake Bay in the American Revolution* (Centreville, Md.: Tidewater Publishers, 1981), 126.

40. Ephraim Douglass to John Armstrong, Jr., May 29, 1784, and Depositions transmitted Aug. 5, 1784, *NDB*, 379–83; Christopher Hayes to President Dickinson, June 14, 1781, and Depositions of James Bell, June 5, and Philip Jenkins, June 7, and Commissioners of Washington County to President Dickinson, June 28, and Proclamation of John Dickinson, June 28, 1784, *PA* 10: 279, 594–95, 584–85, resp.

41. Solon J. Buck and Elizabeth H. Buck, *The Planting of Civilization in Western Pennsylvania* (Pittsburgh, 1939), 449–50.

42. Depositions respecting Aaron Doane, Aug. 14, Statement of John Reynolds, Jailor, Aug. 14, and George Bryan to James Irwin, Oct. 20, 1784, *PA* 10: 597–98, 609, resp.; A. J. Dallas, comp., *Reports of Cases Ruled and Adjudged in the Courts of Pennsylvania* (New York, 1882), 3d ed. vol. 1: 84; Thomas R. Meehan, "Courts, Cases, and Counselors in Revolutionary and Post-Revolutionary Pennsylvania," *PMHB* 91 (1967): 10: Robert A. Rutland, *The Birth of the Bill of Rights* (Chapel Hill: University of North Carolina Press, 1955), 96–97; Henry J. Young, "Treason and Its Punishment in Revolutionary Pennsylvania, *PMHB* 90 (1966): 307.

43. Petition of Aaron Doane, Oct. 17, 1784, *PA* 10: 348.

44. *Respublica v. Doan*, Sept. 1784, in Dallas, *Reports*, 1: 84–95.

45. *Respublica v. Steele*, Sept. 1786, in Dallas, *Reports*, 2: 92; Petition of Aaron Doane, Nov. 8, 1785, *PA* 10: 716–17.

46. Petition in favor of Aaron Doane, Dec. 30, 1785, *PA* 10: 717–18; Reed, "Rogues," 26; Young, "Treason in Revolutionary Pennsylvania," 308.

47. *NDB*, 337; Young, "Treason in Revolutionary Pennsylvania," 308 and n., 309n.

48. Henry Wynkoop to the Council, May 6, and Depositions of James Banes, Jr., and John Hart, May 6, 1786, *PA* 12: 302–3; Charles Biddle, *Autobiography of Charles Biddle, 1745–1821* (Philadelphia, 1883), 233n.; Reed, "Rogues," 26.

49. Merrill Jensen, *The New Nation: History of the United States During the Confederation, 1781–1789* (New York: Vintage Books, 1950), 138.

50. In Council, July 23 and 29 and Aug. 20, 1788, and Benjamin Franklin to Peter Muhlenberg, Sept. 16, 1788, *PCR* 15: 497, 501, 515, and 535, resp.; Vice President Muhlenberg to Chief Justice McKean, July 24, and Resolution of General Assembly, Sept. 23, 1788, *PA* 11: 361, 398; Biddle, *Autobiography*, 202–3, 233–34; Richard A. Ryerson, "Republican Theory and Partisan Reality in Revolutionary Pennsylvania: Toward a New View of the Constitutionalist Party," in Ronald Hoffman and Peter J. Albert, eds., *Sovereign States in an Age of Uncertainty* (Charlottesville: University Press of Virginia, 1981), 96, 99, 109–10, 124, 127; Reed, "Rogues," 27.

51. Biddle, *Autobiography*, 232–33.

52. *NDB*, 332–33.

53. Ibid.; Biddle, *Autobiography*, 234; Young, "Treason in Revolutionary Pennsylvania," 309–10; Reed, "Rogues," 27.

54. In Council, Sept. 24, 1788, *PCR* 15: 544; Young, "Treason in Revolutionary Pennsylvania," 310.

55. Allan Nevins, *The American States During and after the Revolution, 1775–1789* (1924; reprint, New York: Augustus M. Kelley, 1969), 455.

56. Biddle, *Autobiography*, 192, 194.

57. In Council, Nov. 4, 1789, *PCR* 16: 209; *Respublica v. St. Clair*, Sept. 1789, in Dallas, *Reports*, 2: 100; Young, "Treason in Revolutionary Pennsylvania," 308–9.

58. *NDB*, 377; Young, "Treason in Revolutionary Pennsylvania," 309n.

59. *NDB*, 338.

60. Ibid., 335–38; Mercer, "Doans and Their Times," 335–38, including interview of Alfred J. Doan with Levi Doane (1884); Reed, "Rogues," 27–28.

CHAPTER 9

1. Jesse Root to Jonathan Trumbull, May 11, 1782, *LD* 18: 505.

2. *Va. Gaz.* (Purdie), Aug. 2, 1976; *Md. Journal and Baltimore Advertiser*, July 17, 1776; Robert S. Coakley, "Virginia Commerce During the American Revolution" (Ph.D. diss., University of Virginia, 1974), 155; Joseph A. Goldenberg, "Virginia Ports in the American Revolution," in Eller, *Chesapeake Bay in the American Revolution*, 321; John E. Selby, *The Revolution in Virginia, 1775–1783* (Williamsburg, Va.: Colonial Williamsburg Foundation, 1988), 176; John A. McManemin, *Captains of the State Navies: American Revolution* (Spring Lake, N.J.: Ho-Ho-Kus Pub. Co., 1984), 53. The Chesapeake is 200 miles long and between 4 and 40 miles wide.

3. Claude O. Lanciano, Jr., *Captain John Sinclair of Virginia: Patriot, Privateer, and Alleged Pirate* (Gloucester, Va.: Lands End Books 1973), 37–38.

4. *Va. Gaz.* (Purdie), Aug. 2 and 9, 1776; George Weedon to James Hunter Aug. 4, 1776, typescript from manuscript at Mills College, Oakland, California.

5. George M. Curtis, "The Goodrich Family and the Revolution in Virginia, 1774–1776," *VMHB* 84 (1976): 51–52; Ernest M. Eller, "Chesapeake Bay in the American Revolution," in Eller, *Chesapeake Bay in the American Revolution*, 39n.; Francis B. Heitman, *Historical Register of the Officers of the Continental Army* (1914; reprint, Baltimore: Genealogical Pub. Co., 1967), 316.

6. Isle of Wight Committee of Safety, Jan. 4, 1776, "Virginia Legislative Papers," *VMHB* 17 (1909): 253; Jack P. Greene, ed., *Diary of Landon Carter of Sabine Hall, 1752–1778* (Charlottesville: University Press of Virginia, 1965), April 22, 1776, 2: 1021–22; Carey, "Lord Dunmore's Ethiopian Regiment," 65; Curtis, "Goodrich Family," 54–60; Fifth Virginia Convention, April 26, 1776, *RV* 6: 484.

7. Dunmore to Germain, Mar. 30, 1776, in Curtis, "Goodrich Family," 67.

8. *Va. Gaz.* (Purdie), May 3, 1776, and Aug. 22 and 29, 1777; *Pa. Gaz.*, Sept. 10, 1777; Maryland Council of Safety to Col. Hooe, May 30, 1777, *Md. Archives* 16: 268; *RV* 6: 536n. and Fifth Convention, May 20, 1776, 7: 429.

9. *Va. Gaz.* (Purdie), June 19, 1778.

10. Ibid., July 10, 1778.

11. Marine Committee to Navy Board at Boston, Nov. 16, 1778, in Charles O. Paullin, *The Navy of the American Revolution* (1906; reprint, New York: Haskell House Publishers, 1971), 165.

12. JCC, Jan. 15, 1779, 13: 69.

13. *Va. Gaz.* (Dixon and Nicolson), Jan. 30, May 22, June 19, and Sept. 25, 1779; Richard Henry Lee to Henry Laurens, June 18, 1779, James C. Ballagh, ed., *The Letters of Richard Henry Lee* (New York, 1911 and 1914), vol. 2: 72–73; Richard C. Bush, "Revolution and Community in Northumberland County, Virginia, 1776–1782," *Bulletin of the Northumberland Historical Society* 30 (1993): 20, 22.

14. Richard Henry Lee to Samuel Adams, June 18, 1779, in Ballagh, *Letters of Lee*, 2: 73–74.

15. Gardner W. Allen, *A Naval History of the American Revolution* (Williamstown, Mass.: Corner House Publishers, 1970), vol. 2: 569; Adele Hast, *Loyalism in Revolutionary Virginia: The Norfolk Area and the Eastern Shore* (Ann Arbor, Mich.: UMI Research Press, 1982), 129.

16. David J. Mays, ed., *The Letters and Papers of Edmund Pendleton* (Charlottesville, University Press of Virginia, 1967), vol. 1: 133n.; Sabine, *Biographical Sketches of Loyalists*, 2: 481.

17. Donald G. Shomette, *Pirates on the Chesapeake, Being a True History of Pirates, Picaroons, and Raiders on the Chesapeake Bay, 1610–1807* (Centreville, Md.: Tidewater Publishers, 1985), 256.

18. Ibid.; Richard A. Overfield, "The Loyalists of Maryland During the American Revolution" (Ph.D. diss., University of Maryland, 1968), 143, 264.

19. Shomette, *Pirates on the Chesapeake*, 256–58.

20. Ibid., 259; Dorchester Committee of Observation, July 31, and deposition, July 27, *Md. Archives* 12, 151–56; summary from Maryland Convention Executive Papers, Sept. 10 and 12, 1776, and Petition of Joseph Wheland, Oct. 28, 1778, in Calvin W. Mowbray, *The Dorchester County Fact Book* (Silver Spring, Md.: Family Line, 1981), 57–58, 83; Edwin M. Jameson, "Tory Operations on the Bay," in Eller, *Chesapeake Bay in the American Revolution*, 381.

21. *Pa. Gaz. and WA*, Aug. 29, 1781; *Md. Journal and Baltimore Advertiser*, Oct. 24, 1780.

22. Robert B. Douglas, ed., *A French Volunteer of the War of Independence: Chevalier de Pontgibaud* (New York, 1897), 33–37.

23. Robert A. Stewart, *The History of Virginia's Navy of the Revolution* (Richmond, 1933), 128n.; Charles B. Cross, Jr., *A Navy for Virginia: A Colony's Fleet in the Revolution* (Yorktown: Virginia Independence Bicentennial Commission, 1981), 61; C. Keith Wilbur, *Picture Book of the Revolution's Privateers* (Harrisburg, Pa.: Stackpole Books, 1973), 8. Barges in New England were called "shaving-mills." William Coffin to John Cropper, Aug. 30, 1809, John Cropper Papers, VHS.

24. *Md. Gaz.*, Mar. 3, 1780.

25. *Pa. Gaz. and WA*, Aug. 2, 1780; Henry Hoopes to Governor and Council of Maryland, July 26, 1780, *Md. Archives* 45: 31–32; Regina C. Hammett, *History of St. Mary's County, Maryland* (Ridge, Md.: privately printed, 1977), 78, 80; Jameson, "Tory Operations on the Bay," 392; Bush, "Revolution and Community," 23.

26. *Calendar of Maryland State Papers: The Red Books*, no 4, 3; Overfield, "Loyalists

of Maryland," 257–58; Cross, *Navy for Virginia*, 61–62; Shomette, *Pirates on the Chesapeake Bay*, 261; Lanciano, *Captain John Sinclair*, 43–46.

27. *Pa. Gaz. and WA*, Sept. 6, 1780; Jameson, "Tory Operations on the Bay," 388.

28. *Md. Gaz.*, Nov. 17, 1780; *Pa. Gaz. and WA*, Nov. 22, 1780.

29. George Dashiell to Gov. Lee, Dec. 8, 1780, *Md. Archives* 45: 201.

30. Shomette, *Pirates on the Chesapeake*, 266.

31. Ibid.

32. Dashiell to Lee, Dec. 8, 1780, *Md. Archives* 45: 201–2.

33. Depositions on Joseph Wheland's Depredations, Sept. 2, 1780, *Calendar of Maryland State Papers: The Red Books*, no. 5, 137; Overfield, "Loyalists of Maryland," 265–66.

34. Joseph Dashiell to Gov. Lee, Mar. 4, 1781, *Md. Archives* 47: 103–4.

35. *Md. Gaz.*, Mar. 15, and April 5, 1781; *Md. Journal and Baltimore Advertiser*, April 10, 1781; Information of John Anderson, July 2, 1781, *Md. Archives* 47: 334; Concerning Wheland's Raids, Feb. 16, April 8, and 16, and June 18, 1781, cited, from *Md. Archives*, vols. 45 and 47, in Edwin V. Beitzell, *St. Mary's County, Maryland in the American Revolution: Calendar of Events* (Leonardtown, Md.: St. Mary's County Maryland Bicentennial Commission, 1975), 85, 90, and 98; Jean Lee, *The Price of Nationhood: The American Revolution in Charles County* (New York: W.W. Norton and Company, 1994), 35; Jameson, "Tory Operations on the Bay," 393; Overfield, "Loyalists of Maryland," 366–67.

36. Hulbert Footner, *Rivers of the Eastern Shore* (New York, 1944), 49; Overfield, "Loyalists of Maryland," 267.

37. *NG* 7: 477n.

38. "Minutes of the Board of Patuxent Associates," April 21, 1781, *Maryland Historical Magazine* 6 (1911): 305–6 and 309; Myron Smith, Jr., and John G. Earle, "The Maryland State Navy," in Eller, *Chesapeake Bay in the American Revolution*, 205, 232–33; Shomette, *Pirates on the Chesapeake*, 274.

39. George Marshall to Matthew Tilghman, July 21, 1781, *Md. Archives* 47: 36; Shomette, *Pirates on the Chesapeake*, 273; Overfield, "Loyalists of Maryland," 268, 298–99.

40. Donald G. Shomette, *Tidewater Time Capsule: History Beneath the Patuxent* (Centreville, Md.: Tidewater Publishers, 1995), 47.

41. Shomette, *Pirates on the Chesapeake*, 274.

42. Ibid., 287.

43. Isaac J. Greenwood, Jr., "Cruising on the Chesapeake in 1781: Extract of Memoir of John Greenwood," *Maryland Historical Magazine* 5 (1910): 126–30.

44. Shomette, *Pirates on the Chesapeake*, 275.

45. Hast, *Loyalism in Revolutionary Virginia*, 139–40.

46. George Corbin to Jefferson, May 31, 1781, *JP*, 6: 46.

47. George Corbin to Col. William Davies, May 2, 1782, quoted in Davies to the governor, May 16, 1782, in William P. Palmer, ed., *Calendar of Virginia State Papers* (1883; reprint, Richmond, Va.: Kraus Reprint corporation, 1968), 3: 165–66.

48. Gov. Harrison to the Speaker of the House of Delegates of Maryland, May 18, 1782, H. L. McIlwaine, ed., *Official Letters of the Governors of the State of Virginia* (Richmond, 1929), vol. 3: 226; Elizabeth Cometti, "Depredations in Virginia During the

Revolution," in Darrett Rutman, ed., *The Old Dominion: Essays for Thomas Perkins Aber-nethy* (Charlottesville: University Press of Virginia, 1964), 150.

49. Gov. Harrison to General [Lt. Col.] de la Valette, July 16, 1782, in McIlwaine, *Official Letters*, 3: 270; Samuel F. Scott, *From Yorktown to Valmy: The Transformation of the French Army in an Age of Revolution* (Niwot: University of Colorado Press, 1998), 94.

50. William Davies to George Corbin, May 21, 1782, in John Cropper Papers, no. 308, VHS.

51. Eller, "Chesapeake Bay," 53.

52. *Pa. Journal and WA*, May 22, 1782; *Pa. Gaz. and WA*, May 22, 1782; Shomette, *Pirates on the Chesapeake*, 284, 286.

53. Col. John Hull to the Governor, July 31, 1782, in Palmer, *Calendar of Virginia State Papers*, 3: 242.

54. *Md. Gaz.*, July 18, 1782; Richard Henry Lee to the Governor of Virginia, July 2, 1782, in Ballagh, *Letters of Lee*, 2: 273; Shomette, *Pirates on the Chesapeake*, 287; Footner, *Rivers of the Eastern Shore*, 56.

55. *Virginia Gazette of the American Advertiser*, July 27, 1782.

56. *Md. Journal and WA*, Sept. 17, 1782.

57. *Va. Gaz.* and *Virginia Gazette and the Weekly Advertiser*, Sept. 14, 1782.

58. *Md. Archives*, 48: 34; Alton B. P. Barnes, *John Cropper: A Life Fully Lived* (Onley, Va.: Lee Howard Company, 1989), 78; McManemin, *Captains of the State Navies*, 63; Footner, *Rivers of the Eastern Shore*, 57–58; Shomette, *Pirates on the Chesapeake*, 290–94.

59. John Cropper to William Davies, Dec. 6, 1782, in Palmer, *Calendar of Virginia State Papers*, 3: 391–92; Council of Maryland, Dec. 17, 26, and 28, 1782, Md. *Archives*, 48: 323, 328–29; William H. Gaines, "The Battle of the Barges," *Virginia Calvacade* 4, no. 2 (1954): 33–34, 36–37; Barton H. Wise, "Memoir of General John Cropper" (reprint Eastern Shore Virginia Historical Society, 1974) from *Collections of the VHS*, new ser., 11 (1892), 27; "Action Between American and British Barges in the Chesapeake Bay, November, 1782," [firsthand accounts] *Maryland Historical Magazine* 4 (1909): 115–132; Barnes, *Cropper*, 78–80; Shomette, *Pirates on the Chesapeake*, 294–99.

60. *N.J. Gaz.*, Jan. 15, 1783.

61. In Council, Jan. 2, 1783, *Md. Archives*, 48: 336.

62. William Paca to the Merchants of Baltimore, Feb. 19, 1783, *Md. Archives*, 48: 360–64.

63. Ibid.; Paca to Commodore La Ville Brune, Feb. 18, 1783, *Md. Archives* 48: 360; Paca to Washington, Feb. 21, 1783, in Shomette, *Tidewater Time Capsule*, 49; Jameson, "Tory Operations on the Bay," 394; Lee, *Price of Nationhood*, 187.

64. Washington to John Augustine Washington, Jan. 16, 1783, *FWW* 26: 44.

65. Arthur Lee to Washington, Mar. 13, 1783, WP-LC.

66. George Mason to Arthur Lee, Mar. 25, 1783, in Kate M. Rowland, *The Life of George Mason* (New York, 1892), vol. 2: 41.

67. Washington to Gov. William Paca, Mar. 5, 1783, *FWW* 26: 195.

68. Washington to Arthur Lee, Mar. 29, 1783, *FWW* 26: 266.

69. *Royal Gaz. (R)*, April 2, 1783, and *N.Y. Gaz. and Weekly Mercury*, Mar. 31, 1783, quoted in John Greenwood, *The Wartime Service of John Greenwood, 1775–1783* (Richmond, Va.: Westvaco Corporation, 1981), n.p.

70. Woodrow T. Wilson, *History of Crisfield and Surrounding Areas on Maryland's Eastern Shore* (Baltimore: Gateway Press, 1974), 246–47.

71. H. J. Eckenrode, *The Revolution in Virginia* (Boston, 1916), 255.

CHAPTER 10

1. Thomas C. Parramore, *Norfolk: The First Four Centuries* (Charlottesville: University Press of Virginia, 1994), 53, 358; Richard L. Morton, *Colonial Virginia* (Chapel Hill: University of North Carolina Press, 1960), vol. 1: 389.

2. RV 3: 388n.; Hast, *Loyalism in Revolutionary Virginia*, 76, 96. For a discussion of the legal ramifications of the Phillips case, see W. P. Trent, "The Case of Josiah Philips," *AHR* 1 (1895–96): 444–54; Jesse Turner, "A Phantom Precedent," *American Law Review* 48 (1914): 321–44; *JP* 2: 191n.–93n.; William Tyree, "The Case of Josiah Phillips," *Virginia Law Register* 16 (1910–11): 648–58.

3. Third Virginia Convention, Aug. 3, 1775, RV 3: 393; George Gilmer, "Papers, Military and Political, 1775–1778," *Collections of the VHS*, new ser., 6 (1887): 109–10.

4. Fourth Virginia Convention, Jan. 8 and 13, 1776, RV 5: 362–63, 396–97; "Virginia Legislative Papers," 172–73.

5. Resolution for the Evacuation, April 10, 1776, RV 6: 369–71 and Fifth Virginia Convention, May 28, 1776, RV 7, pt. 1: 8, 283–85; Hast, *Loyalism in Revolutionary Virginia*, 62–64; Eckenrode, *Revolution in Virginia*, 139–40.

6. H. R. McIlwaine and Wilmer M. Hall, eds., *Journals of the Council of State of Virginia* (Richmond, 1931–32), June 20, 1777, vol. 1: 435–36 and Jan. 3, 1778, vol. 2: 58; William Wirt Henry, *Patrick Henry: Life, Correspondence, and Speeches* (1891; reprint, Harrisonburg, Va.: Sprinkle Publications, 1993), vol. 1: 611; Trent, "Case of Josiah Philips," 445–46; Hast, *Loyalism in Revolutionary Virginia*, 96–97.

7. Hast, *Loyalism in Revolutionary Virginia*, 96.

8. McIlwaine and Hall, *Journals of Council of State*, May 1, 1778, 2: 127.

9. Ibid., May 1 and May 26, 1778, 127 and 140; Col. John Wilson to Patrick Henry, May 20, 1778, Executive Communications, Library of Virginia; Patrick Henry to the Speaker of the House of Delegates, Benjamin Harrison, May 27, 1778, in McIlwaine, *Official Letters*, 1: 282–83.

10. Col. John Wilson to Patrick Henry, May 20, Executive Communications, Library of Virginia.

11. *Journal of the House of Delegates*, Mar. 1778 session (Richmond, Va., 1821), May 28–30 and June 1, 1778, 22, 24, 28, 33, and 35.

12. "An Act to Attaint Josiah Philips," May 1778 session, in William W. Hening, comp., *The Statutes at Large being a collection of all the Laws of Virginia* (1821; reprint, Richmond, Va.: Whittet and Shepperson, 1969), vol. 9: 403–4; *JP* 2, 193, 283n.; Rutland, *Birth of the Bill of Rights*, 168.

13. Leonard W. Levy, *Jefferson and Civil Liberties: The Darker Side* (Cambridge, Mass.: Harvard University Press, 1963), 35.

14. John H. Creecy, ed., *Virginia Antiquary*, vol. 1, *Princess Anne County Loose Papers, 1700–1789* (Richmond, Va.: Dietz Press, 1954), May 21, 1778, 92–93; Ray A. Billington, *Westward Expansion: History of the American Frontier* (1949; reprint, New York: MacMillan Publishing Company, 1982), 145–46; Selby, *Revolution in Virginia*, 231; Woody

Holton, *Forced Founders: Indians, Debtors, Slaves, and the Making of the American Revolution in Virginia* (Chapel Hill: University of North Carolina Press, 1999), 215.

15. *Va. Gaz.* (Purdie), June 19, 1778; McIlwaine and Hall, *Journals of the Council of State*, Nov. 5, 1778, 2: 210; Levy, *Jefferson and Civil Liberties*, 36.

16. McIlwaine and Hall, *Journals of the Council of State*, July 20 and Nov. 5, 1778, 2: 149 and 211.

17. Princess Anne County Minute Book, no. 10, June 11, 1778, 249, Library of Virginia; William Wirt, *Sketch of the Life and Character of Patrick Henry* (1817; reprint, Philadelphia, 1881), Appendix, 463.

18. *Va. Gaz.* (Dixon and Hunter), Mar. 26, 1779; Hast, *Loyalism in Revolutionary Virginia*, 98.

19. *Va. Gaz.* (Purdie), Oct. 3, 1778. For several published items from the General Court records (no longer extant), see Wirt, *Patrick Henry*, Appendix, 465–67.

20. Levy, *Jefferson and Civil Liberties*, 36; Sabine, *Biographical Sketches of Loyalists*, 2: 184–85.

21. *Va. Gaz.* (Dixon and Hunter), Dec. 4, 1778; Tyree, "Case of Josiah Phillips," 657–58; Trent, "Case of Josiah Philips," 448; General Court Orders, Oct. 27 and 28, 1778, in Wirt, *Patrick Henry*, Appendix, 467.

22. Zechariah Chafee, *Three Human Rights in the Constitution of 1787* (Lawrence: University of Kansas Press, 1956), 93.

23. "Virginia Declaration of Rights," June 12, 1776, in Jack P. Greene, ed., *Colonies to Nation, 1763–1789* (New York: W.W. Norton, 1975), 333.

24. "An Act declaring what shall be treason," Oct. 1776 session, in Hening, *Statutes*, 9: 168; Edmund Pendleton to James Madison, Dec. 9, 1782, in Hutchinson and Rachal, *Papers of James Madison*, 5: 383; Legislative Petition, Princess Anne County, Nov. 15, 1782, Library of Virginia; At a General Court . . . Richmond, July 15 and Oct. 26, 1782, in Palmer, *Calendar of State Papers*, 3: 194, 361; Pendleton's Account of "The Case of the Prisoners" (*Caton v. Commonwealth*) in Court of Appeals, Oct. 29, 1782, in Mays, *Letters and Papers of Pendleton*, 2: 416–27; McBride, "Virginia War Effort," 230; John J. Reardon, *Edmund Randolph: A Biography* (New York: MacMillan Publishing Company, 1974), 61–63; Ward and Greer, *Richmond During the Revolution*, 148–49; David J. Mays, *Edmund Pendleton, 1721–1803: A Biography* (Cambridge, Mass.: Havard University Press, 1950), vol. 2: 190–92.

25. Jonathan Elliot, comp., *The Debates of the Several State Conventions on the Adoption of the Federal Constitution* (1836–45; reprint, New York: Burt Franklin, 1965), vol. 3: 66–67. Edmund Randolph in his *History of Virginia*, ed. Arthur H. Shaffer (Charlottesville: University Press of Virginia, 1970, written about 1809) indicates that Phillips agreed to submit to the attainder rather than stand trial, but Randolph does not clarify the situation. In addition to the Elliot collection, the debates are reproduced, with annotation, in John P. Kaminski and Gaspare J. Saladino, eds., *The Documentary History of the Ratification of the Constitution* (Madison: State Historical Society of Wisconsin, 1990 and 1993), vols. 9 and 10.

26. Hugh B. Grigsby, *The History of the Virginia Federal Convention of 1788* (1890; reprint, New York: Da Capo Press, 1969), vol. 1: 122n.

27. Elliot, *Debates*, 3: 140–41.

28. Ibid., 193.

29. Ibid., 223.

30. Ibid., 236.

31. Ibid., 236–37.

32. Ibid., 298–99.

33. William Blackstone, *Commentaries on the Laws of England*, ed. St. George Tucker (Philadelphia, 1803), Tucker's Appendix to vol. 1, pt. 1, 292–93.

34. Jefferson to William Wirt, Aug. 14, 1814, in Andrew A. Lipscomb and Albert Bergh, eds., *The Writings of Thomas Jefferson* (Washington, D.C., 1903), vol. 14: 169–70.

35. Jefferson to Louis Girardin, Mar. 12, 1815, in ibid., 271–79.

36. McIlwaine and Hall, *Journals of the Council of State*, July 25, 1778, 2: 180.

37. *Journal of the House of Delegates*, Oct. session, Nov. 2 and 11, 1778, 39 and 55.

38. Norfolk County Minute Book, 1776–79, Aug. 3, 1778, Library of Virginia; Hast, *Loyalism in Revolutionary Virginia*, 99.

39. *Va. Gaz.* (Dixon and Hunter), Mar. 26, 1779; Norfolk County Minute Book, June 30, 1778; Hast, *Loyalism in Revolutionary Virginia*, 98.

40. Col. Thomas Newton, Jr., to the Governor, Aug. 9, 1782, in Palmer, *Calendar of State Papers*, 3: 252; Hast, *Loyalism in Revolutionary Virginia*, 120–21; Hugo L. Leaming, *Hidden Americans: Maroons of Virginia and the Carolinas* (New York: Garland Publishing, 1995), 239.

41. Thomas Newton, Jr., to the Governor, Sept. 17, 1781, in Palmer, *Calendar of State Papers*, 2: 450–51.

42. Thomas Newton, Jr., to the Governor, Nov. 10, 1781, Executive Papers, Library of Virginia.

43. Ward and Greer, *Richmond During the Revolution*, 147–49; Hast, *Loyalism in Revolutionary Virginia*, 119–23.

44. George Corbin to William Davies, April 18, 1781, and Levin Joynes to Col. William Davies, Sept. 10, 1781, Executive Papers, Library of Virginia.

45. Malcolm H. Harris, *History of Louisa County, Virginia* (Richmond, 1936), 60; Henry Howe, *Historical Collections of Virginia* (Charleston, S.C., 1845), 358.

46. Sampson, *Escape in America*, 174–75; Selby, *Revolution in Virginia*, 311.

47. *Va. Gaz. and WA*, Aug. 24, 1782.

48. Edmund Pendleton to James Madison, Aug. 26, 1782, in Mays, *Letters and Papers of Pendleton*, 2: 405.

49. *Va. Gaz. and WA*, Aug. 31, 1782.

50. Edmund Randolph to James Madison, Aug. 30, 1782, in Hutchinson and Rachal, *Papers of James Madison*, 5: 91.

51. Thomas Jefferson, *Notes on the State of Virginia*, ed. William Peden (Chapel Hill: University of North Carolina Press, 1955), 155.

CHAPTER 11

1. For the etymology of "maroon" see John D. Duncan, "Servitude and Slavery in Colonial South Carolina, 1670–1776" (Ph.D. diss., Emory University, 1971), 587.

2. *Va. Gaz. and the Amer. Weekly Advertiser*, June 22, 1782; Robert D. Bass, *Ninety-Six: The Struggle for the South Carolina Back Country* (Lexington, S.C.: Sandlapper Store, 1978), 432–37.

3. "Journal of the Second Council of Safety," Dec. 7, 1775, *Collections of the South Carolina Historical Society*, 3 (1859), 63 and letter to Capt. Thornbrough, Dec. 18, 1775, ibid., 94; Council of Safety to William Moultrie, Dec. 7 and by Order of the Council of Safety, Dec. 19, 1775, in David R. Chesnutt, ed., *Papers of Henry Laurens* vols. 1–14 (Columbia, S.C.: University of South Carolina Press, 1985–1992), vol. 10: 546, 576; William Moultrie to Major Charles Cotesworth Pinckney, Dec. 9, 1775, in William Moultrie, *Memoirs of the American Revolution* (1802; reprint, New York: Arno Press, 1968), vol. 1: 113–14; Robert A. Olwell, " 'Domestick Enemies': Slavery and Political Independence in South Carolina, May 1775–March 1776," *Journal of Southern History* 55 (1989): 43; Jeffrey J. Crow, "Slave Rebelliousness and Social Conflict in North Carolina, 1775 to 1802," *WMQ*, 3d ser., 37 (1980): 87.

4. Stephen Bull to Henry Laurens, Mar. 14, and Laurens to Bull, Mar. 16, 1776, in Chesnutt, *Papers of Laurens*, 11: 163, 172.

5. Henry Laurens to Stephen Bull, Mar. 16, 1776, in ibid., 172; Extract of a Letter from the Council of Safety of Georgia and Council of Safety of South Carolina, April 2, 1776, in William B. Clark, ed., *Naval Documents of the American Revolution* (Washington, D.C.: U.S. Government Printing Office, 1969), vol. 4: 636; Journal of HM Sloop *Tamar*, Mar. 25, 1776, in Clark, *Naval Documents*, 4: 515; Edward J. Cashin, *William Bartram and the American Revolution on the Southern Frontier* (Columbia: University of South Carolina Press, 2000), 223, 232–33; William B. Stevens, *A History of Georgia* (Philadelphia, 1859), vol. 2: 136–37, 294.

6. John A. Chapman, *History of Edgefield County* (1897; reprint, Spartanburg, S.C.: Reprint Company 1980), 388–89.

7. *Pa. Gaz.*, June 12, 1779.

8. *Royal Gaz. (R)*, Jan. 30, 1782; Joseph Johnson, *Traditions and Reminiscences of the American Revolution in the South* (Charleston, S.C., 1851), 110–11.

9. Sylvia R. Frey, *Water from the Rock: Black Resistance in a Revolutionary Age* (Princeton, N.J.: Princeton University Press, 1991), 52–53; William S. Willis, "Divide and Rule: Red, White, and Black in the Southeast," *Journal of Negro History* 48 (1963): 161–66, 170.

10. Michael Mullin, *Africa in America: Slave Acculturation in the American South and British Caribbean, 1736–1831* (Urbana: University of Illinois Press, 1992), 44.

11. William Gooch to the Board of Trade, June 29, 1729, in Michael Mullin, ed., *American Negro Slavery: A Documentary History* (Columbia: University of South Carolina Press, 1976), 83; Ira Berlin, *Many Thousands Gone: The First Two Generations of Slavery in North America* (Cambridge, Mass.: Harvard University Press, 1998), 120–1.

12. Herbert Aptheker, "Maroons Within the Present Limit of the United States," in Richard Price, ed., *Maroon Societies: Rebel Slave Communities in the Americas* (New York: Anchor Books, 1973), 152; Freddie L. Parker, *Running for Freedom: Slave Runaways in North Carolina, 1775–1840* (New York: Garland Publishing, 1993), 35–36.

13. Washington quote in Ulrich Troubetzkey, "The Great Dismal Swamp," *Virginia Calvacade* 10 (spring 1961): 23; Johann David Schoepf, *Travels in the Confederation, 1783–1784*, ed. Alfred J. Morison (1911; reprint, New York: Bergman Publishers, 1968), vol. 2: 99; Parker, *Running for Freedom*, 54n.; Freeman, *George Washington*, 3: 93–94, 101–3.

14. Maj. Alexander Dick to Col. William Davies, Dec. 26, 1781, in Palmer, *Calendar of State Papers*, 2: 670–71; Leaming, *Hidden Americans*, 231, 233–35, 239; Charles Roys-

ter, *The Fabulous History of the Dismal Swamp Company: A Story of George Washington's Times* (New York: Alfred A. Knopf Company, 1999), 250.

15. William C. Watson, ed., *Men and Times of the Revolution: Memoirs of Elkanah Watson from 1775 to 1842* (New York, 1856), 36; Marvin C. M. Kay and Lorin E. Cary, "Slave Runaways in Colonial North Carolina, 1748–1775," *NCHR* 63 (1986): 5.

16. Schoepf, *Travels*, 2: 99–100.

17. Smyth, *Tour of the United States*, 2: 100–101.

18. Robert C. McLean, ed., "A Yankee Tutor in the Old South," *NCHR* 47 (1970): 56, Feb. 24, 1817.

19. *NCR*, 23: 201; R. H. Taylor, "Slave Conspiracies in North Carolina," *NCHR* 5 (1928): 23–24; Jeffrey J. Crow et al., *A History of African Americans in North Carolina* (Raleigh: North Carolina Division of Archives and History, 1992), 24–25; Lawrence Lee, *The Lower Cape Fear in Colonial Days* (Chapel Hill: University of North Carolina Press, 1965), 279–81.

20. Col. John Simpson to Col. Richard Cogdell, July 15, 1775, *NCR* 10: 94–95; Evangeline W. Andrews, ed., *Journal of a Lady of Quality* (New Haven, Conn., 1921), 198–200; Crow, "Slave Rebelliousness," 83–86; Leora McEachern and Isabel M. Williams, eds., *Wilmington-New Hanover Safety Committee Minutes, 1774–1776*, July 21, 1775 (Wilmington, Del.: Wilmington-New Hanover County, American Revolution Bicentennial Association, 1974), 47.

21. Quote in Crow et al., *African Americans in North Carolina*, 43.

22. Anthony Allaire, *Diary of Lieut. Anthony Allaire* (1881; reprint, New York: Arno Press, 1968), June 22, 1780, 20; Robert Gray quote in Robert S. Lambert, *South Carolina Loyalists in the American Revolution* (Columbia: University of South Carolina Press, 1987), 222.

23. LT, Aaron Vardy, 47: 266–67.

24. LT, Donald McCrummen, 27: 39–41.

25. LT, Donald Kary, 27: 97–98.

26. LT, Roderick McLenan, 27: 153–57.

27. LT, Ely Branson, 47: 552–56.

28. LT, William Fortune, 52: 105–8.

29. LT, Angus Martin, 48: 561–67.

30. LT, David Fanning, 27: 159–65.

31. Aedanus Burke to Arthur Middleton, May 14, 1782, "Correspondence of Arthur Middleton," *SCHGM* 36 (1925): 201; John C. Meleney, *The Public Life of Aedanus Burke* (Columbia: University of South Carolina Press, 1989), 64.

32. Greene to Robert Morris, Mar. 9, 1782, *NG* 10: 469; Gov. John Mathews to Gen. Marion, April 11 and May 21, 1782, in Gibbes, *Documentary History*, 2: 149, 176; Edward McCrady, *The History of South Carolina in the Revolution, 1775–1780* (1901; reprint, New York: Russell and Russell, 1969), 652; A. S. Salley, *The History of Orangeburg County, South Carolina* (Orangeburg, 1898), 482–86, 526–29; Alexander Gregg, *History of the Old Cheraws* (Columbia, S.C., 1925), 356–67.

33. *NG* 9: 615n.

34. *Pa. Gaz.*, July 31, 1782.

35. Kathleen Deagan and Darcie MacMahon, *Fort Mose: Colonial America's Black Fortress of Freedom* (Gainesville: University Press of Florida, 1995), 37; Jane Landers, *Black Society in Spanish Florida* (Urbana: University of Illinois Press, 1999), 79.

36. Duncan, "Servitude and Slavery," 592–93, 597–600; Betty Wood, *Slavery in Colonial Georgia, 1730–1775* (Athens: University of Georgia Press, 1984), 181; Philip D. Morgan, *Slave Counterpoint* (Chapel Hill: University of North Carolina Press, 1998), 450–51.

37. Stevens, *History of Georgia*, 2: 376–78; Jerome J. Nadelhaft, *Disorders of War: The Revolution in South Carolina* (Orono: University of Maine Press, 1981) 129; Harold E. Davis, *The Fledging Province: Social and Cultural Life in Colonial Georgia, 1733–1776* (Chapel Hill: University of North Carolina Press, 1976), 139.

38. *Charleston Morning Post and Daily Advertiser*, Oct. 26, 1786; Robert Olwell, *Masters, Slaves, & Subjects: The Culture of Power in the South Carolina Low Country, 1740–1790* (Ithaca, N.Y.: Cornell University Press, 1998), 278–79.

39. Joyce E. Chaplin, *In Anxious Pursuit: Agricultural Innovation and Modernity in the Lower South, 1730–1815* (Chapel Hill: University of North Carolina Press, 1993), 323; Landers, *Black Society in Spanish Florida*, 79.

40. Thomas Pinckney to Col. Arnoldus Vanderhorst, Aug. 8, 1787, in Adele S. Edwards, ed., *Journals of the Privy Council [South Carolina], 1783–1789* (Columbia: University of South Carolina Press, 1971), 203.

41. Olwell, *Masters, Slaves, & Subjects*, 279n.–80n.

42. Michael Craton, *Testing the Chains: Resistance to Slavery in the British West Indies* (Ithaca, N.Y.: Cornell University Press, 1982), 62–63.

43. Taylor, "Slave Conspiracies," 25; Crow et al., *African Americans in North Carolina*, 43–45, 47; Crow, *Black Experience in Revolutionary North Carolina*, 86.

44. John Hope Franklin and Loren Schweninger, *Runaway Slaves: Rebels on the Plantation* (New York: Oxford University Press, 1999), 86–87; Crow et al., *History of African Americans in North Carolina*, 47.

45. Greene to Elijah Clarke, June 7, 1786, NG 8: 356; Hugh McCall, *The History of Georgia . . . up to the Present Day [1784]* (Atlanta, 1909, orig. publ. vol. 1, 1811, and vol. 2, 1816), 2: 522–23; Sabine, *Biographical Sketches of Loyalists*, 1: 275; Leaming, *Hidden Americans*, 440; Edward J. Cashin, *The King's Ranger: Thomas Brown and the American Revolution on the Southern Frontier* (Athens: University of Georgia Press, 1989), 135–36.

46. Daniel H. Usner, Jr., *Indians, Settlers, & Slaves in a Frontier Exchange Economy: The Lower Mississippi Valley Before 1783* (Chapel Hill: University of North Carolina Press, 1992), 203; Gilbert C. Din, "Cimarrones and the San Malo Band in Spanish Louisiana," *Louisiana History* 21 (1980), 248; Berlin, *Many Thousands Gone*, 328.

47. James T. McGowan, "Creation of a Slave Society: Louisiana Plantations in the Eighteenth Century" (Ph.D. diss., University of Rochester, 1976), 219, 227, 229, 233–34; Din, "Cimarrones and the San Malo Band," 238–39.

48. McGowan, "Creation of a Slave Society," 235–36, 238; Gwendolyn M. Hall, *Africans in Colonial Louisiana: The Development of Afro-Creole Culture in the Eighteenth Century* (Baton Rouge: Louisiana State University Press, 1992), 212.

49. McGowan, "Creation of a Slave Society," 237–38.

50. Ibid., 237, 239.

51. Ibid., 240; Usner, *Indians, Settlers, & Slaves*, 141; Hall, *Africans in Colonial Louisiana*, 217–20; Gilbert C. Din, *Francisco Bouligny: A Bourbon Soldier in Spanish Louisiana* (Baton Rouge: Louisiana State University Press, 1993), 42 and n.

52. Hall, *Africans in Colonial Louisiana*, 217–18.

53. Ibid., 221–22; Din, "*Cimarrones* and the San Malo Band," 244.

54. Hall, *Africans in Colonial Louisiana*, 222–25.

55. Ibid., 212–13; Jack O. L. Holmes, "*Dramatis Personae* in Spanish Louisiana," *Louisiana Studies* 6 (1967): 175–76; Kimberly S. Hanger, *Bounded Lives: Free Black Society in Colonial New Orleans, 1769–1803* (Durham, N.C.: Duke University Press, 1997), 121–28; Din, "*Cimarrones* and the San Malo Band," 245, 247–49; Din, *Bouligny*, 134–35, 138.

56. Gilbert C. Din and John E. Harkins, *The New Orleans Cabildo: Colonial Louisiana's First City Government, 1769–1803* (Baton Rouge: Louisiana State University Press, 1996), 167; Din, "*Cimarrones* and the San Malo Band," 255–62; Din, *Bouligny*, 133, 135–37; Hall, *Africans in Colonial Louisiana*, 231–32.

57. "Oura St. Malo [The Dirge of San Malo]," in George W. Cable, *Creoles and Cajuns: Stories of Old Louisiana*, ed. Arlin Turner (Garden City, N.Y.: Doubleday, 1959), 418–19; Usner, *Indians, Settlers, & Slaves*, 141–42; Din, "*Cimarrones* and the San Malo Band," 256–57; Hall, *Africans in Colonial Louisiana*, 234–35.

58. Din, "*Cimarrones* and the San Malo Band," 258; Berlin, *Many Thousands Gone*, 240; Caroline M. Burson, *The Stewardship of Don Esteban Miro, 1782–1797* (New Orleans, 1940), 118.

59. Hall, *Africans in Colonial Louisiana*, 236.

60. Craton, *Testing the Chains*, 61–62.

CHAPTER 12

1. Moultrie, *Memoirs*, 1: 203n.

2. Richard J. Hooker, ed., *The Carolina Backcountry on the Eve of the Revolution: The Journal and Other Writings of Charles Woodmason, Anglican Itinerant* (Chapel Hill: University of North Carolina Press, 1953), xxi–xxiii; William Schaper, *Sectionalism and Representation in South Carolina* (1901; reprint, New York: Da Capo Press 1968), 18–20.

3. Richard M. Brown, *The South Carolina Regulators* (Cambridge, Mass.: Harvard University Press, 1963), 27–28.

4. Hooker, *Carolina Backcountry*, 121.

5. Delma E. Presley, "The Crackers of Georgia," *GHQ* 60, (1976), 112–13; Thomas L. Stokes, *The Savannah* (New York: Rinehart and Company, 1951), 160–61.

6. Hooker, *Carolina Backcountry*, 154.

7. Gavin Cochrane to Earl of Dartmouth, June 27, 1766, in Mitford M. Mathews, ed., *A Dictionary of Americanisms on Historical Principles* (Chicago: University of Chicago Press, 1951), vol. 1: 426.

8. James Habersham to James Wright, Aug. 18 and 20, 1772, "The Letters of Hon. James Habersham," *GHSC* 6 (1904): 201–2, 204.

9. Gen. Archibald Campbell to Henry Clinton, Mar. 4, 1779, quoted in Jack M. Sosin, *The Revolutionary Frontier, 1763–1783* (New York: Holt, Rinehart, and Winston, 1967), 102.

10. Uhlendorf, *Letters of Baurmeister*, May 10, 1782, 502.

11. *S.C. Gaz.*, Aug. 10–17, 1767; Hooker, *Carolina Backcountry*, "Remonstrance," 230–33; Brown, *South Carolina Regulators*, 33–39, 76, 82; Robert M. Weir, *Colonial South Carolina: A History* (Millwood, N.J.: KTO Press, 1983), 225–27; George L. Johnston, Jr., *The Frontier in the Colonial South: South Carolina Backcountry, 1736–1800* (Westport, Conn.: Greenwood Press, 1997), 127; Rachel N. Klein, *Unification of a Slave State: The*

Rise of the Planter Class in the South Carolina Backcountry, 1760–1808 (Chapel Hill: University of North Carolina Press, 1990), 43, 74.

12. Brown, *South Carolina Regulators*, 44–47; Hooker, *Carolina Backcountry*, "Remonstrance," 227, 234.

13. *S.C. Gaz.*, Aug. 15, 1768.

14. Hooker, *Carolina Backcountry*, 207; Brown, *South Carolina Regulators*, 205n.; Hooker, *Carolina Backcountry*, 207; Leaming, *Hidden Americans*, 411.

15. *S.C. Gaz.*, Mar. 23, 1769; Hooker, *Carolina Backcountry*, 207.

16. *S.C. Gaz.*, April 6, 1769; Henry Savage, Jr., *River of the Carolinas: The Santee* (New York: Rinehart and Company, 1956), 147–48; Bass, *Ninety-Six*, 65; Klein, *Unification of a Slave State*, 74; Leaming, *Hidden Americans*, 411–13; Hooker, *Carolina Backcountry*, 185; Lambert, *South Carolina Loyalists*, 18; Brown, *South Carolina Regulators*, 94–95.

17. Brown, *South Carolina Regulators*, 103.

18. Ibid., 205n.

19. David Ramsay, *History of South Carolina* (1858; reprint Spartanburg, S.C.: The Reprint Company, 1968), 1: 259.

20. William M. Dabney and Marion Dargan, *William Henry Drayton & the American Revolution* (Albuquerque: University of New Mexico Press, 1962), 92; Rachel N. Klein, "Frontier Planters and the American Revolution: The South Carolina Backcountry, 1775–1789," in Hoffman et al., *An Uncivil War*, 55; James M. Johnson, *Militiamen, Rangers, and Redcoats: The Military in Georgia, 1754–1776* (Macon, Ga.: Mercer University Press, 1992), 121.

21. E. Alfred Jones, ed., *The Journal of Alexander Chesney, a South Carolina Loyalist in the Revolution and After* (Columbus, Ohio, 1921), 66; Lambert, *South Carolina Loyalists*, 43–44; Klein, *Unification of a Slave State*, 96–97; Dabney and Dargan, *Drayton*, 91.

22. Thomas Brown to Lord William Campbell, Sept. 18, 1775, in James H. O'Donnell, "A Loyalist View of the Drayton-Tennent-Hart Mission to the Upcountry," *SCHM* 67 (1966): 17–26; Jones, *Journal of Chesney*, 68–69; Robert W. Barnwell, "Loyalism in South Carolina, 1765–1785" (Ph.D. diss., Duke University, 1941), 107–16; John S. Pancake, *The Destructive War: The British Campaign in the Carolinas* (University: University of Alabama Press, 1985), 74–75.

23. William Moultrie to William H. Drayton, Nov. 9, 1775, in Moultrie, *Memoirs*, 1: 109.

24. Col. William Thompson to Henry Laurens, Nov. 28, 1776, in Gibbes, *Documentary History*, 1: 220; Marvin L. Cann, "Prelude to War: The First Battle of Ninety Six," *SCHM* 76 (1975): 206–13.

25. Declaration of Col. Richardson to Insurgents, Dec. 8, 1775, in Gibbes, *Documentary History*, 1: 224–25; Cann, "Prelude to War," 212–13.

26. Col. Richard Richardson to Henry Laurens, Dec. 12, 1775, in Gibbes, *Documentary History*, 1: 228; John Drayton, *Memoirs of the American Revolution* (Charleston, S.C., 1821), 2: 117–22, 127–36; Lewis P. Jones, *The South Carolina Civil War of 1775* (Lexington, S.C.: The Sandlapper Store, 1975), 72–80; J.B.O. Landrum, *Colonial and Revolutionary History of Upper South Carolina* (Greenville, S.C., 1897), 74–82.

27. "Prisoners Sent to Charleston Town by Col. Richardson," in Gibbes, *Documentary History*, 1: 249–53; Richard Richardson to Henry Laurens, Jan. 2, 1776, in Salley, *History of Orangeburg County*, 327; Lambert, *South Carolina Loyalists*, 48–49.

28. Rachel N. Klein, "Frontier Planters," 58–59; Martha C. Searcy, *The Georgia-Florida Contest in the American Revolution, 1776–1778* (University: University of Alabama Press, 1985), 38; Carole W. Troxler, "Refuge, Resistance, and Reward: The Southern Loyalists' Claim on East Florida," *Journal of Southern History* 55 (1989): 569.

29. Francis Salvador to Chief Justice Drayton, July 18, 1776, in Gibbes, *Documentary History*, 2: 24–25; Lindley S. Butler, ed., *The Narrative of Col. David Fanning* (Davidson, N.C.: Briarpatch Press, 1981), 24 and n.; Tom Hatley, *Dividing Paths: Cherokees and South Carolinians Through the Era of Revolution* (New York: Oxford University Press, 1993), 195 and 197; Sosin, *Revolutionary Frontier*, 91; Charles E. Kovacik and John J. Winberry, *South Carolina: A Geography* (Boulder, Colo.: Westview Press, 1987), 84–85; Grace S. Woodward, *The Cherokees* (Norman: University of Oklahoma Press, 1963), 96–97; John R. Alden, *The South in the Revolution, 1763–1789* (Baton Rouge: Louisiana State University Press, 1957), 272–73; Pancake, *The Destructive War*, 76.

30. Klein, "Frontier Planters," 56.

31. Cashin, *King's Ranger*, 75.

32. Rawlins Lowndes to Henry Laurens, April 13, 1778, PCC r86 i72, 445; Robert Howe to the Continental Congress, April 19, 1778, PCC r178 i160, 450–54; Robert Howe to William Moultrie, April 7, 1778, and Moultrie to Howe, April 10, 1778, in Moultrie, *Memoirs*, 1: 203, 205.

33. John Houstoun to President of Congress, Mar. —, 1778, PCC r87 i73, 191–95; Gov. Patrick Tonyn to Gen. William Howe, April 28, 1778, in *Historical Manuscript Commission Report on American Manuscripts in the Royal Institution of Great Britain* (Hereford, England, 1909), 1: 240; Henry Laurens to John Houstoun, April 16, 1778, in Chesnutt, *Papers of Laurens*, 13: 121; Siebert, *Loyalists in East Florida*, 1: 54.

34. Rawlins Lowndes to Henry Laurens, April 13, 1778, PCC r86 i72, 445–48; "Order Book of Samuel Elbert," *GHSC* 5, pt. 2 (1902): 125–26, April 14, 1778; William Moultrie to Rawlins Lowndes, April 14, 1778, in Moultrie, *Memoirs*, 1: 208; John F. Grimké, "Journal of the Campaign to the Southward, May 9th to July 14th, 1778," *SCHGM* 12 (1911): 65, May 21, 1778; Carole W. Troxler, "Allegiance and Community: East Florida as the Symbol of a Loyalist Contract in the South," in Robert M. Calhoon et al., eds., *Loyalists and Community in North America* (Westport, Conn.: Greenwood Press, 1994), 124; Charles E. Bennett and Donald R. Lennon, *A Quest for Glory: Major General Robert Howe and the American Revolution* (Chapel Hill: University of North Carolina Press, 1991), 71–72.

35. Minutes of the Executive Council, April 7, 1778, RRG 2: 72.

36. William Moultrie to Robert Howe, June 22, 1778, in Moultrie, *Memoirs*, 1: 225; Grimké, "Campaign to the Southward," May 21, 1778, 65.

37. Troxler, "Allegiance and Community," 125; Robert S. Lambert, "The Flight of the Georgia Loyalists," *Georgia Review* 17 (1983): 439.

38. John Houstoun to President of Congress, Mar. 20, 1778, PCC r87 i73, 181–85; Siebert, *Loyalists in East Florida*, 2: 323–24.

39. *Gazette of the State of Georgia*, July 15, 1778, quoted in Robert G. Mitchell, "Loyalist Georgia" (Ph.D. diss., Tulane University, 1964), 99n.

40. LT, Joseph Robinson, 26: 404–7, Isabella McLaurin, 53: 327–31, and Memorial of Jacob Williams, 48: 361–63; Siebert, *Loyalists in East Florida*, 1: 52–53, 375; Cashin, *King's Ranger*, 76; Searcy, *Georgia-Florida Contest*, 132, 151; Troxler, "Refuge, Resistance, and Reward," 572–73; Katcher, *Encyclopedia of British Army Units*, 101.

41. Siebert, *Loyalists in East Florida*, 1: 42–44; Charles C. Pinckney to William Moultrie, May 24, 1778, in Moultrie, *Memoirs*, 1: 214; Cashin, *King's Ranger*, 77; McCall, *History of Georgia*, 2: 357; Bennett and Lennon, *Robert Howe*, 72–73.

42. Letter of Thomas Pinckney, July 1, 1778, and Thomas Pinckney to his sister [Harriott], July 7, 1778, in Jack L. Cross, ed., "Letters of Thomas Pinckney, 1775–1788," *SCHM* 58 (1957): 157–59; Brig. Gen. Augustine Prevost to Gen. Sir William Howe, June 5, 1778, in *Report on American Manuscripts in the Royal Institution*, 1: 260–61; Joseph Habersham to his wife, June 17, 1778, "Some Letters of Joseph Habersham, "GHQ 10 (1926: 147–48; Rawlins Lowndes to Henry Laurens, Dec. 3, 1778, in Chesnutt, *Papers of Laurens*, 14: 552–53; Grimké, "Campaign to the Southward," July 1–6, 11, 1778, 190–94, 200–201; Robert Howe to William Moultrie, July 5, 1778, in Moultrie, *Memoirs*, 1: 228; Cashin, *King's Ranger*, 77–79; Lewis Butler, *The Annals of the King's Royal Rifle Corps* (London, 1913), 1: 305–6.

43. Minutes of the Executive Council, Aug. 31, 1778, RRG 2: 97; Joseph Clay to Henry Laurens, Sept. 9, 1778, "Letters of Joseph Clay of Savannah, 1776–1793," GHSC 8 (1913): 106.

44. Butler, *Royal Rifle Corps*, 1: 34–39; Searcy, *Georgia-Florida Contest*, 161–62; Bennett and Lennon, *Robert Howe*, 91, 169n.; Howard H. Peckham, *The Toll of Independence: Engagements and Battle Casualties of the American Revolution* (Chicago: University of Chicago Press, 1974), 55.

45. LT, John Harrison, 54: 459–63; Siebert, *Loyalists in East Florida*, 1: 74, 78, 85–88, and 2: 375; Peckham, *Toll of Independence*, 74; Lambert, *South Carolina Loyalists*, 217–18; Katcher, *Encyclopedia of British Army Units*, 101–8; Boatner, *Encyclopedia of the Revolution*, 756.

46. LT, George Dawkins, 26: 5–10; *Royal Commission on Losses and Services*, 147n.; Lambert, *South Carolina Loyalists*, 254, 261, 263; Siebert, *Loyalists in East Florida*, 1: 114, 142, 154; Butler, *Royal Rifle Corps*, 1: 303.

47. Butler, *Narrative of Fanning*, 21n.; Robert S. Lambert, "Robert Cunningham," in Richard L. Blanco, *The American Revolution, 1775–1783: An Encyclopedia* (New York: Garland Publishing, 1993), 428–29; Lambert, *South Carolina Loyalists*, 111–12, 217; Boatner, *Encyclopedia of the Revolution*, 575, 579; John S. Ezell, ed., *The New Democracy in America: Travels of Francisco de Miranda in the United States, 1783–1784* (Norman: University of Oklahoma Press, 1963); 24 and n.; Richard M. Brown, *Strain of Violence: Historical Studies of American Violence and Vigilantism* (New York: Oxford University Press, 1975), 76–77.

48. Gov. Thomas Burke to Gov. John Mathews, South Carolina, Mar. 6, 1782, NCR 16: 219.

49. Aedanus Burke to Benjamin Guerard, Dec. 14, 1784, in Klein, *Unification of a Slave State*, 116.

50. Charles I. Bushnell, ed., *Memoirs of Tarleton Brown, Captain in the Revolutionary War* (New York, 1862), 47–51; Larry A. Wise, Jr., "A Sufficient Competence to Make Them Independent: Attitudes Towards Authority, Improvement and Independence in the Carolina-Virginia Backcountry, 1760–1800" (Ph.D. diss., University of Tennessee, 1997), 146–47.

51. Stephen Meats and Edwin T. Arnold, eds., *The Writings of Benjamin F. Perry* (1882; reprint, Spartanburg, S.C.: The Reprint Company, 1980), vol. 1: 55–56.

52. Klein, *Unification of a Slave State*, 118–20; Nadelhaft, *Disorders of War*, 132–33,

135; Meleney, *Aedanus Burke*, 73; Jerome Nadelhaft, "The 'Havoc of War' and Its Aftermath in Revolutionary South Carolina," *Historie Sociale* 12 (1979): 119.

53. Lark E. Adams, ed., *Journal of the House of Representatives [South Carolina], 1785–86* (Columbia: University of South Carolina, 1976), Mar. 7 and 22–23, 1785, 194–96, 276, 285; Rachel Klein, "Ordering the Backcountry: The South Carolina Regulation," *WMQ* 3d ser., 38 (1981): 670n.

54. Nadelhaft, *Disorders of War*, 131.

55. Thomas Burke to Arthur Middleton, July 6, 1782, "Correspondence of Middleton," 204.

CHAPTER 13

1. Jonas Fauche to Col. Charles [Carlos] Howard, Oct. 21, 1795, Jonas Fauche Papers, Georgia Historical Society.

2. *Roman Catholic Records: St. Augustine Parish, White Baptisms, 1792–1799* (Tallahassee, 1941), 123; Daniel Barefoot, *Touring South Carolina Revolutionary War Sites* (Winston-Salem, N.C.: John F. Blair Publisher, 1999), 258; Siebert, *Loyalists in East Florida*, 1: 328; Joseph Ames, "The Cantey Family," *SCHGM* 11 (1910): 224–25.

3. Thomas J. Kirkland and Robert M. Kennedy, *Historic Camden* (Columbia, S.C., 1905), pt. 1: 297; Bushnell, *Memoirs of Tarleton Brown*, 1: 31; Siebert, *Loyalists in East Florida*, 1: 26, 2: 329; Johnson, *Traditions and Reminiscences*, 172–73; Lucian L. Knight, *Georgia's Landmarks, Memorials, and Legends* (Atlanta, 1913–14), 1: 268, 2: 497–98; Ronald G. Killon and Charles T. Waller, *Georgia and the Revolution* (Atlanta: Cherokee Publishing, 1975), 41–42; Joel Chandler Harris, *Stories of Georgia* (New York, 1896), 63–66.

4. Kathryn Braund, "Thomas Brown," in Blanco, *American Revolution: An Encyclopedia*, 1: 187–88; McCall, *History of Georgia*, 2: 315; Siebert, *Loyalists in East Florida*, 1: 38, 173 and 2: 329.

5. John H. Bennett, comp., "A List of Noncommissioned Officers and Private Men of the Second South Carolina Continental Regiment of Foot," *SCHGM* 16 (1915): 27; Stevens, *History of Georgia*, 2: 170–71; Siebert, *Loyalists in East Florida*, 1: 72; McCall, *History of Georgia*, 2: 325–27; Charles C. Jones, Jr., *The Dead Towns of Georgia* (Savannah, 1878), 185–86.

6. *Pa. Packet*, Jan. 28, 1779 (Savannah item, Dec. 3, 1778); "Order Book of John F. Grimke," *SCHGM* 13 (1912): 206.

7. Mary B. Warren, ed., *Revolutionary Memoirs and Muster Rolls* (Athens, Ga.: Heritage Papers, 1994), 161, 163.

8. Lachlan McIntosh to Gen. Lincoln, Aug. 10, 1779, "The Papers of Lachlan McIntosh," *GHQ* 39 (1955): 183–84; Campbell, *Journal of an Expedition Against the Rebels of Georgia*, 122n.; Otis Ashmore and Charles H. Olmstead, "The Battles of Kettle Creek & Brier Creek," *GHQ* 10 (1926): 88–100; Eliza A. Bowen, *The Story of Wilkes County, Georgia* (Marietta, Ga.: Continental Book Company, 1950), 10–13; Stevens, *History of Georgia*, 2: 192; Louise F. Hays, *Hero of Hornet's Nest: A Biography of Elijah Clark* (New York, 1946), 51–52, 56, 58.

9. *S.C. Gaz.*, July 7 and 28, 1779, in Kirkland and Kennedy, *Historic Camden*, 300–301.

10. Klein, "Frontier Planters," 60.

11. *Va. Gaz.* (Dixon and Nicolson), Sept. 25, 1779; *Providence Gaz. and Country Journal*, Oct. 23, 1779; Siebert, *Loyalists in East Florida*, 2: 329; McCall, *History of Georgia*, 2: 424; Lilla M. Hawes, ed., "The Papers of James Jackson, 1781–1798," GHSC 11 (1955): 15.

12. Hays, *Elijah Clark*, 75.

13. Alice N. Waring, *The Fighting Elder: Andrew Pickens (1739–1817)* (Columbia: University of South Carolina Press, 1962), 34; Siebert, *Loyalists in East Florida*, 329; McCall, *History of Georgia*, 2: 468.

14. Bushnell, *Memoirs of Tarleton Brown*, 1: 31; McCall, *History of Georgia*, 2: 472–73; Salley, *Orangeburg County*, 507.

15. James Wright to Lord George Germain, Aug. 20, 1780, "Letters from Governor Sir James Wright," GHSC 3 (1873): 315; Heard Robertson, "The Second British Occupation of Augusta, 1780–1781," GHQ 58 (1974): 429; At a Council, June 17, 1780, Lilla M. Hawes, ed., "Proceedings and Minutes of the Governor and Council of Georgia ... 1774 to 1780," June 17, 1780, GHQ 35 (1951): 201.

16. Caroline Gilman, ed., *Letters of Eliza Wilkinson During the Invasion and Possession of Charleston, South Carolina by the British During the Revolutionary War*, (1839; reprint, New York: Arno Press, 1969), 25–38; Frey, *Water from the Rock*, 116.

17. Col. McGirth's Petition to Governor and Council of Georgia, May 16, 1781, Telamon Cuyler Collection, University of Georgia; Edward J. Cashin and Heard Robertson, *Augusta and the American Revolution: Events in the Georgia Backcountry, 1773–1783* (Darien, Ga.; Ashantilly Press, 1973), 56.

18. Robert Henry, *Narrative of the Battle of Crown's Ford*, Feb. 1, 1781, from the Draper Collection, 17DD28 (Greensboro N.C., 1891), 32.

19. Memorial of Colonels Simon Monro and Roger Kehall, Relative to McGirt and his People, Sept. 5, 1781, and Memorial of Samuel Montgomery to Gov. James Wright, Aug. 7, 1781, Telamon Cuyler Collection, University of Georgia.

20. Col. John Martin to Brig. Gen. Wayne, Mar. 23, Martin to Wayne, Sept. 7, and Martin to Col. Cooper, Sept. 17, 1782, in "Official Letters of Governor John Martin, 1782–1783," GHQ 1 (1917): 302, 327, 328–29; Lambert, *South Carolina Loyalists*, 263; Troxler, "Allegiance and Community," 128–29.

21. Gary D. Olson, "Thomas Brown, Partisans, and the Revolutionary War in Georgia, 1779–1782," GHQ 45 (1970): 200; Patrick Tonyn to John Cruden, May 26, 1784, in Joseph B. Lockey, ed., *East Florida, 1783–1785: A File of Documents* (Berkeley, Calif., 1949), 195–96; Joseph B. Lockey, "The Florida Banditti, 1783," *Florida Historical Quarterly* 24 (1945): 89–92.

22. Tonyn to Zéspedes, Aug. 7, 1784, in Lockey, *East Florida*, 344.

23. Siebert, *Loyalists in East Florida*, 1: 166–67, and deposition of James Hume, Oct. 31, 1786, and testimony of Peter Edwards, Nov. 3, 1786, 2: 44, 47–48; J. Leitch Wright, Jr., *Florida in the American Revolution* (Gainesville: University Press of Florida, 1975), 137.

24. Affidavit of Thomas Clarke, Aug. 4, 1784, in Lockey, *East Florida*, 358–59.

25. Tonyn to Zéspedes, July 5 and 10, Francisco Sanchez to Daniel McGirt, July 1, Decree of Zéspedes, Dec. 8, and Memorial of Francis Sanchez, Dec. 13, 1784, and Reply in the Case of Francis Sanchez, Aug. 10, 1785, in Lockey, *East Florida*, 214–17, 220, 598–600, 654, resp.

26. Tonyn to Zéspedes, July 5, 1784, Lockey, *East Florida*, 214; *S.C. Gaz. and Public*

Advertiser, May 12, 1784, quoted in Kirkland and Kennedy, *Historic Camden*, 304; Lockey, "Florida Banditti," 88–89; Branch Cabell and A. J. Hanna, *The St. Johns: A Paradise of Diversion* (New York, 1943), 131.

27. Reply in the Case of Francis Sanchez, Aug. 10, 1785, in Lockey, *East Florida*, 654–55.

28. William Young to Tonyn, July 21 and 30, Memorial of James McGirtt, Aug. 3, Petition of John Linder, Daniel McGirt, and James McGirt, Aug. 4, Tonyn to Zéspedes, Aug. 7, and Lt. Col. Fernandez to Governor Zéspedes, Aug. 22, 1784, in Lockey, *East Florida*, 349–50, 353–54, 246, 332, 342, and 377–78, resp.; Siebert, *Loyalists in East Florida*, 1: 153, 164; Lockey, "Florida Banditti," 88–89.

29. Tonyn to Zéspedes, Sept. 24, Petition of Samuel Farley, Aug. 16, Memorial of Samuel Farley, Sept. 24, Samuel Farley to Tonyn, Oct. 23, 1784, and Decree, Feb. 4, 1785, in Lockey, *East Florida*, 359–60, 363–64, 366–67, 406–9, 601, resp.; Siebert, *Loyalists in East Florida*, 1: 165.

30. Affidavits of Nathaniel Ashley and Wilson Williams, Dec. 31, 1784, in Lockey, *East Florida*, 505–7.

31. *S.C. Gaz. and General Advertiser*, Oct. 14, 1784.

32. Tonyn to Zéspedes, July 5, 1784, in Lockey, *East Florida*, 19–20.

33. David J. Weber, *The Spanish Frontier in North America* (New Haven, Conn.: Yale University Press, 1992), 278; James W. Covington, *The Seminoles of Florida* (Gainesville, University Press of Florida, 1993), 19–20; Charlton W. Tebeau, *A History of Florida* (Coral Cables, Fla.: University of Miami Press, 1971), 90.

34. Zéspedes to Gálvez, Feb. 9, 1785, in Lockey, *East Florida*, 456–57.

35. Zéspedes to Tonyn, Oct. 11, 1784, in Lockey, *East Florida*, 388–89.

36. William Young to Tonyn, Aug. 5, and Affidavit of Daniel Melyard, Aug. 13, 1784, and Zéspedes to Gálvez, Feb. 9, 1785, in Lockey, *East Florida*, 356, 358, 457; Tebeau, *History of Florida*, 92.

37. Zéspedes to Gálvez, Feb. 9, and to Luis de Vinzaga, Feb. 11, 1785, in Lockey, *East Florida*, 457–58.

38. Petition of Mary McGirrtt to Tonyn, Feb. 21, 1785, in Lockey, *East Florida*, 528–29; Cabell and Hanna, *St. Johns*, 129–30.

39. John Baker to Samuel Elbert, Feb. 16, 1785, "Letter Book of Governor Samuel Elbert from January 1758 to November 1785," GHSC 5, pt. 1 (1901): 195.

40. John Milledge to Florence Sullivan and Gov. Elbert, Feb. 18, 1785, in Harriott M. Salley, ed., *Correspondence of John Milledge, Governor of Georgia, 1802–6* (Charleston, 1949) 19.

41. Tonyn to Zéspedes, Feb. 26, 1785, quoted in Lockey, "Florida Banditti," 92–93.

42. Ibid., 94, 97–98; Bernardo de Troncoso to Zéspedes, Nov. 7, 1785, in Lockey, *East Florida*, 787; Tebeau, *History of Florida*, 92–93.

43. Butler, *Narrative of Fanning*, 30n.–31n.; Robert S. Lambert, "William 'Bloody Bill' Cunningham," in Blanco, *American Revolution: An Encyclopedia*, 1: 429; Pancake, *Destructive War*, 88; Alden, *The South in the Revolution*, 328n.

44. *Spanish Land Grants in Florida*, vol. 1, *Unconfirmed Claims* (Tallahassee, Fla., 1940), 219–20; Lockey, "Florida Banditti," 100–103.

45. Lord Dunmore to Zéspedes, Feb. 16, 1788, quoted in Lockey, "Florida Banditti," 94.

46. Edwin C. McReynolds, *The Seminoles* (Norman: University of Oklahoma Press,

1957), 27; Lyle N. McAlister, "William Augustus Bowles," *Florida Historical Quarterly* 40 (July 1961–April 1962): 317–18.

47. J. Leitch Wright, Jr., *William Augustus Bowles: Director General of the Creek Nation* (Athens: University of Georgia Press, 1967), 64–67; Elisha P. Douglass, "The Adventurer Bowles," *WMQ*, ed. ser., 6 (1949): 7–15; McAlister, "Bowles," 318–19: Siebert, *Loyalists in East Florida*, 1: 178–79; Lockey, "Florida Banditti," 94–95, 98; Luis de Casas to the Conde del Campo de Alanne, Oct. 27, 1791, in Walter C. Hartridge, ed., *The Letters of Don Juan McQueen to His Family, 1791–1807* (Columbia, S.C., 1943), 15; Covington, *Seminoles*, 13; Cashin, *William Bartram*, 98.

48. Lockey, "Florida Banditti," 95–96, 98.

49. George White, *Historical Collections of Georgia* (1855; reprint, Baltimore: Genealogical Publishing Company, 1969), 286; James T. Vocelle, *History of Camden County, Georgia* (St. Marys, Ga., 1914), 43; Stevens, *History of Georgia*, 2: 455; Hays, *Elijah Clark*, 250; Richard K. Murdoch, *The Georgia-Florida Frontier, 1793–1796: Spanish Reaction to French Intrigue and American Designs* (Berkeley: University of California Press, 1951), 133, 154.

50. Charles E. Bennett, *Florida's 'French' Revolution, 1793–1795* (Gainesville: University Presses of Florida, 1981), 103, 114–15, 124–25; Harry Ammon. *The Genet Mission* (New York: W.W. Norton and Company, 1973), 166–67; Meade Minnigerode, *Jefferson, Friend of France 1793* (New York, 1928), 257; Murdoch, *Georgia-Florida Frontier*, 133.

51. Statement of John Peter Wagnon, Feb. 5 and 19, 1794, in Bennett, *Florida's 'French' Revolution*, 108, 111; Robert S. Davis, Jr., "Elijah Clarke," in Blanco, *American Revolution: An Encyclopedia*, 1: 324; Hays, *Elijah Clark*, 242–55, 261–63.

52. Jonas Fauche to Lt. Col. Charles (Carlos) Howard, Oct. 31, and Howard to Fauche, Oct. 31, 1795, in Jonas Fauche Papers, Georgia Historical Society; Murdoch, *Georgia-Florida Frontier*, 124–33, 154n., 175.

53. George Mathews to Jonas Fauche, Nov. 5, 1795, Governor Letter Books, Georgia Department of Archives and History, Savannah, Georgia; Murdoch, *Georgia-Florida Frontier*, 133–35.

54. Ames, *Cantey Family*, 224–25; Kirkland and Kennedy, *Historic Camden*, 304; Johnson, *Traditions and Reminiscences*, 174. The son of James McGirth, also named Daniel, has been mistaken for Daniel McGirth, the subject of this chapter (see, Murdoch, *Georgia-Florida Frontier*, 176n.). Daniel, James's son, remained in East Florida and became a substantial property owner. He married Susana Ashley, a native of South Carolina. Their son, Juan Roberto McGirth, was born in Saint Augustine, Florida, on Sept. 4, 1798, and baptized by a Catholic priest on May 11, 1799. Of the descendants of James McGirth, John McQueen, a North Carolinian who settled in East Florida, noted in 1807: "The family of the McGirths are always pestering me," *Roman Catholic Records, St. Augustine Parish, White Baptisms*, 123; *Spanish Land Grants, Unconfirmed Claims*, 1: 219–21; John McQueen to Robert Mackay, Feb. 4, 1807, in Hartridge, *Letters of Don Juan McQueen*, 73.

55. Incident related by Dr. Boykin, in Kirkland and Kennedy, *Historic Camden*, 304–5.

56. John H. Goff, "Cow Punching in Old Georgia," *Georgia Review* 3 (1949): 341–45.

CHAPTER 14

1. Nathanael Greene to Robert Howe, Dec. 28, 1780, *NG* 7: 17.

2. Lewis Morris, Jr., to Lewis Morris, Dec. 29, 1780, "Letters of Lewis Morris," 474.

3. Joseph L. Boyle, ed., "The Revolutionary War Diaries of Captain Walter Finney," *SCHM* 98 (1997): 134; *NG* 11: 32 and n.

4. Anthony Wayne to Nathanael Greene, Jan. 23, 1782, *NG* 10: 246.

5. Fries, *Records of Moravians*, Bethania Diary, June 9, 1782, 4: 1822.

6. Moultrie, *Memoirs*, 2: 354–55.

7. Rev. John Simpson's Journal, Nov. 5, 1783, in George Howe, *History of the Presbyterian Church in South Carolina* (1870; reprint, Columbia, S.C.: Duffie and Chapman, 1965), 1: 465.

8. Mary Beth Norton, " 'What an Alarming Crisis Is This?' Southern Women and the American Revolution," in Jeffrey J. Crow and Larry E. Tise, eds., *The Southern Experience in the American Revolution* (Chapel Hill: University of North Carolina Press, 1978), 216; Robert O. DeMond, *The Loyalists in North Carolina During the Revolution* (Durham, N.C., Duke University Press, 1940), 98–99.

9. Andrew Armstrong to Gov. Burke, Aug. 22, 1781, *NCR* 15: 616.

10. *LT*, Nicholas Welsh, 47: 535–36.

11. *LT*, John Ross, 48: 382–85.

12. Jeffrey J. Crow, "Liberty Men and Loyalists: Disorder and Disaffection in the North Carolina Backcountry," in Hoffman et al., *Uncivil War*, 144–45.

13. Greene to La Luzerne, June 9, 1781, quoted in A. Roger Ekirch, "Whig Authority and Public Order in Backcountry North Carolina, 1776–1783," in Hoffman et al., *Uncivil War*, 110; Andrew Pickens to Greene, July 25, 1781, *NG* 9: 77; Evelyn M. Acomb, ed., *The Revolutionary Journal of Baron Ludwig von Closen* (Chapel Hill: University of North Carolina Press, 1958), April 12, 1781, 75; John A. Oates, *The Story of Fayetteville and the Upper Cape Fear* (Charlotte, N.C., 1910), 793.

14. Minutes of the Executive Council, Aug. 31, 1782, *RRG* 2: 97; Kenneth Coleman, *The American Revolution in Georgia, 1763–1789* (Athens: University of Georgia Press, 1958), 10, 173.

15. William Moultrie to Col. C. C. Pinckney, Jan 10, 1779, in Moultrie, *Memoirs*, 1: 259; Martin P. Zahniser, *Charles Cotesworth Pinckney: Founding Father* (Chapel Hill: University of North Carolina Press, 1967), 57–58.

16. "Notes on David Ramsay's *History*," in *Miscellaneous Papers of James Jackson*, *GHSC* 11 (1955): 20; Robert S. Davis, Jr., "Elijah Clarke," in Kenneth Coleman and Charles S. Gurr, eds., *Dictionary of Georgia Biography* (Athens: University of Georgia Press, 1983), vol. 1: 191; David B. Mattern, *Benjamin Lincoln and the American Revolution* (Columbia: University of South Carolina Press, 1995), 62, 65; Hays, *Elijah Clark*, 97–109; Bowen, *Wilkes County*, 28–29; Coleman, *American Revolution in Georgia*, 134.

17. John M. Roberts, ed., *Autobiography of a Revolutionary Soldier* [James P. Collins] (1859; reprint, New York: Arno Press, 1979), 66–67.

18. Brown, *Strain of Violence*, 78.

19. Ibid., 78–79.

20. [Anthony Allaire] letter of Jan. 30, 1781, in *Royal Gaz. (R)*, Feb. 24, 1781, in Lyman C. Draper, *King's Mountain and Its Heroes* (1881; reprint, Baltimore: Genealogical Publishing Company, 1983), 517–18; *Royal Gaz. (S.C.)*, April 17, 1782, in Crary, *Price of Loyalty*, 285–90. The British also hanged men naked. See, for example, Aug. 1780, in Samuel C. Williams, ed., "General Richard Winn's Notes—1780," *SCHGM* 43 (1942): 209.

21. Wise, "A Sufficient Competence," 152–53; Johnson, *Traditions and Reminiscences*, 401.

22. *Royal Gaz. (S.C.)*, Feb. 20, 1782.

23. Henry Lee, *Memoirs of the War in the Southern Department of the United States* (New York, 1869), 256–57; Paul J. Sanborn, "Pyle's Massacre," in Blanco, *American Revolution: An Encyclopedia*, 2: 1352–56; Dan L. Morrill, *Southern Campaigns of the American Revolution* (Baltimore: Nautical and Aviation Publishing Company of America, 1993), 147–48.

24. Robert M. Calhoon, *The Loyalists in Revolutionary America, 1760–1781* (New York: Harcourt Brace Jovanovich, 1973), 493; Brown, *Strain of Violence*, 78–79; Anne K. Gregorie, *Thomas Sumter* (Columbia, S.C., 1931), 158.

25. *Royal Gaz. (S.C.)*, May 3, 1782; Cashin, *King's Ranger*, 131; NG 10: 326n.

26. Col. John Collier to Gov. Thomas Burke, Feb. 25, 1782, NCR 16: 203–4; Major Roger Griffith to Brig. Gen. Butler, Mar. 2, 1782, NCR 16: 212; Gov. Thomas Burke to Gen. Allen Jones, Mar. 23, 1782, NCR 16: 558; Samuel Ashe, *A History of North Carolina* (1908; reprint Spartanburg, S.C.: The Reprint Company, 1971), vol. 1: 699–705, 708–10; DeMond, *Loyalists in North Carolina*, 142–43, 149–50.

27. John Rutledge to Delegates of the State of South Carolina, Nov. 20, 1780, in Joseph W. Barnwell, ed., "Letters of John Rutledge," SCHGM 17 (1916): 142–45; Knight, *Georgia's Landmarks*, 2: 493–95; Coleman and Gurr, *Dictionary of Georgia History*, 1: 123–24; Cashin, *King's Ranger*, 120; Edward J. Cashin's reader's report.

28. Col. Le Roy Hammond to Nathanael Greene, Dec. 2, 1781, NG 651–52 and n.; Roberts, *Autobiography of a Revolutionary Soldier*, 41; Brown, *Strain of Violence*, 80–81; Sabine, *Biographical Sketches of Loyalists*, 1; 348–49.

29. For example, Fries, *Records of Moravians*: Memorabilia, Friedberg, Nov. 27, 1780, 4: 1652; Salem Diary, July 22, 1779, 3: 1310; and July 29, 1780, Aug. 15, 1781, and Aug. 21, 1782, 4: 1555–56, 1698, and 1727; Bethania Diary, April 1, 1782, 4: 1819.

30. Gov. Thomas Burke to Gov. John Mathews, Mar. 6, 1782, NCR 16: 219.

31. Meats and Arnold, *Writings of Benjamin F. Perry*, 1: 12–13.

32. Nathanael Greene to Elijah Clarke, June 7, 1781, NG 8: 356.

33. *S.C. and American Gaz.*, Sept. 27, 1780.

34. Lambert, *South Carolina Loyalists*, 224; Barefoot, *South Carolina Revolutionary War Sites*, 158; Landrum, *Upper South Carolina*, 359–60.

35. Meats and Arnold, *Writings of Benjamin F. Perry*, 1: 5–7; Lambert, *South Carolina Loyalists*, 297; Landrum, *Upper South Carolina*, 360, 363.

36. Yates Snowden, *History of South Carolina* (Chicago, 1920), 412–14, 440; Hatley, *Dividing Paths*, 201–3; Stevens, *History of Georgia*, 2: 282–87.

37. *Va. Gaz.*, (Dixon and Nicolson), May 22, 1779, Charleston item, April 30, 1779; Tom Martin, "Creek Indians," in Blanco, *American Revolution: An Encyclopedia*, 1: 422–23; Coleman, *American Revolution in Georgia*, 141; David H. Corkran, *The Creek Frontier, 1540–1783* (Norman: University of Oklahoma Press, 1967), 319–20.

38. James Blair to James Iredell, July 21, 1781, in Don Higginbotham, ed., *The Papers of James Iredell* (Raleigh: North Carolina Division of Archives and History, 1976), vol. 1: 266–69: Benjamin Quarles, *The Negro in the American Revolution* (1961; reprint, Chapel Hill: University of North Carolina Press, 1996), 140–41; Newsome, "British Orderly Book," Feb. 5, 1781, 296; Frey, *Water from the Rock*, 97–102, 139; Crow, "Slave Rebelliousness," 88–89.

39. Capt. John Meals to Nathanael Greene, Feb. 2, 1782, NG 10: 308; Wesley Laing, "Cattle in Early Virginia" (Ph.D. diss., University of Virginia, 1958), 151–55, 162; Lewis

C. Gray, *History of Agriculture in the Southern United States to 1860* (Washington, D.C., 1933), vol. 1: 115, 144, 149.

40. Proclamation of Gen. Cornwallis, July 18, 1780, in Tarleton, *Campaigns of 1780 and 1781*, 121–22; E. Wayne Carp, *To Starve the Army at Pleasure: Continental Army Administration and Political Culture* (Chapel Hill: University of North Carolina Press, 1984), 98.

41. Benjamin Lincoln to Gov. Rutledge, April 16, and B. Beekman to Benjamin Lincoln, Aug. 7, 1779, Benjamin Lincoln Papers, MHS.

42. *Providence Gaz. and Country Journal*, Oct. 23, 1779, Charleston item, Aug. 24, 1779.

43. Chapman, *History of Edgefield County*, 70–71.

44. Gov. John Martin to Elijah Clarke, Mar. 22, 1782, "Official Letters of Governor John Martin," *GHQ* 1 (1917): 1–2.

45. "An Act Amending the Act [1768] to prevent stealing of Horses and Neat Cattle," *Acts, Ordinances and Resolves of the General Assembly of the State of South Carolina Passed in the Year 1784* (Charleston, 1784); *S.C. Weekly Gaz.*, Feb. 27, 1784; Davis, *Fledging Province*, 83–84; Johnson, *Traditions and Reminiscences*, 400; Nadelhaft, *Disorders of War*, 132.

46. For example, Extract from Court Records of Craven County, Nov. 15, 1779, *NCR* 14: 302–3.

47. James Iredell to Hannah Iredell, Nov. 25, 1779, and Oct. 9, 1782, in Higginbotham, *Papers of Iredell*, 2: 128, 354.

48. For example, at Cane-acre, *S.C. Weekly Gaz.*, Feb. 13, 1784, and case in point, the activity of Benjamin Cleveland.

49. *S.C. Weekly Gaz.*, Feb. 13 and 27 and Mar. 6, 1784; Klein, *Unification of a Slave State*, 117.

50. Meleney, *Aedanus Burke*, 247–48, including quote.

51. Col. Wade Hampton to Greene, July 29, 1781, *NG* 9: 105.

52. Gen. Griffith Rutherford to Gov. Caswell, June 28, 1779, *NCR* 14: 132.

53. "Presentments of a Grand Jury of Georgia, March 1780," Richmond County, in Lilla M. Hawes, ed., *The Papers of Lachlan McIntosh, 1774–1779*, *GHSC* 12 (1957): 87.

54. Gov. James Wright to Lord Germain, Mar. 5, and Address of Assembly to Gov. James Wright, Mar. 5, 1781, "Letters from James Wright," 335, 338–39.

55. Bushnell, *Memoirs of Tarleton Brown*, 39, 42.

56. Meats and Arnold, *Writings of Benjamin F. Perry*, 1: 95–98.

57. *Royal Georgia Gaz.*, Feb. 11, 1779.

58. Robert D. Bass, "The South Carolina Rangers: A Forgotten Loyalist Regiment," *Proceedings of the South Carolina Historical Association* (1977): 68 and 70, includes quote from Wemyss to Cornwallis, Sept. 30, 1780; Johnston, *Frontier in the Colonial South*, 130; McCrady, *South Carolina in the Revolution*, 642, 650; Lambert, *South Carolina Loyalists*, 85, 115; Robert D. Bass, *Swamp Fox: The Life and Campaigns of General Francis Marion* (New York: Henry Holt and Company, 1959), 62, 71; Katcher, *Encyclopedia of British Army Units*, 100.

59. E. F. Rockwell, "Sam Brown: A Legend about 'Look-Out Shoals of the Catawba River,'" *Historical Magazine* 2 (1873): 227–28; Draper, *King's Mountain and Its Heroes*, 134–38; Pancake, *Destructive War*, 85, 89; Landrum, *Upper South Carolina*, 131–32.

60. Klein, *Unification of a Slave State*, 97–98, including quote.

61. Col. Wade Hampton to Nathanael Greene, Aug. 5, 1781, NG 9: 132.

62. Minutes of the Executive Council, Oct. 22, 1782, RRG 2: 384–86.

63. Fries, *Records of Moravians*, Bethania Diary, June 10, 1782, 4: 1823.

64. Draper Coll., 1DD51, Samuel Hammond.

65. Davis, *Fledging Province*, 47.

66. NG 7: 42n.; Weir, *Colonial South Carolina*, 158; Charles C. Crittenden, "Overland Travel and Transportation in North Carolina, 1763–1789," *NCHR* 8 (1931): 239; Carl Bridenbaugh, *Myths & Realities: Societies of the Colonial South* (New York: Atheneum, 1963), 141, 145–47.

67. Fries, *Records of Moravians*, Bethania Diary, June 8, 1782, 4: 1822.

68. Excerpt from the diary of Anthony Allaire, Nov. 15, 1780, in Draper, *King's Mountain and Its Heroes*, 514.

69. Quote in Nadelhaft, "The 'Havoc of War,' " 115.

70. Quote in Crittenden, "Overland Travel and Transportation," 249.

71. Davis, *Fledging Province*, 119, including quote.

72. Ibid., 47–50; Alan D. Watson, "Ordinances in Colonial Eastern North Carolina," *NCHR* 45 (1968): 67–69; G. M. Trevelyan, *English Social History: A Survey of Six Centuries, Chaucer to Queen Victoria* (1941; reprint London: Longmans, 1961), 161.

73. Gregg, *Old Cheraws*, 397–98.

74. Fries, *Records of Moravians*, Salem Diary, Jan. 19, 1781, 4: 1669.

75. For example, Boyle, "Diaries of Walter Finney," 134; Nathanael Greene to Col. John Cox, Jan. 9, 1781, NG 7: 82.

76. Gregg, *Old Cheraws*, 361–64.

77. James Wright to Lord George Germain, Aug. 20, 1780, RRG 3: 315; John Martin to Col. Stephen Johnson, Aug. 26, and to Patrick Carr, Aug. 28, 1782, in "Official Letters of Martin," 321 and 323; Patrick Carr to Gov. Martin, Aug. 11, 1782, in "Letters of Patrick Carr, Terror to British Loyalists, to Governors John Martin and Lyman Hall, 1782 and 1783," *GHQ* 1 (1917): 338.

78. Lachlan McIntosh to Nathanael Greene, Oct. 30, 1782, in Hawes, *Papers of McIntosh*, 103.

79. Gov. John Martin to Col. Stephen Johnson, Aug. 26, 1782, in "Official Letters of Martin," 321.

80. Nathanael Greene to Samuel Huntington, Dec. 28, 1780, NG 7: 9.

81. E. W. Caruthers, *Interesting Revolutionary Incidents and Sketches of Character Chiefly in the Old North State* (Philadelphia, 1856), 306–14.

82. Daniel B. Thorp, *The Moravian Community in Colonial North Carolina: Pluralism on the Southern Frontier* (Knoxville: University of Tennessee Press, 1989), 114–46.

83. Fries, *Records of Moravians*: Salem Diary, June 8, 1777, Sept. 8 and Nov. 27, 1780, and Jan. 19, 1781, 3: 1152 and 4: 1564–65, 1578, and 1669; Bethabara Diary, Aug. 31, 1780, 4: 1645; Bethania Diary, Feb. 15 and 18, 1781, and April 25, 1779, 4: 1767 and 1890; Friedberg Diary, Dec. 27, 1781, 4: 1782; and Memorabilia—Wachovia, Jan. 1782, 4: 1786 and 4: 1708n.

84. William Bratton to Gov. Guerard, Feb. 13, 1784, quoted in Nadelhaft, " 'Havoc of War,' " 115.

85. Minutes of the Executive Council, Mar. 23, 1784, RRG 2: 622.

86. Smyth, *Tour of the United States*, 2: 89.

87. Quote in Meleney, *Aedanus Burke*, 73.

88. Ralph Izard to Thomas Jefferson, April 27, 1784, *JP*: 130.

EPILOGUE

1. Richard Slotkin, *Regeneration Through Violence: The Mythology of the American Frontier, 1600–1860* (Middletown, Conn.: Wesleyan University Press, 1973), 5.

2. Charles Royster, "Founding a Nation in Blood: Military Conflict and American Nationality," in Ronald Hoffman and Peter J. Albert, eds., *Arms and Independence: The Military Character of the American Revolution* (Charlottesville: University Press of Virginia, 1984), 26.

3. Tebbenhoff, "Associated Loyalists," 119.

4. Terry G. Jordan and Matti E. Kaups, *The American Backwoods Frontier: An Ethnic and Ecological Interpretation* (Baltimore: Johns Hopkins University Press, 1989), 70.

5. David Hackett Fischer, *Albion's Seed: Four British Folkways in America* (New York: Oxford University Press, 1989), 767.

6. Fries, *Records of Moravians*, from the Bagge manuscript, 1776, 3: 1036.

7. Meats and Arnold, *Writings of Benjamin F. Perry*, 1: 27.

8. Fortescue Cuming, *Sketches of a Tour in the Western Country, 1807–1809*, in Reuben G. Thwaites, ed., *Early Western Travels, 1748–1846* (Cleveland, Ohio, 1904), 4: 137–38.

9. Elliot J. Gorn, " 'Gouge and Bite, Pull Hair and Scratch': The Social Significance of Fighting in the Southern Backcountry," *AHR* 90 (1985): 31.

10. Jack K. Williams, *Vogues in Villainy: Crime and Retribution in Ante-Bellum South Carolina* (Columbia: University of South Carolina Press, 1959), 33.

11. Gorn, "Gouge and Bite," 20–21.

12. Williams, *Vogues in Villainy*, 17, 28.

13. Thomas P. Slaughter, *The Whiskey Rebellion: Frontier Epilogue to the American Revolution* (New York: Oxford University Press, 1986), 65, 69.

14. Buck and Buck, *Planting Civilization in Western Pennsylvania*, 442.

15. Allan W. Eckert, *That Dark and Bloody River* (New York: Bantam Books, 1996), 232–33, 552, 556, 591–93.

16. Elenore L. Kinietz, "Robin Hood of Pennsylvania," *Keystone Folklore Quarterly* 2, no. 3 (1957): 68–78.

17. Wise, "A Sufficient Competence," 154; Pat S. Elder, *Melungeons: Examining an Appalachian Legend* (Blountville, Tenn.: Continuity Press, 1999), 14–15, 177, 295–98 and *passim*; John Stoutenburgh, Jr., *Dictionary of the American Indian* (New York: Bonanza Books, 1960), 221; Kenneth W. Porter, "Relations Between Negroes and Indians Within the Present Limits of the United States," *Journal of Negro History* 17 (1932): 315; "Melungeons Gather to Discover History," *Richmond Times-Dispatch*, July 27, 1997.

18. Antonio Pace, ed., *Luigi Castiglioni's Viaggio: Travels in the United States of America, 1785–1787* (1790; reprint, Syracuse, N.Y.: Syracuse University Press, 1983), 165.

19. *Charleston Morning Post and Daily Advertiser*, July 3, 1786.

20. Michael Mullin, "British Caribbean and North American Slaves in an Era of War and Revolution, 1775–1807," in Crow and Tise, *Southern Experience in the American*

Revolution, 261; *RRG* July 8, 1783, 2: 510–11; Waring, *Fighting Elder*, 125; Kathryn E. Braund, *Deerskins and Duffels: The Creek Indian Trade with Anglo-America, 1685–1815* (Lincoln: University of Nebraska Press, 1993), 182.

21. Narrative of Mr. Walton, (Feb. 1797), *Letters of Benjamin Hawkins, 1796–1806* (Savannah, Ga., 1916), 79–80.

22. Arthur K. Moore, *The Frontier Mind: A Cultural Analysis of Kentuckian Frontiersmen* (Lexington: University of Kentucky Press, 1957), 42.

23. "A Memorandum of M. Austin's Journey from the Lead Mines in Virginia to the Lead Mines . . . Louisiana, 1796–1797," *AHR* 5 (1899–1900): 525.

24. William Faux, *Memorable Days in America, Being a Journal of a Tour of the United States*, in Thwaites, *Early Western Travels*, Jan. 1, 1820, 12: 13.

25. Moore, *Frontier Mind*, 39.

26. Adolph P. Gratiot, "Criminal Justice on the Kentucky Frontier" (Ph.D. diss., University of Pennsylvania, 1952), 44–46, 91–92.

27. Hazel Dicken-Garcia, *To Western Woods: The Breckinridge Family Moves to Kentucky in 1793* (Rutherford, N.J.: Fairleigh Dickinson University Press, 1991), 55.

28. Gratiot, "Criminal Justice on the Kentucky Frontier," 322–23.

29. Charles L. Wallis, ed., *Autobiography of Peter Cartwright* (Nashville, Tenn.: Abingdon Press, 1986), 30; Boynton Merrill, Jr., *Jefferson's Nephews: A Frontier Tragedy* (Princeton, N.J.: Princeton University Press, 1976), 402n.

30. Malcolm J. Rohrbough, *The Trans-Appalachian Frontier: People, Societies, and Institutions, 1775–1850* (Belmont, Calif.: 1990), 15; Harriette S. Arnow, *Seedtime on the Cumberland* (New York: Macmillan Company, 1960), 205, 214n.

31. Rohrbough, *Trans-Appalachian Frontier*, 17; Harriette S. Arnow, *Flowering of the Cumberland* (1963; reprint, Lincoln: University of Nebraska Press, 1996), 197–98, 210–11.

32. Arnow, *Seedtime on the Cumberland*, 205, 214n., 225, 248; Samuel C. Williams, *Tennessee During the Revolutionary War* (1944; reprint, Knoxville: University of Tennessee Press, 1974), 216.

33. Samuel C. Williams, *Beginnings of West Tennessee in the Land of the Chickasaws, 1541–1841* (Johnson City, Tenn., 1930), 174, 234.

34. Robert V. Haynes, "Law Enforcement in Frontier Mississippi," *Journal of Mississippi History* 22 (1960): 30–31; James F. Doster, "Early Settlements on the Tombigbee and Tensaw Rivers," *Alabama Review* 12 (1959): 92.

35. Ephraim Kirby to President Thomas Jefferson, May 1, 1804, in Clarence E. Carter, ed., *The Territorial Papers of the United States* (Washington, D.C., 1937), 5: 323–34.

36. William C. Davis, *A Way Through the Wilderness: The Natchez Trace and the Civilization of the Southern Frontier* (New York: HarperCollins, 1995), 268–71; James W. Bragg, "Captain Slick: Arbiter of Early Alabama Morals," *Alabama Review* 11 (1958): 125–34.

37. Jack D. L. Holmes, "Law and Order in Spanish Natchez, 1781–1798," *Journal of Mississippi History* 25 (1963): 191–92; Joseph T. Hatfield, *William Claiborne: Jefferson Centurion in the American West* (Lafayette: University of Southwestern Louisiana Press, 1976), 48; Mrs. Dunbar Rowland, *Life, Letters and Papers of William Dunbar* (Jackson, Miss., 1930), Diary, May 1, 1778, 62.

38. Gov. Claiborne to Richard Sparks and to Governor of Louisiana, Feb. 10, to Governor De Salcedo, Feb. 28, to Daniel Burnet, April 27, and to Seymour Rennick

[April], 1802, in Mrs. Dunbar Rowland, ed., *The Official Letter Books of W.C.C. Claiborne* (Jackson, Miss., 1917), 1: 44–46, 61, and 91–93, resp.

39. Thomas Hulme, *A Journal Made During a Tour in the Western Country, Sept. 30, 1818–Aug. 7, 1819*, in Thwaites, *Early Western Travels*, 10 (1907): 46–47.

40. James A. Rose, "The Regulators and Flatheads in Southern Illinois," *Transactions of the Illinois State Historical Society for the Year 1906* (Springfield, 1906): 108–9; James E. Davis, *Frontier Illinois* (Bloomington: Indiana University Press, 1998), 177 and 287; Paul Wellman, *Spawn of Evil: The Invisible Empire of Soulless Men Which for a Generation Held the Nation in a Spell of Terror* (Garden City, N.Y.: Doubleday and Company, 1964), 134–37.

41. Elias P. Fordham, *Personal Narrative of Travels . . . 1817–1818*, ed. Frederic A. Ogg (Cleveland, 1906), Jan. 26, 1818, 154–55.

42. William D. Snively, Jr., and Louanna Furbee, *Satan's Ferryman: A True Tale of the Old Frontier* (New York: Frederick Ungar Publishing Company, 1968), 36.

43. Otto A. Rothert, *The Outlaws of Cave-in-Rock* (Carbondale: Southern Illinois University Press, 1996), 18–20, 37; Walter Havighurst, *Land of Promise: The Story of the Northwest Territory* (New York, 1947), 226; Wellman, *Spawn of Evil*, 117–19.

44. Committee Report on Petition of Elisha Winters, April 17, 1810, U.S. Senate, in James F. Hopkins, ed., *The Papers of Henry Clay* (Lexington: University Press of Kentucky, 1959), 1: 468; Draper Collection, 2CC: 34 and 29CC: 75–76; Jonathan Daniels, *The Devil's Backbone: The Story of the Natchez Trace* (New York: McGraw-Hill Book Company, 1962), 114–24; Michael Allen, *Western Rivermen, 1763–1801: Ohio and Mississippi Boatmen and the Myth of the Alligator Horse* (Baton Rouge: Louisiana State University Press, 1990), 81–83; Raymond M. Bell, "Captain Samuel Mason," typescript (Washington, Pa., 1992), 4, 9, 14–15; Rothert, *Outlaws of Cave-in-Rock*, 107–27, 175, 250–63; Wellman, *Spawn of Evil*, 43–49, 100–13; Davis, *Way Through the Wilderness*, 14–15, 272–75.

45. Draper Collection, 5S: 70–72 and 30S: 114, 183–93: Chester R. Young, ed., *Westward into Kentucky: The Narrative of Daniel Trabue* (Lexington: University Press of Kentucky, 1981), 195–96; Robert L. Kincaid, *The Wilderness Road* (Indianapolis, 1947), 196–99; Robert M. Coates, *The Outlaw Years: The History of the Land Pirates of the Natchez Trace* (1930; reprint, Lincoln: University of Nebraska Press, 1986), 24–34; Wellman, *Spawn of Evil*, 13–20; Rothert, *Outlaws of Cave-in-Rock*, 107–27.

46. Faux, *Memorable Days in America*, Dec. 16, 1818, 11: 293; Shadrach L. Jackson, *The Life of Logan Belt* (1888; reprint, Utica, Ky.: McDowell Publications, 1979), 92–93; Rothert, *Outlaws of Cave-in-Rock*, 284–306; Wellman, *Spawn of Evil*, 123–38; Snively and Furbee, *Satan's Ferryman, passim*.

47. Henry D. Southerland, Jr., and Jerry E. Brown, *The Federal Road Through Georgia, the Creek Nation, and Alabama, 1806–1836* (Tuscaloosa: University of Alabama Press, 1989), 17–20, 98–101; Thomas P. Abernethy, *The Formative Period in Alabama, 1815–1828*, rev. ed. (University: University of Alabama Press, 1965), 38: Daniels, *Devil's Backbone*, 104–6; Coates, *Outlaw Years*, 79–105.

48. For example, the Bear River Valley in Tennessee. William L. Montell, *Killings: Folk Justice in the Upper South* (Lexington: University Press of Kentucky, 1986), 9.

49. Quote in Reginald Horsman, *The Frontier in the Formative Years, 1783–1815* (Albuquerque: University of New Mexico Press, 1975), 128–29.

50. James Iredell to Francis Iredell, June 15, 1771, in Higginbotham, *Papers of Iredell*, 1: 71.

Index

Hampton, Col. Wade, 231, 233
Hampton, Va., 141
Hand, Gen. Edward, 19
Hankinson, Col. Aaron, 93
Hankinson, Kenneth, 115
Harding, George (alias Thomas), 76–77
Hardwick Township, N.J., 90
Hare, Joseph Thompson, 251
Hargrove, James, 158
Harlem River, 30, 32
Harpe, Micajah, 249–51
Harpe, Wiley, 249–51
Harrill, Noah, 233
Harrington, Henry, 236–37
Harrison, Gov. Benjamin, 145, 162
Harrison, John, 232
Harrison, Robert, 232
Harrison's Rangers, 232
Hart, Col. William, 124–25
Hart, John, 121
Hartford, Conn., 21
Harwood, Jacob, 119
Harwood, William, 137–38
Hatfield, Cornelius, 25–59
Hatfield, Smith, 58–59
Havana, Cuba, 217
Haverstraw, N.Y., 70
Haw River, N.C., 226
Hawley, Capt. David, 43
Haynie, Charles, 138
Head of Elk, Md., 8, 174
Heath, Gen. William, 24, 26
Heer, Capt. Bartholomew von, 10
Heiliker, William, 82
Hellings, Mary, 121
Hemlock Swamp, N.J., 112
Hempstead, L.I., 14
Henderson, Archibald, 123
Hendricks, Baker, 41
Hendrickson, Lt., 95
Henry, Gov. Patrick, 155–56, 158, 161–
64
Hessians, 1, 2, 4, 8, 22, 33
Heyward, Thomas, 200
Hicks, Thomas, 44
Highlands area, N.Y., 18–19, 23–24, 69–

84, 242, 277 n.31; eastern Highlands
banditti, 80–84
Highwarden, John, 159
Highwaymen, 212, 231, 233–34, 236–39,
248–50, 252
Hillsborough (Hillsboro), N.C., 8, 226,
237–38
Hobart, John, 73
Hobkirk's Hill, battle of, 198
Hodges, Graham R., 63
Hodges, James, 158
Hodges, Robert, 158
Holbrook, Thomas, 142
Hole, Nicholas, 122
Holloway, Charles, 232
Holmes, James, 21–22
Holmes, John, 106, 108
Holston River, Tenn., 194, 224, 247
Honeywell, Israel, 31
Hooper's Strait (Chesapeake Bay), 140
Hoops, Maj. Robert, 91
Hope, N.C., 227
Hopkins, Joshua, 160
Horseneck (Greenwich), Conn., 25–26
Horse stealing, 11, 73, 98, 105, 159,
188, 191, 195, 200, 230–34, 236, 246–
49
Hough, Daniel, 122
Houston, James (1), 46
Houston, James (2), 82
Houstoun, Gov. John, 196–98
Howard, Capt. Carlos, 218
Howe, Gen. Robert, 195, 197, 221
Howe, Gen. Sir William, 4, 8, 14, 51,
62, 87; and loyalty, 51–52
Huddy, Capt. Joshua, 63–67
Hudson River, 7, 18–19, 56, 58, 61, 69–
70, 72, 76, 78, 80–81, 90, 94
Hulce, Joseph, 38
Hull, Col. William, 31–32
Humberstone, Ontario, 133
Hume, James, 209
Hunt, William, 193
Huntington, N.Y., 35, 46
Hurricane Island (Ohio River), 249
Hutchinson, William (1), 87, 89

About the Author

HARRY M. WARD is William Binford Vest Professor of History, Emeritus at the University of Richmond. He is the author of numerous books and other publications relating to Colonial and Revolutionary America.